CORRIE TEN BOOM

CORRIE TEN BOOM

Her Story

The Hiding Place

Tramp for the Lord

Jesus is Victor

Inspirational Press · New York

First Inspirational Press edition published in 1995.
Inspirational Press
A division of Budget Book Service, Inc.
386 Park Avenue South
New York, NY 10016

Inspirational Press is a registered trademark of Budget Book Service, Inc.
Published by arrangement with Chosen Books, Inc., and Fleming H. Revell, a division of Baker Book House Company.

Library of Congress Catalog Card Number: 95-78088
ISBN: 0-88486-126-0

Designed by Hannah Lerner

Printed in the United States of America

Contents

The Hiding Place

Contents

Preface

When we were doing the research for *God's Smuggler*, a name kept cropping up: Corrie ten Boom. This Dutch lady—in her mid-seventies when we first began to hear of her—was Brother Andrew's favorite traveling companion. Brother Andrew is a missionary behind the Iron Curtain; his fascinating stories about her in Vietnam, where she had earned that most honorable title "Double-old Grandmother"— and in a dozen other Communist countries—came to mind so often that we finally had to hold up our hands to stop his flow of reminiscence. "We could never fit her into the book," we said. "She sounds like a book in herself." It's the sort of thing you say. Not meaning anything.

It was in May, 1968, that we attended a church service in Germany. A man was speaking about his experiences in a Nazi concentration camp. His face told the story more eloquently than his words: pain-haunted eyes, shaking hands that could not forget. He was followed at the lectern by a white-haired woman, broad of frame and sensible of shoe, with a face that radiated love, peace, joy. But—the story that these two people were relating was the same! She too had been in a concentration camp, seen the same savagery, suffered the same losses. His response was easy to understand. But hers?

We stayed behind to talk with her. And as we did, we realized that we were meeting Andrew's Corrie. Cornelia ten Boom's world-wide ministry of comfort and counsel had begun there in the concentration camp where she had found, as the prophet Isaiah promised, "a hiding place from the wind, a covert from the tempest . . . the shadow of a great rock in a weary land."

On subsequent visits we got to know this amazing woman well. Together we visited the crooked little Dutch house—one room wide—where till her fifties she lived the uneventful life of a spinster watchmaker, little dreaming as she cared for her older sister and their elderly father that a world of high adventure lay just around the corner. We went to the garden in south Holland where young Corrie gave her heart away forever. To the big brick house in Haarlem where Pickwick served real coffee in the middle of the war. . . .

And all the while we had the extraordinary feeling that we were not looking into the past but into the future. As though these people and places were speaking to us not about things that had already happened but about the world that lay ahead of us in the 1970s. Already we found ourselves actually putting into practice how-to's we learned from her about:
- handling separation
- getting along with less
- security in the midst of insecurity

- forgiveness
- how God can use weakness
- dealing with difficult people
- facing death
- how to love your enemies
- what to do when evil wins

We commented to her about the practicalness of everything she recalled, how her memories seemed to throw a spotlight on problems and decisions we faced here and now. "But," she said, "this is what the past is for! Every experience God gives us, every person He puts in our lives is the perfect preparation for the future that only He can see."

Every experience, every person. . . . Father, who did the finest watch repairs in Holland and then forgot to send the bill. Mama, whose body became a prison, but whose spirit soared free. Betsie, who could make a party out of three potatoes and some twice-used tea leaves. As we looked into the twinkling blue eyes of this undefeatable woman, we wished that these people were part of our own lives.

And then, of course, we realized that they could be. . . .

John and Elizabeth Sherrill

July, 1971
Chappaqua, New York

1. The One Hundredth Birthday Party

I JUMPED OUT of bed that morning with one question in my mind—sun or fog? Usually it was fog in January in Holland, dank, chill, and gray. But occasionally—on a rare and magic day—a white winter sun broke through. I leaned as far as I could from the single window in my bedroom; it was always hard to see the sky from the Beje. Blank brick walls looked back at me, the backs of other ancient buildings in this crowded center of old Haarlem. But up there where my neck craned to see, above the crazy roofs and crooked chimneys, was a square of pale pearl sky. It was going to be a sunny day for the party!

I attempted a little waltz as I took my new dress from the tipsy old wardrobe against the wall. Father's bedroom was directly under mine but at seventy-seven he slept soundly. That was one advantage to growing old, I thought, as I worked my arms into the sleeves and surveyed the effect in the mirror on the wardrobe door. Although some Dutch women in 1937 were wearing their skirts knee-length, mine was still a cautious three inches above my shoes.

You're not growing younger yourself, I reminded my reflection. Maybe it was the new dress that made me look more critically at myself than usual: forty-five years old, unmarried, waistline long since vanished.

My sister Betsie, though seven years older than I, still had that slender grace that made people turn and look after her in the street. Heaven knows it wasn't her clothes; our little watch shop had never made much money. But when Betsie put on a dress something wonderful happened to it.

On me—until Betsie caught up with them—hems sagged, stockings tore, and collars twisted. But today, I thought, standing back from the mirror as far as I could in the small room, the effect of dark maroon was very smart.

Far below me down on the street, the doorbell rang. Callers? Before 7:00 in the morning? I opened my bedroom door and plunged down the steep twisting stairway. These stairs were an afterthought in this curious old house. Actually it was two houses. The one in front was a typical tiny old-Haarlem structure, three stories high, two rooms deep, and only one room wide. At some unknown point in its long history its rear wall had been knocked through to join it with the even thinner, steeper house in back of it—which had only three rooms, one on top of the other—and this narrow corkscrew staircase squeezed between the two.

Quick as I was, Betsie was at the door ahead of me. An enormous spray of flowers filled the doorway. As Betsie took them, a small delivery boy appeared. "Nice day for the party, Miss," he said, trying to peer past the flowers as though coffee and cake might already be set out. He would be coming to the party later, as indeed, it seemed, would all of Haarlem.

Betsie and I searched the bouquet for the card. "Pickwick!" we shouted together.

Pickwick was an enormously wealthy customer who not only bought the very finest watches but often came upstairs to the family part of the house above the shop. His real name was Herman Sluring; Pickwick was the name Betsie and I used between ourselves because he looked so incredibly like the illustrator's drawing in our copy of Dickens. Herman Sluring was without doubt the ugliest man in Haarlem. Short, immensely fat, head bald as a Holland cheese, he was so wall-eyed that you were never quite sure whether he was looking at you or someone else—and as kind and generous as he was fearsome to look at.

The flowers had come to the side door, the door the family used, opening onto a tiny alleyway, and Betsie and I carried them from the little hall into the shop. First was the workroom where watches and clocks were repaired. There was the high bench over which Father had bent for so many years, doing the delicate, painstaking work that was known as the finest in Holland. And there in the center of the room was my bench, and next to mine Hans the apprentice's, and against the wall old Christoffels'.

Beyond the workroom was the customers' part of the shop with its glass case full of watches. All the wall clocks were striking 7:00 as Betsie and I carried the flowers in and looked for the most artistic spot to put them. Ever since childhood I had loved to step into this room where a hundred ticking voices welcomed me. It was still dark inside because the shutters had not been drawn back from the windows on the street. I unlocked the street door and stepped out into the Barteljorisstraat. The other shops up and down the narrow street were shuttered and silent: the optician's next door, the dress shop, the baker's, Weil's Furriers across the street.

I folded back our shutters and stood for a minute admiring the window display that Betsie and I had at last agreed upon. This window was always a great source of debate between us, I wanting to display as much of our stock as could be squeezed onto the shelf, and Betsie maintaining that two or three beautiful watches, with perhaps a piece of silk or satin swirled beneath, was more elegant and more inviting. But this time the window satisfied us both: it held a collection of clocks and pocketwatches all at least a hundred years old, borrowed for the occasion from friends and antique dealers all over the city. For today was the shop's one hundredth birthday. It was on this day in January 1837 that Father's father had placed in this window a sign: TEN BOOM. WATCHES.

For the last ten minutes, with a heavenly disregard for the precisions of passing time, the church bells of Haarlem had been pealing out 7:00 o'clock, and now half a block away in the town square, the great bell of St. Bavo's solemnly donged seven times. I lingered in the street to count them, though it was cold in the January dawn. Of course everyone in Haarlem had radios now, but I could remember when the life of the city had run on St. Bavo time, and only trainmen and others who needed to know the exact hour had come here to read the "astronomical clock." Father would take the train to Amsterdam each week to bring back the time from the Naval Observatory and it was a source of pride to him that the astronomical clock was never more than two seconds off in the seven days. There it stood now, as I stepped back into the shop, still tall and gleaming on its concrete block, but shorn now of eminence.

The doorbell on the alley was ringing again; more flowers. So it went for an hour, large bouquets and small ones, elaborate set pieces and home-grown plants in clay pots. For although the party was for the shop, the affection of a city was for Father. "Haarlem's Grand Old Man" they called him and they were setting about to prove it. When the shop and the workroom would not hold another bouquet, Betsie and I started carrying them upstairs to the two rooms above the shop. Though it was twenty years since her death, these were still "Tante Jans's rooms." Tante Jans was Mother's older sister and her presence lingered in the massive dark furniture she had left behind her. Betsie set down a pot of greenhouse-grown tulips and stepped back with a little cry of pleasure.

"Corrie, just look how much brighter!"

Poor Betsie. The Beje was so closed in by the houses around that the window plants she started each spring never grew tall enough to bloom.

At 7:45 Hans, the apprentice, arrived and at 8:00 Toos, our saleslady-bookkeeper. Toos was a sour-faced, scowling individual whose ill-temper had made it impossible for her to keep a job until—ten years ago—she had come to work for Father. Father's gentle courtesy had disarmed and mellowed her and, though she would have died sooner than admit it, she loved him as fiercely as she disliked the rest of the world. We left Hans and Toos to answer the doorbell and went upstairs to get breakfast.

Only three places at the table, I thought, as I set out the plates. The dining room was in the house at the rear, five steps higher than the shop but lower than Tante

Jans's rooms. To me this room with its single window looking into the alley was the heart of the home. This table, with a blanket thrown over it, had made me a tent or a pirate's cove when I was small. I'd done my homework here as a school-child. Here Mama read aloud from Dickens on winter evenings while the coal whistled in the brick hearth and cast a red glow over the tile proclaiming, "Jesus is Victor."

We used only a corner of the table now, Father, Betsie and I, but to me the rest of the family was always there. There was Mama's chair, and the three aunts' places over there (not only Tante Jans but Mama's other two sisters had also lived with us). Next to me had sat my other sister, Nollie, and Willem, the only boy in the family, there beside Father.

Nollie and Willem had had homes of their own many years now, and Mama and the aunts were dead, but still I seemed to see them here. Of course their chairs hadn't stayed empty long. Father could never bear a house without children and whenever he heard of a child in need of a home a new face would appear at the table. Somehow, out of his watch shop that never made money he fed and dressed and cared for eleven more children after his own four were grown. But now these, too, had grown up and married or gone off to work, and so I laid three plates on the table.

Betsie brought the coffee in from the tiny kitchen, which was little more than a closet off the dining room, and took bread from the drawer in the sideboard. She was setting them on the table when we heard Father's step coming down the stair-case. He went a little slowly now on the winding stairs; but still as punctual as one of his own watches, he entered the dining room, as he had every morning since I could remember, at 8:10.

"Father!" I said kissing him and savoring the aroma of cigars that always clung to his long beard, "a sunny day for the party!"

Father's hair and beard were now as white as the best tablecloth Betsie had laid for this special day. But his blue eyes behind the thick round spectacles were as mild and merry as ever, and he gazed from one of us to the other with frank delight.

"Corrie, dear! My dear Betsie! How gay and lovely you both look!"

He bowed his head as he sat down, said the blessing over bread, and then went on eagerly, "Your mother—how she would have loved these new styles and see-ing you both looking so pretty!"

Betsie and I looked hard into our coffee to keep from laughing. These "new styles" were the despair of our young nieces, who were always trying to get us into brighter colors, shorter skirts, and lower necklines. But conservative though we were, it was true that Mama had never had anything even as bright as my deep maroon dress or Betsie's dark blue one. In Mama's day married women—and unmarried ones "of a certain age"—wore black from the chin to the ground. I had never seen Mama and the aunts in any other color.

"How Mama would have loved everything about today!" Betsie said. "Remember how she loved 'occasions'?"

Mama could have coffee on the stove and a cake in the oven as fast as most people could say, "best wishes." And since she knew almost everyone in Haarlem, especially the poor, sick and neglected, there was almost no day in the year that was not for somebody, as she would say with eyes shining, "a very special occasion!"

And so we sat over our coffee, as one should on anniversaries, and looked back—back to the time when Mama was alive, and beyond. Back to the time when Father was a small boy growing up in this same house. "I was born right in this room," he said, as though he had not told us a hundred times. "Only of course it wasn't the dining room then, but a bedroom. And the bed was in a kind of cupboard set into the wall with no windows and no light or air of any kind. I was the first baby who lived. I don't know how many there were before me, but they all died. Mother had tuberculosis you see, and they didn't know about contaminated air or keeping babies away from sick people."

It was a day for memories. A day for calling up the past. How could we have guessed as we sat there—two middle-aged spinsters and an old man—that in place of memories we were about to be given adventure such as we had never dreamed of? Adventure and anguish, horror and heaven were just around the corner, and we did not know.

Oh Father! Betsie! If I had known would I have gone ahead? Could I have done the things I did?

But how could I know? How could I imagine this white-haired man, called Opa—Grandfather—by all the children of Haarlem, how could I imagine this man thrown by strangers into a grave without a name?

And Betsie, with her high lace collar and her gift for making beauty all around her, how could I picture this dearest person on earth to me standing naked before a roomful of men? In that room on that day, such thoughts were not even thinkable.

Father stood up and took the big brass-hinged Bible from its shelf as Toos and Hans rapped on the door and came in. Scripture reading at 8:30 each morning for all who were in the house was another of the fixed points around which life in the Beje revolved. Father opened the big volume and Betsie and I held our breaths. Surely, today of all days, when there was still so much to do, it would not be a whole chapter! But he was turning to the Gospel of Luke where we'd left off yesterday—such long chapters in Luke too. With his finger at the place, Father looked up.

"Where is Christoffels?" he said.

Christoffels was the third and only other employee in the shop, a bent, wizened little man who looked older than Father though actually he was ten years younger. I remembered the day six or seven years earlier when he had first come into the shop, so ragged and woebegone that I'd assumed that he was one of the beggars who had the Beje marked as a sure meal. I was about to send him up to the kitchen where Betsie kept a pot of soup simmering when he announced with great dignity that he was considering permanent employment and was offering his services first to us.

It turned out that Christoffels belonged to an almost vanished trade, the itinerant clockmender who trudged on foot throughout the land, regulating and repairing the tall pendulum clocks that were the pride of every Dutch farmhouse. But if I was surprised at the grand manner of this shabby little man I was even more astonished when Father hired him on the spot.

"They're the finest clockmen anywhere," he told me later, "these wandering clocksmiths. There's not a repair job they haven't handled with just the tools in their sack."

And so it had proved through the years as people from all over Haarlem brought their clocks to him. What he did with his wages we never knew; he had remained as tattered and threadbare as ever. Father hinted as much as he dared—for next to his shabbiness Christoffels' most notable quality was his pride—and then gave it up.

And now, for the first time ever, Christoffels was late.

Father polished his glasses with his napkin and started to read, his deep voice lingering lovingly over the words. He had reached the bottom of the page when we heard Christoffels' shuffling steps on the stairs. The door opened and all of us gasped. Christoffels was resplendent in a new black suit, new checkered vest, a snowy white shirt, flowered tie, and stiff starched collar. I tore my eyes from the spectacle as swiftly as I could, for Christoffels' expression forbade us to notice anything out of the ordinary.

"Christoffels, my dear associate," Father murmured in his formal, old-fashioned way, "what joy to see you on this—er—auspicious day." And hastily he resumed his Bible reading.

Before he reached the end of the chapter the doorbells were ringing, both the shop bell on the street and the family bell in the alley. Betsie ran to make more coffee and put her taartjes in the oven while Toos and I hurried to the doors. It seemed that everyone in Haarlem wanted to be first to shake Father's hand. Before long a steady stream of guests was winding up the narrow staircase to Tante Jans's rooms where he sat almost lost in a thicket of flowers. I was helping one of the older guests up the steep stairs when Betsie seized my arm.

"Corrie! We're going to need Nollie's cups right away! How can we—?"

"I'll go get them!"

Our sister Nollie and her husband were coming that afternoon as soon as their six children got home from school. I dashed down the stairs, took my coat and my bicycle from inside the alley door, and was wheeling it over the threshold when Betsie's voice reached me, soft but firm.

"Corrie, your new dress!"

And so I whirled back up the stairs to my room, changed into my oldest skirt and set out over the bumpy brick streets. I always loved to bike to Nollie's house. She and her husband lived about a mile and a half from the Beje, outside the cramped old center of the city. The streets there were broader and straighter; even the sky seemed bigger. Across the town square I pedaled, over the canal on the Grote Hout bridge and along the Wagenweg, reveling in the thin winter sunshine. Nollie lived on Bos en Hoven Straat, a block of identical attached houses with white curtains and potted plants in the windows.

How could I foresee as I zipped around the corner, that one summer day, when the hyacinths in the commercial bulb flats nearby were ripe and brown, I would brake my bicycle here and stand with my heart thudding in my throat, daring to go no closer for fear of what was taking place behind Nollie's starched curtains?

Today I careened onto the sidewalk and burst through the door with never a knock. "Nollie, the Beje's jammed already! You ought to see! We need the cups right now!"

Nollie came out of the kitchen, her round pretty face flushed with baking. "They're all packed by the door. Oh I wish I could go back with you—but I've got batches of cookies still to bake and I promised Flip and the children I'd wait for them."

"You're—all coming, aren't you?"

"Yes, Corrie, Peter will be there." Nollie was loading the cups into the bicycle bags. As a dutiful aunt I tried to love all my nieces and nephews equally. But Peter . . . well, was Peter. At thirteen he was a musical prodigy and a rascal and the pride of my life.

"He's even written a special song in honor of the day," Nollie said.

"Here now, you'll have to carry this bagful in your hand, so be careful."

The Beje was more crowded than ever when I got back, the alley so jammed with bicycles I had to leave mine at the corner. The mayor of Haarlem was there in his tailcoat and gold watch chain. And the postman and the trolley motorman and half a dozen policemen from the Haarlem Police Headquarters just around the corner.

After lunch the children started coming and, as children always did, they went straight to Father. The older ones sat on the floor around him, the smallest ones climbed into his lap. For in addition to his twinkling eyes and long cigar-sweet beard, Father ticked. Watches lying on a shelf run differently from watches carried about, and so Father always wore the ones he was regulating. His suit jackets had four huge inside pockets, each fitted with hooks for a dozen watches, so that wherever he went the hum of hundreds of little wheels went gaily with him. Now with a child on each knee and ten more crowded close, he drew from another pocket his heavy cross-shaped winding key, each of the four ends shaped for a different size clock. With a flick of his finger he made it spin, gleaming, glinting. . . .

Betsie stopped in the doorway with a tray of cakes. "He doesn't know there's anyone else in the room," she said.

I was carrying a stack of soiled plates down the stairs when a little shriek below told me that Pickwick had arrived. We used to forget, we who loved him, what a shock the first sight of him could be to a stranger. I hurried down to the door, introduced him hastily to the wife of an Amsterdam wholesaler, and got him upstairs. He sank his ponderous bulk into a chair beside Father, fixed one eye on me, the other on the ceiling, and said, "Five lumps, please."

Poor Pickwick! He loved children as much as Father did, but while children took to Father on sight, Pickwick had to win them. He had one trick, though, that never failed. I brought him his cup of coffee, thick with sugar, and watched him look around in mock consternation. "But my dear Cornelia!" he cried. "There's no table to set it on!" He glanced out of one wide-set eye to make sure the children were watching. "Well, it's a lucky thing I brought my own!" And with that he set cup and saucer on his own protruding paunch. I had never known a child who could resist it; soon a respectful circle had gathered round him.

A little later Nollie and her family arrived. "Tante Corrie!" Peter greeted me innocently. "You don't *look* one hundred years old!" And before I could swat him he was sitting at Tante Jans's upright piano filling the old house with melody. People called out requests—popular songs, selections from Bach chorales, hymns—and soon the whole room was joining in the choruses.

How many of us were there, that happy afternoon, who were soon to meet under very different circumstances! Peter, the policemen, dear ugly Pickwick, all of us were there except my brother Willem and his family. I wondered why they should be so late. Willem and his wife and children lived in the town of Hilversum, thirty miles away: still, they should have been here by now.

Suddenly the music stopped and Peter from his perch on the piano bench hissed across the room, "Opa! Here's the competition!"

I glanced out the window. Turning into the alley were Mr. and Mrs. Kan, owners of the other watch shop on the street. By Haarlem standards they were newcomers, having opened their store only in 1910 and so been on the Barteljorisstraat a mere twenty-seven years. But since they sold a good many more watches than we did, I considered Peter's comment factual enough.

Father, however, was distressed. "Not competitors, Peter!" he said reprovingly. "Colleagues!" And lifting children quickly off his knees, he got up and hurried to the head of the stairs to greet the Kans.

Father treated Mr. Kan's frequent visits to the shop below as social calls from a cherished friend. "Can't you see what he's doing?" I would rage after Mr. Kan had gone. "He's finding out how much we're charging so he can undersell us!" Mr. Kan's display window always featured in bold figures prices exactly five guilders below our own.

And Father's face would light up with a kind of pleased surprise as it always did on those rare occasions when he thought about the business side of watchmaking.

"But Corrie, people will save money when they buy from him!" And then he would always add, "I wonder how he does it."

Father was as innocent of business know-how as his father had been before him. He would work for days on a difficult repair problem and then forget to send a bill. The more rare and expensive a watch, the less he was able to think of it in terms of money. "A man should pay for the privilege of working on such a watch!" he would say.

As for merchandising methods, for the first eighty years of the shop's history the shutters on the streets had been closed each evening promptly at 6:00. It was not until I myself had come into the business twenty years ago that I had noticed the throngs of strollers crowding the narrow sidewalks each evening and had seen how the other stores kept their windows lighted and open. When I pointed this out to Father he was as delighted as though I had made a profound discovery. "And if people see the watches it might make them want to buy one! Corrie, my dear, how very clever you are!"

Mr. Kan was making his way toward me now, full of cake and compliments. Guilty for the jealous thoughts I harbored I took advantage of the crowd and made my escape downstairs. The workroom and shop were even more crowded with well-wishers than the upstairs rooms. Hans was passing cakes in the back room, as was Toos in the front, wearing the nearest thing to a smile that her perpetually down-drawn lips would permit. As for Christoffels, he had simply and astonishingly expanded. It was impossible to recognize that stooped and shabby little man in the glorious figure at the door, greeting newcomers with a formal welcome followed by a relentless tour of the shop. Quite obviously it was the greatest day of his life.

All through the short winter afternoon they kept coming, the people who counted themselves Father's friends. Young and old, poor and rich, scholarly gentlemen and illiterate servant girls—only to Father did it seem that they were all alike. That was Father's secret: not that he overlooked the differences in people; that he didn't know they were there.

And still Willem was not here. I said goodbye to some guests at the door and stood for a moment gazing up and down the Barteljorisstraat. Although it was only 4:00 in the afternoon the lights in the shops were coming on against the January dusk. I still had a great deal of little-sister worship for this big brother, five years older than I, an ordained minister and the only ten Boom who had ever been to college. Willem saw things, I felt. He knew what was going on in the world.

Oftentimes, indeed, I wished that Willem did not see quite so well, for much that he saw was frightening. A full ten years ago, way back in 1927, Willem had written in his doctoral thesis, done in Germany, that a terrible evil was taking root in that land. Right at the university, he said, seeds were being planted of a contempt for human life such as the world had never seen. The few who had read his paper had laughed.

Now of course, well, people weren't laughing about Germany. Most of the good clocks came from there, and recently several firms with whom we had dealt for years were simply and mysteriously "out of business." Willem believed it was part of a deliberate and large-scale move against Jews; every one of the closed businesses was Jewish. As head of the Dutch Reformed Church's program to reach Jews, Willem kept in touch with these things.

Dear Willem, I thought, as I stepped back inside and closed the door, he was about as good a salesman of the church as Father was of watches. If he'd converted a single Jew in twenty years I hadn't heard about it. Willem didn't try to change people, just to serve them. He had scrimped and saved enough money to build a home for elderly Jews in Hilversum—for the elderly of all faiths, in fact, for Willem was against any system of segregation. But in the last few months the home had been deluged with younger arrivals—all Jews and all from Germany. Willem and his family had given up their own living quarters and were sleeping in a corridor. And still the frightened, homeless people kept coming, and with them tales of a mounting madness.

I went up to the kitchen where Nollie had just brewed a fresh pot of coffee, picked it up, and continued with it upstairs to Tante Jans's rooms. "What does he want?" I asked a group of men gathered around the cake table as I set down the pot. "This man in Germany, does he want war?" I knew it was poor talk for a party, but somehow thoughts of Willem always set my mind on hard subjects.

A chill of silence fell over the table and spread swiftly around the room.

"What does it matter?" a voice broke into it. "Let the big countries fight it out. It won't affect us."

"That's right!" from a watch salesman. "The Germans let us alone in the Great War. It's to their advantage to keep us neutral."

"Easy for you to talk," cried a man from whom we bought clock parts. "Your stock comes from Switzerland. What about us? What do I do if Germany goes to war? A war could put me out of business!"

And at that moment Willem entered the room. Behind him came Tine, his wife, and their four children. But every eye in the room had settled on the figure whose arm Willem held in his. It was a Jew in his early thirties in the typical broad-brimmed black hat and long black coat. What glued every eye to this man was his face. It had been burned. In front of his right ear dangled a gray and frizzled ringlet, like the hair of a very old man. The rest of his beard was gone, leaving only a raw and gaping wound.

"This is Herr Gutlieber," Willem announced in German. "He just arrived in Hilversum this morning. Herr Gutlieber, my father."

"He got out of Germany on a milk truck," Willem told us rapidly in Dutch. "They stopped him on a streetcorner—teen-aged boys in Munich—set fire to his beard."

Father had risen from his chair and was eagerly shaking the newcomer's hand. I brought him a cup of coffee and a plate of Nollie's cookies. How grateful I was now for Father's insistence that his children speak German and English almost as soon as Dutch.

Herr Gutlieber sat down stiffly on the edge of a chair and fixed his eyes on the cup in his lap. I pulled up a chair beside him and talked some nonsense about the unusual January weather. And around us conversation began again, a hum of party talk rising and falling.

"Hoodlums!" I heard the watch salesman say. "Young hooligans! It's the same in every country. The police'll catch up with 'em—you'll see. Germany's a civilized country."

And so the shadow fell across us that winter afternoon in 1937, but it rested lightly. Nobody dreamed that this tiny cloud would grow until it blocked out the sky. And nobody dreamed that in this darkness each of us would be called to play a role: Father and Betsie and Mr. Kan and Willem—even the funny old Beje with its unmatching floor levels and ancient angles.

In the evening after the last guest had gone I climbed the stairs to my room thinking only of the past. On my bed lay the new maroon dress; I had forgotten to put it back on. "I never did care about clothes," I thought. "Even when I was young. . . ."

Childhood scenes rushed back at me out of the night, strangely close and urgent. Today I know that such memories are the key not to the past, but to the future. I know that the experiences of our lives, when we let God use them, become the mysterious and perfect preparation for the work He will give us to do.

I didn't know it then—nor, indeed, that there was any new future to prepare for in a life as humdrum and predictable as mine. I only knew as I lay in my bed at the top of the house that certain moments from long ago stood out in focus against the blur of years. Oddly sharp and near they were, as though they were not yet finished, as though they had something more to say. . . .

2. *Full Table*

IT WAS 1898 and I was six years old. Betsie stood me in front of the wardrobe mirror and gave me a lecture.

"Just look at your shoes! You've missed every other button. And those old torn stockings your very first day at school? See how nice Nollie looks!"

Nollie and I shared this bedroom at the top of the Beje. I looked at my eight-year-old sister: sure enough, her high-buttoned shoes were neatly fastened. Reluctantly I pulled off mine while Betsie rummaged in the wardrobe.

At thirteen, Betsie seemed almost an adult to me. Of course Betsie had always seemed older because she couldn't run and roughhouse the way other children did. Betsie had been born with pernicious anemia. And so while the rest of us played tag or bowl-the-hoop or had skate races down frozen canals in winter, Betsie sat and did dull grown-up things like embroidery. But Nollie played as hard as anyone and wasn't much older than I and it didn't seem fair that she should always do everything right.

"Betsie," she was saying earnestly, "I'm *not* going to wear that great ugly hat to school just because Tante Jans paid for it. Last year it was that ugly gray one— and this year's is even worse!"

Betsie looked at her sympathetically. "Well, but . . . you can't go to school without a hat. And you know we can't afford another one."

"We don't have to!"

With an anxious glance at the door, Nollie dropped to her knees, reached beneath the single bed which was all our tiny room would hold, and drew out a little round

18

hat box. Inside nestled the smallest hat I had ever seen. It was of fur, with a blue satin ribbon for under the chin.

"Oh, the darling thing!" Betsie lifted it reverently from the box and held it up to the patch of light that struggled into the room over the surrounding rooftops. "Where did you ever——"

"Mrs. van Dyver gave it to me." The van Dyvers owned the millinery shop two doors down. "She saw me looking at it and later she brought it here, after Tante Jans picked out . . . *that.*"

Nollie pointed to the top of the wardrobe. A deep-rimmed brown bonnet with a cluster of lavender velvet roses proclaimed in every line the personage who had picked it out. Tante Jans, Mama's older sister, had moved in with us when her husband died to spend, as she put it, "what few days remain to me," though she was still only in her early forties.

Her coming had greatly complicated life in the old house—already crowded by the earlier arrivals of Mama's other two sisters, Tante Bep and Tante Anna—since along with Tante Jans had come quantities of furniture, all of it too large for the little rooms at the Beje.

For her own use Tante Jans took the two second-story rooms of the front house, directly over the watch shop and workroom. In the first room she wrote the flaming Christian tracts for which she was known all over Holland, and in the second received the well-to-do ladies who supported this work. Tante Jans believed that our welfare in the hereafter depended on how much we could accomplish here on earth. For sleep she partitioned off a cubicle from her writing room just large enough to hold a bed. Death, she often said, was waiting to snatch her from her work, and so she kept her hours of repose as brief and businesslike as possible.

I could not remember life in the Beje before Tante Jans's arrival, nor whose these two rooms had been before. Above them was a narrow attic beneath the steep, sloping roof of the first house. For as long as I could recall, this space had been divided into four truly miniature rooms. The first one, looking out over the Barteljorisstraat—and the only one with a real window—was Tante Bep's. Behind it, strung like railroad compartments off a narrow aisle, were Tante Anna's, Betsie's, and our brother Willem's. Five steps up from these rooms, in the second house behind, was Nollie's and my small room, beneath ours Mama's and Father's room, and beneath theirs the dining room with the kitchen tacked like an afterthought to the side of it.

If Tante Jans's share in this crowded house was remarkably large, it never seemed so to any of us living there. The world just naturally made place for Tante Jans. All day long the horse-drawn trolley clopped and clanged past our house to stop at the Grote Markt, the central town square half a block away. At least that was where it stopped for other people. When Tante Jans wished to go somewhere she stationed herself on the sidewalk directly in front of the watch-shop door and as the horses thundered close, held up a single gloved finger. It looked to me more possible to stop the sun in the sky than to halt the charge of that trolley before its appointed place. But it stopped for Tante Jans, brakes squealing, horses nearly falling over one another, and the driver tipped his tall hat as she swept aboard.

And this was the commanding eye past which Nollie had to get the little fur hat. Tante Jans had bought most of the clothing for us three girls since coming to live with us, but her gifts had a price. To Tante Jans, the clothes in fashion when she was young represented God's final say on human apparel; all change since then came from the style-book of the devil. Indeed, one of her best-known pamphlets exposed him as the inventor of the mutton sleeve and the bicycle skirt.

"I know!" I said now as the buttonhook in Betsie's swift fingers sped up my shoes, "you could fit the fur hat right inside the bonnet! Then when you get outside, take the bonnet off!"

"Corrie!" Nollie was genuinely shocked. "That wouldn't be honest!" And with a baleful glance at the big brown hat she picked up the little fur one and started after Betsie round the stairs down to breakfast.

I picked up my own hat—the despised gray one from last year—and trailed after them, one hand clinging to the center post. Let Tante Jans see the silly hat then. I didn't care. I never could understand all the fuss over clothes.

What I did understand, what was awful and alarming, was that this was the day I was to start school. To leave this old house above the watch shop, leave Mama and Father and the aunts, in fact leave behind everything that was certain and well-loved. I gripped the post so tight that my palm squeaked as I circled around. The elementary school was only a block and a half away, it was true, and Nollie had gone there two years without difficulty. But Nollie was different from me; she was pretty and well-behaved and always had her handkerchief.

And then, as I rounded the final curve, the solution came to me, so clear and simple that I laughed out loud. I just wouldn't go to school! I'd stay here and help Tante Anna with the cooking and Mama would teach me to read and I'd never go into that strange ugly building at all. Relief and comfort flooded me and I took the last three steps in a bound.

"Shhh!" Betsie and Nollie were waiting for me outside the dining room door. "For heaven's sake, Corrie, don't do anything to get Tante Jans started wrong," Betsie said. "I'm sure," she added doubtfully, "that Father and Mama and Tante Anna will like Nollie's hat."

"Tante Bep won't," I said.

"She never likes anything," Nollie said, "so she doesn't count."

Tante Bep, with her perpetual, disapproving scowl, was the oldest of the aunts and the one we children liked least. For thirty years she had worked as a governess in wealthy families and she continually compared our behavior with that of the young ladies and gentlemen she was used to.

Betsie pointed to the Frisian clock on the stairwall, and with a finger on her lips silently opened the dining room door. It was 8:12: breakfast had already begun.

"Two minutes late!" cried Willem triumphantly.

"The Waller children were never late," said Tante Bep.

"But they're here!" said Father. "And the room is brighter!"

The three of us hardly heard: Tante Jans's chair was empty.

"Is Tante Jans staying in bed today?" asked Betsie hopefully as we hung our hats on their pegs.

"She's making herself a tonic in the kitchen," said Mama. She leaned forward to pour our coffee and lowered her voice. "We must all be specially considerate of dear Jans today. This is the day her husband's sister died some years ago—or was it his cousin?"

"I thought it was his aunt," said Tante Anna.

"It was a cousin and it was a mercy," said Tante Bep.

"At any rate," Mama hurried on, "you know how these anniversaries upset dear Jans, so we must all try to make it up to her."

Betsie cut three slices from the round loaf of bread while I looked around the table trying to decide which adult would be most enthusiastic about my decision to stay at home. Father, I knew, put an almost religious importance on education. He himself had had to stop school early to go to work in the watch shop, and though he had gone on to teach himself history, theology, and literature in five languages, he always regretted the missed schooling. He would want me to go— and whatever Father wanted, Mama wanted too.

Tante Anna then? She'd often told me she couldn't manage without me to run errands up and down the steep stairs. Since Mama was not strong, Tante Anna did most of the heavy housework for our family of nine. She was the youngest of the four sisters, with a spirit as generous as Mama's own. There was a myth in our family, firmly believed in by all, that Tante Anna received wages for this work— and indeed every Saturday Father faithfully paid her one guilder. But by Wednesday when the greengrocer came he often had to ask for it back, and she always had it, unspent and waiting. Yes, she would be my ally in this business.

"Tante Anna," I began, "I've been thinking about you working so hard all day when I'm in school and——"

A deep dramatic intake of breath made us all look up. Tante Jans was standing in the kitchen doorway, a tumbler of thick brown liquid in her hand. When she had filled her chest with air she closed her eyes, lifted the glass to her lips and drained it down. Then with a sigh she let out the breath, set the glass on the sideboard and sat down.

"And yet," she said, as though we had been discussing the subject, "what do doctors know? Dr. Blinker prescribed this tonic—but what can medicine really do? What good does anything do when one's Day arrives?"

I glanced round the table; no one was smiling. Tante Jans's preoccupation with death might have been funny, but it wasn't. Young as I was I knew that fear is never funny.

"And yet, Jans," Father remonstrated gently, "medicine has prolonged many a life."

"It didn't help Zusje! And she had the finest doctors in Rotterdam. It was this very day when she was taken—and she was no older than I am now, and got up and dressed for breakfast that day, just as I have."

She was launching into a minute-by-minute account of Zusje's final day when her eyes lit on the peg from which dangled Nollie's new hat.

"A fur muff?" she demanded, each word bristling with suspicion. "At this time of year!"

"It isn't a muff, Tante Jans," said Nollie in a small voice.

"And is it possible to learn what it is?"

"It's a hat, Tante Jans," Betsie answered for her, "a surprise from Mrs. van Dyver. Wasn't it nice of——"

"Oh no. Nollie's hat has a brim, as a well-brought-up girl's should. I know. I bought—and paid—for it myself."

There were flames in Tante Jans's eyes, tears in Nollie's when Mama came to the rescue. "I'm not at *all* sure this cheese is fresh!" She sniffed at the big pot of yellow cheese in the center of the table and pushed it across to Father. "What do you think, Casper?"

Father, who was incapable of practicing deceit or even recognizing it, took a long and earnest sniff. "I'm sure it's perfectly fine, my dear! Fresh as the day it came. Mr. Steerwijk's cheese is always——" Catching Mama's look he stared from her to Jans in confusion. "Oh—er—ah, Jans—ah, what do you think?"

Tante Jans seized the pot and glared into it with righteous zeal. If there was one subject which engaged her energies even more completely than modern clothing it was spoiled food. At last, almost reluctantly it seemed to me, she approved the cheese, but the hat was forgotten. She had plunged into the sad story of an acquaintance "my very age" who had died after eating a questionable fish, when the shop people arrived and Father took down the heavy Bible from its shelf.

There were only two employees in the watch shop in 1898, the clock man and Father's young apprentice-errand boy. When Mama had poured their coffee, Father put on his rimless spectacles and began to read:

"Thy word is a lamp unto my feet, and a light unto my path. . . . Thou art my hiding place and my shield: I hope in thy word. . . ."

What kind of hiding place, I wondered idly as I watched Father's brown beard rise and fall with the words. What was there to hide from?

It was a long, long psalm; beside me Nollie began to squirm. When at last Father closed the big volume, she, Willem, and Betsie were on their feet in an instant and snatching up their hats. Next minute they had raced down the last five stairs and out the alley door.

More slowly the two shopworkers got up and followed them down the stairs to the shop's rear entrance. Only then did the five adults notice me still seated at the table.

"Corrie!" cried Mama. "Have you forgotten you're a big girl now? Today you go to school too! Hurry, or you must cross the street alone!"

"I'm not going."

There was a short, startled silence, broken by everybody at once.

"When I was a girl——" Tante Jans began.

"Mrs. Waller's children——" from Tante Bep.

But Father's deep voice drowned them out. "Of course she's not going alone! Nollie was excited today and forgot to wait, that's all. Corrie is going with me."

And with that he took my hat from its peg, wrapped my hand in his and led me from the room. My hand in Father's! That meant the windmill on the Spaarne, or swans on the canal. But this time he was taking me where I didn't want to go! There was a railing along the bottom five steps: I grabbed it with my free hand and held on. Skilled watchmaker's fingers closed over mine and gently unwound them. Howling and struggling I was led away from the world I knew into a bigger, stranger, harder one . . . .

Mondays, Father took the train to Amsterdam to get the time from the Naval Observatory. Now that I had started school it was only in the summer that I could go with him. I would race downstairs to the shop, scrubbed, buttoned, and pronounced passable by Betsie. Father would be giving last-minute instructions to the apprentice. "Mrs. Staal will be in this morning to pick up her watch. This clock goes to the Bakker's in Bloemendaal."

And then we would be off to the station, hand in hand, I lengthening my strides and he shortening his to keep in step. The train trip to Amsterdam took only half an hour, but it was a wonderful ride. First the close-wedged buildings of old Haarlem gave way to separate houses with little plots of land around them. The spaces between houses grew wider. And then we were in the country, the flat Dutch farmland stretching to the horizon ruler-straight canals sweeping past the window. At last, Amsterdam, even bigger than Haarlem, with its bewilderment of strange streets and canals.

Father always arrived a couple of hours before the time signal in order to visit the wholesalers who supplied him with watches and parts. Many of these were Jews, and these were the visits we both liked best. After the briefest possible discussion of business, Father would draw a small Bible from his traveling case; the wholesaler, whose beard would be even longer and fuller than Father's, would snatch a book or a scroll out of a drawer, clap a prayer cap onto his head; and the two of them would be off, arguing, comparing, interrupting, contradicting— reveling in each other's company.

And then, just when I had decided that this time I had really been forgotten, the wholesaler would look up, catch sight of me as though for the first time, and strike his forehead with the heel of his hand.

"A guest! A guest in my gates and I have offered her no refreshment!" And springing up he would rummage under shelves and into cupboards and before long I would be holding on my lap a plate of the most delicious treats in the world—honey cakes and date cakes and a kind of confection of nuts, fruits, and sugar. Desserts were rare in the Beje, sticky delights like these unknown.

By five minutes before noon we were always back at the train station, standing at a point on the platform from which we had a good view of the tower of the Naval Observatory. On the top of the tower where it could be seen by all the ships in the harbor was a tall shaft with two movable arms. At the stroke of 12:00 noon each day the arms dropped. Father would stand at his vantage point on the platform almost on tiptoe with the joy of precision, holding his pocket watch and a pad and pencil. There! Four seconds fast. Within an hour the "astronomical clock" in the shop in Haarlem would be accurate to the second.

On the train trip home we no longer gazed out the window. Instead we talked—about different things as the years passed. Betsie's graduation from secondary school in spite of the months missed with illness. Whether Willem, when he graduated, would get the scholarship that would let him go on to the university. Betsie starting work as Father's bookkeeper in the shop.

Oftentimes I would use the trip home to bring up things that were troubling me, since anything I asked at home was promptly answered by the aunts. Once—I must have been ten or eleven—I asked Father about a poem we had read at school the winter before. One line had described "a young man whose face was not shadowed by sexsin." I had been far too shy to ask the teacher what it meant, and Mama had blushed scarlet when I consulted her. In those days just after the turn of the century sex was never discussed, even at home.

So the line had stuck in my head. "Sex," I was pretty sure, meant whether you were a boy or a girl, and "sin" made Tante Jans very angry, but what the two together meant I could not imagine. And so, seated next to Father in the train compartment, I suddenly asked, "Father, what is sexsin?"

He turned to look at me, as he always did when answering a question, but to my surprise he said nothing. At last he stood up, lifted his traveling case from the rack over our heads, and set it on the floor.

"Will you carry it off the train, Corrie?" he said.

I stood up and tugged at it. It was crammed with the watches and spare parts he had purchased that morning.

"It's too heavy," I said.

"Yes," he said. "And it would be a pretty poor father who would ask his little girl to carry such a load. It's the same way, Corrie, with knowledge. Some knowledge is too heavy for children. When you are older and stronger you can bear it. For now you must trust me to carry it for you."

And I was satisfied. More than satisfied—wonderfully at peace. There were answers to this and all my hard questions—for now I was content to leave them in my father's keeping.

Evenings at the Beje there was always company and music. Guests would bring their flutes or violins and, as each member of the family sang or played an instrument, we made quite an orchestra gathered around the upright piano in Tante Jans's front room.

The only evenings when we did not make our own music was when there was a concert in town. We could not afford tickets but there was a stage door at the side of the concert hall through which sounds came clearly. There in the alley outside this door we and scores of other Haarlem music lovers followed every note. Mama and Betsie were not strong enough to stand so many hours, but some of us from the Beje would be there, in rain and snow and frost, and while from inside we would hear coughs and stirrings, there was never a rustle in the listeners at the door.

Best of all was when there were concerts at the cathedral, because a relative was sexton there. Just inside his small private entrance a wooden bench ran along the wall. Here we sat, our backs chilled by the ancient stone, our ears and hearts warmed by the music.

The great golden organ was one that Mozart had played, and some of its notes seemed to come from heaven itself. Indeed, I was sure that heaven was like St. Bavo's, and probably about the same size. Hell, I knew, was a hot place, so heaven must be like this cold, dank, holy building, where smoke rose like incense from the footwarmers of the paying customers. In heaven, I fervently believed, everybody had footwarmers. Even in the summer the chill never left the marble grave slabs on the floor. But when the organist touched the keys we scarcely noticed—and when he played Bach, not at all.

I was following Mama and Nollie up a dark, straight flight of stairs where cobwebs clutched at our hair and mice scuttled away ahead of us. The building was less than a block from the Beje, and probably a century newer, but here was no Tante Anna to wax and scrub.

We were going to see one of the many poor families in the neighborhood whom Mama had adopted. It never occurred to any of us children that we ourselves were poor; "the poor" were people you took baskets to. Mama was always cooking up nourishing broths and porridges for forgotten old men and pale young mothers—on days, that is, when she herself was strong enough to stand at the stove.

The night before, a baby had died, and with a basket of her own fresh bread Mama was making the prescribed call on the family. She toiled painfully up the railless stairs, stopping often for breath. At the top a door opened into a single room that was obviously cooking, eating, and sleeping quarters all at once. There were already many visitors, most of them standing for lack of chairs. Mama went at once to the young mother, but I stood frozen on the threshold. Just to the right of the door, so still in the homemade crib, was the baby.

It was strange that a society which hid the facts of sex from children made no effort to shield them from death. I stood staring at the tiny unmoving form with my heart thudding strangely against my ribs. Nollie, always braver than I, stretched out her hand and touched the ivory-white cheek. I longed to do it too, but hung back, afraid. For a while curiosity and terror struggled in me. At last I put one finger on the small curled hand.

It was cold.

Cold as we walked back to the Beje, cold as I washed for supper, cold even in the snug gas-lit dining room. Between me and each familiar face around the table crept those small icy fingers. For all Tante Jans's talk about it, death had been only a word. Now I knew that it could really happen—if to the baby, then to Mama, to Father, to Betsie!

Still shivering with that cold, I followed Nollie up to our room and crept into bed beside her. At last we heard Father's footsteps winding up the stairs. It was the best moment in every day, when he came up to tuck us in. We never fell asleep until he had arranged the blankets in his special way and laid his hand for a moment on each head. Then we tried not to move even a toe.

But that night as he stepped through the door I burst into tears. "I need you!" I sobbed. "You can't die! You can't!"

Beside me on the bed Nollie sat up. "We went to see Mrs. Hoog," she explained. "Corrie didn't eat her supper or anything."

Father sat down on the edge of the narrow bed. "Corrie," he began gently, "when you and I go to Amsterdam—when do I give you your ticket?"

I sniffed a few times, considering this.

"Why, just before we get on the train."

"Exactly. And our wise Father in heaven knows when we're going to need things, too. Don't run out ahead of Him, Corrie. When the time comes that some of us will have to die, you will look into your heart and find the strength you need— just in time."

3. Karel

I FIRST MET Karel at one of the "occasions" for which Mama was famous. Afterward I never could remember whether it was a birthday, a wedding anniversary, a new baby—Mama could make a party out of anything. Willem introduced him as a friend from Leiden and he shook hands with us one by one. I took that long strong hand, looked up into those deep brown eyes and fell irretrievably in love.

As soon as everyone had coffee I sat down just to gaze at him. He seemed quite unaware of me, but that was only natural. I was a child of fourteen, while he and Willem were already university men, sprouting straggly beards and breathing out cigar smoke with their conversation.

It was enough, I felt, to be in the same room with Karel. As for being unnoticed, I was thoroughly used to that. Nollie was the one boys noticed, though like so many pretty girls, she seemed not to care. When a boy asked for a lock of her hair— the standard method in those days of declaring passion—she would pull a few strands from the ancient gray carpet in our bedroom, tie them with a sentimental blue ribbon, and make me the messenger. The carpet was quite threadbare by now, the school full of broken hearts.

I, on the other hand, fell in love with each boy in my class in turn, in a kind of hopeless, regular rhythm. But since I was not pretty, and far too bashful to express my feelings, a whole generation of boys was growing up unaware of the girl in seat thirty-two.

Karel, though, I thought as I watched him spooning sugar into his cup, was different. I was going to love Karel forever.

It was two years before I saw Karel again. That was the winter, 1908, that Nollie and I made a trip to the university at Leiden to pay Willem a visit. Willem's sparsely furnished room was on the fourth floor of a private home. He gathered both Nollie and me into a bear-hug and then ran to the window.

"Here," he said, taking in from the sill a cream bun he had been keeping cold there. "I bought this for you. You'd better eat it quick before my starving friends arrive."

We sat on the edge of Willem's bed gulping down the precious bun; I suspected that to buy it Willem had had to go without lunch. A second later the door slammed open and in burst four of his friends—tall, deep-voiced young men in coats with twice-turned collars and threadbare cuffs. Among them was Karel.

I swallowed the last bite of cream bun, wiped my hands on the back of my skirt and stood up. Willem introduced Nollie and me around. But when he came to Karel, Karel interrupted.

"We know each other already." He bowed ever so slightly. "Do you remember? We met at a party at your home." I glanced from Karel to Nollie—but no, he was looking straight at me. My heart poured out a rapturous reply, but my mouth was still filled with the sticky remains of bun and it never reached my lips. Soon the young men were seated at our feet on the floor, all talking eagerly and at once.

Perched beside me on the bed, Nollie joined in as naturally as though visiting a university was an everyday event for us. For one thing, she looked the part: at eighteen she was already in long skirts, while I was acutely conscious of the six inches of thick black school-girl stockings between the hem of my dress and the top of my shoes.

Also, Nollie had things to talk about: the year before she had started Normal School. She didn't really want to be a teacher, but in those days universities did not offer scholarships to girls and Normal Schools were inexpensive. And so she chatted easily and knowledgeably about things of interest to students—this new theory of relativity by a man called Einstein, and whether Admiral Peary would really reach the North Pole.

"And you, Corrie. Will you go on to be a teacher, too?"

Sitting on the floor at my feet, Karel was smiling at me. I felt a blush rise beneath my high collar.

"Next year, I mean," he persisted. "This is your final year in secondary school, isn't it?"

"Yes. I mean—no. I'll stay home with Mama and Tante Anna."

It came out so short and flat. Why did I say so little when I wanted to say so very much? . . .

That spring I finished school and took over the work of the household. It had always been planned that I would do this, but now there was an added reason. Tante Bep had tuberculosis.

The disease was regarded as incurable: the only known treatment was rest at a sanatorium and that was only for the rich. And so for many months Tante Bep lay in her little closet of a room, coughing away her life.

To keep down the risk of infection, only Tante Anna went in or out. Around the clock she nursed her older sister, many nights getting no sleep at all, and so the cooking and washing and cleaning for the family fell to me. I loved the work, and except for Tante Bep would have been completely happy. But over everything lay her shadow: not only the illness, but her whole disgruntled and disappointed life.

Often I would catch a glimpse inside when I handed in a tray or Tante Anna passed one out. There were the few pathetic mementos of thirty years in other people's homes. Perfume bottles—empty many years—because well-bred families always gave the governess perfume for Christmas. Some faded Daguerrotypes of children who by now must have children and grandchildren of their own. Then the door would shut. But I would linger in that narrow passage under the eaves, yearning to say something, to heal something. Wanting to love her better.

I spoke once about my feelings to Mama. She too was more and more often in bed. Always before when pain from the gallstones had got too bad she'd had an operation. But a small stroke after the last one made further surgery impossible, and many days, making up a tray for Tante Bep, I carried one upstairs to Mama also.

This time when I brought in her lunch she was writing letters. When Mama wasn't supplying the neighborhood with caps and baby dresses from her flying needles, she was composing cheery messages for shut-ins all over Haarlem. The fact that she herself had been shut-in much of her life never seemed to occur to her. "Here's a poor man, Corrie," she cried as I came in, "who's been cooped up in a single room for three years. Just think, shut away from the sky!"

I glanced out Mama's single window at the brick wall three feet away. "Mama," I said as I set the tray on the bed and sat down beside it, "can't we do something for Tante Bep? I mean, isn't it sad that she has to spend her last days here where she hates it, instead of where she was so happy? The Wallers' or someplace?"

Mama laid down her pen and looked at me. "Corrie," she said at last, "Bep has been just as happy here with us—no more and no less—than she was anywhere else."

I stared at her, not understanding.

"Do you know when she started praising the Wallers so highly?" Mama went on. "The day she left them. As long as she was there, she had nothing but complaints. The Wallers couldn't compare with the van Hooks where she'd been before. But at the van Hooks she'd actually been miserable. Happiness isn't something that depends on our surroundings, Corrie. It's something we make inside ourselves."

Tante Bep's death affected her sisters in characteristic fashion. Mama and Tante Anna redoubled their cooking and sewing for the needy in the neighborhood, as though realizing how brief was anyone's lifetime of service. As for Tante Jans, her own particular specter moved very close. "My own sister," she would exclaim at odd moments of the day. "Why, it might as well have been me!"

A year or so after Tante Bep's death, a new doctor took over Dr. Blinker's house calls. The new man's name was Jan van Veen and with him came his young sister and nurse, Tine van Veen. With him also came a new gadget for taking blood pressure. We had no idea what this meant but everyone in the household submitted to having the strip of cloth wrapped around his arm and air pumped into it.

Tante Jans, who loved medical paraphernalia of every kind, took a tremendous fancy to the new doctor and from then on consulted him as often as her finances would permit. And so it was Dr. van Veen, a couple of years later, who first discovered that Tante Jans had diabetes.

In those days this was a death sentence as surely as tuberculosis had been. For days the household was numb with the shock of it. After all these years of fearing even the idea, here was the dread thing itself. Tante Jans went straight to bed on hearing the news.

But inaction went poorly with her vigorous personality and one morning to everyone's surprise she appeared for breakfast in the dining room precisely at 8:10, with the announcement that doctors were often wrong. "All these tests and tubes," said Tante Jans, who believed in them implicitly, "what do they really prove?"

And from then on she threw herself more forcefully than ever into writing, speaking, forming clubs, and launching projects. Holland in 1914, like the rest of Europe, was mobilizing for war, and the streets of Haarlem were suddenly filled with young men in uniform. From her windows overlooking the Barteljorisstraat, Tante Jans watched them idling by, gazing aimlessly into the shop windows, most of them young, penniless, and lonesome. And she conceived the idea of a soldiers' center.

It was a novel idea for its day and Tante Jans threw all the passion of her nature into it. The horse-drawn trolley on the Barteljorisstraat had recently been replaced with a big new electric one. But it still squealed to a stop, spitting sparks from rails and wire, when Tante Jans stood imperiously before the Beje. She would sweep aboard, her long black skirts in one hand, in the other a list of the well-to-do ladies who were about to become patronesses of the new venture. Only those of us who knew her best were aware, beneath all the activity, of the monstrous fear which drove her on.

And meanwhile her disease posed financial problems. Each week a fresh test had to be made to determine the sugar-content of her blood, and this was a complicated and expensive process requiring either Dr. van Veen or his sister to come to the house.

At last Tine van Veen taught me to run the weekly test myself. There were several steps involved, the most crucial being to heat the final compound to exactly the right temperature. It was hard to make the old coal-burning range in our dark kitchen do anything very precisely, but I finally learned how and from then on each Friday mixed the chemicals and conducted the test myself. If the mixture remained clear when heated, all was well. It was only if it turned black that I was to notify Dr. van Veen.

It was that spring that Willem came home for his final holiday before ordination. He had graduated from the university two years before and was now in his last months of theological school. One warm evening during his visit we were all sitting around the dining room table. Father with thirty watches spread out before him was marking in a little notebook in his precise, beautiful script: "two seconds lost," "five seconds gained," while Willem read aloud from a history of the Dutch Reformation.

All at once the bell in the alley rang. Outside the dining room window a mirror faced the alley door so that we could see who was there before going down to open it. I glanced into it and sprang up from the table.

"Corrie!" said Betsie reprovingly. "Your skirt!"

I could never remember that I was wearing long skirts now, and Betsie spent many evenings mending the rips I put in them when I moved too fast. Now I took all five steps in a bound. For at the door, a bouquet of daffodils in her hands, was Tine van Veen. Whether it was the soft spring night that put it in my mind, or Willem's dramatic, pulpit-trained voice, I suddenly knew that the meeting of these two people had to be a very special moment.

"For your mother, Corrie," Tine said, holding out the flowers as I opened the door. "I hope she's——"

"No, no, you carry the flowers! You look beautiful with them!" And without even taking her coat I pushed the startled girl up the stairs ahead of me.

I prodded her through the dining room door, almost treading on her heels to see Willem's reaction. I knew exactly how it would be. My life was lived just then in romantic novels; I borrowed them from the library in English, Dutch, and German, often reading ones I liked in all three languages, and I had played this scene where hero meets heroine a thousand times.

Willem rose slowly to his feet, his eyes never leaving Tine's. Father stood up too. "Miss van Veen," Father said in his old-fashioned manner, "allow me to present to you our son, Willem. Willem, this is the young lady of whose talent and kindness you have heard us speak."

I doubt if either one heard the introduction. They were staring at each other as though there were not another soul in the room or in the world.

Willem and Tine were married two months after his ordination. During all the weeks of getting ready, one thought stood out in my mind: Karel will be there. The wedding day dawned cool and sparkling. My eyes picked Karel immediately from the crowd in front of the church, dressed in top hat and tails as were all the male guests, but incomparably the handsomest there.

As for me, I felt that a transformation had taken place since he had seen me last. The difference between my twenty-one years and his twenty-six was not, after all, as big as it had once been.

But more than that, I felt—no, not beautiful. Even on such a romantic day as this I could not persuade myself of that. I knew that my jaw was too square, my legs too long, my hands too large. But I earnestly believed—and all the books agreed—that I would look beautiful to the man who loved me.

Betsie had done my hair that morning, laboring for an hour with the curling iron until it was piled high on my head—and so far, for a wonder, it had stayed. She'd made my silk dress too, as she'd made one for each of the women in the family, working by lamplight in the evenings because the shop was open six days a week and she would not sew on Sundays.

Now looking around me I decided that our homemade outfits were as stylish as any there. Nobody would guess, I thought as the gentle press toward the door began, that Father had given up his cigars and Tante Jans the coal fire in her rooms in order to buy the silk that swished so elegantly with us now.

"Corrie?"

In front of me stood Karel, tall black hat in his hands, his eyes searching my face as though he were not quite sure.

"Yes, it's me!" I said, laughing up at him. It's me, Karel, and it's you, and it's the moment I've been dreaming of!

"But you're so—so grown up. Forgive me, Corrie, of course you are! It's just that I've always thought of you as the little girl with the enormous blue eyes." He stared at me a little longer and then added softly, "And now the little girl is a lady, and a lovely one."

Suddenly the organ music swelling from the open door was for us, the arm he offered me was the moon, and my gloved hand resting upon it the only thing that kept me from soaring right over the peaked rooftops of Haarlem.

It was a windy, rainy Friday morning in January when my eyes told me what at first my brain refused to grasp. The liquid in the glass beaker on the kitchen stove was a muddy, sullen black.

I leaned against the old wooden sink and shut my eyes. "Please God, let me have made a mistake!" I went over in my mind the different steps, looked at the vials of chemicals, the measuring spoons. No. All just the same as I'd always done.

It was this wretched room then—it was always dark in this little cupboard of a kitchen. With a pot holder I snatched up the beaker and ran to the window in the dining room.

Black. Black as fear itself.

Still clutching the beaker I pounded down the five steps and through the rear door of the shop. Father, his jeweler's glass in his eye, was bent over the shoulder of the newest apprentice, deftly selecting an infinitesimal part from the array before them on the workbench.

I looked through the glass in the door to the shop, but Betsie, behind her little cashier's desk, was talking to a customer. Not a customer, I corrected myself, a nuisance—I knew the woman. She came here for advice on watches and then bought them at that new place, Kan's, across the street. Neither Father nor Betsie seemed to care that this was happening more and more.

As the woman left I burst through the door with the telltale beaker.

"Betsie!" I cried. "Oh Betsie, it's black! How are we going to tell her? What are we going to do?"

Betsie came swiftly from behind the desk and put her arms around me. Behind me Father came into the shop. His eyes traveled from the beaker to Betsie to me.

"And you did it exactly right, Corrie? In every detail?"

"I'm afraid so, Father."

"And I am sure of it, my dear. But we must have the doctor's verdict too."

"I'll take it at once," I said.

And so I poured the ugly liquid into a small bottle and ran with it over the slippery, rain-washed streets of Haarlem.

There was a new nurse at Dr. van Veen's and I spent a miserable, silent half-hour in the waiting room. At last his patient left and Dr. van Veen took the bottle into his small laboratory.

"There is no mistake, Corrie," he said as he emerged. "Your aunt has three weeks at the very most."

We held a family conference in the watch shop when I got back: Mama, Tante Anna, Father, Betsie, and me (Nollie did not get home from her teaching job until evening). We agreed that Tante Jans must know at once.

"We will tell her together," Father decided, "though I will speak the necessary words. And perhaps," he said, his face brightening, "perhaps she will take heart from all she has accomplished. She puts great store on accomplishment, Jans does, and who knows but that she is right!"

And so the little procession filed up the steps to Tante Jans's rooms. "Come in," she called to Father's knock, and added as she always did, "and close the door before I catch my death of drafts."

She was sitting at her round mahogany table, working on yet another appeal for her soldiers' center. As she saw the number of people entering the room, she laid down her pen. She looked from one face to another, until she came to mine and gave a little gasp of comprehension. This was Friday morning, and I had not yet come up with the results of the test.

"My dear sister-in-law," Father began gently, "there is a joyous journey which each of God's children sooner or later sets out on. And, Jans, some must go to their Father empty-handed, but you will run to Him with hands full!"

"All your clubs . . . ," Tante Anna ventured.

"Your writings . . . ," Mama added.

"The funds you've raised . . . ," said Betsie.

"Your talks . . . ," I began

But our well-meant words were useless. In front of us the proud face crumpled; Tante Jans put her hands over her eyes and began to cry. "Empty, empty!" she choked at last through her tears. "How can we bring anything to God? What does He care for our little tricks and trinkets?"

And then as we listened in disbelief she lowered her hands and with tears still coursing down her face whispered, "Dear Jesus, I thank You that we must come with empty hands. I thank You that You have done all—all—on the Cross, and that all we need in life or death is to be sure of this."

Mama threw her arms around her and they clung together. But I stood rooted to the spot, knowing that I had seen a mystery.

It was Father's train ticket, given at the moment itself.

With a flourish of her handkerchief and a forceful clearing of her nose, Tante Jans let us know that the moment for sentiment had passed.

"If I had a moment's privacy," she said, "I might get some work accomplished."

She glanced at Father, and into those stern eyes crept the nearest thing to a twinkle I had ever seen. "Not that the work matters, Casper. Not that it matters at all. But," she dismissed us crisply, "I'm not going to leave an untidy desk behind for someone else to clean up."

It was four months after Tante Jans' funeral that the long-awaited invitation came to Willem's First Sermon. After less than a year as assistant to a minister in Uithuizen, he had been given a church of his own in Brabant, the beautiful rural southern part of Holland. And in the Dutch Reformed Church, a minister's first sermon in his first church was the most solemn, joyous, emotional occasion that an unemotional people could conceive. Family and friends would come from great distances and stay for days.

From his own assistant pastorate, Karel wrote that he would be there and looked forward to seeing us all again. I endowed that word "all" with special meaning and pressed dresses and packed trunks in a delirium of anticipation.

It was one of Mama's bad times. She huddled in the corner of our train compartment, the hand that gripped Father's whitening at the knuckles each time the train lurched or swayed. But while the rest of us gazed out at long rows of poplars in their bright June green, Mama's eyes never left the sky. What to us was a trip through the country, to her was a feast of clouds and light and infinite blue distances.

Both the village of Made and the congregation of Willem's church had declined in recent years. But the church building itself, dating back to better days, was large, and so was Willem and Tine's house across the street. Indeed by Beje standards it was enormous; for the first few nights the ceiling seemed so far overhead that I could not sleep. Uncles and cousins and friends arrived each day, but no matter how many people moved in, the rooms always looked to me half empty.

Three days after we got there I answered the front door knocker and there stood Karel, coal dust from the train trip still speckling his shoulders. He tossed his brown carpetbag past me into the hall, seized my hand, and drew me out into the June sunshine. "It's a lovely day in the country, Corrie!" he cried. "Come walking!"

From then on it seemed taken for granted that Karel and I would go walking each day. Each time we wandered a little farther down the country lanes that wound in every direction away from the village, the dirt beneath our feet so different from the brick streets of Haarlem. It was hard to believe, at such moments, that the rest of Europe was locked in the bloodiest war in history. Even across the ocean the madness seemed to be spreading: the papers said America would enter.

Here in neutral Holland one sunlit June day followed another. Only a few people—like Willem—insisted that the war was Holland's tragedy too. His first sermon was on this theme. Europe and the world were changing, he said: no matter which side won, a way of life was gone forever. I looked around at his congregation of sturdy villagers and farmers and saw that they did not care for such ideas.

After the sermon, friends and more distant family started home. But Karel lingered on. Our walks lasted longer. Often we talked about Karel's future, and suddenly we were speaking not about what Karel was going to do, but about what we were going to do. We imagined that we had a huge old manse like this one to decorate, and rejoiced to discover that we had the same ideas about furniture, flowers, even the same favorite colors. Only about children did we disagree: Karel wanted four, while I held out stubbornly for six.

And all this while the word "marriage" was never spoken.

One day when Karel was in the village, Willem came out of the kitchen with two cups of coffee in his hands. Tine with a cup of her own was just behind him.

"Corrie," Willem said, handing me the coffee and speaking as though with effort, "has Karel led you to believe that he is——"

"Serious?" Tine finished his sentence for him.

The hateful blush that I could never control set my cheeks burning. "I . . . no . . . we . . . why?"

Willem's face reddened too. "Because, Corrie, this is something that can never be. You don't know Karel's family. They've wanted one thing since he was a small child. They've sacrificed for it, planned for it, built their whole lives around it. Karel is to . . . 'marry well' is the way I think they put it."

The big barren parlor seemed suddenly emptier still. "But—what about what Karel wants? He's not a small child now!"

Willem fixed his sober, deep-set eyes on mine. "He will do it, Corrie. I don't say he wants it. To him it's just a fact of life like any other. When we'd talk about girls we liked—at the university—he'd always say at the end, 'Of course I could never marry her. It would kill my mother.'"

The hot coffee scalded my mouth but I gulped it down and made my escape to the garden. I hated that gloomy old house and sometimes I almost hated Willem for always seeing the dark, hard side of things. Here in the garden it was different. There wasn't a bush, hardly a flower, that Karel and I hadn't looked at together, that didn't have a bit of our feeling for each other still clinging to it. Willem might know more than I did about theology and war and politics—but when it came to romance! Things like money, social prestige, family expectations, why, in the books they vanished like rainclouds, every time. . . .

Karel left Made a week or so later, and his last words made my heart soar. Only months afterward did I remember how strangely he spoke them, the urgency, almost desperation in his voice. We were standing in the driveway of the manse waiting for the horse and cart which Made still regarded as the only dependable conveyance when there was a train to be caught. We had said goodbye after breakfast and if part of me was disappointed that he still had not proposed, another part of me was content just to be beside him. Now suddenly in the driveway he seized both my hands.

"Corrie, write to me!" he said, but not gaily. Pleadingly. "Write me about the Beje! I want to know everything. I want every detail of that ugly, beautiful, crumbling old house! Write about your father, Corrie! Write how he forgets to send the bills. Oh Corrie, it's the happiest home in Holland!"

And so it was, indeed, when Father, Mama, Betsie, Nollie, Tante Anna, and I returned. It had always been a happy place, but now each little event seemed to glow because I could share it with Karel. Every meal I cooked was an offering to him, each shining pot a poem, every sweep of the broom an act of love.

His letters did not come as often as mine went singing to him, but I put this down to his work. The minister he was assisting, he wrote, had turned the parish calling over to him: it was a wealthy congregation and large contributors expected frequent and unhurried visits from the clergy.

As time went by his letters came more seldom. I made up for it with mine and went humming my way through the summer and fall. One glorious, nippy November day when all of Holland was singing with me, the doorbell rang. I was washing the lunch dishes in the kitchen, but I ran through the dining room and down the steps before the rest of the family could stir.

I flung open the alley door and there was Karel.

Beside him was a young woman.

She stood smiling at me. I took in the hat with its sweeping feather, the ermine collar, the white-gloved hand resting on his arm. Then a blur seemed to move over the scene, for Karel was saying, "Corrie, I want you to meet my fiancée."

I must have said something. I must have led them up to Tante Jans's front room that we used now as a parlor. I only recall how my family came to the rescue, talking, shaking hands, taking coats, finding chairs, so that I would not have to do or say anything. Mama broke even her own record for making coffee. Tante Anna passed cakes. Betsie engaged the young woman in a discussion of winter fashions and Father pinned Karel in a corner with questions of the most international and impersonal nature. What did he make of the news that President Wilson was sending American troops to France?

Somehow the half-hour passed. Somehow I managed to shake her hand, then Karel's hand, and to wish them every happiness. Betsie took them down to the door. Before it clicked shut I was fleeing up the stairs to my own room at the top of the house where the tears could come.

How long I lay on my bed sobbing for the one love of my life I do not know. Later, I heard Father's footsteps coming up the stairs. For a moment I was a little girl again waiting for him to tuck the blankets tight. But this was a hurt that no blanket could shut out, and suddenly I was afraid of what Father would say. Afraid he would say, "There'll be someone else soon," and that forever afterward this untruth would lie between us. For in some deep part of me I knew already that there would not—soon or ever—be anyone else.

The sweet cigar-smell came into the room with Father. And of course he did not say the false, idle words.

"Corrie," he began instead, "do you know what hurts so very much? It's love. Love is the strongest force in the world, and when it is blocked that means pain.

"There are two things we can do when this happens. We can kill the love so that it stops hurting. But then of course part of us dies, too. Or, Corrie, we can ask God to open up another route for that love to travel.

"God loves Karel—even more than you do—and if you ask Him, He will give you His love for this man, a love nothing can prevent, nothing destroy. Whenever we cannot love in the old, human way, Corrie, God can give us the perfect way."

I did not know, as I listened to Father's footsteps winding back down the stairs, that he had given me more than the key to this hard moment. I did not know that he had put into my hands the secret that would open far darker rooms than this— places where there was not, on a human level, anything to love at all.

I was still in kindergarten in these matters of love. My task just then was to give up my feeling for Karel without giving up the joy and wonder that had grown with it. And so, that very hour, lying there on my bed, I whispered the enormous prayer:

"Lord, I give to You the way I feel about Karel, my thoughts about our future— oh, You know! Everything! Give me Your way of seeing Karel instead. Help me to love him that way. That much."

And even as I said the words I fell asleep.

4. The Watch Shop

I WAS STANDING on a chair washing the big window in the dining room, waving now and then to passersby in the alley, while in the kitchen Mama peeled potatoes for lunch. It was 1918; the dreadful war was finally over: even in the way people walked you could sense a new hope in the air.

It wasn't like Mama, I thought, to let the water keep running that way; she never wasted anything.

"Corrie."

Her voice was low, almost a whisper.

"Yes, Mama?"

"Corrie," she said again.

And then I heard the water spilling out of the sink onto the floor. I jumped down from the chair and ran into the kitchen. Mama stood with her hand on the faucet, staring strangely at me while the water splashed from the sink over her feet.

"What is it, Mama!" I cried, reaching for the faucet. I pried her fingers loose, shut off the water, and drew her away from the puddle on the floor.

"Corrie," she said again.

"Mama, you're ill! We've got to get you to bed!"

"Corrie."

I put an arm beneath her shoulder and guided her through the dining room and up the stairs. At my cry Tante Anna came running down them and caught Mama's other arm. Together we got her onto her bed and then I raced down to the shop for Father and Betsie.

For an hour the four of us watched the effect of the cerebral hemorrhage spread slowly over her body. The paralysis seemed to affect her hands first, traveling from them along her arms and then down into her legs. Dr. van Veen, for whom the apprentice had gone running, could do no more than we.

Mama's consciousness was the last thing to go, her eyes remaining open and alert, looking lovingly at each one of us until very slowly they closed and we were sure she was gone forever. Dr. van Veen, however, said that this was only a coma, very deep, from which she could slip either into death or back to life.

For two months Mama lay unconscious on that bed, the five of us, with Nollie on the evening shift, taking turns at her side. And then one morning, as unexpectedly as the stroke had come, her eyes opened and she looked around her. Eventually she regained the use of her arms and legs enough to be able to move about with assistance, though her hands would never again hold her crochet hook or knitting needles.

We moved her out of the tiny bedroom facing the brick wall, down to Tante Jans's front room where she could watch the busy life of the Barteljorisstraat. Her mind, it was soon clear, was as active as ever, but the power of speech did not return—with the exception of three words. Mama could say "yes," "no," and—perhaps because it was the last one she had pronounced—"Corrie." And so Mama called everybody "Corrie."

To communicate, she and I invented a little game, something like Twenty Questions. "Corrie," she would say.

"What is it, Mama? You're thinking of someone!"

"Yes."

"Someone in the family."

"No."

"Somebody you saw on the street?"

"Yes."

"Was it an old friend?"

"Yes."

"A man?"

"No."

A woman Mama had known for a long time. "Mama, I'll bet it's someone's birthday!" And I would call out names until I heard her delighted, "Yes!" Then I would write a little note saying that Mama had seen the person and wished her a happy birthday. At the close I always put the pen in her stiffened fingers so she could sign it. An angular scrawl was all that was left of her beautiful curling signature, but it was soon recognized and loved all over Haarlem.

It was astonishing, really, the quality of life she was able to lead in that crippled body, and watching her during the three years of her paralysis, I made another discovery about love.

Mama's love had always been the kind that acted itself out with soup pot and sewing basket. But now that these things were taken away, the love seemed as whole as before. She sat in her chair at the window and loved us. She loved the people she saw in the street—and beyond: her love took in the city, the land of Holland, the world. And so I learned that love is larger than the walls which shut it in.

More and more often, Nollie's conversation at the dinner table had been about a young fellow teacher at the school where she taught, Flip van Woerden. By the time Mr. van Woerden paid the formal call on Father, Father had rehearsed and polished his little speech of blessing a dozen times.

The night before the wedding, as Betsie and I lifted her into bed, Mama suddenly burst into tears. With Twenty Questions we discovered that no, she was not unhappy about the marriage; yes, she liked Flip very much. It was that the solemn mother-daughter talk promised over the years for this night, the entire sex education which our taciturn society provided, was now not possible.

In the end, that night, it was Tante Anna who mounted the stairs to Nollie's room, eyes wide and cheeks aflame. Years before, Nollie had moved from our room at the top of the stairs down to Tante Bep's little nook, and there she and Tante Anna were closeted for the prescribed half-hour. There could have been no one in all Holland less informed about marriage than Tante Anna, but this was ritual: the older woman counseling the younger one down through the centuries—one could no more have got married without it than one could have dispensed with the ring.

Nollie was radiant, the following day, in her long white dress. But it was Mama I could not take my eyes off. Dressed in black as always, she was nevertheless suddenly young and girlish, eyes sparkling with joy at this greatest Occasion the ten Booms had ever held. Betsie and I took her into the church early and I was sure that most of the van Woerden family and friends never dreamed that the gracious and smiling lady in the first pew could neither walk alone nor speak.

It was not until Nollie and Flip came down the aisle together that I thought for the very first time of my own dreams of such a moment with Karel. I glanced at Betsie, sitting so tall and lovely on the other side of Mama. Betsie had always known that, because of her health, she could not have children, and for that reason had decided long ago never to marry. Now I was twenty-seven, Betsie in her mid-thirties, and I knew that this was the way it was going to be: Betsie and I the unmarried daughters living at home in the Beje.

It was a happy thought, not a sad one. And that was the moment when I knew for sure that God had accepted the faltering gift of my emotions made four years ago. For with the thought of Karel—all shining round with love as thoughts of him had been since I was fourteen—came not the slightest trace of hurt. "Bless Karel, Lord Jesus," I murmured under my breath. "And bless her. Keep them close to one another and to You." And that was a prayer, I knew for sure, that could not have sprung unaided from Corrie ten Boom.

But the great miracle of the day came later. To close the service we had chosen Mama's favorite hymn, "Fairest Lord Jesus." And now as I stood singing it I heard, behind me in the pew, Mama's voice singing too. Word after word, verse after verse, she joined in, Mama who could not speak four words, singing the beautiful lines without a stammer. Her voice which had been so high and clear was hoarse and cracked, but to me it was the voice of an angel.

All the way through she sang, while I stared straight ahead, not daring to turn around for fear of breaking the spell. When at last everyone sat down, Mama's eyes, Betsie's, and mine were brimming with tears.

At first we hoped it was the beginning of Mama's recovery. But the words she had sung she was not able to say, nor did she ever sing again. It had been an isolated moment, a gift to us from God, His own very special wedding present. Four weeks later, asleep with a smile on her lips, Mama slipped away from us forever.

It was in late November that year that a common cold made a big difference. Betsie began to sniff and sneeze and Father decided that she must not sit behind the cashier's table where the shop door let in the raw winter air.

But Christmas was coming, the shop's busiest time: with Betsie bundled up in bed, I took to running down to the shop as often as I could to wait on customers and wrap packages and save Father clambering up and down from his tall workbench a dozen times an hour.

Tante Anna insisted she could cook and look after Betsie. And so I settled in behind Betsie's table, writing down sales and repair charges, recording cash spent for parts and supplies, and leafing through past records in growing disbelief.

But—there was no system here anywhere! No way to tell whether a bill had been paid or not, whether the price we were asking was high or low, no way in fact to tell if we were making money or losing it.

I hurried down the street to the bookseller one wintry afternoon, bought a whole new set of ledgers, and started in to impose method on madness. Many nights after the door was locked and the shutters closed I sat on in the flickering gaslight, poring over old inventories and wholesalers' statements.

Or I would question Father. "How much did you charge Mr. Hoek for that repair work last month?"

Father would look at me blankly. "Why . . . ah . . . my dear . . . I can't really . . ."

"It was a Vacheron, Father, an old one. You had to send all the way to Switzerland for the parts and here's their bill and——"

His face lit up. "Of course I remember! A beautiful watch, Corrie! A joy to work on. Very old, only he'd let dust get into it. A fine watch must be kept clean, my dear!"

"But how much did you charge, Father?"

I developed a system of billing and, increasingly, my columns of figures began to correspond to actual transactions. And increasingly, I discovered that I loved it. I had always felt happy in this little shop with its tiny voices and shelves of small shining faces. But now I discovered that I liked the business side of it too, liked catalogues and stock listings, liked the whole busy, energetic world of trade.

Every now and then when I remembered that Betsie's cold had settled in her chest and threatened, as hers always did, to turn into pneumonia, I would reproach myself for being anything but distressed at the present arrangement. And at night when I would hear the hard, racking cough from her bedroom below I would pray with all my heart for her to be better at once.

And then one evening two days before Christmas, when I had closed up the shop for the night and was locking the hallway door, Betsie came bursting in from the alley with her arms full of flowers. Her eyes when she saw me there were like a guilty child's.

"For Christmas, Corrie!" she pleaded. "We have to have flowers for Christmas!"

"Betsie ten Boom!" I exploded. "How long has this been going on? No wonder you're not getting better!"

"I've stayed in bed most of the time, honestly——" she stopped while great coughs shook her. "I've only got up for really important things."

I put her to bed and then prowled the rooms with new-opened eyes, looking for Betsie's "important things." How little I had really noticed about the house! Betsie had wrought changes everywhere. I marched back up to her room and confronted her with the evidence. "Was it important, Betsie, to rearrange all the dishes in the corner cupboard?"

She looked up at me and her face went red. "Yes it was," she said defiantly. "You just put them in any old way."

"And the door to Tante Jans's rooms? Someone's been using paint remover on it, and sandpaper too—and that's hard work!"

"But there's beautiful wood underneath, I just know it! For years I've wanted to get that old varnish off and see. Oh Corrie," she said, her voice suddenly small and contrite, "I know it's horrid and selfish of me when you've had to be in the shop day after day. And I will take better care of myself so you won't have to do it much longer; but, oh, it's been so glorious being here all day, pretending I was in charge, you know, planning what I'd do. . . .

And so it was out. We had divided the work backwards. It was astonishing, once we'd made the swap, how well everything went. The house had been clean under my care; under Betsie's it glowed. She saw beauty in wood, in pattern, in color, and helped us to see it too. The small food budget which had barely survived my visits to the butcher and disappeared altogether at the bakery, stretched under Betsie's management to include all kinds of delicious things that had never been on our table before. "Just wait till you see what's for dessert this noon!" she'd tell us at the breakfast table, and all morning in the shop the question would shimmer in the back of our minds.

The soup kettle and the coffee pot on the back of the stove, which I never seemed to find time for, were simmering again the first week Betsie took over, and soon a stream of postmen and police, derelict old men and shivering young errand boys were pausing inside our alley door to stamp their feet and cup their hands around hot mugs, just as they'd done when Mama was in charge.

And meanwhile, in the shop, I was finding a joy in work that I'd never dreamed of. I soon knew that I wanted to do more than wait on customers and keep the accounts. I wanted to learn watch repair itself.

Father eagerly took on the job of teaching me. I eventually learned the moving and stationary parts, the chemistry of oils and solutions, tool and grindwheel and magnifying techniques. But Father's patience, his almost mystic rapport with the harmonies of watchworks, these were not things that could be taught.

Wristwatches had become fashionable and I enrolled in a school which specialized in this kind of work. Three years after Mama's death I became the first licensed woman watchmaker in Holland.

And so was established the pattern our lives were to follow for over twenty years. When Father had put the Bible back on its shelf after breakfast he and I would go down the stairs to the shop while Betsie stirred the soup pot and plotted magic with three potatoes and a pound of mutton. With my eye on income-and-outlay the shop was doing better and soon we were able to hire a saleslady to preside over the front room while Father and I worked in back.

There was a constant procession through this little back room. Sometimes it was a customer; most often it was simply a visitor—from a laborer with wooden klompen on his feet to a fleet owner—all bringing their problems to Father. Quite unabashedly, in the sight of customers in the front room and the employes working with us, he would bow his head and pray for the answer.

He prayed over the work, too. There weren't many repair problems he hadn't encountered. But occasionally one would come along that baffled even him. And then I would hear him say: "Lord, You turn the wheels of the galaxies. You know what makes the planets spin and You know what makes this watch run. . . ."

The specifics of the prayer were always different, for Father—who loved science—was an avid reader of a dozen university journals. Through the years he took his stopped watches to "the One who set the atoms dancing," or "Who keeps the great currents circling through the sea." The answers to these prayers seemed often to come in the middle of the night: many mornings I would climb onto my stool to find the watch that we had left in a hundred despairing pieces fitted together and ticking merrily.

One thing in the shop I never learned to do as well as Betsie, and that was to care about each person who stepped through the door. Often when a customer entered I would slip out the rear door and up to Betsie in the kitchen. "Betsie!

Who is the woman with the Alpina lapel-watch on a blue velvet band—stout, around fifty?"

"That's Mrs. van den Keukel. Her brother came back from Indonesia with malaria and she's been nursing him. Corrie," as I sped back down the stairs, "ask her how Mrs. Rinker's baby is!"

And Mrs. van den Keukel, leaving the shop a few minutes later would comment mistakenly to her husband, "That Corrie ten Boom is just like her sister!"

Even before Tante Anna's death in the late 1920s, the empty beds in the Beje were beginning to fill up with the succession of foster children who for over ten years kept the old walls ringing with laughter and Betsie busy letting down hems and pants cuffs.

And meanwhile Willem and Nollie were having families—Willem and Tine four children, Nollie and Flip six. Willem had long since left the parish ministry, where his habit of speaking the hard truth had made a succession of congregations unhappy, and had started his nursing home in Hilversum, thirty miles from Haarlem.

Nollie's family we saw more often, as their school—of which Flip was now principal—was right in Haarlem. It was a rare day when one or another of their six was not at the Beje to visit Opa at his workbench or peer into Tante Betsie's mixing bowl or race up and down the winding steps with the foster children.

Indeed it was at the Beje that we first discovered young Peter's musical gift. It happened around our radio. We had first heard this modern wonder at a friend's house. "A whole orchestra," we kept repeating to each other—somehow that seemed especially difficult to produce inside a box. We began to put pennies aside toward a radio of our own.

Long before the sum was raised Father came down with the hepatitis that almost cost his life: during the long stay in the hospital his beard turned snow white. The day he returned home—a week after his seventieth birthday—a little committee paid us a visit. They represented shopkeepers, street sweepers, a factory owner, a canal bargeman—all people who had realized during Father's illness what he meant to them. They had pooled their resources and bought him a radio.

It was a large table model with an ornate shell-shaped speaker and it brought us many years of joy. Every Sunday Betsie would scour the papers, British, French, and German as well as our own, since the radio brought in stations from all over Europe, and plan the week's program of concerts and recitals.

It was one Sunday afternoon when Nollie and her family were visiting that Peter suddenly spoke up in the middle of a Brahms concerto.

"It's funny they put a bad piano on the radio."

"Sshhh," said Nollie, but, "What do you mean, Peter?" asked Father.

"One of the notes is wrong."

The rest of us exchanged glances: what could an eight-year-old know? But Father led the boy to Tante Jans's old upright. "Which note, Peter?"

Peter struck the keys up the scale till he reached B above middle C. "This one," he said.

And then everyone in the room heard it too: the B on the concert grand was flat.

I spent the rest of the afternoon sitting beside Peter on the piano bench giving him simple musical quizzes, uncovering a phenomenal musical memory and perfect pitch. Peter became my music student until—in about six months—he had learned everything I knew and went on to more expert teachers.

The radio brought another change to our lives, one that Father at first resisted. Every hour, over the BBC, we could hear the striking hours of Big Ben. And with his stopwatch in his hand corrected to the astronomical clock in the shop, Father conceded that the first stroke of the English clock time after time coincided with the hour.

Father remained, however, mistrustful of this English time. He knew several Englishmen—and they were invariably late. As soon as he was strong enough to travel by train again, he resumed his weekly trips to Amsterdam to get Naval Observatory time.

But as the months passed and Big Ben and the Observatory continued in perfect agreement, he went less regularly, and finally not at all. The astronomical clock in any case was so jarred and jiggled by the constant rattle of automobile traffic in the narrow street outside that it was no longer the precision instrument it had been. The ultimate ignominy came the day Father set the astronomical clock by the radio.

In spite of this and other changes, life for the three of us—Father, Betsie, and me—stayed essentially the same. Our foster children grew up and went away to jobs or to marry, but they were often in the house for visits. The Hundredth Anniversary came and went; the following day Father and I were back at our workbenches as always.

Even the people we passed on our daily walks were perfectly predictable. Though it was years now since his illness, Father still walked unsteadily and I still went with him on his daily stroll through the downtown streets. We took our walk always at the same time, after the midday dinner and before the shop reopened at two, and always over the same route. And since other Haarlemers were just as regular in their habits, we knew exactly whom we would meet.

Many of those we nodded to were old friends or customers, others we knew only from this daily encounter—the woman sweeping her steps on Koning Straat, the man who read the *World Shipping News* at the trolley stop on the Grote Markt. And our favorite, the man we called The Bulldog. This was not only because we never saw him without two large bulldogs on the end of a leash but because, with his wrinkled, jowly face and short bowlegs he looked exactly like one of his own pets. His obvious affection for the animals was what touched us: as they went along he constantly muttered and fussed at them. Father and The Bulldog always tipped their hats to one another ceremoniously as we passed.

And while Haarlem and the rest of Holland strolled and bowed and swept its steps, the neighbor on our east geared for war. We knew what was happening— there was no way to keep from knowing. Often in the evening, turning the dial on the radio, we would pick up a voice from Germany. The voice did not talk, or even shout. It screamed. Oddly, it was even-tempered Betsie who reacted most strongly, hurtling from her chair and flinging herself at the radio to shut off the sound.

And yet, in the interludes, we forgot. Or, when Willem was visiting and would not let us forget, or when letters to Jewish suppliers in Germany came back marked "Address Unknown," we still managed to believe that it was primarily a German problem. "How long are they going to stand for it?" we said. "They won't put up with that man for long."

Only once did the changes taking place in Germany reach inside the little shop on the Barteljorisstraat, and that was in the person of a young German watch- maker. Germans frequently came to work under Father for a while, for his repu- tation reached even beyond Holland. So when this tall good-looking young man appeared with apprentice papers from a good firm in Berlin, Father hired him without hesitation. Otto told us proudly that he belonged to the Hitler Youth. Indeed it was a puzzle to us why he had come to Holland, for he found nothing but fault with Dutch people and products. "The world will see what Germans can do," he said often.

His first morning at work he came upstairs for coffee and Bible reading with the other employes; after that he sat alone down in the shop. When we asked him why, he said that though he had not understood the Dutch words, he had seen that Father was reading from the Old Testament which, he informed us, was the Jews' "Book of Lies."

I was shocked, but Father was only sorrowful. "He has been taught wrong," he told me. "By watching us, seeing that we love this Book and are truthful people, he will realize his error."

It was several weeks later that Betsie opened the door from the hallway and beckoned to Father and me. Upstairs on Tante Jans's tall mahogany chair sat the lady who ran the rooming house where Otto lived. Changing the bed sheets that morning, she said, she had found something under his pillow. And she drew from her market satchel a knife with a curving ten-inch blade.

Again, Father put the best interpretation on it. "The boy is probably only fright- ened, alone in a strange country. He probably bought it to protect himself."

It was true enough that Otto was alone. He spoke no Dutch, nor made any effort to learn, and besides Father, Betsie, and me, few people in this working-class part of the city spoke German. We repeated our invitation to join us upstairs in the evenings, but whether he did not care for our choice of radio programs, or because the evening ended as the morning began, with prayer and Bible reading, he sel- dom did.

In the end, Father did fire Otto—the first employe he had ever discharged in more than sixty years in business. And it was not the knife or the anti-Semitism that finally brought it about, but Otto's treatment of the old clock mender, Christoffels.

From the very first I had been baffled by his brusqueness with the old man. It wasn't anything he did—not in our presence anyway—but what he didn't do. No standing back to let the older man go first, no helping on with a coat, no picking up a dropped tool. It was hard to pin down. One Sunday when Father, Betsie, and I were having dinner at Hilversum I commented on what I had concluded was simple thoughtlessness.

Willem shook his head. "It's very deliberate," he said. "It's because Christoffels is old. The old have no value to the State. They're also harder to train in the new ways of thinking. Germany is systematically teaching disrespect for old age."

We stared at him, trying to grasp such a concept. "Surely you are mistaken, Willem!" Father said. "Otto is extremely courteous to me—unusually so. And I'm a good deal older than Christoffels."

"You're different. You're the boss. That's another part of the system: respect for authority. It is the old and the weak who are to be eliminated."

We rode the train home in stunned silence—and we started watching Otto more closely. But how could we know, how in the Holland of 1939 could we have guessed, that it was not in the shop where we could observe him but in the streets and alleys outside that Otto was subjecting Christoffels to a very real, small persecution. "Accidental" collisions and trippings, a shove, a heel ground into a toe, were making the old clockman's journeys to and from work times of terror.

The erect and shabby little man was too proud to report any of this to us. It was not until the icy February morning that Christoffels stumbled into the dining room with a bleeding cheek and a torn coat that the truth came out. Even then, Christoffels said nothing. But running down to the street to pick up his hat, I encountered Otto surrounded by an indignant little cluster of people who had seen what happened. Rounding the corner into the alley, the young man had deliberately forced the older one into the side of the building and ground his face against the rough bricks.

Father tried to reason with Otto as he let him go, to show him why such behavior was wrong. Otto did not answer. In silence he collected the few tools he had brought with him and in silence left the shop. It was only at the door that he turned to look at us, a look of the most utter contempt I had ever seen.

5. Invasion

THE SLENDER HANDS of the clock on the stair wall pointed to 9:25 as we left the dining room that night. That in itself was unusual in our orderly lives. Father was eighty years old now, and promptly at 8:45 each evening—an hour sooner than formerly—he would open the Bible, the signal for prayers, read one chapter, ask God's blessing on us through the night, and by 9:15 be climbing the stairs to his bedroom. Tonight, however, the Prime Minister was to address the nation at 9:30. One question ached through all of Holland like a long-held breath: Would there be war?

We circled up the steps to Tante Jans's rooms and Father went to warm up the big table radio. We did not so often spend the evenings up here listening to music now. England, France, and Germany were at war; their stations carried mostly war reports or code messages and many frequencies were jammed. Even Dutch stations carried mostly war news, and that we could hear just as well on the small portable radio we kept now in the dining room, a gift from Pickwick the Christmas before.

This, though, was to be a major broadcast; somehow we all felt it merited the large old set with its elaborate speaker. We sat now, waiting for 9:30, tense and upright in the high-backed wooden chairs, avoiding as if by a kind of premonition the cushioned and comfortable seats.

Then the Prime Minister's voice was speaking to us, sonorous and soothing. There would be no war. He had had assurances from high sources on both sides. Holland's neutrality would be respected. It would be the Great War all over again. There was nothing to fear. Dutchmen were urged to remain calm and to——

The voice stopped. Betsie and I looked up, astonished. Father had snapped off the set and in his blue eyes was a fire we had never seen before.

"It is wrong to give people hope when there is no hope," he said. "It is wrong to base faith upon wishes. There will be war. The Germans will attack and we will fall."

He stamped out his cigar stub in the ashtray beside the radio and with it, it seemed, the anger too, for his voice grew gentle again. "Oh, my dears, I am sorry for all Dutchmen now who do not know the power of God. For we will be beaten. But He will not." He kissed us both goodnight and in a moment we heard the steps of an old man climbing the stairs to bed.

Betsie and I sat rooted to our chairs. Father, so skilled at finding good in every situation, so slow to believe evil. If Father saw war and defeat, then there was no other possibility at all.

I sat bolt upright in my bed. What was that? There! There it was again! A brilliant flash followed a second later by an explosion which shook the bed. I scrambled over the covers to the window and leaned out. The patch of sky above the chimney tops glowed orange-red.

I felt for my bathrobe and thrust my arms through the sleeves as I whirled down the stairs. At Father's room I pressed my ear against the door. Between bomb bursts I heard the regular rhythm of his breathing.

I dived down a few more steps and into Tante Jans's rooms. Betsie had long since moved into Tante Jans's little sleeping cubicle where she would be nearer the kitchen and the doorbell. She was sitting up in the bed. I groped toward her in the darkness and we threw our arms round each other.

Together we said it aloud:

"War."

It was five hours after the Prime Minister's speech. How long we clung together, listening, I do not know. The bombing seemed mostly to be coming from the direction of the airport. At last we tiptoed uncertainly out to Tante Jans's front room. The glowing sky lit the room with a strange brilliance. The chairs, the mahogany bookcase, the old upright piano, all pulsed with an eerie light.

Betsie and I knelt down by the piano bench. For what seemed hours we prayed for our country, for the dead and injured tonight, for the Queen. And then, incredibly, Betsie began to pray for the Germans, up there in the planes, caught in the fist of the giant evil loose in Germany. I looked at my sister kneeling beside me in the light of burning Holland. "Oh Lord," I whispered, "listen to Betsie, not me, because I cannot pray for those men at all."

And it was then that I had the dream. It couldn't have been a real dream because I was not asleep. But a scene was suddenly and unreasonably in my mind. I saw the Grote Markt, half a block away, as clearly as though I were standing there, saw the town hall and St. Bavo's and the fish mart with its stair-stepped facade.

Then as I watched, a kind of odd, old farm wagon—old fashioned and out of place in the middle of a city—came lumbering across the square pulled by four enormous black horses. To my surprise I saw that I myself was sitting in the wagon. And Father too! And Betsie! There were many others, some strangers, some friends. I recognized Pickwick and Toos, Willem and young Peter. All together we were slowly being drawn across the square behind those horses. We couldn't get off the wagon, that was the terrible thing. It was taking us away—far away, I felt—but we didn't want to go. . . .

"Betsie!" I cried, jumping up, pressing my hands to my eyes. "Betsie, I've had such an awful dream!"

I felt her arm around my shoulder. "We'll go down to the kitchen where the light won't show, and we'll make a pot of coffee."

The booming of the bombs was less frequent and farther away as Betsie put on the water. Closer by was the wail of fire alarms and the beep of the hose trucks. Over coffee, standing at the stove, I told Betsie what I had seen.

"Am I imagining things because I'm frightened? But it wasn't like that! It was real. Oh Betsie, was it a kind of vision?"

Betsie's finger traced a pattern on the wooden sink worn smooth by generations of ten Booms. "I don't know," she said softly. "But if God has shown us bad times ahead, it's enough for me that He knows about them. That's why He sometimes shows us things, you know—to tell us that this too is in His hands."

For five days Holland held out against the invader. We kept the shop open, not because anyone was interested in watches, but because people wanted to see Father. Some wanted him to pray for husbands and sons stationed at the borders of the country. Others, it seemed to me, came just to see him sitting there behind his workbench as he had for sixty years and to hear in the ticking clocks a world of order and reason.

I never opened my workbench at all but joined Betsie making coffee and carrying it down. We brought down the portable radio, too, and set it up on the display case. Radio was Haarlem's eyes and ears and very pulse-rate, for after that first night, although we often heard planes overhead, the bombing never came so close again.

The first morning over the radio came instructions that ground-floor windows must be taped. Up and down the Barteljorisstraat shopowners were out on the sidewalk; there was an unaccustomed neighborhood feel as advice, rolls of adhesive, and tales of the night's terror passed from door to door. One store owner, an outspoken anti-Semite, was helping Weil the Jewish furrier put up boards where a pane of glass had shaken loose. The optician next door to us, a silent, withdrawn individual, came over and taped the top of our display window where Betsie and I could not reach.

A few nights later the radio carried the news we dreaded: the Queen had left. I had not cried the night of the invasion but I cried now, for our country was lost. In the morning the radio announced tanks advancing over the border.

And suddenly all of Haarlem was in the streets. Even Father, whose daily stroll was as predictable as his own clock chimes, broke his routine to go walking at the unheard-of hour of 10:00 A.M. It was as though we wanted to face what was coming together, the whole city united, as though each would draw strength from each other Hollander.

And so the three of us walked, jostled by the crowd, over the bridge on the Spaarne, all the way to the great wild cherry tree whose blossoms each spring formed such a white glory that it was called the Bride of Haarlem. A few faded petals clung now to the new-leafed branches, but most of the Bride's flowers had fallen, forming a wilted carpet beneath us.

A window down the street flew open.

"We've surrendered!"

The procession in the street stopped short. Each told his neighbor what we had all heard for ourselves. A boy of maybe fifteen turned to us with tears rolling down his cheeks. "I would have fought! I wouldn't ever have given up!" Father stooped down to pick up a small bruised petal from the brick pavement; tenderly he inserted it in his buttonhole.

"That is good, my son," he told the youngster. "For Holland's battle has just begun."

But during the first months of occupation, life was not so very unbearable. The hardest thing to get used to was the German uniform everywhere, German trucks and tanks in the street, German spoken in the shops. Soldiers frequently visited our store, for they were getting good wages and watches were among the first things they bought. Toward us they took a superior tone as though we were not-quite-bright children. But among themselves, as I listened to them excitedly discussing their purchases, they seemed like young men anywhere off on a holiday. Most of them selected women's watches for mothers and sweethearts back home.

Indeed, the shop never made so much money as during that first year of the war. With no new shipments coming in, people bought up everything we had in stock, even the *winkeldochters*, the "shop-daughters," merchandise that had lain around so long it seemed part of the furniture. We even sold the green marble mantle clock with the twin brass cupids.

The curfew too, at first, was no hardship for us, since it was originally set at 10:00 P.M., long after we were indoors in any case. What we did object to were the identity cards each citizen was issued. These small folders containing photograph and fingerprints had to be produced on demand. A soldier or a policeman—the Haarlem police were now under the direct control of the German Commandant—

might stop a citizen at any time and ask to see his card; it had to be carried in a pouch about the neck. We were issued ration cards too, but at least that first year, the coupons represented food and merchandise actually available in the stores. Each week the newspapers announced what the current coupons could be exchanged for.

That was another thing it was hard to adjust to—newspapers that no longer carried news. Long glowing reports of the successes of the German army on its various fronts. Eulogies of German leaders, denunciations of traitors and saboteurs, appeals for the unity of the "Nordic peoples." But not news that we could trust.

And so we depended again on the radio. Early in the occupation, Haarlemers were ordered to turn in all private sets. Realizing it would look strange if our household produced none at all, we decided to turn in the portable and hide the larger, more powerful instrument in one of the many hollow spaces beneath the old twisting staircase.

Both suggestions were Peter's. He was sixteen at the time of the invasion and shared with other Dutch teenagers the restless energy of anger and impotence. Peter installed the table radio beneath a curve in the stairs just above Father's room and expertly replaced the old boards, while I carried the smaller one down to the big Vroom en Dreesman department store where the radio collection was being made. The army clerk looked at me across the counter.

"Is this the only radio you own?"

"Yes."

He consulted a list in front of him. "Ten Boom, Casper, Ten Boom, Elizabeth, at the same address. Do either of them own a radio?"

I had known from childhood that the earth opened and the heavens rained fire upon liars, but I met his gaze.

"No."

Only as I walked out of the building did I begin to tremble. Not because for the first time in my life I had told a conscious lie. But because it had been so dreadfully easy.

But we had saved our radio. Every night Betsie or I would remove the stair tread and crouch over the radio, the volume barely audible, while the other one thumped the piano in Tante Jans's room as hard as she could, to hear the news from England. And at first the news over the radio and the news in our captive press was much the same. The German offensive was everywhere victorious. Month after month the Free Dutch broadcasts could only urge us to wait, to have courage, to believe in the counter-offensive which must surely some day be mounted.

The Germans had repaired the bomb damage to the airport and were using it now as a base for air raids against England. Night after night we lay in bed listening to the growl of engines heading west. Occasionally English planes retaliated and then the German fighters might intercept them right over Haarlem.

One night I tossed for an hour while dogfights raged overhead, streaking my patch of sky with fire. At last I heard Betsie stirring in the kitchen and ran down to join her.

She was making tea. She brought it into the dining room where we had covered the windows with heavy black paper and set out the best cups. Somewhere in the night there was an explosion; the dishes in the cupboard rattled. For an hour we sipped our tea and talked, until the sound of planes died away and the sky was silent. I said goodnight to Betsie at the door to Tante Jans's rooms and groped my way up the dark stairs to my own. The fiery light was gone from the sky. I felt for my bed: there was the pillow. Then in the darkness my hand closed over something hard. Sharp too! I felt blood trickle along a finger.

It was a jagged piece of metal, ten inches long.

"Betsie!"

I raced down the stairs with the shrapnel shard in my hand. We went back to the dining room and stared at it in the light while Betsie bandaged my hand. "On your pillow," she kept saying.

"Betsie, if I hadn't heard you in the kitchen——"

But Betsie put a finger on my mouth. "Don't say it, Corrie! There are no 'if's' in God's world. And no places that are safer than other places. The center of His will is our only safety—O Corrie, let us pray that we may always know it!"

The true horror of occupation came over us only slowly. During the first year of German rule there were only minor attacks on Jews in Holland. A rock through the window of a Jewish-owned store. An ugly word scrawled on the wall of a synagogue. It was as though they were trying us, testing the temper of the country. How many Dutchmen would go along with them?

And the answer, to our shame, was many. The National Socialist Bond, the quisling organization of Holland, grew larger and bolder with each month of occupation. Some joined the NSB simply for the benefits: more food, more clothing coupons, the best jobs and housing. But others became NSBers out of conviction. Nazism was a disease to which the Dutch too were susceptible, and those with an anti-Semitic bias fell sick of it first.

On our daily walk Father and I saw the symptoms spread. A sign in a shop window: JEWS WILL NOT BE SERVED. At the entrance to a public park: NO JEWS. On the door of the library. In front of restaurants, theaters, even the concert hall whose alley we knew so much better than its seats.

A synagogue burned down and the fire trucks came. But only to keep the flames from spreading to the buildings on either side.

One noon as Father and I followed our familiar route, the sidewalks were bright with yellow stars sewn to coats and jacket fronts. Men, women, and children wore the six-pointed star with the word *Jood* ("Jew") in the center. We were surprised, as we walked, at how many of the people we had passed each day were Jews. The

man who read the *World Shipping News* in the Grote Markt wore a star on his
neatly pressed business suit. So did The Bulldog, his jowly face more deeply lined
than ever, his voice as he fussed at his dogs, sharp with strain.

Worst were the disappearances. A watch, repaired and ready, hanging on its
hook in the back of the shop, month after month. A house in Nollie's block mysteriously deserted, grass growing in the rose garden. One day Mr. Kan's shop up
the street did not open. Father knocked on his door as we passed that noon, to see
if someone were ill, but there was no answer. The shop remained shuttered, the
windows above dark and silent for several weeks. Then, although the shop stayed
closed, an NSB family moved into the apartment above.

We never knew whether these people had been spirited away by the Gestapo or
gone into hiding before this could happen. Certainly public arrests, with no attempt
to conceal what was happening, were becoming more frequent. One day as Father
and I were returning from our walk we found the Grote Markt cordoned off by a
double ring of police and soldiers. A truck was parked in front of the fish mart;
into the back were climbing men, women, and children, all wearing the yellow
star. There was no reason we could see why this particular place at this particular
time had been chosen.

"Father! Those poor people!" I cried.

The police line opened, the truck moved through. We watched till it turned the
corner.

"Those poor people," Father echoed. But to my surprise I saw that he was looking
at the soldiers now forming into ranks to march away. "I pity the poor Germans,
Corrie. They have touched the apple of God's eye."

We talked often, Father, Betsie and I, about what we could do if a chance should
come to help some of our Jewish friends. We knew that Willem had found hiding
places at the beginning of the occupation for the German Jews who had been living in his house. Lately he had also moved some of the younger Dutch Jews away
from the nursing home. "Not my old people," he would say. "Surely they will not
touch my old people."

Willem had addresses. He knew of farms in rural areas where there were few
occupying troops. Willem would be the one to ask.

It was a drizzly November morning in 1941, a year and a half after the invasion, as I stepped outside to fold back the shutters, that I saw a group of four
German soldiers coming down the Barteljorisstraat. They were wearing combat
helmets low over their ears, rifles strapped to their shoulders. I shrank back into
the doorway and watched. They were checking shop numbers as they walked. At
Weil's Furriers directly across the street the group stopped. One of the soldiers
unstrapped his gun and with the butt banged on the door. He was drawing it back
for another blow when the door opened and all four pushed inside.

I dashed back through our shop and up to the dining room where Betsie was setting out three places. "Betsie! Hurry! Something awful is happening at Weil's!" We reached the front door again in time to see Mr. Weil backing out of his shop, the muzzle of a gun pressed against his stomach. When he had prodded Mr. Weil a short way down the sidewalk, the soldier went back into the store and slammed the door. Not an arrest, then.

Inside, we could hear glass breaking. Soldiers began carrying out armloads of furs. A crowd was gathering in spite of the early morning hour. Mr. Weil had not moved from the spot on the sidewalk where the soldier had left him.

A window over his head opened and a small shower of clothes rained down on him—pajamas, shirts, underwear. Slowly, mechanically, the old furrier stooped and began to gather up his clothing. Betsie and I ran across the street to help him.

"Your wife!" Betsie whispered urgently. "Where is Mrs. Weil?"

The man only blinked at her.

"You must come inside!" I said, snatching socks and handkerchiefs from the sidewalk. "Quick, with us!"

And we propelled the bewildered old man across to the Beje. Father was in the dining room when we reached it and greeted Mr. Weil without the slightest sign of surprise. His natural manner seemed to relax the furrier a bit. His wife, he said, was visiting a sister in Amsterdam.

"We must find a telephone and warn her not to come home!" Betsie said.

Like most private telephones ours had been disconnected early in the occupation. There were public phones at several places in the city, but of course messages went to a public reception center at the other end. Was it right to connect a family in Amsterdam with the trouble here? And if Mrs. Weil could not come home, where was she to go? Where were the Weils to live? Certainly not with the sister where they could so easily be traced. Father and Betsie and I exchanged glances. Almost with a single breath we said, "Willem."

Again it was not the kind of matter that could be relayed through the public phone system. Someone had to go, and I was the obvious choice. Dutch trains were dirty and overcrowded under the occupation; the trip that should have taken under an hour took nearly three. Willem was not there when I finally reached the big nursing home just after noon, but Tine and their twenty-two-year-old son Kik were. I told them what had happened on the Barteljorisstraat and gave them the Amsterdam address.

"Tell Mr. Weil to be ready as soon as it's dark," Kik said.

But it was nearly 9:00 P.M.—the new curfew hour—before Kik rapped at the alley door. Tucking Mr. Weil's clothing bundle beneath his arm, he led the man away into the night.

It was more than two weeks before I saw Kik again to ask him what had happened. He smiled at me, the broad, slow smile I had loved since he was a child.

"If you're going to work with the underground, Tante Corrie, you must learn not to ask questions."

That was all we ever learned of the Weils. But Kik's words went round and round in my head. "The underground. . . . If you're going to work with the underground." Was Kik working with this secret and illegal group? Was Willem?

We knew of course that there was an underground in Holland—or suspected it. Most cases of sabotage were not reported in our controlled press, but rumors abounded. A factory had been blown up. A train carrying political prisoners had been stopped and seven, or seventeen, or seventy, had made it away. The rumors tended to get more spectacular with each repetition. But always they featured things we believed were wrong in the sight of God. Stealing, lying, murder. Was this what God wanted in times like these? How should a Christian act when evil was in power?

It was about a month after the raid on the fur shop that Father and I, on our usual walk, saw something so very unusual that we both stopped in mid-stride. Walking toward us along the sidewalks, as so many hundreds of times before, came The Bulldog with his rolling short-legged gait. The bright yellow star had by now ceased to look extraordinary, so what—and then I knew what was wrong. The dogs. The dogs were not with him!

He passed without seeming to see us. With one accord Father and I turned around and walked after him. He turned a number of corners while we grew more and more embarrassed at following him without any real excuse. Although Father and he had tipped their hats to each other for years, we had never spoken and did not even know his name.

At last the man stopped in front of a small secondhand shop, took out a ring of keys, and let himself in. We looked through the window at the cluttered interior. Only a glance showed us that this was more than the usual hodgepodge of bric-a-brac and hollow-seated chairs. Someone who loved beautiful things had chosen everything here. "We must bring Betsie!" I said.

A little bell over the door jingled as we stepped in. Astonishing to see The Bulldog hatless and indoors, unlocking a cash drawer at the rear of the store.

"Permit an introduction, Sir," Father began. "I am Casper ten Boom and this is my daughter, Cornelia."

The Bulldog shook hands and again I noticed the deep creases in the sagging cheeks. "Harry de Vries," he said.

"Mr. de Vries, we've so often admired your—er—affection for your bulldogs. We hope they are well?"

The squat little man stared from one of us to the other. Slowly the heavy-rimmed eyes filled with tears. "Are they well?" he repeated. "I believe they are well. I hope that they are well. They are dead."

"Dead!" we said together.

"I put the medicine in their bowl with my own hands and I petted them to sleep. My babies. My little ones. If you could only have seen them eat! I waited, you know, till we had enough coupons for meat. They used to have meat all the time."

We stared at him dumbly. "Was it," I ventured at last, "was it because of the rationing?"

With a gesture of his hands the little man invited us into a small room in back of the shop and gave us chairs. "Miss ten Boom, I am a Jew. Who knows when they will come to take me away? My wife too—although she is a Gentile—is in danger because of her marriage."

The Bulldog raised his chin so high his jowls stretched taut. "It is not for ourselves we mind. We are Christians, Cato and I. When we die we will see Jesus, and this is all that matters.

"But I said to Cato, 'What about the dogs? If we are taken away who will feed them? Who will remember their water and their walk? They will wait and we will not come and they will not understand.' No! This way my mind is at ease."

"My dear friend!" Father grasped The Bulldog's hand in both of his. "Now that these dear companions may no longer walk with you, will you not do my daughter and me the great honor of accompanying us?"

But this The Bulldog would not do. "It would put you in danger," he kept saying. He did, however, accept an invitation to come to visit us. "After dark, after dark," he said.

And so one evening the following week Mr. de Vries came to the alley door of the Beje bringing his sweet, shy wife, Cato, and soon she and Harry were almost nightly visitors in Tante Jans's front room.

The Bulldog's chief delight at the Beje, after talking with Father, were the tomes of Jewish theology now housed in Tante Jans's big mahogany case. For he had become a Christian, some forty years earlier, without ceasing in the least to be a loyal Jew. "A completed Jew!" he would tell us smilingly. "A follower of the one perfect Jew."

The books belonged to the rabbi of Haarlem. He had brought them to Father more than a year before: "Just in case I should not be able to care for them—ah—indefinitely." He had waved a bit apologetically at the procession of small boys behind him, each staggering under the weight of several huge volumes. "My little hobby. Book collecting. And yet, old friend, books do not age as you and I do. They will speak still when we are gone, to generations we will never see. Yes, the books must survive."

The rabbi had been one of the first to vanish from Haarlem.

How often it is a small, almost unconscious event that marks a turning point. As arrests of Jews in the street became more frequent, I had begun picking up and delivering work for our Jewish customers myself so that they would not have to venture into the center of town. And so one evening in the early spring of 1942 I was in the home of a doctor and his wife. They were a very old Dutch family: the portraits on the walls could have been a textbook of Holland's history.

The Heemstras and I were talking about the things that were discussed whenever a group of people got together in those days, rationing and the news from England, when down the stairs piped a childish voice.

"Daddy! You didn't tuck us in!"

Dr. Heemstra was on his feet in an instant. With an apology to his wife and me he hurried upstairs and in a minute we heard a game of hide-and-seek going and the shrill laughter of two children.

That was all. Nothing had changed. Mrs. Heemstra continued with her recipe for stretching the tea ration with rose leaves. And yet everything was changed. For in that instant, reality broke through the numbness that had grown in me since the invasion. At any minute there might be a rap on this door. These children, this mother and father, might be ordered to the back of a truck.

Dr. Heemstra came back to the living room and the conversation rambled on. But under the words a prayer was forming in my heart.

"Lord Jesus, I offer myself for Your people. In any way. Any place Any time."

And then an extraordinary thing happened.

Even as I prayed, that waking dream passed again before my eyes. I saw again those four black horses and the Grote Markt. As I had on the night of the invasion I scanned the passengers drawn so unwillingly behind them. Father, Betsie, Willem, myself—leaving Haarlem, leaving all that was sure and safe—going where?

6. *The Secret Room*

IT WAS SUNDAY, May 10, 1942, exactly two years after the fall of Holland. The sunny spring skies, the flowers in the lamppost boxes, did not at all reflect the city's mood. German soldiers wandered aimlessly through the streets, some looking as if they had not yet recovered from a hard Saturday night, some already on the lookout for girls, a few hunting for a place to worship.

Each month the occupation seemed to grow harsher, restrictions more numerous. The latest heartache for Dutchmen was an edict making it a crime to sing the "Wilhelmus," our national anthem.

Father, Betsie, and I were on our way to the Dutch Reformed church in Velsen, a small town not far from Haarlem, where Peter had won the post of organist in competition against forty older and more experienced musicians. The organ at Velsen was one of the finest in the country; though the train seemed slower each time, we went frequently.

Peter was already playing, invisible in the tall organ loft, when we squeezed into the crowded pew. That was one thing the occupation had done for Holland: churches were packed.

After hymns and prayers came the sermon, a good one today, I thought. I wished Peter would pay closer attention. He regarded sermons as interesting only to venerable relics like his mother and me. I had reached fifty that spring, to Peter the age at which life had definitely passed by. I would beg him to remember that death and ultimate issues could come for any of us at any age—especially these days— but he would reply charmingly that he was too fine a musician to die young.

The closing prayers were said. And then, electrically, the whole church sat at attention. Without preamble, every stop pulled out to full volume, Peter was playing the "Wilhelmus"!

Father, at eighty-two, was the first one on his feet. Now everyone was standing. From somewhere in back of us a voice sang out the words. Another joined in, and another. Then we were all singing together, the full voice of Holland singing her forbidden anthem. We sang at the top of our lungs, sang our oneness, our hope, our love for Queen and country. On this anniversary of defeat it seemed almost for a moment that we were victors.

Afterward we waited for Peter at the small side door of the church. It was a long time before he was free to come away with us, so many people wanted to embrace him, to shake his hand and thump his back. Clearly he was enormously pleased with himself.

But now that the moment had passed I was, as usual, angry with him. The Gestapo was certain to hear about it, perhaps already had: their eyes and ears were everywhere. I thought of Nollie, home fixing Sunday dinner for us all. I thought of Peter's brothers and sisters. And Flip—what if he lost the principalship of the school for this? And for what had Peter risked so much? Not for people's lives but for a gesture. For a moment's meaningless defiance.

At Bos en Hoven Straat, however, Peter was a hero as one by one his family made us describe again what had happened. The only members of the household who felt as I did were the two Jewish women staying at Nollie's. One of these was an elderly Austrian lady whom Willem had sent into hiding here. "Katrien," as the family had rechristened her, was posing as the van Woerdens' housemaid—although Nollie confided to me that she had yet so much as to make her own bed. Probably she did not know how, as she came from a wealthy and aristocratic family.

The other woman was a young, blonde, blue-eyed Dutch Jew with flawless false identity papers supplied by the Dutch national underground itself. The papers were so good and Annaliese looked so unlike the Nazi stereotype of a Jew, that she went freely in and out of the house, shopping and helping out at the school, giving herself out to be a friend of the family whose husband had died in the bombing of Rotterdam. Katrien and Annaliese could not understand any more than I could Peter's deliberately doing something which would attract the attention of the authorities.

I spent an anxious afternoon, tensing at the sound of every motor, for only the police, Germans, and NSBers had automobiles nowadays. But the time came to go home to the Beje and still nothing had happened.

I worried two more days, then decided either Peter had not been reported or that the Gestapo had more important things to occupy them. It was Wednesday morning just as Father and I were unlocking our workbenches that Peter's little sister Cocky burst into the shop.

"Opa! Tante Corrie! They came for Peter! They took him away!"

"Who? Where?"

But she didn't know and it was three days before the family learned that he had been taken to the federal prison in Amsterdam.

It was 7:55 in the evening, just a few minutes before the new curfew hour of 8:00. Peter had been in prison for two weeks. Father and Betsie and I were seated around the dining room table, Father replacing watches in their pockets and Betsie doing needlework, our big, black, slightly-Persian cat curled contentedly in her lap. A knock on the alley door made me glance in the window mirror. There in the bright spring twilight stood a woman. She carried a small suitcase and—odd for the time of year—wore a fur coat, gloves, and a heavy veil.

I ran down and opened the door. "Can I come in?" she asked. Her voice was high-pitched in fear.

"Of course." I stepped back. The woman looked over her shoulder before moving into the little hallway.

"My name is Kleermaker. I'm a Jew."

"How do you do?" I reached out to take her bag, but she held onto it. "Won't you come upstairs?"

Father and Betsie stood up as we entered the dining room. "Mrs. Kleermaker, my father and my sister."

"I was about to make some tea!" cried Betsie. "You're just in time to join us!"

Father drew out a chair from the table and Mrs. Kleermaker sat down, still gripping the suitcase. The "tea" consisted of old leaves which had been crushed and reused so often they did little more than color the water. But Mrs. Kleermaker accepted it gratefully, plunging into the story of how her husband had been arrested some months before, her son gone into hiding. Yesterday the S.D.—the political police who worked under the Gestapo—had ordered her to close the family clothing store. She was afraid now to go back to the apartment above it. She had heard that we had befriended a man on this street. . . .

"In this household," Father said, "God's people are always welcome."

"We have four empty beds upstairs," said Betsie. "Your problem will be choosing which one to sleep in!" Then to my astonishment she added, "First though, give me a hand with the tea things."

I could hardly believe my ears. Betsie never let anyone help in her kitchen: "I'm just a fussy old maid," she'd say.

But Mrs. Kleermaker had jumped to her feet with pathetic eagerness and was already stacking plates and cups. . . .

Just two nights later the same scene was repeated. The time was again just before 8:00 on another bright May evening. Again there was a furtive knock at the side door. This time an elderly couple was standing outside.

"Come in!"

It was the same story: the same tight-clutched possessions, the same fearful glance and tentative tread. The story of neighbors arrested, the fear that tomorrow their turn would come.

That night after prayer-time the six of us faced our dilemma. "This location is too dangerous," I told our three guests. "We're half a block from the main police headquarters. And yet I don't know where else to suggest."

Clearly it was time to visit Willem again. So the next day I repeated the difficult trip to Hilversum. "Willem," I said, "we have three Jews staying right at the Beje. Can you get places for them in the country?"

Willem pressed his fingers to his eyes and I noticed suddenly how much white was in his beard. "It's getting harder," he said. "Harder every month. They're feeling the food shortage now even on the farms. I still have addresses, yes, a few. But they won't take anyone without a ration card."

"Without a ration card! But, Jews aren't issued ration cards!"

"I know." Willem turned to stare out the window. For the first time I wondered how he and Tine were feeding the elderly men and women in their care.

"I know," he repeated. "And ration cards can't be counterfeited. They're changed too often and they're too easy to spot. Identity cards are different. I know several printers who do them. Of course you need a photographer."

A photographer? Printers? What was Willem talking about? "Willem, if people need ration cards and there aren't any counterfeit ones, what do they do?"

Willem turned slowly from the window. He seemed to have forgotten me and my particular problem. "Ration cards?" He gestured vaguely. "You steal them."

I stared at this Dutch Reformed clergyman, "Then, Willem, could you steal . . . I mean . . . could you get three stolen cards?"

"No, Corrie! I'm watched! Don't you understand that? Every move I make is watched!"

He put an arm around my shoulder and went on more kindly, "Even if I can continue working for a while, it will be far better for you to develop your own sources. The less connection with me—the less connection with anyone else—the better."

Joggling home on the crowded train I turned Willem's words over and over in my mind. "Your own sources." That sounded so—so professional. How was I going to find a source of stolen ration cards? Who in the world did I know. . . .

And at that moment a name appeared in my mind.

Fred Koornstra.

Fred was the man who used to read the electric meter at the Beje. The Koornstras had a retarded daughter, now a grown woman, who attended the "church" I had been conducting for the feeble-minded for some twenty years. And now Fred had a new job working for the Food Office. Wasn't it in the department where ration books were issued?

That evening after supper I bumped over the brick streets to the Koornstra house. The tires on my faithful old bicycle had finally given out and I had joined the hundreds clattering about town on metal wheel rims. Each bump reminded me jarringly of my fifty years.

Fred, a bald man with a military bearing, came to the door and stared at me blankly when I said I wanted to talk to him about the Sunday service. He invited me in, closed the door, and said, "Now Corrie, what is it you really came to see me about?"

("Lord," I prayed silently, "if it is not safe to confide in Fred, stop this conversation now before it is too late.")

"I must first tell you that we've had some unexpected company at the Beje. First it was a single woman, then a couple, when I got back this afternoon, another couple." I paused for just an instant. "They are Jews."

Fred's expression did not change.

"We can provide safe places for these people but they must provide something too. Ration cards."

Fred's eyes smiled. "So. Now I know why you came here."

"Fred, is there any way you can give out extra cards? More than you report?"

"None at all, Corrie. Those cards have to be accounted for a dozen ways. They're checked and double-checked."

The hope that had begun to mount in me tumbled. But Fred was frowning.

"Unless——" he began.

"Unless?"

"Unless there should be a hold-up. The Food Office in Utrecht was robbed last month—but the men were caught."

He was silent a while. "If it happened at noon," he said slowly, "when just the record clerk and I are there . . . and if they found us tied and gagged . . ." He snapped his fingers. "And I know just the man who might do it! Do you remember the——"

"Don't!" I said, remembering Willem's warning. "Don't tell me who. And don't tell me how. Just get the cards if you possibly can."

Fred stared at me a moment. "How many do you need?"

I opened my mouth to say, "Five." But the number that unexpectedly and astonishingly came out instead was, "One hundred."

When Fred opened the door to me just a week later, I gasped at the sight of him. Both eyes were a greenish purple, his lower lip cut and swollen.

"My friend took very naturally to the part," was all he would say.

But he had the cards. On the table in a brown manila envelope were one hundred passports to safety. Fred had already torn the "continuing coupon" from each one. This final coupon was presented at the Food Office the last day of each month in exchange for the next month's card. With these coupons Fred could "legally" continue to issue us one hundred cards.

We agreed that it would be risky for me to keep coming to his house each month. What if he were to come to the Beje instead, dressed in his old meterman uniform?

The meter in the Beje was in the back hall at the foot of the stairs. When I got home that afternoon I pried up the tread of the bottom step, as Peter had done higher to hide the radio, and found a hollow space inside. Peter would be proud of me I thought as I worked—and was flooded by a wave of lonesomeness for that brave and cocksure boy. But even he would have to admit, I concluded as I stepped back at last to admire the completed hideaway, that a watchmaker's hand and eye were worth something. The hinge was hidden deep in the wood, the ancient riser undisturbed. I was ridiculously pleased with it.

We had our first test of the system on July 1. Fred was to come in through the shop as he always had, carrying the cards beneath his shirt. He would come at 5:30, when Betsie would have the back hall free of callers. To my horror at 5:25 the shop door opened and in stepped a policeman.

He was a tall man with close-cropped orange-red hair whom I knew by name—Rolf van Vliet—but little else. He had come to the Hundredth Birthday Party, but so had half the force. Certainly he was not one of Betsie's "regulars" for winter morning coffee.

Rolf had brought in a watch that needed cleaning, and he seemed in a mood to talk. My throat had gone dry, but Father chatted cheerfully as he took off the back of Rolf's watch and examined it. What were we going to do? There was no way to warn Fred Koornstra. Promptly at 5:30 the door of the shop opened and in he walked, dressed in his blue workclothes. It seemed to me that his chest was too thick by a foot at least.

With magnificent aplomb Fred nodded to Father, the policeman, and me. "Good evening." Courteous but a little bored.

He strode through the door at the rear of the shop and shut it behind him. My ears strained to hear him lift the secret lid. There! Surely Rolf must have heard it too.

The door behind us opened again. So great was Fred's control that he had not ducked out the alleyway exit, but came strolling back through the shop.

"Good evening," he said again.

"Evening."

He reached the street door and was gone. We had got away with it this time, but somehow, some way, we were going to have to work out a warning system.

For meanwhile, in the weeks since Mrs. Kleermaker's unexpected visit, a great deal had happened at the Beje. Supplied with ration cards, Mrs. Kleermaker and the elderly couple and the next arrivals and the next had found homes in safer locations. But still the hunted people kept coming, and the needs were often more complicated than rations cards and addresses. If a Jewish woman became pregnant where could she go to have her baby? If a Jew in hiding died, how could he be buried?

"Develop your own sources," Willem had said. And from the moment Fred Koornstra's name had popped into my mind, an uncanny realization had been growing in me. We were friends with half of Haarlem! We knew nurses in the maternity hospital. We knew clerks in the Records Office. We knew someone in every business and service in the city.

We didn't know, of course, the political views of all these people. But—and here I felt a strange leaping of my heart—God did! My job was simply to follow His leading one step at a time, holding every decision up to Him in prayer. I knew I was not clever or subtle or sophisticated; if the Beje was becoming a meeting place for need and supply, it was through some strategy far higher than mine.

A few nights after Fred's first "meterman" visit the alley bell rang long after curfew. I sped downstairs expecting another sad and stammering refugee. Betsie and I had already made up beds for four new overnight guests that evening: a Jewish woman and her three small children.

But to my surprise, close against the wall of the dark alley, stood Kik. "Get your bicycle," he ordered with his usual young abruptness. "And put on a sweater. I have some people I want you to meet."

"Now? After curfew?" But I knew it was useless to ask questions. Kik's bicycle was tireless too, the wheel rims swathed in cloth. He wrapped mine also to keep down the clatter, and soon we were pedaling through the blacked-out streets of Haarlem at a speed that would have scared me even in daylight.

"Put a hand on my shoulder," Kik whispered. "I know the way."

We crossed dark side streets, crested bridges, wheeled round invisible corners. At last we crossed a broad canal and I knew we had reached the fashionable suburb of Aerdenhout.

We turned into a driveway beneath shadowy trees. To my astonishment Kik picked up my bicycle and carried both his and mine up the front steps. A serving girl with starched white apron and ruffled cap opened the door. The entrance hall was jammed with bicycles.

Then I saw him. One eye smiling at me, the other at the door, his vast stomach hastening ahead of him. Pickwick!

He led Kik and me into the drawing room where, sipping coffee and chatting in small groups, was the most distinguished-looking group of men and women I had ever seen. But all my attention, that first moment, was on the inexpressibly fragrant aroma in that room. Surely, was it possible, they were drinking real coffee?

Pickwick drew me a cup from the silver urn on the sideboard. It was coffee. After two years, rich, black, pungent Dutch coffee. He poured himself a cup too, dropping in his usual five lumps of sugar as though rationing had never been invented. Another starched and ruffled maid was passing a tray heaped high with cakes.

Gobbling and gulping I trailed about the room after Pickwick, shaking the hands of the people he singled out. They were strange introductions for no names were mentioned, only, occasionally, an address, and "Ask for Mrs. Smit." When I had met my fourth Smit, Kik explained with a grin, "It's the only last name in the underground."

So this was really and truly the underground! But—where were these people from? I had never laid eyes on any of them. A second later I realized with a shiver down my spine that I was meeting the national group.

Their chief work, I gleaned from bits of conversation, was liaison with England and the Free Dutch forces fighting elsewhere on the continent. They also maintained the underground route through which downed Allied plane crews reached the North Sea coast.

But they were instantly sympathetic with my efforts to help Haarlem's Jews. I blushed to my hair roots to hear Pickwick describe me as "the head of an operation here in this city." A hollow space under the stairs and some haphazard friendships were not an operation. The others here were obviously competent, disciplined, and professional.

But they greeted me with grave courtesy, murmuring what they had to offer as we shook hands. False identity papers. The use of a car with official government plates. Signature forgery.

In a far corner of the room Pickwick introduced me to a frail-appearing little man with a wispy goatee. "Our host informs me," the little man began formally, "that your headquarters building lacks a secret room. This is a danger for all, those you are helping as well as yourselves and those who work with you. With your permission I will pay you a visit in the coming week. . . ."

Years later I learned that he was one of the most famous architects in Europe. I knew him only as Mr. Smit.

Just before Kik and I started our dash back to the Beje, Pickwick slipped an arm through mine. "My dear, I have good news. I understand that Peter is about to be released." . . .

So he was, three days later, thinner, paler, and not a whit daunted by his two months in a concrete cell. Nollie, Tine, and Betsie used up a month's sugar ration baking cakes for his welcome-home party.

And one morning soon afterward the first customer in the shop was a small thin-bearded man named Smit. Father took his jeweler's glass from his eye. If there was one thing he loved better than making a new acquaintance, it was discovering a link with an old one.

"Smit," he said eagerly. "I know several Smits in Amsterdam. Are you by any chance related to the family who——"

"Father," I interrupted, "this is the man I told you about. He's come to, ah, inspect the house."

"A building inspector? Then you must be the Smit with offices in the Grote Hout Straat. I wonder that I haven't——"

"Father!" I pleaded, "he's not a building inspector, and his name is not Smit."

"Not Smit?"

Together Mr. Smit and I attempted to explain, but Father simply could not understand a person's being called by a name not his own. As I led Mr. Smit into the back hall we heard him musing to himself, "I once knew a Smit on Koning Straat. . . ."

Mr. Smit examined and approved the hiding place for ration cards beneath the bottom step. He also pronounced acceptable the warning system we had worked out. This was a triangle-shaped wooden sign advertising "Alpina Watches" which I had placed in the dining room window. As long as the sign was in place, it was safe to enter.

But when I showed him a cubby hole behind the corner cupboard in the dining room, he shook his head. Some ancient redesigning of the house had left a crawl space in that corner and we'd been secreting jewelry, silver coins, and other valuables there since the start of the occupation. Not only the rabbi had brought us his library but other Jewish families had brought their treasures to the Beje for safe-keeping. The space was large enough that we had believed a person could crawl in there if necessary, but Mr. Smit dismissed it without a second glance.

"First place they'd look. Don't bother to change it though. It's only silver. We're interested in saving people, not things."

He started up the narrow corkscrew stairs, and as he mounted so did his spirits. He paused in delight at the odd-placed landings, pounded on the crooked walls, and laughed aloud as the floor levels of the two old houses continued out of phase.

"What an impossibility!" he said in an awestruck voice. "What an improbable, unbelievable, unpredictable impossibility! Miss ten Boom, if all houses were constructed like this one, you would see before you a less worried man."

At last, at the very top of the stairs, he entered my room and gave a little cry of delight. "This is it!" he exclaimed.

"You want your hiding place as high as possible," he went on eagerly. "Gives you the best chance to reach it while the search is on below. He leaned out the window, craning his thin neck, the little faun's beard pointing this way and that.

"But . . . this is my bedroom. . . ."

Mr. Smit paid no attention. He was already measuring. He moved the heavy, wobbly old wardrobe away from the wall with surprising ease and pulled my bed into the center of the room. "This is where the false wall will go!" Excitedly he drew out a pencil and drew a line along the floor thirty inches from the back wall. He stood up and gazed at it moodily.

"That's as big as I dare," he said. "It will take a cot mattress, though. Oh yes. Easily!"

I tried again to protest, but Mr. Smit had forgotten I existed. Over the next few days he and his workmen were in and out of our house constantly. They never knocked. At each visit each man carried in something. Tools in a folded newspaper. A few bricks in a briefcase. "Wood!" he exclaimed when I ventured to wonder if a wooden wall would not be easier to build. "Wood sounds hollow. Hear it in a minute. No, no. Brick's the only thing for false walls."

After the wall was up, the plasterer came, then the carpenter, finally the painter. Six days after he had begun, Mr. Smit called Father, Betsie, and me to see.

We stood in the doorway and gaped. The smell of fresh paint was everywhere. But surely nothing in this room was newly painted! All four walls had that streaked and grimy look that old rooms got in coal-burning Haarlem. The ancient molding ran unbroken around the ceiling, chipped and peeling here and there, obviously undisturbed for a hundred and fifty years. Old water stains streaked the back wall, a wall that even I who had lived half a century in this room, could scarcely believe was not the original, but set back a precious two-and-a-half feet from the true wall of the building.

Built-in bookshelves ran along this false wall, old, sagging shelves whose blistered wood bore the same water stains as the wall behind them. Down in the far lefthand corner, beneath the bottom shelf, a sliding panel, two feet high and two wide, opened into the secret room.

Mr. Smit stooped and silently pulled this panel up. On hands and knees Betsie and I crawled into the narrow room behind it. Once inside we could stand up, sit, or even stretch out one at a time on the single mattress. A concealed vent, cunningly let into the real wall, allowed air to enter from outside.

"Keep a water jug there," said Mr. Smit, crawling in behind us. "Change the water once a week. Hardtack and vitamins keep indefinitely. Anytime there is anyone in the house whose presence is unofficial, all possessions except the clothes actually on his back must be stored in here."

Dropping to our knees again we crawled single file out into my bedroom. "Move back into this room," he told me. "Everything exactly as before."

With his fist he struck the wall above the bookshelves.

"The Gestapo could search for a year," he said. "They'll never find this one."

7. Eusie

PETER WAS HOME, yet he was not safe, any more than any healthy young male was safe. In Germany the munitions factories were desperate for workers. Without warning soldiers would suddenly surround a block of buildings and sweep through them, herding every male between sixteen and thirty into trucks for transport. This method of lightning search and seizure was called "the razzia," and every family with young men lived in dread of it.

Flip and Nollie had rearranged their kitchen to give them an emergency hiding place as soon as the razzias started. There was a small potato cellar beneath the kitchen floor: they enlarged the trapdoor letting into it, put a large rug on top of it and moved the kitchen table to stand on this spot.

Since Mr. Smit's work at the Beje I realized that this hole under the kitchen floor was a totally inadequate hiding place. Too low in the house for one thing, and probably as Mr. Smit would say, "the first place they'd look." However, it was not a sustained search by trained people it was intended for, but a swoop by soldiers, a place to get out of sight for half an hour. And for that, I thought, it was probably sufficient. . . .

It was Flip's birthday when the razzia came to that quiet residential street of identical attached homes. Father, Betsie, and I had come early with a quarter-pound of real English tea from Pickwick.

Nollie, Annaliese, and the two older girls were not yet back when we arrived. A shipment of men's shoes had been announced by one of the department stores and Nollie had determined to get Flip a pair "if I have to stand in line all day."

We were chatting in the kitchen with Cocky and Katrien when all at once Peter and his older brother, Bob, raced into the room, their faces white. "Soldiers! Quick! They're two doors down and coming this way!"

They jerked the table back, snatched away the rug and tugged open the trap-door. Bob lowered himself first, lying down flat, and Peter tumbled in on top of him. We dropped the door shut, yanked the rug over it and pulled the table back in place. With trembling hands Betsie, Cocky, and I threw a long tablecloth over it and started laying five places for tea.

There was a crash in the hall as the front door burst open and a smaller crash close by as Cocky dropped a teacup. Two uniformed Germans ran into the kitchen, rifles leveled.

"Stay where you are. Do not move."

We heard boots storming up the stairs. The soldiers glanced around disgustedly at this room filled with women and one old man. If they had looked closer at Katrien she would surely have given herself away: her face was a mask of terror. But they had other things on their minds.

"Where are your men?" the shorter soldier asked Cocky in clumsy, thick-accented Dutch.

"These are my aunts," she said, "and this is my grandfather. My father is at his school, and my mother is shopping, and——"

"I didn't ask about the whole tribe!" the man exploded in German. Then in Dutch: "Where are your brothers?"

Cocky stared at him a second, then dropped her eyes. My heart stood still. I knew how Nollie had trained her children—but surely, surely now of all times a lie was permissible!

"Do you have brothers?" the officer asked again.

"Yes," Cocky said softly. "We have three."

"How old are they?"

"Twenty-one, nineteen, and eighteen."

Upstairs we heard the sounds of doors opening and shutting, the scrape of furniture dragged from walls.

"Where are they now?" the soldier persisted.

Cocky leaned down and began gathering up the broken bits of cup. The man jerked her upright. "Where are your brothers?"

"The oldest one is at the Theological College. He doesn't get home most nights because——"

"What about the other two?"

Cocky did not miss a breath.

"Why, they're under the table."

Motioning us all away from it with his gun, the soldier seized a corner of the cloth. At a nod from him the taller man crouched with his rifle cocked. Then he flung back the cloth.

At last the pent-up tension exploded: Cocky burst into spasms of high hysterical laughter. The soldiers whirled around. Was this girl laughing at them?

"Don't take us for fools!" the short one snarled. Furiously he strode from the room and minutes later the entire squad trooped out—not, unfortunately, before the silent soldier had spied and pocketed our precious packet of tea.

It was a strange dinner party that evening, veering as it did from heartfelt thanksgiving to the nearest thing to a bitter argument our close-knit family had ever had. Nollie stuck by Cocky, insisting she would have answered the same way. "God honors truth-telling with perfect protection!"

Peter and Bob, from the viewpoint of the trapdoor, weren't so sure. And neither was I. I had never had Nollie's bravery—no, nor her faith either. But I could spot illogic. "And it isn't logical to *say* the truth and *do* a lie! What about Annaliese's false papers—and that maid's uniform on Katrien?"

" 'Set a watch, O Lord, before my mouth,' " Nollie quoted. " 'Keep the door of my lips.' Psalm One Hundred Forty-one!" she finished triumphantly.

"All right, what about the radio? I had to lie with my lips to keep that!"

"And yet whatever came from your lips, Corrie, I am sure it was spoken in love!" Father's kindly voice reproached my flushed face.

Love. How did one show it? How could God Himself show truth and love at the same time in a world like this?

By dying. The answer stood out for me sharper and chiller than it ever had before that night: the shape of a Cross etched on the history of the world.

It was getting harder and harder to find safe homes in the country for the scores of Jews who were passing through our underground station by early 1943. Even with ration cards and forged papers there were not enough places for them all. Sooner or later we knew we were going to have to start hiding people here in the city. How sad that the very first should have been the dearest of all.

It was in the middle of a busy morning in the shop when Betsie slipped through the workshop door. "Harry and Cato are here!" she said.

We were surprised. Harry had never come to the Beje in the daytime because he feared his yellow star would cause awkwardness for us. Father and I hurried behind Betsie up the stairs.

Harry de Vries related the familiar story. The visit the evening before from an NSB quisling. The announcement that the shop was confiscated. Who cared if Harry were a Christian? Any Jew can convert to avoid trouble, the NSBer said. This morning the appearance of a uniformed German to make it official: the shop was closed "in the interest of national security."

"But—if I am a security risk," said poor Harry, "surely they will not stop with taking my store."

Doubtless they would not. But just then there was absolutely no available place outside the city. In fact the only underground address we had at the moment was the home of a woman named De Boer, not four blocks from the Beje.

That afternoon I knocked on Mrs. De Boer's door. She was a dumpy woman dressed in a blue cotton smock and bedroom slippers. We supplied Mrs. De Boer with ration cards and had arranged an emergency appendectomy from there. She showed me the living quarters in her attic. Eighteen Jews were staying there, most of them in their early twenties. "They've been cooped up too long," she said. "They sing and dance and make all sorts of noise."

"If you think one more couple is too much. . . ."

"No. No . . . how can I turn them away? Bring them tonight. We'll manage."

And so Harry and Cato began their life at Mrs. De Boer's, living in one of the narrow dormers in the attic. Betsie went every day to take them some homemade bread, a bit of tea, a slice of sausage. But Betsie's main concern was not for the morale of Harry and Cato, it was for their very lives.

"They're in danger, you know," she told Father and me. "It's true that these young people are at the bursting point. This afternoon they were making such a commotion I could hear them down on the street!"

There were other concerns, that bitter gray winter. Though there was little snow, the cold came early and stayed late, and fuel was scarce. Here and there in the parks and along the canals trees began to disappear as people cut them down to heat cookstoves and fireplaces.

The damp unheated rooms were hardest on the very young and the very old. One morning Christoffels did not appear for Bible reading in the dining room, nor later in the workshop. His landlady found him dead in his bed, the water in his washbasin frozen solid. We buried the old clockmaker in the splendid suit and vest he had worn to the Hundredth Birthday Party, six years and another lifetime ago.

Spring came slowly. We celebrated my fifty-first birthday with a little party in the de Vrieses' alcove home.

It was one week later, April 22, that Cato arrived alone at the Beje. Inside the door she burst into tears. "Those foolish young people went crazy! Last night eight of them left the house. Naturally they were stopped and arrested—the boys hadn't even bothered to cut their side-burns. The Gestapo didn't have any trouble getting information out of them."

The house had been raided, she said, at 4:00 that morning. Cato was released when they discovered she was not Jewish. "But everyone else—Harry, Mrs. De Boer too—oh what will become of them!"

For the next three days Cato was at the Haarlem police station from early morning until curfew, pestering Dutch and Germans alike to let her see her husband. When they sent her away, she stepped across the street and waited silently on the sidewalk.

Friday just before the noon closing when the shop was crowded a policeman pushed open the street door, hesitated, then continued back into the rear room. It was Rolf van Vliet, the officer who had been here when our ration cards were first delivered. He took off his cap and I noticed again that startling orange-red hair.

"This watch is still not keeping time," Rolf said. He took off his wristwatch, placed it on my workbench, and leaned forward. Was he saying something? It was all I could do to hear. "Harry de Vries will be taken to Amsterdam tomorrow. If you want to see him, come promptly at three this afternoon." And then, "Do you see? The second hand still hesitates at the top of the dial."

At three that afternoon Cato and I stepped through the tall double doors of the police station. The policeman on duty at the guard post was Rolf himself.

"Come with me," he said gruffly. He led us through a door and along a high-ceilinged corridor. At a locked metal gate he stopped. "Wait here," Rolf said.

Someone on the other side opened the gate and Rolf passed through. He was gone several minutes. Then the door opened again and we were face to face with Harry. Rolf stood back as Harry took Cato into his arms.

"You have only a few seconds," whispered Rolf.

They drew apart, looking into each other's eyes.

"I'm sorry," said Rolf. "He'll have to go back."

Harry kissed his wife. Then he took my hand and shook it solemnly. Tears filled our eyes. For the first time Harry spoke "I shall use this place—wherever they're taking us," he said. "It will be my witness stand for Jesus."

Rolf took Harry by the elbow.

"We will pray for you many times every day, Harry!" I cried as the gate swung shut.

An instinct which I shared with no one told me that this was the last time I would ever see our friend The Bulldog.

That night we held a meeting about Rolf: Betsie and I and the dozen or so teen-age boys and girls who acted as messengers for this work. If Rolf had risked his own safety to tell us about Harry's transport, perhaps he should work with us.

"Lord Jesus," I said aloud, "this could be a danger for all of us and for Rolf too." But even with the words came a flood of assurance about this man. How long, I wondered, would we be led by this Gift of Knowledge.

I assigned one of our younger boys to follow Rolf home from work next day and learn where he lived. The older boys, the ones susceptible to the factory draft, we sent out only after dark now, and then most often dressed as girls.

The following week I visited Rolf at home. "You have no idea how much it meant to see Harry," I said when I was safe inside. "How can we repay this kindness?"

Rolf ran his hands through his bright hair. "Well, there is a way. The cleaning woman at the jail has a teenage son and they've almost picked him up twice. She's desperate to find another place for him to live."

"Perhaps I can help," I said. "Do you think she could find that her watch needs repairing?"

The next day Toos came to the door of Tante Jans's room where I was talking with two new volunteers for our work. More and more I was leaving the watch shop to her and Father as our underground "operation" required more time. "There's a funny looking little woman downstairs," Toos said. "She says her name is Mietje. She says to tell you 'Rolf sent her.'"

I met Mietje in the dining room. The hand that I shook was ridged and leathery from years of scrubbing floors. A tuft of hair grew from her chin. "I understand," I said, "that you have a son you're very proud of."

"Oh yes!" Mietje's face lit up at the mention of him.

I took the bulky old alarm clock she had brought with her. "Come for your clock tomorrow afternoon and I'll hope to have good news."

That night we listened to our messengers' reports. The long, cruel winter had opened up places at several addresses. There was a place on a nearby tulip farm, but the farmer had decided he must be paid for the risk he was taking. We would have to provide a fee—in silver rijksdaalders, not paper money—plus an additional ration card. It didn't happen often that a "host" would require money for his services; when one did we paid gladly.

When Mietje appeared the following morning I took a small banknote from my purse and tore off a corner. "This is for your son," I said. "Tonight he is to go to the Gravenstenenbrug. There is a tree stump right next to the bridge—they cut down the tree last winter. He is to wait beside it, looking into the canal. A man will come up and ask if he has change for a bankbill. Your son is to match the missing corner, and then follow this man without asking questions."

Betsie came into the dining room as Mietje was grasping my hand in her two sandpaper ones. "I'll make it up to you! Somehow, some day, I'll find a way to repay you!"

Betsie and I exchanged smiles. How could this simple little soul help with the kind of need we faced?

And so the work grew. As each new need arose, a new answer was found, too. Through Pickwick, for example, we met the man at the central telephone exchange whose department handled orders to connect and disconnect lines. With a little rewiring and juggling of numbers, he soon had our instrument in operation.

What a day it was when the old wall phone in the rear hall jangled joyously for the first time in three years! And how we needed it! For by now there were eighty Dutchmen—elderly women and middle-aged men along with our teenagers—working in "God's underground" as we sometimes laughingly called ourselves. Most of these people never saw one another; we kept face-to-face contacts as few as possible. But all knew the Beje. It was headquarters, the center of a spreading web: the knot where all threads crossed.

But if the telephone was a boon, it was also a fresh risk—as was each added worker and connection. We set the phone's ring as low as we could and still hear it; but who might happen to be passing through the hall when it rang?

For that matter how long would curious eyes up and down the street continue to believe that one small watch shop was quite as busy as it appeared? It was true that repair work was in demand: plenty of legitimate customers still passed in and out. But there was altogether too much coming and going, especially in the early evening. The curfew was now 7:00 P.M., which in spring and summer left no nighttime hours at all in which workers could move legally through the streets.

It was an hour and a half before that time on the first of June, 1943, and I was thinking of all this as I sat impatiently behind my workbench. Six workers still not back and so many loose ends to tie up before 7:00. For one thing, being the first of the month, Fred Koornstra should be arriving with the new ration cards. The hundred cards which had seemed such an extravagant request a year ago were now far too few for our needs and Fred was only one of our suppliers, some of the stolen cards coming from as far away as Delft. How long can we go on this way? I wondered. How long can we continue to count on this strange protection?

My thoughts were interrupted by the side entrance bell. Betsie and I reached it at the same instant. In the alley stood a young Jewish woman cradling a tiny blanketed bundle in her arms. Behind her I recognized an intern from the maternity hospital.

The baby, he told us in the hallway, had come prematurely. He had kept mother and child in the hospital longer than permitted already because she had nowhere else to go.

Betsie held out her arms for the baby and at that moment Fred Koornstra opened the door from the shop. He blinked a moment at seeing people in the hall, then turned with great deliberation to the meter on the wall. The young doctor, seeing what he took to be an actual meterman, turned as white as his own collar. I longed to reassure both him and Fred, but knew that the fewer of the group who knew one another the safer it was for all. The poor intern gulped a hasty goodbye while Betsie and I got mother and baby up to the dining room and closed the door on Fred and his work.

Betsie poured a bowl of the soup she had cooked for supper from a much-boiled bone. The baby began a thin high wail; I rocked it while the mother ate. Here was a new danger, a tiny fugitive too young to know the folly of making a noise. We had had many Jewish children over a night or several nights at the Beje and even the youngest had developed the uncanny silence of small hunted things. But at two weeks this one had yet to discover how unwelcoming was its world: we would need a place for them far removed from other houses.

And the very next morning into the shop walked the perfect solution. He was a clergyman friend of ours, pastor in a small town outside of Haarlem, and his home was set back from the street in a large wooded park.

"Good morning, Pastor," I said, the pieces of the puzzle falling together in my mind. "Can we help you?"

I looked at the watch he had brought in for repair. It required a very hard-to-find spare part. "But for you, Pastor, we will do our very best. And now I have something I want to confess."

The pastor's eyes clouded. "Confess?"

I drew him out the back door of the shop and up the stairs to the dining room.

"I confess that I too am searching for something." The pastor's face was now wrinkled with a frown. "Would you be willing to take a Jewish mother and her baby into your home? They will almost certainly be arrested otherwise."

Color drained from the man's face. He took a step back from me. "Miss ten Boom! I do hope you're not involved with any of this illegal concealment and undercover business. It's just not safe! Think of your father! And your sister— she's never been strong!"

On impulse I told the pastor to wait and ran upstairs. Betsie had put the new-comers in Willem's old room, the farthest from windows on the street. I asked the mother's permission to borrow the infant: the little thing weighed hardly anything in my arms.

Back in the dining room I pulled back the coverlet from the baby's face.

There was a long silence. The man bent forward, his hand in spite of himself reaching for the tiny fist curled round the blanket. For a moment I saw compassion and fear struggle in his face. Then he straightened. "No. Definitely not. We could lose our lives for that Jewish child!"

Unseen by either of us, Father had appeared in the doorway. "Give the child to me, Corrie," he said.

Father held the baby close, his white beard brushing its cheek, looking into the little face with eyes as blue and innocent as the baby's own. At last he looked up at the pastor. "You say we could lose our lives for this child. I would consider that the greatest honor that could come to my family."

The pastor turned sharply on his heels and walked out of the room.

So we had to accept a bad solution to our problem. On the edge of Haarlem was a truck farm which hid refugees for short periods of time. It was not a good location, since the Gestapo had been there already. But there was nowhere else available on short notice. Two workers took the woman and child there that afternoon.

A few weeks later we heard that the farm had been raided. When the Gestapo came to the barn where the woman was hidden, not the baby but the mother began to shriek with hysteria. She, the baby, and her protectors were all taken.

We never learned what happened to them.

Although we had a friend at the telephone exchange, we could never be sure that our line was not tapped. So we developed a system for coding our underground messages in terms of watches.

"We have a woman's watch here that needs repairing. But I can't find a mainspring. Do you know who might have one?" (We have a Jewish woman in need of a hiding place and we can't find one among our regular contacts.)

"I have a watch here with a face that's causing difficulty. One of the numbers has worked loose and it's holding back the hand. Do you know anyone who does this kind of repair work?" (We have a Jew here whose features are especially Semitic. Do you know anyone who would be willing to take an extra risk?)

"I'm sorry, but the child's watch you left with us is not repairable. Do you have the receipt?" (A Jewish child has died in one of our houses. We need a burial permit.)

One morning in the middle of June the telephone rang with this message. "We have a man's watch here that's giving us trouble. We can't find anyone to repair it. For one thing, the face is very old-fashioned. . . ."

So, a Jew whose features gave him away. This was the hardest kind of person to place. "Send the watch over and I'll see what we can do in our own shop," I said.

Promptly at 7:00 that evening the side doorbell rang. I glanced at the mirror in the window of the dining room where we were still sitting over tea of rose leaves and cherry stems. Even from the side of his head I could tell that this was our old-fashioned watch. His form, his clothes, his very stance were music-hall-comedy Jewish.

I ran down to the door. "Do come in."

The smiling slender man in his early thirties, with his protruding ears, balding head, and minuscule glasses, gave an elaborate bow. I liked him instantly.

Once the door was closed he took out a pipe. "The very first thing I must ask," he said, "is whether or not I should leave behind my good friend the pipe? Meyer Mossel and his pipe are not easily separated. But for you, kind lady, should the smell get into your drapes, I would gladly say goodbye to my friend nicotine."

I laughed. Of all the Jews who had come to our house this was the first to enter gaily and with a question about our own comfort.

"Of course you must keep your pipe!" I said. "My father smokes a cigar—when he can get one these days."

"Ah! These days!" Meyer Mossel raised arms and shoulders in an enormous shrug. "What do you expect, when the barbarians have overrun the camp?"

I took him up to the dining room. There were seven seated at the table, a Jewish couple waiting placement and three underground workers in addition to Father and Betsie. Meyer Mossel's eyes went straight to Father.

"But," he cried. "One of the Patriarchs!"

It was exactly the right thing to say to Father. "But," he returned with equal good humor, "a brother of the Chosen People!"

"Can you recite the One Hundred and Sixty-sixth Psalm, Opa?" Meyer said.

Father beamed. Of course there is no Psalm 166; the Psalter stops with 150. It must be a joke, and nothing could please Father better than a scriptural joke. "The Hundred and Sixty-sixth Psalm?"

"Shall I recite it for you?" Meyer asked.

Father gave a bow of assent and Meyer plunged into verse.

"But that's Psalm One Hundred!" Father interrupted. And then his face lit up. Of course! Psalm 66 started with the identical words. Meyer had asked for the One Hundredth *and* the Sixty-sixth Psalm. For the rest of the evening I could hear Father chuckling, "Psalm One Hundred and Sixty-six!"

At 8:45 Father took the old brass-bound Bible from its shelf. He opened to the reading in Jeremiah where we had left off the night before, then with sudden inspiration passed the Bible across the table to Meyer.

"I would consider it an honor if you would read for us tonight," Father said.

Lifting the Book lovingly, Meyer rose to his feet. From a pocket came a small prayer cap, and then, from deep in his throat, half-sung, half-pleaded, came the words of the ancient prophet, so feelingly and achingly that we seemed to hear the cry of the Exile itself.

Meyer Mossel, he told us afterward, had been cantor in the synagogue in Amsterdam. For all his lightheartedness he had suffered much. Most of his family had been arrested; his wife and children were in hiding on a farm in the north which had declined to accept Meyer—"for obvious reasons," he said with a grimace at his own unmistakable features.

And gradually it dawned on all of us that this endearing man was at the Beje to stay. It was certainly not an ideal place, but for Meyer nothing could be ideal right now.

"At least," I told him one evening, "your name doesn't have to give you away too." Ever since the days when Willem was studying church history, I had remembered the venerable fourth-century church father, Eusebius.

"I think we'll call you Eusebius," I decided. We were sitting in Tante Jans's front room with Kik and some other young men who had made us a delivery of forged travel-permits too late to get home by curfew.

Meyer leaned back and stared at the ceiling pensively. He took his pipe out of his mouth. "Eusebius Mossel," he said, tasting the words. "No, it doesn't sound quite right. Eusebius Gentile Mossel."

We all laughed. "Don't be a goose," Betsie said. "You must change both names!"

Kik looked slyly at Father. "Opa! How about Smit? That seems a popular name these days."

"It does seem so!" said Father, not catching the joke. "Extraordinarily popular!" And Eusebius Smit it became.

Changing Meyer's name was easy—at once he became "Eusie." But getting Eusie to eat non-kosher food was something else. The problem of course was that we were grateful for food of any kind: we stood in line for hours, this third year of the occupation, to get whatever was available.

One day the paper announced that coupon number four was good for pork sausage. It was the first meat we'd had in weeks. Lovingly Betsie prepared the feast, saving every drop of fat for flavoring other foods later.

"Eusie," Betsie said as she carried the steaming casserole of pork and potatoes to the table, "the day has come."

Eusie knocked the ashes out of his pipe and considered his plight out loud. He, who had always eaten kosher, he, the oldest son of an oldest son of a respected family, in fact, he Meyer Mossel Eusebius Smit, was seriously being asked to eat pork.

Betsie placed a helping of sausage and potato before him. "Bon appetit."

The tantalizing odor reached our meat-starved palates. Eusie wet his lips with his tongue. "Of course," he said, "there's a provision for this in the Talmud." He speared the meat with his fork, bit hungrily and rolled his eyes heavenward in pure pleasure. "And I'm going to start hunting for it, too," he said, "just as soon as dinner's over."

As if Eusie's arrival had broken down a last hesitation, within a week there were three new permanent additions to the household. First there was Jop, our current apprentice, whose daily trip from his parents' home in the suburbs had twice nearly ended in seizure for the factory transport. The second time it happened his parents asked if he could stay at the Beje and we agreed. The other two were Henk, a young lawyer, and Leendert, a schoolteacher. Leendert made an especially important contribution to the secret life of the Beje. He installed our electric warning system.

By now I had learned to make the nighttime trip out to Pickwick's almost as skillfully as could Kik. One evening when I had gratefully accepted a cup of coffee, my wall-eyed friend sat me down for a lecture.

"Cornelia," he said, settling his bulk on a velvet chair too small for him, "I understand you have no alarm system in your house. This is purest folly. Also I am given to believe that you are not carrying on regular drills for your guests."

I was always amazed at how well Pickwick knew what went on at the Beje.

"You know that a raid may come any day," Pickwick continued. "I don't see how you can avoid one. Scores of people in and out—and an NSB agent living over Kan's up the street.

"Your secret room is no good to you if people can't get to it in time. I know this Leendert. He's a good man and a very passable electrician. Get him to put a buzzer in every room with a door or a window on the street. Then hold practice drills until your people can disappear into that room without a trace in less than a minute. I'll send someone to get you started."

Leendert did the electrical work that weekend. He installed a buzzer near the top of the stairs—loud enough to be heard all over the house but not outside. Then he placed buttons to sound the buzzer at every vantage point where trouble might first be spotted. One button went beneath the dining room windowsill, just below the mirror which gave onto the side door. Another went in the downstairs hall just inside that door and a third inside the front door on the Barteljorisstraat. He also put a button behind the counter in the shop and one in each workbench as well as beneath the windows in Tante Jans's rooms.

We were ready for our first trial run. The four unacknowledged members of our household were already climbing up to the secret room two times a day: in the morning to store their night clothes, bedding and toilet articles, and in the evening to put away their day things. Members of our group, too, who had to spend the night, kept raincoats, hats, anything they had brought with them, in that room. Altogether that made a good deal of traffic in and out of my small bedroom—smaller now indeed by nearly a yard. Many nights my last waking sight would be Eusie in long robe and tasseled nightcap, handing his day clothes through the secret panel.

But the purpose of the drills was to see how rapidly people could reach the room at any hour of the day or night without prior notice. A tall sallow-faced young man arrived from Pickwick one morning to teach me how to conduct the drills.

"Smit!" Father exclaimed when the man introduced himself. "Truly it's most astonishing! We've had one Smit after another here lately. Now you bear a great resemblance to. . . ."

Mr. Smit disentangled himself gently from Father's genealogical inquiries and followed me upstairs.

"Mealtimes," he said. "That's a favorite hour for a raid. Also the middle of the night." He strode from room to room pointing everywhere to evidence that more than three people lived in the house. "Watch wastebaskets and ashtrays."

He paused in a bedroom door. "If the raid comes at night they must not only take their sheets and blankets but get the mattress turned. That's the S.D.'s favorite trick—feeling for a warm spot on a bed."

Mr. Smit stayed for lunch. There were eleven of us at the table that day, including a Jewish lady who had arrived the night before and a Gentile woman and her small daughter, members of our underground, who acted as "escorts." The three of them were leaving for a farm in Brabant right after lunch.

Betsie had just passed around a stew so artfully prepared you scarcely missed the meat when, without warning, Mr. Smit leaned back in his chair and pushed the button below the window.

Above us the buzzer sounded. People sprang to their feet, snatching up glasses and plates, scrambling for the stairs, while the cat clawed halfway up the curtain in consternation. Cries of "Faster!" "Not so loud!" and "You're spilling it!" reached us as Father, Betsie, and I hastily rearranged table and chairs to look like a lunch for three in progress.

"No, leave my place," Mr. Smit instructed. "Why shouldn't you have a guest for lunch? The lady and the little girl could have stayed too."

At last we were seated again and silence reigned upstairs.

The whole process had taken four minutes.

A little later we were all gathered again around the dining room table. Mr. Smit set out before him the incriminating evidence he had found: two spoons and a piece of carrot on the stairs, pipe ashes in an "unoccupied" bedroom. Everyone looked at Eusie who blushed to the tips of his large ears.

"Also those," he pointed to the hats of mother and daughter still dangling from the pegs on the dining room wall. "If you have to hide, stop and think what you arrived with. Besides which, you're all simply too slow."

The next night I sounded the alarm again and this time we shaved a minute thirty-three seconds off our run. By our fifth trial we were down to two minutes. We never did achieve Pickwick's ideal of under a minute, but with practice we learned to jump up from whatever we were doing and get those who had to hide into the secret room in seventy seconds. Father, Toos, and I worked on "stalling techniques" which we would use if the Gestapo came through the shop door; Betsie invented a similar strategy for the side door. With these delaying tactics we hoped we could gain a life-saving seventy ticks of a second hand.

Because the drills struck so close to the fear which haunted each of our guests— never spoken, always present—we tried to keep these times from becoming altogether serious. "Like a game!" we'd tell each other: "a race to beat our own record!" One of our group owned the bakery in the next street. Early in the month I would deposit a supply of sugar coupons with him. Then when I decided it was time for a drill I would go to him for a bag of cream puffs—an inexpressible treat in those sweetless days—to be secreted in my workbench and brought out as a reward for a successful practice.

Each time the order of cream puffs was larger. For by now, in addition to the workers whom we wanted to initiate into the system, we had three more permanent boarders: Thea Dacosta, Meta Monsanto, and Mary Itallie.

Mary Itallie, at seventy-six the oldest of our guests, was also the one who posed the greatest problem. The moment Mary stepped through our door I heard the asthmatic wheezing which had made other hosts unwilling to take her in.

Since her ailment compromised the safety of the others, we took up the problem in caucus. The seven most concerned—Eusie, Jop, Henk, Leendert, Meta, Thea, and Mary herself—joined Father, Betsie, and me in Tante Jans's front room.

"There is no sense in pretending," I began. "Mary has a difficulty—especially after climbing stairs—that could put you all in danger."

In the silence that followed, Mary's labored breathing seemed especially loud.

"Can I speak?" Eusie asked.

"Of course."

"It seems to me that we're all here in your house because of some difficulty or other. We're the orphan children—the ones nobody else wanted. Any one of us is jeopardizing all the others. I vote that Mary stay."

"Good," said lawyer Henk, "let's put it to the vote."

Hands began rising but Mary was struggling to speak. "Secret ballots," she brought out at last. "No one should be embarrassed."

Henk brought a sheet of paper from the desk in the next room and tore it into nine small strips. "You too," he said, handing ballots to Betsie, Father, and me. "If we're discovered, you suffer the same as us."

He handed around pencils. "Mark 'No' if it's too great a risk, 'Yes' if you think she belongs here."

For a moment pencils scratched, then Henk collected the folded ballots. He opened them in silence, then reached over and dropped them into Mary's lap.

Nine little scraps of paper, nine times the word, "Yes."

And so our "family" was formed. Others stayed with us a day or a week, but these seven remained, the nucleus of our happy household.

That it could have been happy, at such a time and in such circumstances, was largely a tribute to Betsie. Because our guests' physical lives were so very restricted, evenings under Betsie's direction became the door to the wide world. Sometimes we had concerts, with Leendert on the violin, and Thea, a truly accomplished musician, on the piano. Or Betsie would announce "an evening of Vondel" (the Dutch Shakespeare), with each of us reading a part. One night a week she talked Eusie into giving Hebrew lessons, another night Meta taught Italian.

The evening's activity had to be kept brief because the city now had electricity only a short while each night, and candles had to be hoarded for emergencies. When the lamps flickered and dimmed we would wind back down to the dining room where my bicycle was set up on its stand. One of us would climb onto it, the others taking chairs, and then while the rider pedaled furiously to make the headlight glow bright, someone would pick up the chapter from the night before. We changed cyclist and reader often as legs or voice grew tired, reading our way through histories, novels, plays.

Father always went upstairs after prayers at 9:15, but the rest of us lingered, reluctant to break the circle, sorry to see the evening end. "Oh well," Eusie would say hopefully as we started at last to our rooms, "maybe there'll be a drill tonight! I haven't had a cream puff in nearly a week. . . ."

8. *Storm Clouds Gather*

IF EVENINGS WERE pleasant, daytimes grew increasingly tense. We were too big; the group was too large, the web too widespread. For a year and a half now we had got away with our double lives. Ostensibly we were still an elderly watchmaker living with his two spinster daughters above his tiny shop. In actuality the Beje was the center of an underground ring that spread now to the farthest corners of Holland. Here daily came dozens of workers, reports, appeals. Sooner or later we were going to make a mistake.

It was mealtimes especially when I worried. There were so many now for every meal that we had to set the chairs diagonally around the dining room table. The cat loved this arrangement. Eusie had given him the Hebrew name "Maher Shalal Hashbaz," meaning appropriately enough, "hastening to the spoils, hurrying to the prey." With the chairs set so close M. S. Hashbaz could circle the entire table on our shoulders, purring furiously, traveling round and round.

But I was uneasy at being so many. The dining room was only five steps above street-level; a tall passerby could see right in the window. We'd hung a white curtain across it providing a kind of screen while letting in light. Still, only when the heavy blackout shades were drawn at night did I feel truly private.

At lunch one day, looking through the thin curtain I thought I saw a figure standing just outside in the alley. When I looked again a minute later it was still there. There was no reason for anyone to linger there unless he was curious about what went on in the Beje. I got up and parted the curtain an inch.

Standing a few feet away, seemingly immobilized by some terrible emotion, was old Katrien from Nollie's house!

I bolted down the stairs, threw open the door, and pulled her inside. Although the August day was hot, the old lady's hands were cold as ice. "Katrien! What are you doing here? Why were you just standing there?"

"She's gone mad!" she sobbed. "Your sister's gone mad!"

"Nollie? Oh, what's happened!"

"They came!" she said. "The S.D.! I don't know what they knew or who told them. Your sister and Annaliese were in the living room and I heard her!" The sobs broke out again. "I heard her!"

"Heard what?" I nearly screamed.

"Heard what she told them! They pointed at Annaliese and said, 'Is this a Jew?' And your sister said, 'Yes.'"

I felt my knees go weak. Annaliese, blonde, beautiful young Annaliese with the perfect papers. And she'd trusted us! Oh Nollie, Nollie, what has your rigid honesty done! "And then?" I asked.

"I don't know. I ran out the back door. She's gone mad!"

I left Katrien in the dining room, wheeled my bicycle down the stairs and bumped as fast as I could the mile and a half to Nollie's. Today the sky did not seem larger above the Wagenweg. At the corner of Bos en Hoven Straat I leaned my bike against a lamppost and stood panting, my heart throbbing in my throat. Then, as casually as I was able, I strolled up the sidewalk toward the house. Except for a car parked at the street curb directly in front, everything looked deceptively normal. I walked past. Not a sound from behind the white curtains. Nothing to distinguish this house from the replicas of it on either side.

When I got to the corner I turned around. At that moment the door opened and Nollie came out. Behind her walked a man in a brown business suit. A minute later a second man appeared, half pulling, half supporting Annaliese. The young woman's face was white as chalk; twice before they reached the car I thought she would faint. The car doors slammed, the motor roared, and they were gone.

I pedaled back to the Beje fighting back tears of anxiety. Nollie, we soon learned, had been taken to the police station around the corner, to one of the cells in back. But Annaliese had been sent to the old Jewish theater in Amsterdam from which Jews were transported to extermination camps in Germany and Poland.

It was Mietje, stooped, care-worn little Mietje whose offer of help we had discounted, who kept us in touch with Nollie. She was in wonderful spirits, Mietje said, singing hymns and songs in her high sweet soprano.

How could she sing when she had betrayed another human being! Mietje delivered the bread that Betsie baked for Nollie each morning, and the blue sweater Nollie asked for, her favorite, with flowers embroidered over the pocket.

Mietje relayed another message from Nollie, one especially for me: "No ill will happen to Annaliese. God will not let them take her to Germany. He will not let her suffer because I obeyed Him."

Six days after Nollie's arrest, the telephone rang. Pickwick's voice was on the other end. "I wonder, my dear, if I could trouble you to deliver that watch yourself?"

A message, then, that he could not relay over the phone. I biked at once out to Aerdenhout, taking along a man's watch for safe measure.

Pickwick waited until we were in the drawing room with the door shut. "The Jewish theater in Amsterdam was broken into last night. Forty Jews were rescued. One of them—a young woman—was most insistent that Nollie know: 'Annaliese is free.'"

He fixed me with one of his wide-set eyes. "Do you understand this message?"

I nodded, too overcome with relief and joy to speak. How had Nollie known? How had she been so sure?

After ten days in the Haarlem jail, Nollie was transferred to the federal prison in Amsterdam.

Pickwick said that the German doctor in charge of the prison hospital was a humane man who occasionally arranged a medical discharge. I went at once to Amsterdam to see him. But what could I say, I wondered, as I waited in the entrance hall of his home. How could I get into the good graces of this man?

Lolling about the foyer, sniffing from time to time at my legs and hands, were three perfectly huge Doberman pinschers. I remembered the book we were reading aloud by bicycle lamp, *How to Win Friends and Influence People*. One of the techniques advocated by Dale Carnegie was: find the man's hobby. Hobby, dogs . . . I wonder. . . .

At last the maid returned and showed me into a small sitting room. "How smart of you, Doctor!" I said in German to the grizzle-haired man on the sofa.

"Smart?"

"Yes, to bring these lovely dogs with you. They must be good company when you have to be away from your family."

The doctor's face brightened. "You like dogs then?"

About the only dogs I had ever known were Harry de Vries' bulldogs. "Bulls are my favorite. Do you like bulls?"

"People don't realize it," the doctor said eagerly, "but bulldogs are very affectionate."

For perhaps ten minutes, while I racked my brain for everything I had ever heard or read on the subject, we talked about dogs. Then abruptly the doctor stood up. "But I'm sure you haven't come here to talk about dogs. What's on your mind?"

I met his eye. "I have a sister in prison here in Amsterdam. I was wondering if . . . I don't think she's well."

The doctor smiled. "So, you aren't interested in dogs at all."

"I'm interested now," I said, smiling too. "But I'm far more interested in my sister."

"What's her name?"

"Nollie van Woerden."

The doctor went out of the room and came back with a brown notebook. "Yes. One of the recent arrivals. Tell me something about her. What is she in prison for?"

Taking a chance, I told the doctor that Nollie's crime had been hiding a Jew. I also told him that she was the mother of six children, who if left without aid could become a burden to the State. (I did not mention that the youngest of these children was now seventeen.)

"Well, we'll see." He walked to the door of the sitting room. "You must excuse me now."

I was more encouraged than at any time since Nollie's arrest as I rode the train back to Haarlem. But days, then a week, then two weeks passed and there was no further news. I went back to Amsterdam. "I've come to see how those Dobermans are," I told the doctor.

He was not amused. "You mustn't bother me. I know that you have not come to talk about dogs. You must give me time."

So there was nothing to do but wait.

It was a bright September noon when seventeen of us were squeezed around the dining room table. All of a sudden Nils, seated across from me, turned pale. Nils, one of our workers, had come to report old Katrien safely arrived at a farm north of Alkmaar. Now Nils spoke in a low normal voice.

"Do not turn around. Someone is looking over the curtain."

Over the curtain! But—that was impossible! He'd have to be ten feet high. The table felt silent.

"He's on a ladder, washing the window," Nils said.

"I didn't order the windows washed," said Betsie.

Whoever it was, we mustn't sit here in this frozen, guilty silence! Eusie had an inspiration. "Happy Birthday!" he sang. "Happy Birthday to you!" We all got the idea and joined in lustily. "Happy Birthday, dear Opa . . . ," the song was still echoing through the Beje when I went out the side door and stood next to the ladder, looking up at the man holding bucket and sponge.

"What are you doing? We didn't want the windows washed. Especially not during the party!"

The man took a piece of paper from his hip pocket and consulted it. "Isn't this Kuiper's?"

"They're across the street. But—anyhow, come in and help us celebrate." The man shook his head. He thanked me, but he had work to do. I watched him crossing the Barteljorisstraat with his ladder to Kuiper's candy store.

"Did it work?" a clamor of voices asked when I got back to the dining room. "Do you think he was spying?"

I didn't answer. I didn't know.

* * *

That was the hardest. Never knowing. And one of the biggest unknowns was my own performance under questioning. As long as I was awake I felt fairly sure of myself. But if they should come at night . . . Over and over again the group worked with me—Nils, Henk, Leendert—bursting into my room without warning, shaking me awake, hurling questions at me.

The first time it happened I was sure the real raid had come. There was a terrific pounding on my door, then the beam of a flashlight in my eyes. "Get up! On your feet!" I could not see the man who was speaking.

"Where are you hiding your nine Jews?"

"We only have six Jews now."

There was an awful silence. The room light came on to show Rolf clutching his head with his hands. "Oh no. Oh no," he kept saying. "It can't be that bad."

"Think now," said Henk just behind him. "The Gestapo is trying to trap you. The answer is, 'What Jews! We don't have Jews here.'"

"Can I try again?"

"Not now," said Rolf. "You're wide-awake now."

They tried again a few nights later. "The Jews you're hiding, where do they come from?"

I sat up groggily. "I don't know. They just come to the door."

Rolf flung his hat to the floor. "No, no, no!" he shouted. " 'What Jews! There are no Jews! Can't you learn?"

"I'll learn," I promised. "I'll do better."

And sure enough the next time I woke a little more completely. Half a dozen shadowy forms filled the room. "Where do you hide the ration cards?" a voice demanded.

Under the bottom stair, of course. But this time I would not be trapped into saying so. A crafty reply occurred to me: "In the Frisian clock on the stairwell!"

Kik sat down beside me on the bed and put an arm around me. "That was better, Tante Corrie," he said. "You tried, this time. But remember—you *have* no cards except the three for you, Opa, and Tante Betsie. There *is* no underground activity here, you don't understand what they're talking about. . . ."

Gradually, with repeated drills, I got better. Still, when the time actually came, when they were real Gestapo agents really trained in getting the truth from people, how would I perform?

Willem's underground work brought him frequently to Haarlem. There was an expression of something like despair mingled now with the worry lines in his face. Twice soldiers had been to the nursing home, and although he had managed to deceive them about most of the Jews still in residence there, one sick blind old woman had been taken away.

"Ninety-one!" Willem kept saying. "She couldn't even walk—they had to carry her to the car."

So far, Willem's position as a minister had prevented direct action against him and Tine, but he was watched, he said, more closely than ever. To provide an official reason for his visits to Haarlem he started conducting a weekly prayer fellowship at the Beje each Wednesday morning.

But Willem could do nothing routinely—especially pray—and soon the meeting was attended by dozens of Haarlemers hungry for something to believe in, this fourth year of the occupation. Most of those coming to the services had no idea of the double life of the Beje. In a way they posed a fresh danger as they passed workers and couriers from other underground groups coming and going on the narrow stairs. But in another way, we thought, it might be an advantage to have these flocks of obviously innocent people in and out. That, at least, was our hope.

We were sitting around the supper table after curfew one night, three ten Booms, the seven "permanent guests," and two Jews for whom we were seeking homes, when the shop doorbell chimed.

A customer after closing? And one bold enough to stand on the Barteljorisstraat after curfew? Taking the keys from my pocket I hurried down to the hall, unlocked the workshop door, and felt my way through the dark store. At the front door I listened a moment.

"Who's there?" I called.

"Do you remember me?"

A man's voice speaking German. "Who it it?" I asked in the same language.

"An old friend, come for a visit. Open the door!"

I fumbled with the lock and drew the door gingerly back. It was a German soldier in uniform. Before I could reach the alarm button behind the door, he had pushed his way inside. Then he took off his hat and in the October twilight I recognized the young German watchmaker whom Father had discharged four years ago.

"Otto!" I cried.

"Captain Altschuler," he corrected me. "Our positions are slightly reversed, Miss ten Boom, are they not?"

I glanced at his insignia. He was not a captain or anything close to it, but I said nothing. He looked around the shop.

"Same stuffy little place," he said. He reached for the wall switch, but I put my hand over it.

"No! We don't have blackout shades in the shop!"

"Well, let's go upstairs where we can talk over old times. That old clock cleaner still around?"

"Christoffels? He died in the fuel shortage last winter."

Otto shrugged. "Good riddance then! What about the pious old Bible reader?"

I was edging my way to the sales counter where another bell was located. "Father is very well, thank you."

"Well, aren't you going to invite me up to pay my respects?"

Why was he so eager to go upstairs? Had the wretched fellow come just to gloat, or did he suspect something? My finger found the button.

"What was that!" Otto whirled around suspiciously.

"What was what?"

"That sound! I heard a kind of buzzing."

"I didn't hear anything."

But Otto had started back through the workshop.

"Wait!" I shouted. "Let me get the front door locked and I'll go up with you! I—I want to see how long it takes them to recognize you."

I dawdled at the door as long as I dared: definitely his suspicions were aroused. Then I followed him through the rear door into the hall. Not a sound from the dining room or the stairs. I dashed past him up the steps and rapped on the door.

"Father! Betsie!" I cried in what I hoped was a playful voice. "I'll give you three— no, uh—six guesses who's standing here!"

"No guessing games!" Otto reached past me and flung open the door.

Father and Betsie looked up from their meal. The table was set for three, my unfinished plate on the other side. It was so perfect that even I, who had just seen twelve people eating here, could scarcely believe this was anything but an innocent old man dining with his daughters. The "Alpina" sign stood on the sideboard: they had remembered everything.

Uninvited, Otto pulled out a chair. "Well!" he crowed. "Things happened just like I said, didn't they?"

"So it would seem," said Father mildly.

"Betsie," I said, "give Captain Altschuler some tea!"

Otto took a sip of the brew Betsie poured him and glared round the table at us. "Where did you get real tea! No one else in Holland has tea."

How stupid of me. The tea had come from Pickwick.

"If you must know," I said, "it comes from a German officer. But you mustn't ask any further questions." I tried to imply clandestine dealings with a high occupation official.

Otto lingered another fifteen minutes. And then, feeling perhaps that he had underlined his victory sufficiently, sauntered out into the empty streets.

It was only after another half-hour that we dared give the all clear to nine cramped and shaky people.

The second week in October, during a particularly hectic morning with underground problems, the secret telephone number rang downstairs in the hall. I hurried down to pick it up; only Father, Betsie, or I ever answered it.

"Well!" said a voice. "Aren't you coming to pick me up?"

It was Nollie.

"Nollie! When—How—Where are you?"

"At the train station in Amsterdam! Only I have no money for the trainfare."

"Stay right there! Oh, Nollie, we're coming!"

I biked to Bos en Hoven Straat and then with Flip and the children who happened to be at home, hurried to the Haarlem station. We saw Nollie even before our train came to a stop in Amsterdam—her bright blue sweater like a patch of blue sky in the big dark shed.

Seven weeks in prison had left her pallid-faced, but as radiantly Nollie as ever. A prison doctor, she said, had pronounced her low blood pressure a serious condition, one that might leave her permanently disabled and her six children a burden to society. Her face wrinkled in puzzlement as she said it.

Christmas, 1943, was approaching. The light snow which had fallen was the only festive quality of the season. Every family it seemed had someone in jail, in a work camp, or in hiding. For once the religious side of the holidays was uppermost in every mind.

At the Beje, we had not only Christmas to celebrate but also Hanukkah, the Jewish "Festival of Lights." Betsie found a Hanukkah candlestand among the treasures stored with us behind the dining room cupboard and set it up on the upright piano. Each night we lighted one more candle as Eusie read the story of the Maccabees.

Then we would sing, haunting, melancholy desert music. We were all very Jewish those evenings.

About the fifth night of the Festival, as we were gathered round the piano, the doorbell in the alley rang. I opened it to find Mrs. Beukers, wife of the optician next door, standing in the snow. Mrs. Beukers was as round and placid as her husband was thin and worried, but tonight her plump face was twisted with anxiety.

"Do you think," she whispered, "your Jews could sing a little more softly? We can hear them right through the walls and—well, there are all kinds of people on this street. . . ."

Back in Tante Jans's rooms we considered this news in consternation. If the Beukers family knew all about our affairs, how many other people in Haarlem did too?

It wasn't long before we discovered that one who did was the chief of police himself. One dark January morning when it was trying to snow again, Toos burst into underground "headquarters" in Tante Jans's rear room clutching a letter in her hand. The envelope bore the seal of the Haarlem police.

I tore it open. Inside, on the police chief's stationery, was a hand written note. I read it silently, then aloud.

"You will come to my office this afternoon at three o'clock."

For twenty minutes we tried to analyze that note. Some felt it was not a prelude to arrest. Why would the police give you a chance to escape? Still, it was safest to prepare for search and imprisonment. Workers slipped out of the house, one at a time. Boarders emptied wastebaskets and picked up scraps of sewing in preparation for a quick flight to the secret room. I burned incriminating papers in the long-empty coal hearth in the dining room. The cat caught the tension in the air and sulked beneath the sideboard.

Then I took a bath, perhaps the last for months, and packed a prison bag according to what Nollie and others had learned: a Bible, a pencil, needle and thread, soap—or what we called soap these days—toothbrush, and comb. I dressed in my warmest clothes with several sets of underwear and a second sweater beneath the top one. Just before 3:00 I hugged Father and Betsie tight, and walked through the gray slush to the Smedestraat.

The policeman on duty was an old acquaintance. He looked at the letter, then at me with a curious expression. "This way," he said.

He knocked at a door marked "Chief." The man who sat behind the desk had red-gray hair combed forward over a bald spot. A radio was playing. The chief reached over and twisted the volume knob not down but up.

"Miss ten Boom," he said. "Welcome."

"How do you do, Sir."

The chief had left his desk to shut the door behind me. "Do sit down," he said. "I know all about you, you know. About your work."

"The watchmaking you mean. You're probably thinking more about my father's work than my own."

The chief smiled. "No, I mean your 'other' work."

"Ah, then you're referring to my work with retarded children? Yes. Let me tell you about that——"

"No, Miss ten Boom," the chief lowered his voice. "I am not talking about your work with retarded children. I'm talking about still another work, and I want you to know that some of us here are in sympathy."

The chief was smiling broadly now. Tentatively I smiled back. "Now, Miss ten Boom," he went on, "I have a request."

The chief sat down on the edge of his desk and looked at me steadily. He dropped his voice until it was just audible. He was, he said, working with the underground himself. But an informer in the police department was leaking information to the Gestapo. "There's no way for us to deal with this man but to kill him."

A shudder went down my spine.

"What alternative have we?" the chief went on in a whisper. "We can't arrest him—there are no prisons except those controlled by the Germans. But if he remains at large many others will die. That is why I wondered, Miss ten Boom, if in your work you might know of someone who could——"

"Kill him?"

"Yes."

I leaned back. Was this all a trap to trick me into admitting the existence of a group, into naming names?

"Sir," I said at last, seeing the chief's eyes flicker impatiently, "I have always believed that it was my role to save life, not destroy it. I understand your dilemma, however, and I have a suggestion. Are you a praying man?"

"Aren't we all, these days?"

"Then let us pray together now that God will reach the heart of this man so that he does not continue to betray his countrymen."

There was a long pause. Then the chief nodded. "That I would very much like to do."

And so there in the heart of the police station, with the radio blaring out the latest news of the German advance, we prayed. We prayed that this Dutchman would come to realize his worth in the sight of God and the worth of every other human being on earth.

At the end of the prayer the chief stood up. "Thank you, Miss ten Boom." He shook my hand. "Thank you again. I know now that it was wrong to ask you."

Still clutching my prison bag, I walked through the foyer and around the corner to the Beje.

Upstairs, people crowded around wanting to know everything. But I did not tell them. Not everything—I did not want Father and Betsie to know that we had been asked to kill. It would have been an unnecessary burden for them to bear.

The episode with the chief of police should have been encouraging. Apparently we had friends in high places. As a matter of fact the news had the opposite effect upon us. Here was one more illustration of how our secret was no secret at all. All of Haarlem seemed to know what we were up to.

We knew we should stop the work, but how could we? Who would keep open the network of supplies and information on which the safety of hundreds depended? If a hideaway had to be abandoned, as happened all the time, who would coordinate the move to another address? We had to go on, but we knew that disaster could not be long in coming.

As a matter of fact, it came first to Jop, the seventeen-year-old apprentice who had sought a safe home at the Beje.

Late one afternoon near the end of January, 1944, Rolf stepped stealthily into the workshop. He glanced at Jop. I nodded: Jop was party to everything that went on in the house.

"There's an underground home in Ede that is going to be raided this evening. Do you have anyone who can go?"

But I did not. Not a single courier or escort person was at the Beje this late in the day.

"I'll go," Jop said.

I opened my mouth to protest that he was inexperienced, and liable to the factory transport himself if stopped on the street. Then I thought of the unsuspecting people at Ede. We had a wardrobe of girls' scarves and dresses upstairs. . . .

"Then quickly, boy," Rolf said. "You must leave immediately." He gave Jop the details and hurried away. In a few moments Jop reappeared, making a very pretty brunette in long coat and kerchief, a fur muff hiding his hands. Did the lad have some kind of premonition? To my astonishment he turned at the door and kissed me.

Jop was supposed to be back by the 7:00 P.M. curfew. Seven came and went. Perhaps he had been delayed and would return in the morning.

We did have a visitor early the next day but it was not Jop. I knew the minute Rolf stepped through the door that bad news was weighing him down.

"It's Jop, isn't it?"

"Yes."

"What happened?"

Rolf had learned the story from the sergeant at the night desk. When Jop got to the address in Ede the Gestapo was already there. Jop had rung the bell; the door opened. Pretending to be the owner of the house, the S.D. man had invited Jop in.

"And Corrie," Rolf said, "we must face it. The Gestapo will get information out of Jop. They have already taken him to Amsterdam. How long will he be able to hold his tongue?"

Once again we considered stopping the work. Once again we discovered we could not.

That night Father and Betsie and I prayed long after the others had gone to bed. We knew that in spite of daily mounting risks we had no choice but to move forward. This was evil's hour: we could not run away from it. Perhaps only when human effort had done its best and failed, would God's power alone be free to work.

9. The Raid

AT THE SOUND of someone in my room I opened my eyes painfully. It was Eusie, carrying up his bedding and night clothes to store in the secret room. Behind him came Mary and Thea with their bundles.

I shut my eyes again. It was the morning of February 28, 1944. For two days I had been in bed with influenza. My head throbbed, my joints were on fire. Every little sound, Mary's wheeze, the scrape of the secret panel, made me want to shriek. I heard Henk and Meta come in, then Eusie's laugh as he handed the day things out to the others through the low door.

Go away all of you! Leave me alone! I bit my lip to keep from saying it.

At last they collected their clothes and belongings and trooped out, closing the door behind them. Where was Leendert? Why hadn't he come up? Then I remembered that Leendert was away for a few days setting up electrical warning systems like ours in several of our host homes. I drifted back into a feverish sleep.

The next thing I knew, Betsie was standing at the foot of the bed, a steaming cup of herb tea in her hand. "I'm sorry to wake you, Corrie. But there's a man down in the shop who insists he will talk only to you."

"Who is he?"

"He says he's from Ermelo. I've never seen him before."

I sat up shakily. "That's all right. I have to get up anyway. Tomorrow the new ration cards come."

I sipped the scalding tea, then struggled to my feet. There by the bed lay my prison bag, packed and ready as it had been since the summons from the chief of police. In fact I'd been adding to it. Besides the Bible, clothing, and toilet things, it now held vitamins, aspirins, iron pills for Betsie's anemia and much else. It had become a kind of talisman for me, a safeguard against the terrors of prison.

I got slowly into my clothes and stepped out onto the landing. The house seemed to reel around me. I crept down, clinging to the handrail. At the door to Tante Jans's rooms I was surprised to hear voices. I looked in. Of course, I'd forgotten. It was Wednesday morning, people were gathering for Willem's weekly service. I saw Nollie passing around "occupation coffee" as we called the current brew of roots and dried figs. Peter was already at the piano, as he was most weeks to provide the music. I continued down around the stairs, passing new arrivals streaming up.

As I arrived, wobble-kneed, in the shop, a small sandy-haired man sprang forward to meet me. "Miss ten Boom!"

"Yes?" There was an old Dutch expression: you can tell a man by the way he meets your eyes. This man seemed to concentrate somewhere between my nose and my chin. "Is it about a watch?" I asked.

"No, Miss ten Boom, something far more serious!" His eyes seemed to make a circle around my face. "My wife has just been arrested. We've been hiding Jews, you see. If she is questioned, all of our lives are in danger."

"I don't know how *I* can help," I said.

"I need six hundred guilders. There's a policeman at the station in Ermelo who can be bribed for that amount. I'm a poor man—and I've been told you have certain contacts."

"Contacts?"

"Miss ten Boom! It's a matter of life and death! If I don't get it right away she'll be taken to Amsterdam and then it will be too late."

Something about the man's behavior made me hesitate. And yet how could I risk being wrong? "Come back in half an hour. I'll have the money," I said.

For the first time the man's eyes met mine.

"I'll never forget this," he said.

The amount was more than we had at the Beje so I sent Toos to the bank with instructions to hand the man the money, but not to volunteer any information.

Then I struggled back up the stairs. Where ten minutes earlier I'd been burning with fever, now I was shaking with cold. I stopped at Tante Jans's rooms just long enough to take a briefcase of papers from the desk. Then with apologies to Willem and the others I continued to my room. I undressed again, refilled the vaporizer where it was hissing on its small spirit-stove, and climbed back into bed. For a while I tried to concentrate on the names and addresses in the briefcase. Five cards needed this month in Zandvoort. None in Overveen. We would need eighteen in. . . . The flu roared behind my eyes, the papers swam in front of me. The briefcase slipped from my hand and I was asleep.

*   *   *

In my fevered dream a buzzer kept ringing. On and on it went. Why wouldn't it stop? Feet were running, voices whispering. "Hurry! Hurry!"

I sat bolt upright. People were running past my bed. I turned just in time to see Thea's heels disappear through the low door. Meta was behind her, then Henk.

But—I hadn't planned a drill for today! Who in the world—unless—unless it wasn't a drill. Eusie dashed past me, white-faced, his pipe rattling in the ashtray that he carried in shaking hands.

And at last it penetrated my numbed brain that the emergency had come. One, two, three people already in the secret room; four as Eusie's black shoes and scarlet socks disappeared. But Mary—where was Mary? The old woman appeared in the bedroom door, mouth open, gasping for air. I sprang from my bed and half-pulled, half-shoved her across the room.

I was sliding the secret panel down behind her when a slim white-haired man burst into the room. I recognized him from Pickwick's, someone high in the national Resistance. I'd had no idea he was in the house. He dived after Mary. Five, six. Yes, that was right with Leendert away.

The man's legs vanished and I dropped the panel down and leapt back into bed. Below I heard doors slamming, heavy footsteps on the stairs. But it was another sound that turned my blood to water: the strangling, grating rasp of Mary's breathing.

"Lord Jesus!" I prayed. "You have the power to heal! Heal Mary now!"

And then my eye fell on the briefcase, stuffed with names and addresses. I snatched it up, yanked up the sliding door again, flung the case inside, shoved the door down and pushed my prison bag up against it. I had just reached the bed again when the bedroom door flew open.

"What's your name?"

I sat up slowly and—I hoped—sleepily.

"What?"

"Your name!"

"Cornelia ten Boom." The man was tall and heavy-set with a strange, pale face. He wore an ordinary blue business suit. He turned and shouted down the stairs, "We've got one more up here, Willemse."

He turned back to me. "Get up! Get dressed!"

As I crawled out from under the covers, the man took a slip of paper from his pocket and consulted it. "So you're the ring leader!" He looked at me with new interest. "Tell me now, where are you hiding the Jews?"

"I don't know what you're talking about."

The man laughed. "And you don't know anything about an underground ring, either. We'll see about that!"

He had not taken his eyes off me, so I began to pull on my clothes over my pajamas, ears straining for a sound from the secret room.

"Let me see your papers!"

I pulled out the little sack that I wore around my neck. When I took out my identification folder, a roll of bills fell out with it. The man stooped, snatched up the money from the floor, and stuffed it into his pocket. Then he took my papers and looked at them. For a moment the room was silent. Mary Itallie's wheeze— why wasn't I hearing it?

The man threw the papers back at me. "Hurry up!"

But he was not in half the hurry I was to get away from that room. I buttoned my sweater all wrong in my haste and stuffed my feet into my shoes without bothering to tie them. Then I was about to reach for my prison bag.

Wait.

It stood where I had shoved it in my panic: directly in front of the secret panel. If I were to reach down under the shelf to get it now, with this man watching my every move, might not his attention be attracted to the last place on earth I wanted him to look?

It was the hardest thing I had ever done to turn and walk out of that room leaving the bag behind.

I stumbled down the stairs, my knees shaking as much from fear as from flu. A uniformed soldier was stationed in front of Tante Jans's rooms; the door was shut. I wondered if the prayer meeting had ended, if Willem and Nollie and Peter had got away. Or were they all still in there? How many innocent people might be involved?

The man behind me gave me a little push and I hurried on down the stairs to the dining room. Father, Betsie, and Toos were sitting on chairs pulled back against the wall. Beside them sat three underground workers who must have arrived since I had gone upstairs. On the floor beneath the window, broken in three pieces, lay the "Alpina" sign. Someone had managed to knock it from the sill.

A second Gestapo agent in plain clothes was pawing eagerly through a pile of silver rijksdaalders and jewelry heaped on the dining room table. It was the cache from the space behind the corner cupboard: it had been indeed the first place they looked.

"Here's the other one listed at the address," said the man who had brought me down. "My information says she's the leader of the whole outfit."

The man at the table, the one called Willemse, glanced at me, then turned back to the loot in front of him. "You know what to do, Kapteyn."

Kapteyn seized me by the elbow and shoved me ahead of him down the remaining five steps and into the rear of the shop. Another soldier in uniform stood guard just inside this door. Kapteyn prodded me through to the front room and pushed me against the wall.

"Where are the Jews?"

"There aren't any Jews here."

The man struck me hard across the face.

"Where do you hide the ration cards?"

"I don't know what you're——"

Kapteyn hit me again. I staggered up against the astronomical clock. Before I could recover he slapped me again, then again, and again, stinging blows that jerked my head backward.

"Where are the Jews?"

Another blow.

"Where is your secret room?"

I tasted blood in my mouth. My head spun, my ears rang—I was losing consciousness. "Lord Jesus," I cried out, "protect me!"

Kapteyn's hand stopped in midair.

"If you say that name again I'll kill you!"

But instead his arm slowly dropped to his side. "If you won't talk, that skinny one will."

I stumbled ahead of him up the stairs. He pushed me into one of the chairs against the dining room wall. Through a blur I saw him lead Betsie from the room.

Above us hammer blows and splintering wood showed where a squad of trained searchers was probing for the secret room. Then down in the alley the doorbell rang. But the sign! Didn't they see the "Alpina" sign was gone and—I glanced at the window and caught my breath. There on the sill, the broken pieces fitted carefully together, sat the wooden triangle.

Too late I looked up to see Willemse staring intently at me. "I thought so!" he said. "It was a signal, wasn't it?"

He ran down the stairs. Above us the hammering and the tramp of boots had stopped. I heard the alley door open and Willemse's voice, smooth and ingratiating.

"Come in, won't you?"

"Have you heard!" A woman's voice. "They've got Oom Herman!"

Pickwick? Not Pickwick!

"Oh?" I heard Willemse say. "Who was with him?" He pumped her as hard as he could, then placed her under arrest. Blinking with fright and confusion, the woman was seated with us along the wall. I recognized her only as a person who occasionally took messages for us about the city. I stared in anguish at the sign in the window announcing to the world that all was as usual at the Beje. Our home had been turned into a trap: how many more would fall into it before this day was over? And Pickwick! Had they really caught Pickwick!

Kapteyn appeared with Betsie in the dining room door. Her lips were swollen and puffy, a bruise was darkening on her cheek. She half fell into the chair next to mine.

"Oh Betsie! He hurt you!"

"Yes." She dabbed at the blood on her mouth. "I feel so sorry for him."

Kapteyn whirled, his white face even paler. "Prisoners will remain silent!" he shrieked. Two men were clumping down the stairs and into the dining room carrying something between them. They had discovered the old radio beneath the stairs.

"Law-abiding citizens, are you?" Kapteyn went on. "You! The old man there. I see you believe in the Bible." He jerked his thumb at the well-worn book on its shelf. "Tell me, what does it say in there about obeying the government?"

" 'Fear God,' " Father quoted, and on his lips in that room the words came as blessing and reassurance. " 'Fear God and honor the Queen.' "

Kapteyn stared at him. "It doesn't say that. The Bible doesn't say that."

"No." Father admitted. "It says, 'Fear God, honor the King.' But in our case, that is the Queen."

"It's not King or Queen!" roared Kapteyn. "We're the legal government now, and you're all lawbreakers!"

The doorbell rang again. Again there were the questions and the arrest. The young man—one of our workers—had barely been assigned a chair when again the bell sounded. It seemed to me that we had never had so many callers: the dining room was getting crowded. I felt sorriest for those who had come simply on social visits. An elderly retired missionary was brought in, jaw quivering with fear. At least, from the banging and thumping above, they had not yet discovered the secret room.

A new sound made me jump. The phone down in the hall was ringing.

"That's a telephone!" cried Willemse.

He glared around the room, then grabbing me by the wrist yanked me down the stairs behind him. He thrust the receiver up against my ear but kept his own hand on it.

"Answer!" he said with his lips.

"This is the ten Boom residence and shop," I said as stiffly as I dared.

But the person on the other end did not catch the strangeness. "Miss ten Boom, you're in terrible danger! They've arrested Herman Sluring! They know everything! You've got to be careful!" On and on the woman's voice babbled, the man at my side hearing everything.

She had scarcely hung up when the phone rang again. A man's voice, and again the message, "Oom Herman's been taken to the police station. That means they're on to everything. . . . "

At last, the third time I repeated my formal and untypical little greeting, there was a click on the other end. Willemse snatched the earpiece from my hand.

"Hello! Hello!" he shouted. He jiggled the cradle on the wall. The line had gone dead. He shoved me back up the stairs and into my chair again. "Our friends wised up," he told Kapteyn. "But I heard enough."

Apparently Betsie had received permission to leave her chair: she was slicing bread at the sideboard. I was surprised to realize it was already lunchtime. Betsie passed the bread around the room but I shook my head. The fever was raging again. My throat ached and my head throbbed.

A man appeared in the doorway. "We've searched the whole place, Willemse," he said. "If there's a secret room here, the devil himself built it."

Willemse looked from Betsie to Father to me. "There's a secret room," he said quietly. "And people are using it or they would have admitted it. All right. We'll set a guard around the house till they've turned to mummies."

In the hush of horror which followed there was a gentle pressure on my knees. Maher Shalal Hashbaz had jumped up into my lap to rub against me. I stroked the shining black fur. What would become of him now? I would not let myself think about the six people upstairs.

It had been half an hour since the doorbell had rung last. Whoever had caught my message over the phone must have spread the alarm. Word was out: no one else would walk into the trap at the Beje.

Apparently Willemse had come to the same conclusion because abruptly he ordered us on our feet and down to the hallway with our coats and hats. Father, Betsie, and me he held in the dining room till last. In front of us down the stairs came the people from Tante Jans's rooms. I held my breath scanning them. Apparently most of those at the prayer service had left before the raid. But by no means all. Here came Nollie, behind her, Peter. Last in the line came Willem.

The whole family then. Father, all four of his children, one grandchild. Kapteyn gave me a shove.

"Get moving."

Father took his tall hat from the wall peg. Outside the dining room door he paused to pull up the weights on the old Frisian clock.

"We mustn't let the clock run down," he said.

Father! Did you really think we would be back home when next the chain ran out?

The snow had gone from the streets; puddles of dirty water stood in the gutters as we marched through the alley and into the Smedestraat. The walk took only a minute, but by the time we got inside the double doors of the police station I was shaking with cold. I looked anxiously around the foyer for Rolf and the others we knew, but saw no one. A contingent of German soldiers seemed to be supplementing the regular police force.

We were herded along a corridor and through the heavy metal door where I had last seen Harry de Vries. At the end of this hall was a large room that had obviously been a gymnasium. Windows high in the walls were covered with wire mesh; rings and basketball hoops were roped to the ceiling. Now a desk stood in the center of the room with a German army officer seated behind it. Tumbling mats had been spread out to cover part of the floor and I collapsed onto one of them.

For two hours the officer took down names, addresses, and other statistics. I counted those who had been arrested with us: thirty-five people from the raid on the Beje.

People from previous arrests were sitting or lying about on the mats too, some of them faces we knew. I looked for Pickwick but he was not among them. One of them, a fellow watchmaker who often came to the Beje on business, seemed especially distressed at what had happened to us. He came and sat down beside Father and me.

At last the officer left. For the first time since the alarm buzzer sounded we could talk among ourselves. I struggled to sit up. "Quick!" I croaked. "We've got to agree on what to say! Most of us can simply tell the truth but——" My voice died in my throat. It seemed to my flu-addled brain that Peter was giving me the most ferocious frown I had ever seen.

"But if they learn that Uncle Willem was teaching this morning from the Old Testament, it could make trouble for him," Peter finished for me.

He jerked his head to one side and I clamored unsteadily to my feet. "Tante Corrie!" he hissed when we were on the other side of the room. "That man, the watchmaker! He's a Gestapo plant." He patted my head as though I were a sick child. "Lie down again, Tante Corrie. Just for heaven's sake don't do any talking."

I was waked by the heavy door of the gym slamming open. In strode Rolf.

"Let's have it quiet in here!" he shouted. He leaned close to Willem and said something I could not hear. "Toilets are out back," he continued in a loud voice. "You can go one at a time under escort."

Willem sat down beside me. "He says we can flush incriminating papers if we shred them fine enough." I fumbled through my coat pockets. There were several scraps of paper and a billfold containing a few paper rijksdaalders. I went over each item, trying to think how I would explain it in a court process. Beside the row of outdoor toilets was a basin with a tin cup on a chain. Gratefully I took a long drink—the first since the tea Betsie had brought me that morning.

Toward evening a policeman carried into the gym a large basket of fresh hot rolls. I could not swallow mine. Only the water tasted good to me, though I grew embarrassed at asking again and again to be taken outside.

When I got back the last time, a group had gathered around Father for evening prayers. Every day of my life had ended like this: that deep steady voice, that sure and eager confiding of us all to the care of God. The Bible lay at home on its shelf, but much of it was stored in his heart. His blue eyes seemed to be seeing beyond the locked and crowded room, beyond Haarlem, beyond earth itself, as he quoted from memory: "Thou art my hiding place and my shield: I hope in thy word. . . . Hold thou me up, and I shall be safe. . . ."

None of us slept much. Each time someone left the room he had to step over a dozen others. At last light crept through the high, screened windows at the top of the room. The police again brought rolls. As the long morning wore on I dozed with my back up against the wall; the worst pain now seemed to be in my chest. It was noon when soldiers entered the room and ordered us on our feet. Hastily we struggled into our coats and filed again through the cold corridors.

In the Smedestraat a wall of people pressed against police barricades set across the street. As Betsie and I stepped out with Father between us, a murmur of horror greeted the sight of "Haarlem's Grand Old Man" being led to prison. In front of the door stood a green city bus with soldiers occupying the rear seats. People were climbing aboard while friends and relatives in the crowd wept or simply stared. Betsie and I gripped Father's arms to start down the steps. Then we froze. Stumbling past us between two soldiers, hatless and coatless, came Pickwick. The top of his bald head was a welter of bruises, dried blood clung to the stubble on his chin. He did not look up as he was hauled onto the bus.

Father, Betsie, and I squeezed into a double seat near the front. Through the window I caught a glimpse of Tine standing in the crowd. It was one of those radiant winter days when the air seemed to shimmer with light. The bus shuddered and started up. Police cleared a path and we inched forward. I gazed hungrily out the window, holding onto Haarlem with my eyes. Now we were crossing the Grote Markt, the walls of the great cathedral glowing a thousand shades of gray in the crystal light. In a strange way it seemed to me that I had lived through this moment before.

Then I recalled.

The vision. The night of the invasion. I had seen it all. Willem, Nollie, Pickwick, Peter—all of us here—drawn against our wills across this square. It had all been in the dream—all of us leaving Haarlem, unable to turn back. Going where?

10. *Scheveningen*

OUTSIDE HAARLEM THE bus took the south road, paralleling the sea. On our right rose the low sandy hills of the dune country, soldiers silhouetted on the ridges. Clearly we were not being taken to Amsterdam.

A two-hour drive brought us instead into the streets of The Hague. The bus stopped in front of a new, functional building; word was whispered back that this was Gestapo headquarters for all of Holland. We were marched—all but Pickwick, who seemed unable to rise out of his seat—into a large room where the endless process of taking down names, addresses, and occupations began all over again.

On the other side of the high counter running the length of the room I was startled to see both Willemse and Kapteyn. As each of the prisoners from Haarlem reached the desk, one or the other would lean forward and speak to a man seated at a typewriter and there would be a clatter of sound from the machine.

Suddenly the chief interrogator's eye fell on Father. "That old man!" he cried. "Did he have to be arrested? You, old man!"

Willem led Father up to the desk. The Gestapo chief leaned forward. "I'd like to send you home, old fellow," he said. "I'll take your word that you won't cause any more trouble."

I could not see Father's face, only the erect carriage of his shoulders and the halo of white hair above them. But I heard his answer.

"If I go home today," he said evenly and clearly, "tomorrow I will open my door again to any man in need who knocks."

The amiability drained from the other man's face. "Get back in line!" he shouted. "*Schnell!* This court will tolerate no more delays!"

But delays seemed all that this court existed for. As we inched along the counter there were endless repetitions of questions, endless consulting of papers, endless coming and going of officials. Outside the windows the short winter day was fading. We had not eaten since the rolls and water at dawn.

Ahead of me in line, Betsie answered, "Unmarried," for the twentieth time that day.

"Number of children?" droned the interrogator.

"I'm unmarried," Betsie repeated.

The man did not even look up from his papers. "Number of children!" he snapped.

"No children," said Betsie resignedly.

Toward nightfall a stout little man wearing the yellow star was led past us to the far end of the room. A sound of scuffling made us all look up. The wretched man was attempting to hold onto something clutched in his hands.

"It's mine!" he kept shouting. "You can't take it! You can't take my purse!"

What madness possessed him? What good did he imagine money would do him now? But he continued to struggle, to the obvious glee of the men around him.

"Here Jew!" I heard one of them say. He lifted his booted foot and kicked the small man in the back of his knees. "This is how we take things from a Jew."

It made so much noise. That was all I could think as they continued to kick him. I clutched the counter to keep from falling myself as the sounds continued. Wildly, unreasonably, I hated the man being kicked, hated him for being so helpless and so hurt. At last I heard them drag him out.

Then all at once I was standing in front of the chief questioner. I looked up and met Kapteyn's eyes, just behind him.

"This woman was the ringleader," he said.

Through the turmoil inside me I realized it was important for the other man to believe him. "What Mr. Kapteyn says is true," I said. "These others—they know nothing about it. It was all my——"

"Name?" the interrogator inquired imperturbably.

"Cornelia ten Boom, and I'm the—"

"Age?"

"Fifty-two. The rest of these people had nothing to do——"

"Occupation?"

"But I've told you a dozen times!" I burst out in desperation.

"Occupation?" he repeated.

It was dark night when we were marched at last out of the building. The green bus was gone. Instead we made out the bulk of a large canvas-roofed army truck. Two soldiers had to lift Father over the tailgate. There was no sign of Pickwick. Father, Betsie, and I found places to sit on a narrow bench that ran around the sides.

The truck had no springs and bounced roughly over the bomb-pitted streets of The Hague. I slipped my arm behind Father's back to keep him from striking the edge. Willem, standing near the back, whispered back what he could see of the blacked-out city. We had left the downtown section and seemed to be headed west toward the suburb of Scheveningen. That was our destination then, the federal penitentiary named after this seaside town.

The truck jerked to a halt; we heard a screech of iron. We bumped forward a few feet and stopped again. Behind us massive gates clanged shut.

We climbed down to find ourselves in an enormous courtyard surrounded by a high brick wall. The truck had backed up to a long low building; soldiers prodded us inside. I blinked in the white glare of bright ceiling lights.

"*Nasen gegen Mauer!*"—"Noses to the wall!"

I felt a shove from behind and found myself staring at cracked plaster. I turned my eyes as far as I could, first left and then right. There was Willem. Two places away from him, Betsie. Next to me on the other side was Toos. All like me standing with their faces to the wall. Where was Father?

There was an endless wait while the scars on the wall before my eyes became faces, landscapes, animal shapes. Then somewhere to the right a door opened.

"Women prisoners follow me!"

The matron's voice sounded as metallic as the squealing door. As I stepped away from the wall I glanced swiftly round the room for Father. There he was—a few feet out from the wall, seated in a straight-backed chair. One of the guards must have brought it for him.

Already the matron was starting down the long corridor that I could see through the door. But I hung back, gazing desperately at Father, Willem, Peter, all our brave underground workers.

"Father!" I cried suddenly. "God be with you!"

His head turned toward me. The harsh overhead light flashed from his glasses.

"And with you, my daughters," he said.

I turned and followed the others. Behind me the door slammed closed. And with you! And with you! Oh Father, when will I see you next?

Betsie's hand slipped around mine. A strip of coconut-palm matting ran down the center of the wide hall. We stepped onto it off the damp concrete.

"Prisoners walk to the side." It was the bored voice of the guard behind us. "Prisoners must not step on the matting."

Guiltily we stepped off the privileged path.

Ahead of us in the corridor was a desk, behind it a woman in uniform. As each prisoner reached this point she gave her name for the thousandth time that day and placed on the desk whatever she was wearing of value. Nollie, Betsie, and I unstrapped our beautiful wristwatches. As I handed mine to the officer, she pointed to the simple gold ring that had belonged to Mama. I wriggled it from my finger and laid it on the desk along with my wallet and paper guilders.

The procession down the corridor continued. The walls on both sides of us were lined with narrow metal doors. Now the column of women halted: the matron was fitting a key into one of them. We heard the thud of a bolt drawn back, the screech of hinges. The matron consulted a list in her hand, then called the name of a lady I didn't even know, one of those who had been at Willem's prayer meeting.

Was it possible that that had been only yesterday? Was this only Thursday night? Already the events at the Beje seemed part of another lifetime. The door banged shut; the column moved on. Another door unlocked, another human being closed behind it. No two from Haarlem in the same cell.

Among the very first names read from the list was Betsie's. She stepped through the door; before she could turn or say goodbye, it had closed. Two cells farther on, Nollie left me. The clang of those two doors rang in my ears as the slow march continued.

Now the corridor branched and we turned left. Then right, then left again, an endless world of steel and concrete.

"Ten Boom, Cornelia."

Another door rasped open. The cell was deep and narrow, scarcely wider than the door. A woman lay on the single cot, three others on straw ticks on the floor. "Give this one the cot," the matron said. "She's sick."

And indeed, even as the door slammed behind me a spasm of coughing seized my chest and throat.

"We don't want a sick woman in here!" someone shouted. They were stumbling to their feet, backing as far from me as the narrow cubicle would allow.

"I'm . . . I'm so very sorry—— " I began, but another voice interrupted me.

"Don't be. It isn't your fault. Come on, Frau Mikes, give her the cot." The young woman turned to me. "Let me hang up your hat and coat."

Gratefully I handed her my hat, which she added to a row of clothes hanging from hooks along one wall. But I kept my coat wrapped tight around me. The cot had been vacated and I moved shakily toward it, trying not to sneeze or breathe as I squeezed past my cell-mates. I sank down on the narrow bed, then went into a fresh paroxysm of coughs as a cloud of choking black dust rose from the filthy straw mattress. At last the attack passed and I lay down. The sour straw smell filled my nostrils. I felt each slat of wood through the thin pallet.

"I will never be able to sleep on such a bed," I thought, and the next thing I knew it was morning and there was a clattering at the door "Food call," my cellmates told me. I struggled to my feet. A square of metal had dropped open in the door, forming a small shelf. Onto this someone in the hall was placing tin plates filled with a steaming gruel.

"There's a new one here!" the woman called Frau Mikes called through the aperture. "We get five portions!" Another tin plate was slammed onto the shelf. "If you're not hungry," Frau Mikes added, "I'll help you with it."

I picked up my plate, stared at the watery gray porridge and handed it silently to her. In a little while the plates were collected and the pass-through in the door slammed shut.

Later in the morning a key grated in the lock, the bolt banged, and the door opened long enough for the sanitary bucket to be passed out. The wash basin was also emptied and returned with clean water. The women picked up their straw pallets from the floor and piled them in a corner, raising a fresh storm of dust which started me coughing helplessly again.

Then a prison boredom—which I soon learned to fear above all else—settled over the cell. At first I attempted to relieve it by talking with the others, but though they were as courteous as people can be who are living literally on top of one another, they turned aside my questions and I never learned much about them.

The young woman who had spoken kindly to me the night before, I did discover, was a baroness, only seventeen years old. This young girl paced constantly, from morning until the overhead light bulb went off at night, six steps to the door, six steps back, dodging those sitting on the floor, back and forth like an animal in a cage.

Frau Mikes turned out to be an Austrian woman who had worked as a char-woman in an office building. She often cried for her canary. "Poor little thing! What will become of him! They'll never think to feed him."

This would start me thinking of our cat. Had Maher Shalal Hashbaz made his escape into the street—or was he starving inside the sealed house? I would picture him prowling among the chairlegs in the dining room, missing the shoulders he loved to walk on. I tried not to let my mind venture higher in the house, not to let it climb the stairs to see if Thea, Mary, Eusie—no! I could do nothing for them here in this cell. God knew they were there.

One of my cellmates had spent three years here in Scheveningen. She could hear the rattle of the meal cart long before the rest of us and tell by the footstep who was passing in the corridor. "That's the trusty from medical supply. Someone's sick." . . . "This is the fourth time someone in 316 has gone for a hearing."

Her world consisted of this cubicle and the corridor outside—and soon I began to see the wisdom of this narrowed vision, and why prisoners instinctively shied away from questions about their larger lives. For the first days of my imprison-ment I stayed in a frenzy of anxiety about Father, Betsie, Willem, Pickwick. Was Father able to eat this food? Was Betsie's blanket as thin as this one?

But these thoughts led to such despair that I soon learned not to give in to them. In an effort to fix my mind on something I asked Frau Mikes to teach me the card game that she played hour after hour. She had made the cards herself with the squares of toilet paper that were issued two a day to each prisoner; all day she sat on a corner of the cot endlessly laying them out in front of her and gathering them up again.

I was a slow learner, since no cards of any kind had been played at the Beje.

Now as I began to grasp the solitaire game I wondered what Father's resistance to them had been—surely nothing could be more innocent than this succession of shapes called clubs, spades, diamonds. . . .

But as the days passed I began to discover a subtle danger. When the cards went well my spirits rose. It was an omen: someone from Haarlem had been released! But if I lost. . . . Maybe someone was ill. The people in the secret room had been found. . . .

At last I had to stop playing. In any case I was finding it hard to sit up so long. Increasingly I was spending the days as I did the nights, tossing on the thin straw pallet trying in vain to find a position in which all aches at once were eased. My head throbbed continually, pain shot up and down my arms, my cough brought up blood.

I was thrashing feverishly on the cot one morning when the cell door opened and there stood the steel-voiced matron I had seen the night I entered the cell two weeks before.

"Ten Boom, Cornelia."

I struggled to my feet.

"Bring your hat and your coat and come with me."

I looked around at the others for a hint as to what was happening. "You're going to the outside," our prison expert said. "When you take your hat you always go outside."

My coat I was wearing already, but I took my hat from its hook and stepped out into the corridor. The matron relocked the door then set off so rapidly that my heart hammered as I trotted after her, careful to stay off the precious matting. I stared yearningly at the locked doors on either side of us; I could not remember behind which ones my sisters had disappeared.

At last we stepped out into the broad, high-walled courtyard. Sky! For the first time in two weeks, blue sky! How high the clouds were, how inexpressibly white and clean. I remembered suddenly how much sky had meant to Mama.

"Quick!" snapped the matron.

I hurried to the shiny black automobile beside which she was standing. She opened the rear door and I got in. Two others were already in the back seat, a soldier and a woman with a gaunt gray face. In front next to the driver slumped a desperately ill-looking man whose head lolled strangely on the seat back. As the car started up the woman beside me lifted a blood-stained towel to her mouth and coughed into it. I understood: the three of us were ill. Perhaps we were going to a hospital!

The massive prison gate opened and we were in the outside world, spinning along broad city streets. I stared in wonderment through the window. People walking, looking in store windows, stopping to talk with friends. Had I truly been as free as that only two weeks ago?

The car parked before an office building; it took both the soldier and the driver to get the sick man up three flights of stairs. We entered a waiting room jammed with people and sat down under the watchful eyes of the soldier. When nearly an hour had passed I asked permission to use the lavatory. The soldier spoke to the trim white-uniformed nurse behind the reception desk.

"This way," she said crisply. She took me down a short hall, stepped into the bathroom with me and shut the door. "Quick! Is there any way I can help?"

I blinked at her. "Yes. Oh yes! A Bible! Could you get me a Bible? And—a needle and thread! And a toothbrush! And soap!"

She bit her lip doubtfully. "So many patients today—and the soldier—but I'll do what I can." And she was gone.

But her kindness shone in the little room as brightly as the gleaming white tiles and shiny faucets. My heart soared as I scrubbed the grime off my neck and face.

A man's voice at the door: "Come on! You've been in there long enough!"

Hastily I rinsed off the soap and followed the soldier back to the waiting room. The nurse was back at her desk, coolly efficient as before; she did not look up. After another long wait my name was called. The doctor asked me to cough, took my temperature and blood pressure, applied his stethoscope, and announced that I had pleurisy with effusion, pre-tubercular.

He wrote something on a sheet of paper. Then with one hand on the doorknob he laid the other for an instant on my shoulder. "I hope," he said in a low voice, "that I am doing you a favor with this diagnosis."

In the waiting room the soldier was on his feet ready for me. As I crossed the room the nurse rose briskly from her desk and swished past me. In my hand I felt a small knobby something wrapped in paper.

I slid it into my coat pocket as I followed the soldier down the stairs. The other woman was already back in the car; the sick man did not reappear. All during the return ride my hand kept straying to the object in my pocket, stroking it, tracing the outline. "Oh Lord, it's so small, but still it could be—let it be a Bible!"

The high walls loomed ahead, the gate rang shut behind us. At last, at the end of the long echoing corridors, I reached my cell and drew the package from my pocket. My cellmates crowded round me as I unwrapped the newspaper with trembling hands. Even the baroness stopped her pacing to watch.

As two bars of precious prewar soap appeared, Frau Mikes clapped her hand over her mouth to suppress her yelp of triumph. No tooth-brush or needle but— unheard-of wealth—a whole packet of safety pins! And, most wonderful of all, not indeed a whole Bible, but in four small booklets, the four Gospels.

I shared the soap and pins among the five of us but, though I offered to divide the books as well, they refused. "They catch you with those," the knowledgeable one said, "and it's double sentence and *kalte kost* as well." *Kalte kost*—the bread ration alone without the daily plate of hot food—was the punishment constantly held over our heads. If we made too much noise we'd have *kalte kost*. If we were slow with the bucket it would be *kalte kost*. But even *kalte kost* would be a small price to pay, I thought as I stretched my aching body on the foul straw, for the precious books I clutched between my hands.

It was two evenings later, near the time when the light bulb usually flickered off, that the cell door banged open and a guard strode in.

"Ten Boom, Cornelia," she snapped. "Get your things."

I stared at her, an insane hope rising in me. "You mean——

"Silence! No talking!"

It did not take long to gather my "things": my hat and an undervest that was drying after a vain attempt to get it clean in the much-used basin water. My coat with the precious contents of its pockets had never yet been off my back. Why such strict silence, I wondered. Why should I not be allowed even a goodbye to my cellmates? Would it be so very wrong for a guard to smile now and then, or give a few words of explanation?

I said farewell to the others with my eyes and followed the stiff-backed woman into the hall. She paused to lock the door, then marched off down the corridor. But—the wrong way! We were not heading toward the outside entrance at all, but deeper into the maze of prison passageways.

Still without a word she halted in front of another door and opened it with a key. I stepped inside. The door clanged behind me. The bolt slammed shut.

The cell was identical with the one I had just left, six steps long, two wide, a single cot at the back. But this one was empty. As the guard's footsteps died away down the corridor I leaned against the cold metal of the door. Alone. Alone behind these walls. . . .

I must not let my thoughts run wildly; I must be very mature and very practical. Six steps. Sit down on the cot. This one reeked even worse than the other: the straw seemed to be fermenting. I reached for the blanket: someone had been sick on it. I thrust it away but it was too late. I dashed for the bucket near the door and leaned weakly over it.

At that moment the light bulb in the ceiling went out. I groped back to the cot and huddled there in the dark, setting my teeth against the stink of the bedding, wrapping my coat tighter about me. The cell was bitter cold, wind hammered against the wall. This must be near the outside edge of the prison: the wind had never shrieked so in the other one.

What had I done to be separated from people this way? Had they discovered the conversation with the nurse at the doctor's office? Or perhaps some of the prisoners from Haarlem had been interrogated and the truth about our group was known. Maybe my sentence was solitary confinement for years and years. . . .

In the morning my fever was worse. I could not stand even long enough to get my food from the shelf in the door and after an hour or so the plate was taken away untouched.

Toward evening the pass-through dropped open again and the hunk of coarse prison bread appeared. By now I was desperate for food but less able to walk than ever. Whoever was in the hall must have seen the problem. A hand picked up the bread and hurled it toward me. It landed on the floor beside the cot where I clawed for it and gnawed it greedily.

For several days while the fever raged my supper was delivered in this manner. Mornings the door squealed open and a woman in a blue smock carried the plate of hot gruel to the cot. I was as starved for the sight of a human face as for the food and tried in a hoarse croak to start a conversation. But the woman, obviously a fellow prisoner, would only shake her head with a fearful glance toward the hall.

The door also opened once a day to let in the trusty from Medical Supply with a dose of some stinging yellow liquid from a very dirty bottle. The first time he entered the cell I clutched at his sleeve. "Please!" I rasped. "Have you seen an eighty-four-year-old man—white hair, a long beard? Casper ten Boom! You must have taken medicine to him!"

The man tugged loose. "I don't know! I don't know anything!"

The cell door slammed back against the wall, framing the guard. "Solitary prisoners are not permitted to talk! If you say another word to one of the work-duty prisoners it will be *kalte kost* for the duration of your sentence!" And the door banged behind the two of them.

This same trusty was also charged with recording my temperature each time he came. I had to take off my shirt and place the thermometer between my arm and the side of my body. It did not look to me like an accurate system: sure enough, by the end of the week an irritable voice called through the food slot, "Get up and get the food yourself! Your fever's gone—you won't be waited on again!"

I felt sure that the fever had not gone, but there was nothing for it but to creep, trembling, to the door for my plate. When I had replaced it I would lie down again on the smelly straw, steeling myself for the bawling out I knew would come. "Look at the great lady, back in bed again! Are you going to lie there all day long?" Why lying down was such a crime I could never understand. Nor indeed what one was supposed to accomplish if one got up. . . .

Thoughts, now that I was alone, were a bigger problem than ever. I could no longer even pray for family and friends by name, so great was the fear and longing wrapped round each one. "Those I love, Lord," I would say. "You know them. You see them. Oh—bless them all!"

Thoughts were enemies. That prison bag . . . how many times I opened it in my mind and pawed through all the things I had left behind. A fresh blouse. Aspirin, a whole bottle of them. Toothpaste with a kind of pepperminty taste, and——

Then I would catch myself. How ridiculous, such thoughts! If I had it to do again would I really put these little personal comforts ahead of human lives? Of course not. But in the dark nights, as the wind howled and the fever pulsed, I would draw that bag out of some dark corner of my mind and root through it once again. A towel to lay on this scratchy straw. An aspirin . . .

In only one way was this new cell an improvement over the first one. It had a window. Seven iron bars ran across it, four bars up and down. It was high in the wall, much too high to look out of, but through those twenty-eight squares I could see the sky.

All day I kept my eyes fixed on that bit of heaven. Sometimes clouds moved across the squares, white or pink or edged with gold, and when the wind was from the west I could hear the sea. Best of all, for nearly an hour each day, gradually lengthening as the spring sun rose higher, a shaft of checkered light streamed into the dark little room. As the weather turned warmer and I grew stronger I would stand up to catch the sunshine on my face and chest, moving along the wall with the moving light, climbing at last onto the cot to stand on tiptoe in the final rays.

As my health returned, I was able to use my eyes longer. I had been sustaining myself from my Scriptures a verse at a time; now like a starving man I gulped entire Gospels at a reading, seeing whole the magnificent drama of salvation.

And as I did, an incredible thought prickled the back of my neck. Was it possible that this—all of this that seemed so wasteful and so needless—this war, Scheveningen prison, this very cell, none of it was unforeseen or accidental? Could it be part of the pattern first revealed in the Gospels? Hadn't Jesus—and here my reading became intent indeed—hadn't Jesus been defeated as utterly and unarguably as our little group and our small plans had been?

But . . . if the Gospels were truly the pattern of God's activity, then defeat was only the beginning. I would look around at the bare little cell and wonder what conceivable victory could come from a place like this.

The prison expert in the first cell had taught me to make a kind of knife by rubbing a corset stay against the rough cement floor. It seemed to me strangely important not to lose track of time. And so with a sharp-honed stay I scratched a calendar on the wall behind the cot. As each long featureless day crawled to a close, I checked off another square. I also started a record of special dates beneath the calendar:

February 28,1944	Arrest
February 29, 1944	Transport to Scheveningen
March 16, 1944	Beginning of Solitary

And now a new date:

April 15, 1944	My Birthday in Prison

A birthday had to mean a party, but I searched in vain for a single cheerful object. At least in the other cell there had been bright bits of clothing: the baroness' red hat, Frau Mikes' yellow blouse. How I regretted now my own lack of taste in clothes.

At least I would have a song at my party! I chose one about the Bride of Haarlem tree—she would be in full bloom now. The child's song brought it all close: the bursting branches, the petals raining like snow on the brick sidewalk——

"Quiet in there!" A volley of blows sounded on my iron door. "Solitary prisoners are to keep silent!"

I sat on the cot, opened the Gospel of John, and read until the ache in my heart went away.

Two days after my birthday I was taken for the first time to the big, echoing shower room. A grim-faced guard marched beside me, her scowl forbidding me to take pleasure in the expedition. But nothing could dim the wonder of stepping into that wide corridor after so many weeks of close confinement.

At the door to the shower room several women were waiting. Even in the strict silence this human closeness was joy and strength. I scanned the faces of those coming out, but neither Betsie nor Nollie was there, nor anyone else from Haarlem. And yet, I thought, they are all my sisters. How rich is anyone who can simply see human faces!

The shower too was glorious: warm clean water over my festering skin, streams of water through my matted hair. I went back to my cell with a new resolve: the next time I was permitted a shower I would take with me three of my Gospels. Solitary was teaching me that it was not possible to be rich alone.

And I was not alone much longer: into my solitary cell came a small busy black ant. I had almost put my foot where he was one morning as I carried my bucket to the door when I realized the honor being done me. I crouched down and admired the marvelous design of legs and body. I apologized for my size and promised I would not so thoughtlessly stride about again.

After a while he disappeared through a crack in the floor. But when my evening piece of bread appeared on the door shelf, I scattered some crumbs and to my joy he popped out almost at once. He picked up a heroic piece, struggled down the hole with it and came back for more. It was the beginning of a relationship.

Now in addition to the daily visit of the sun I had the company of this brave and handsome guest—in fact soon of a whole small committee. If I was washing out clothes in the basin or sharpening the point on my homemade knife when the ants appeared, I stopped at once to give them my full attention. It would have been unthinkable to squander two activities on the same bit of time!

One evening as I was crossing another long, long day from the calendar scratched on my wall, I heard shouts far down the corridor. They were answered closer by. Now noisy voices came from every direction. How unusual for the prisoners to be making a racket! Where were the guards?

The shelf in my door had not been closed since the bread came two hours ago. I pressed my ear to it and listened but it was hard to make sense of the tumult outside. Names were being passed from cell to cell. People were singing, others pounding on their doors. The guards must all be away!

"Please! Let's be quiet!" a voice nearby pleaded. "Let's use this time before they get back!"

"What's happening?" I cried through the open slot. "Where are the guards?"

"At the party," the same voice answered me. "It's Hitler's birthday."

Then—these must be their own names people were shouting down the corridor. This was our chance to tell where we were, to get information.

"I'm Corrie ten Boom!" I called through the food shelf. "My whole family is here somewhere! Oh, has anyone seen Casper ten Boom! Betsie ten Boom! Nollie van Woerden! Willem ten Boom!" I shouted names until I was hoarse and heard them repeated from mouth to mouth down the long corridor. I passed names too, to the right and left, as we worked out a kind of system.

After a while answers began to filter back. "Mrs. van der Elst is in Cell 228. . . ." "Pietje's arm is much better. . . ." Some of the messages I could hardly bear to relay: "The hearing was very bad: he sits in the cell without speaking." "To my husband Joost: our baby died last week. . . ."

Along with personal messages were rumors about the world outside, each more wildly optimistic than the last.

"There is a revolution in Germany!"

"The Allies have invaded Europe!"

"The war cannot last three weeks longer!"

At last some of the names I had shouted out began to return. "Betsie ten Boom is in cell 312. She says to tell you that God is good."

Oh, that was Betsie! That was every inch Betsie!

Then: "Nollie van Woerden was in cell 318, but she was released more than a month ago." Released! Oh, thank God!

Toos, too, released!

News from the men's section was longer returning, but as it did my heart leapt higher and higher:

Peter van Woerden. Released!

Herman Sluring. Released!

Willem ten Boom. Released!

As far as I could discover, every single one taken in the raid on the Beje—with the exception of Betsie and me—had been freed. Only about Father could I discover no news at all, although I called his name over and over into the murmuring hall. No one seemed to have seen him. No one seemed to know. . . .

It was perhaps a week later that my cell door opened and a prison trusty tossed a package wrapped in brown paper onto the floor. I picked it up, hefted it, turned it over and over. The wrapping paper had been torn open and carelessly retied, but even through the disarray I could spot Nollie's loving touch. I sat on the cot and opened it.

There, familiar and welcoming as a visit from home, was the light blue embroidered sweater. As I put it on I seemed to feel Nollie's arms circling my shoulders. Also inside the package were cookies and vitamins, needle and thread, and a bright red towel. How Nollie understood the gray color-hunger of prison! She had even wrapped the cookies in gay red cellophane.

I was biting into the first one when an inspiration came to me. I dragged the cot out from the wall to stand under the naked overhead bulb. Climbing on it I fashioned a lampshade with the paper: a cheery red glow at once suffused the bleak little room.

I was rewrapping the cookies in the brown outer paper when my eyes fell on the address written in Nollie's careful hand, slanting upward toward the postage stamp. But—Nollie's handwriting did not slant. . . . The stamp! Hadn't a message once come to the Beje under a stamp, penciled in the tiny square beneath? Laughing at my own overwrought imagination I moistened the paper in the basin water and worked the stamp gently free.

Words! There was definitely writing there—but so tiny I had to climb again onto the cot and hold the paper close to the shaded bulb.

"All the watches in your closet are safe."

Safe. Then—then Eusie, and Henk, and Mary, and—they'd got out of the secret room! They'd escaped! They were free!

I burst into racking sobs, then heard heavy footsteps bearing down the corridor. Hastily I jumped down from the cot and shoved it back to the wall. The pass-through clattered open.

"What's the commotion in here!"

"It's nothing. I—won't do it again."

The slot in the door snapped shut. How had they managed it? How had they got past the soldiers? Never mind, dear Lord, You were there, and that was all that mattered. . . .

The cell door opened to let in a German officer followed by the head matron herself. My eyes ran hungrily over the well-pressed uniform with its rows of brilliant-colored battle ribbons.

"Miss ten Boom," the officer began in excellent Dutch, "I have a few questions I believe you can help me with."

The matron was carrying a small stool which she leapt to set down for the officer. I stared at her. Was this obsequious creature the terrible-voiced terror of the women's wing?

The officer sat down, motioning me to take the cot. There was something in that gesture that belonged to the world outside the prison. As he took out a small notebook and began to read names from it I was suddenly conscious of my rumpled clothes, my long, ragged fingernails.

To my relief I honestly did not know any of the names he read—now I understood the wisdom of the ubiquitous "Mr. Smit." The officer stood up. "Will you be feeling well enough to come for your hearing soon?"

Again that ordinary human manner. "Yes—I—I hope so." The officer stepped out into the hall, the matron bobbing and scurrying after him with the stool.

It was the third of May; I was sitting on my cot sewing. Since Nollie's package had been delivered I had a wonderful new occupation: one by one I was pulling the threads from the red towel and with them embroidering bright figures on the pajamas that I had only recently stopped wearing beneath my clothes. A window with ruffled curtains. A flower with an impossible number of petals and leaves. I had just started work on the head of a cat over the right pocket when the food shelf in the door banged open and shut with a single motion.

And there on the floor of the cell lay a letter.

I dropped the pajamas and sprang forward. Nollie's writing. Why should my hand tremble as I picked it up?

The letter had been opened by the censor—held by them too: the postmark was over a week old. But it was a letter, a letter from home—the very first one! Why this sudden fear?

I unfolded the paper. "Corrie, can you be very brave?"

No! No, I couldn't be brave! I forced my eyes to read on.

"I have news that is very hard to write you. Father survived his arrest by only ten days. He is now with the Lord. . . ."

I stood with the paper between my hands so long that the daily shaft of sunlight entered the cell and fell upon it. Father . . . Father . . . the letter glittered in the criss-cross light as I read the rest. Nollie had no details, not how or where he had died, not even where he was buried.

Footsteps were passing on the coconut matting. I ran to the door and pressed my face to the closed pass-through. "Please! Oh please!"

The steps stopped. The shelf dropped open. "What's the matter?"

"Please! I've had bad news—oh please, don't go away!"

"Wait a minute." The footsteps retreated, then returned with a jangle of keys. The cell door opened.

"Here." The young woman handed me a pill with a glass of water. "It's a sedative."

"This letter just came," I explained. "It says that my father—it says my father has died."

The girl stared at me. "Your father!" she said in astonished tones.

I realized how very old and decrepit I must look to this young person. She stood in the doorway a while, obviously embarrassed at my tears. "Whatever happens," she said at last, "you brought it on yourself by breaking the laws!"

Dear Jesus, I whispered as the door slammed and her footsteps died away, how foolish of me to have called for human help when You are here. To think that Father sees You now, face to face! To think that he and Mama are together again, walking those bright streets. . . .

I pulled the cot from the wall and below the calendar scratched another date:

March 9, 1944   Father. Released.

11. *The Lieutenant*

I WAS WALKING with a guard—behind and a little to the right of her so my feet would not touch the sacrosanct mat—down a corridor I had not seen before. A turn to the right, a few steps down, right again . . . what an endless labyrinth this prison was. At last we stepped out into a small interior courtyard. A drizzle of rain was falling. It was a chill raw morning in late May: after three months in prison I had been called for my first hearing.

Barred windows stared from tall buildings on three sides of the courtyard, along the fourth was a high wall and against this stood a row of small huts. So these were where the infamous interrogations took place. My breath came short and hard as I thought back to the reports I had passed on, the night of Hitler's birthday.

"Lord Jesus, You were called to a hearing too. Show me what to do."

And then I saw something. Whoever used the fourth of the huts had planted a row of tulips along the side. They were wilted now, only tall stems and yellowing leaves, but . . . "Dear Lord, let me go to hut number four!"

The guard had paused to unstrap a long military cape fastened to the shoulder of her uniform. Protected from the rain, she crunched up the gravel path. Past the first hut, the second, the third. She halted in front of the hut with the flowerbed and rapped on the door.

"*Ja! Herrein!*" called a man's voice.

The guard pushed open the door, gave a straight-armed salute and marched smartly off. The man wore a gun in a leather holster and a beribboned uniform.

He removed his hat and I was staring into the face of the gentle-mannered man who had visited me in my cell.

"I am Lieutenant Rahms," he said, stepping to the door to close it behind me. "You're shivering! Here, let me get a fire going."

He filled a pot-bellied stove from a small coal scuttle, for all the world a kindly German householder entertaining a guest. What if this were all a subtle trap? This kind, human manner—perhaps he had simply found it more effective than brutality in tricking the truth from affection-starved people. "Oh Lord, let no weak gullibility on my part endanger another's life."

"I hope," the officer was saying, "we won't have many more days this spring as cold as this one." He drew out a chair for me to sit on.

Warily I accepted it. How strange after three months, to feel a chair-back behind me, chair-arms for my hands! The heat from the stove was quickly warming the little room. In spite of myself I began to relax. I ventured a timid comment about the tulips: "So tall, they must have been beautiful."

"Oh they were!" he seemed ridiculously pleased. "The best I've ever grown. At home we always have Dutch bulbs."

We talked about flowers for a while and then he said, "I would like to help you, Miss ten Boom. But you must tell me everything. I may be able to do something, but only if you do not hide anything from me."

So there it was already. All the friendliness, the kindly concern that I had half-believed in—all a device to elicit information. Well, why not? This man was a professional with a job to do. But I, too, in a small way, was a professional.

For an hour he questioned me, using every psychological trick that the young men of our group had drilled me in. In fact, I felt like a student who has crammed for a difficult exam and then is tested on only the most elementary material. It soon became clear that they believed the Beje had been a headquarters for raids on food ration offices around the country. Of all the illegal activities I had on my conscience, this was probably the one I knew least about. Other than receiving the stolen cards each month and passing them on, I knew no details of the operation. Apparently my real ignorance began to show; after a while Lieutenant Rahms stopped making notes of my hopelessly stupid answers.

"Your other activities, Miss ten Boom. What would you like to tell me about them?"

"Other activities? Oh, you mean—you want to know about my church for mentally retarded people!" And I plunged into an eager account of my efforts at preaching to the feeble-minded.

The lieutenant's eyebrows rose higher and higher. "What a waste of time and energy!" he exploded at last. "If you want converts, surely one normal person is worth all the half-wits in the world!"

I stared into the man's intelligent blue-gray eyes: true National-Socialist philosophy I thought, tulip bed or no. And then to my astonishment I heard my own voice saying boldly, "May I tell you the truth, Lieutenant Rahms?"

"This hearing, Miss ten Boom, is predicated on the assumption that you will do me that honor."

"The truth, Sir," I said, swallowing, "is that God's viewpoint is sometimes different from ours—so different that we could not even guess at it unless He had given us a Book which tells us such things."

I knew it was madness to talk this way to a Nazi officer. But he said nothing so I plunged ahead. "In the Bible I learn that God values us not for our strength or our brains but simply because He has made us. Who knows, in His eyes a half-wit may be worth more than a watchmaker. Or—a lieutenant."

Lieutenant Rahms stood up abruptly. "That will be all for today." He walked swiftly to the door. "Guard!"

I heard footsteps on the gravel path.

"The prisoner will return to her cell."

Following the guard through the long cold corridors, I knew I had made a mistake. I had said too much. I had ruined whatever chance I had that this man might take an interest in my case.

And yet the following morning it was Lieutenant Rahms himself who unlocked my cell door and escorted me to the hearing. Apparently he did not know of the regulation that forbade prisoners to step on the mat, for he indicated that I was to walk ahead of him down the center of the hall. I avoided the eyes of the guards along the route, guilty as a well-trained dog discovered on the living room sofa.

In the courtyard this time a bright sun was shining. "Today," he said, "we will stay outside. You are pale. You are not getting enough sun."

Gratefully I followed him to the farthest corner of the little yard where the air was still and warm. We settled our backs against the wall. "I could not sleep last night," the lieutenant said, "thinking about that Book where you have read such different ideas. What else does it say in there?"

On my closed eyelids the sun glimmered and blazed. "It says," I began slowly, "that a Light has come into this world, so that we need no longer walk in the dark. Is there darkness in your life, Lieutenant?"

There was a very long silence.

"There is great darkness," he said at last. "I cannot bear the work I do here."

Then all at once he was telling me about his wife and children in Bremen, about their garden, their dogs, their summer hiking vacations. "Bremen was bombed again last week. Each morning I ask myself, are they still alive?"

"There is One Who has them always in His sight, Lieutenant Rahms. Jesus is the Light the Bible shows to me, the Light that can shine even in such darkness as yours."

The man pulled the visor of his hat lower over his eyes; the skull-and-crossbones glinted in the sunlight. When he spoke it was so low I could hardly hear. "What can you know of darkness like mine. . . . "

Two more mornings the hearings continued. He had dropped all pretense of questioning me on my underground activities and seemed especially to enjoy hearing about my childhood. Mama, Father, the aunts—he wanted to hear stories about them again and again. He was incensed to learn that Father had died right here in Scheveningen; the documents on my case made no mention of it.

These documents did answer one question: the reason for solitary confinement. "Prisoner's condition contagious to others in cell." I stared at the brief typed words where Lieutenant Rahms's finger rested. I thought of the long wind-haunted nights, the scowling guards, the rule of silence. "But, if it wasn't punishment, why were they so angry with me? Why couldn't I talk?"

The lieutenant squared the edges of the papers in front of him. "A prison is like any institution, Miss ten Boom, certain rules, certain ways of doing things—"

"But I'm not contagious now! I've been better for weeks and weeks, and my own sister is so close! Lieutenant Rahms, if I could only see Betsie! If I could just talk with her a few minutes!"

He lifted his eyes from the desk and I saw anguish in them. "Miss ten Boom, it is possible that I appear to you a powerful person. I wear a uniform, I have a certain authority over those under me. But I am in prison, dear lady from Haarlem, a prison stronger than this one."

It was the fourth and final hearing, and we had come back into the small hut for the signing of the *procès-verbal*. He gathered up the completed transcript and went out with it, leaving me alone. I was sorry to say goodbye to this man who was struggling so earnestly for truth. The hardest thing for him seemed to be that Christians should suffer. "How can you believe in God now?" he'd ask. "What kind of a God would have let that old man die here in Scheveningen?"

I got up from the chair and held my hands out to the squat little stove. I did not understand either why Father had died in such a place. I did not understand a great deal.

And suddenly I was thinking of Father's own answer to hard questions: "Some knowledge is too heavy . . . you cannot bear it . . . your Father will carry it until you are able." Yes! I would tell Lieutenant Rahms about the traincase—he always liked stories about Father.

But when the lieutenant returned to the room a guard from the women's wing was with him. "Prisoner ten Boom has completed her hearings," he said, "and will return to her cell."

The young woman snapped to attention. As I stepped through the door, Lieutenant Rahms leaned forward.

"Walk slowly," he said, "in Corridor F."

Walk slowly? What did he mean? The guard strode down the long door-lined halls so swiftly I had to trot to keep up with her. Ahead of us a prison trusty was unlocking the door to a cell. I trailed behind the guard as much as I dared, my heart thumping wildly. It would be Betsie's cell—I knew it!

Then I was abreast of the door. Betsie's back was to the corridor. I could see only the graceful upswept bun of her chestnut hair. The other women in the cell stared curiously into the corridor; her head remained bent over something in her lap. But I had seen the home Betsie had made in Scheveningen.

For unbelievably, against all logic, this cell was charming. My eyes seized only a few details as I inched reluctantly past. The straw pallets were rolled instead of piled in a heap, standing like little pillars along the walls, each with a lady's hat atop it. A headscarf had somehow been hung along the wall. The contents of several food packages were arranged on a small shelf; I could just hear Betsie saying, "The red biscuit tin here in the center!" Even the coats hanging on their hooks were part of the welcome of that room, each sleeve draped over the shoulder of the coat next to it like a row of dancing children——

"*Schneller! Aber schnell!*"

I jumped and hurried after my escort. It had been a glimpse only, two seconds at the most, but I walked through the corridors of Scheveningen with Betsie's singing spirit at my side.

All morning I heard doors opening and closing. Now keys rattled outside my own: a very young guard in a very new uniform bounded in.

"Prisoner stand at attention!" she squeaked. I stared at her wide, blinking eyes; the girl was in mortal fear of something or someone.

Then a shadow filled the doorway and the tallest woman I had ever seen stepped into the cell. Her features were classically handsome, the face and height of a goddess—but one carved in marble. Not a flicker of feeling registered in her eyes.

"No sheets here either, I see," she said in German to the guard. "See that she has two by Friday. One to be changed every two weeks."

The ice-cold eyes appraised me exactly as they had the bed. "How many showers does the prisoner get?"

The guard wet her lips. "About one a week, *Wachtmeisterin.*"

One a week! One shower a month was closer!

"She will go twice a week."

Sheets! Regular showers! Were conditions going to be better? The new head matron took two strides into the cell; she did not need the cot to reach the overhead bulb. Rip! Off came my red-cellophane lampshade. She pointed to a box of soda crackers that had come in a second package from Nollie.

"No boxes in the cells!" cried the little guard in Dutch, as indignantly as though this had been a long-standing rule.

Not knowing what else to do I dumped the crackers out onto the cot. At the matron's unspoken command I emptied a bottle of vitamins and a sack of peppermint drops the same way.

Unlike the former head matron, who shrieked and scolded endlessly in her rusted-hinge voice, this woman worked in a terrifying silence. With a gesture she directed the guard to feel beneath the mattress. My heart wedged in my throat; my precious remaining Gospel was hidden there. The guard knelt and ran her hands the length of the cot. But whether she was too nervous to do a thorough job or whether there was a more mysterious explanation, she straightened up empty-handed.

And then they were gone.

I stood gazing numbly at the jumble of food on my cot. I thought of this woman reaching Betsie's cell, reducing it again to four walls and a prison cot. A chill wind was blowing through Scheveningen, cleaning, ordering, killing.

It was this tall, ramrod-straight woman who unlocked the door to my cell one afternoon in the second half of June and admitted Lieutenant Rahms. At the severity in his face I swallowed the greeting that had almost burst from me.

"You will come to my office," he said briefly. "The notary has come."

We might as well have been total strangers. "Notary?" I said stupidly.

"For the reading of your Father's will." He made an impatient gesture; obviously this minor matter had interrupted a busy day. "It's the law—family present when a will is opened."

Already he was heading from the cell and down the corridor. I broke into a clumsy run to keep up with the strides of the silent woman beside me. The law? What law? And since when had the German occupation government concerned itself with Dutch legal procedures? Family. Family present. . . . No, don't let yourself think of it!

At the door to the courtyard the matron turned, erect and impassive, back along the corridor. I followed Lieutenant Rahms into the dazzling early summer afternoon. He opened the door for me into the fourth hut. Before my eyes adjusted to the gloom I was drowning in Willem's embrace.

"Corrie! Corrie! Baby sister!" It was fifty years since he had called me that.

Now Nollie's arm was around me too, the other one still clinging to Betsie, as though by the strength of her grip she would hold us together forever. Betsie! Nollie! Willem! I did not know which name to cry first. Tine was in that little room too—and Flip! And another man; when I had time to look I recognized the Haarlem notary who had been called in on the watchshop's few legal consultations. We held each other at arms length to look, we babbled questions all at once.

Betsie was thin and prison-pale. But it was Willem who shocked me. His face was gaunt, yellow, and pain-haunted. He had come home this way from Scheveningen, Tine told me. Two of the eight men crowded into his tiny cell had died of jaundice while he was there.

Willem! I could not bear to see him this way. I crooked my arm through his, standing close so that I did not have to look at him, loving the sound of his deep rolling voice. Willem did not seem aware of his own illness: his concern was all for Kik. This handsome blond son had been seized the month before while helping an American parachutist reach the North Sea. They believed he had been on one of the recent prison trains into Germany.

As for Father, they had learned a few more facts about his last days. He had apparently become ill in his cell and been taken by car to the municipal hospital in The Hague. There, no bed had been available. Father had died in a corridor, separated somehow from his records or any clue as to his identity. Hospital authorities had buried the unknown old man in the paupers' cemetery. The family believed they had located the particular grave.

I glanced over at Lieutenant Rahms. He was standing with his back to us as we talked, staring down at the cold unlit stove. Swiftly I opened the package that Nollie had pressed into my hand with the first embrace. It was what my leaping heart had told me: a Bible, the entire Book in a compact volume, tucked inside a small pouch with a string for wearing around the neck as we had once carried our identity cards. I dropped it quickly over my head and down my back beneath my blouse. I couldn't even find words with which to thank her: the day before, in the shower line, I had given away my last remaining Gospel.

"We don't know all the details," Willem was saying in a low voice to Betsie, "just that after a few days the soldiers were taken off guard duty at the Beje and police stationed there instead." The fourth night, he believed, the chief had succeeded in assigning Rolf and another of our group to the same shift. They had found all the Jews well, though cramped and hungry, and seen them to new hiding places.

"And now?" I whispered back. "They're all right now?"

Willem lowered his deep-sunk eyes to mine. He had never been good at concealing difficult truths. "They're all right, Corrie—all except Mary." Old Mary Itallie, he said, had been arrested one day walking down a city street. Where she had been going and why she had exposed herself this way in broad daylight, nobody knew.

"The time is up." Lieutenant Rahms left his perusal of the stove and nodded to the notary. "Proceed with the reading of the will."

It was a brief, informal document: the Beje was to be home for Betsie and me as long as we wanted it; should there ever be any money realized from the sale of house or watch shop, he knew we would recall his equal love for us all; he committed us with joy to the constant care of God.

In the silence which followed, we all suddenly bowed our heads. "Lord Jesus," Willem said, "we praise You for these moments together under the protection of this good man. How can we thank him? We have no power to do him any service. Lord, allow us to share this inheritance from our father with him as well. Take him too, and his family, into Your constant care."

Outside, a guard's footsteps sounded on the crunchy gravel walk.

12. *Vught*

"GET YOUR THINGS together! Get ready to evacuate! Collect all possessions in pillowcases!" The shouts of the guards echoed up and down the long corridor.

I stood in the center of my cell in a frenzy of excitement. Evacuate! Then—then something was happening! We were leaving the prison! The counter-invasion must have begun!

I snatched the pillowcase from the little wad of straw I had stuffed into it. What riches this coarse bit of muslin had been in the two weeks since it had been provided: a shield for my head from the scratch and smell of the bedding. It almost didn't matter that the promised sheets had never arrived.

With trembling hands I dropped my few belongings into it, the blue sweater, the pajamas covered now back and front with embroidered figures—toothbrush, comb, a few remaining crackers wrapped in toilet paper. My Bible was in its pouch on my back where it remained except when I was reading it.

I put on my coat and hat and stood at the iron door clutching the pillowcase in both hands. It was still early in the morning; the tin breakfast plate had not yet been removed from the shelf in the door. Getting ready had taken no time at all.

An hour passed. I sat on the cot. Two hours. Three. It was warm in the cell this late June day. I took off my hat and coat and folded them next to me on the cot.

More time passed. I kept my eyes on the ant hole, hoping for a last visit from my small friends, but they did not appear. Probably I had frightened them by my early dashing about. I reached into the pillowcase, took one of the crackers and crumbled it about the little crack. No ants. They were staying safely hidden.

And suddenly I realized that this too was a message, a last wordless communication among neighbors. For I too had a hiding place when things were bad. Jesus was this place, the Rock cleft for me. I pressed a finger to the tiny crevice.

The afternoon sun appeared on the wall and moved slowly across the cell. And then all at once there was a clanging out in the corridor. Doors scraped. Bolts banged. "Out! *Schnell!* All out! No talking!"

I snatched up my hat and coat.

My door screeched open. "Form ranks of five—" the guard was already at the next cell.

I stepped out into the hall. It was jammed from wall to wall: I had never dreamed so many women occupied this corridor. We exchanged looks. "In-va-sion," we mouthed silently, the soundless word sweeping through the massed women like an electric charge. Surely the invasion of Holland had begun! Why else would they be emptying the prison!

Where would we be taken? Where were we headed? Not into Germany! Dear Jesus, not Germany.

The command was given and we shuffled forward down the long chill halls, each carrying a pillowcase, with her belongings forming a little bulge at the bottom. At last we emerged into the wide courtyard inside the front gate of the prison and another long wait began. But this wait was pleasant with the late afternoon sun on our backs. Far to the right I could see the columns of the men's section. But crane my neck though I would, I could not see Betsie anywhere.

At last the huge gate swung in and a convoy of gray transport buses drove through. I was herded aboard the third one. The seats had been removed, the windows painted over. The bus lurched dreadfully as it started up but we were standing too close together to fall. When the bus ground to a stop we were at a freight yard somewhere on the outskirts of the city.

Again we were formed into ranks. The guards' voices were tense and shrill. We had to keep our heads facing forward, eyes front. Behind us we could hear buses arriving, then lumbering away again. It was still light, but I knew by the ache in my stomach that it was long past suppertime.

And then, ahead and to the left of me, in the newest group of arriving prisoners, I spotted a chestnut bun. Betsie! Somehow, some way, I was going to get to her! Now instead of wanting the day to end, I prayed that we stay where we were until dark.

Slowly the long June day faded. Thunder rumbled and a few drops of rain fell. At last a long row of unlit coaches rolled slowly over the tracks in front of us. They banged to a stop, rolled forward a little farther, then stopped again. After a while they began backing. For an hour or more the train switched back and forth.

By the time the order came to board, it was pitch dark. The ranks of prisoners surged forward. Behind us the guards shouted and cursed: obviously they were nervous at transporting so many prisoners at one time. I wriggled and shoved to the left. Elbows and shoulders were in my way but I squirmed past. At the very steps of the train I reached out and seized Betsie's hand.

Together we climbed onto the train, together found seats in a crowded compartment, together wept tears of gratitude. The four months in Scheveningen had been our first separation in fifty-three years; it seemed to me that I could bear whatever happened with Betsie beside me.

More hours passed as the loaded train sat on the siding. For us they flew, there was so much to share. Betsie told me about each of her cellmates—and I told her about mine and the little hole into which they scrambled at any emergency. As always, Betsie had given to others everything she had. The Bible that Nollie had smuggled to her she had torn up and passed around, book by book.

It must have been 2:00 or 3:00 in the morning that the train at last began to move. We pressed our faces to the glass, but no lights showed and clouds covered the moon. The thought uppermost in every mind was: Is it Germany? At one point we made out a tower that Betsie was sure was the cathedral at Delft. An hour or more later the clack of the train changed pitch: we were crossing a trestle. But— a very long one! As the minutes passed and still we had not reached the other side Betsie and I exchanged looks. The Moerdijk Bridge! Then we were headed south. Not east into Germany, but south to Brabant. For the second time that night we wept tears of joy.

I leaned my head back against the wooden slats of the seat and shut my eyes, reliving another train trip to Brabant. Mama's hand had gripped Father's, then, as the train swayed. Then, too, it was June—the June of the First Sermon, of the garden back of the manse, of Karel. . . .

I must have fallen asleep, back in that other June, for when I opened my eyes the train had stopped. Voices were shouting at us to move: *Schneller! Aber schnell!* An eerie glare lit the windows. Betsie and I stumbled after the others along the aisle and down the iron steps. We seemed to have stopped in the middle of a woods. Floodlights mounted in trees lit a broad rough-cleared path lined by soldiers with leveled guns.

Spurred by the shouts of the guards Betsie and I started up the path between the gun barrels. "*Schneller!* Close ranks! Keep up! Five abreast!" Betsie's breath was coming short and hard and still they yelled at us to go faster. It had rained hard here, for there were deep puddles in the path. Ahead of us a white-haired woman stepped to the side to avoid one; a soldier struck her in the back with a gun butt. I took Betsie's pillowcase along with mine, hooked my other arm through hers and hauled her along beside me.

The nightmare march lasted a mile or more. At last we came to a barbed-wire fence surrounding a row of wooden barracks. There were no beds in the one we entered, only long tables with backless benches pulled up to them. Betsie and I collapsed onto one of these. Under my arm I could feel the irregular flutter of her heart. We fell into an exhausted sleep, our heads on the table.

The sun was streaming through the barracks windows when we woke up. We were thirsty and hungry: we had had nothing to eat or drink since the early meal at Scheveningen the morning before. But all that day no guard or any official person appeared inside the barracks. At last, when the sun was low in the sky, a prisoner crew arrived with a great vat of some thick steamy substance that we gobbled ravenously.

And so began our stay in this place that, we learned, was named Vught after the nearest small village. Unlike Scheveningen, which had been a regular Dutch prison, Vught had been constructed by the occupation especially as a concentration camp for political prisoners. We were not yet in the camp proper but in a kind of quarantine compound outside. Our biggest problem was idleness, wedged together as we were around the long rows of tables with nothing to do. We were guarded by the same young women who had patrolled the corridors at Scheveningen. They had been adequate enough as long as we were behind locked doors; here they seemed at a loss. Their only technique for maintaining discipline was to shriek obscenities and hand out punishments to all alike. Half rations for the entire barracks. An extra roll call at rigid attention. A ban on talking for twenty-four hours.

Only one of our overseers never threatened or raised her voice. This was the tall, silent head matron from Scheveningen. She appeared in Vught the third morning during the predawn roll call and at once something like order seized our rebellious and untidy ranks. Lines straightened, hands were clamped to sides, whispers ceased as those cold blue eyes swept across us.

Among ourselves we nicknamed her "The General." During one long roll call a pregnant woman at our table slumped to the floor, striking her head against the edge of the bench. The General did not so much as pause in her expressionless reading of names.

We had been in this outer camp at Vught almost two weeks when Betsie and I along with a dozen others were called out by name during morning roll call. When the rest had been dismissed The General distributed typewritten forms among us and instructed us to present them at the administration barracks at 9:00 o'clock.

A worker on the food crew—a long-term prisoner from the main camp—smiled encouragingly as he ladled out our breakfast. "You're free!" he whispered. "Those pink forms mean release!"

Betsie and I stared disbelievingly at the sheets of paper in our hands. Free? Free to leave—free to go home? Others crowded around, congratulating us, embracing us. The women from Betsie's cell at Scheveningen wept unabashedly. How cruel to have to leave all these behind!

"Surely the war will be over very soon," we told them. We emptied our pillowcases, passing out our few belongings among those who had to stay.

Long before 9:00 we were standing in the big wooden anteroom of Administration. At last we were summoned to an inner office where our forms were examined, stamped, and handed over to a guard. We followed this man down a corridor into another office. For hours the process continued as we were shuttled from one room and official to another, questioned, fingerprinted, sent on to the next post. The group of prisoners grew until there were forty or fifty of us standing in line beside a high anchor-chain fence topped with barbed wire. On the other side of the fence was a white birch woods, above our heads the blue Brabant sky. We too belonged to that wide free world.

The next barracks we entered held a row of desks with women clerks seated behind them. At one of these I was handed a brown paper envelope. I emptied it into my hand and the next moment was staring in disbelief at my Alpina watch. Mama's ring. Even my paper guilders. I had not seen these things since the night we arrived at Scheveningen. Money . . . why, that belonged to the world of shops and trolley cars. We could go to a train station with this money. Two fares to Haarlem, please. . . .

We marched along a path between twisted rolls of barbed wire and through a wide gate into a compound of low tin-roofed barracks. There were more lines, more waits, more shuffling from desk to desk, but already the camp and its procedures had become unreal to me.

Then we were standing before a high counter and a young male clerk was saying, "Leave all personal effects at the window marked 'C'."

"But they just gave them back to me!"

"Watches, purses, jewelry . . ."

Mechanically, like a machine with no will of its own, I handed watch, ring, and money through the small barred window. A uniformed woman swept them into a metal box. "Move along! Next!"

Then—were we not to be released? Outside this building a florid-faced officer formed us into a double column and marched us across a broad parade ground. At one end of it a crew of men with shaved heads and striped overalls were digging a ditch. What did it mean? What did any of it mean, this whole long day of lines and waits? Betsie's face was gray with weariness and she stumbled as we marched.

Through another fence we arrived in a yard surrounded on three sides by low concrete buildings. A young woman in a military cape was waiting for us.

"Prisoners halt!" barked the red-faced officer. "Explain to the newcomers, *Fraulein*, the function of the bunkers."

"The bunkers," the girl began in the bored voice of a museum guide, "are for the accommodation of those who fail to cooperate with camp rules. The rooms are cozy, if a bit small: about the size of a gym locker. To hasten the educational process the hands are tied above the head. . . ."

Even as the horrid recital continued, two guards came out of the bunkers, carrying between them the form of a man. He was alive, for his legs were moving, but he seemed to have no conscious control over them. His eyes were sunken and rolled back in his head.

"Not everyone," the girl observed in the same detached drawl, "seems to appreciate the accommodations at the bunkers."

I seized Betsie's arm as the command to march came again, more to steady myself than her. It was Father's traincase once again. Such cruelty was too much to grasp, too much to bear. Heavenly Father, carry it for me!

We followed the officer down a wide street lined with barracks on either side and halted at one of the gray, featureless sheds. It was the end of the long day of standing, waiting, hoping: we had simply arrived in the main camp at Vught.

The barracks appeared almost identical with the one we had left this morning, except that this one was furnished with bunks as well as tables and benches. And still we were not allowed to sit: there was a last wait while the matron with maddening deliberateness checked off our documents against a list.

"Betsie!" I wailed, "how long will it take?"

"Perhaps a long, long time. Perhaps many years. But what better way could there be to spend our lives?"

I turned to stare at her. "Whatever are you talking about?"

"These young women. That girl back at the bunkers. Corrie, if people can be taught to hate, they can be taught to love! We must find the way, you and I, no matter how long it takes. . . ."

She went on, almost forgetting in her excitement to keep her voice to a whisper, while I slowly took in the fact that she was talking about our guards. I glanced at the matron seated at the desk ahead of us. I saw a gray uniform and a visored hat; Betsie saw a wounded human being.

And I wondered, not for the first time, what sort of a person she was, this sister of mine . . . what kind of road she followed while I trudged beside her on the all-too-solid earth.

A few days later Betsie and I were called up for work assignments. One glance at Betsie's pallid face and fragile form, and the matron waved her contemptuously back inside the barracks where the elderly and infirm spent the day sewing prison uniforms. The women's uniform here in Vught was a blue overall with a red stripe down the side of the leg, practical and comfortable, and a welcome change after our own clothes that we had worn since the day of our arrest.

Apparently I looked strong enough for harder work; I was told to report to the Phillips factory. This "factory" turned out to be no more than another large barracks inside the camp complex. Early in the morning though it was, the tar beneath the shingled roof was beginning to bubble in the hot July sun. I followed my escort into the single large room where several hundred men and women sat at long plank tables covered with thousands of tiny radio parts. Two officers, one male, one female, were strolling the aisles between the benches while the prisoners bent to their tasks.

I was assigned a seat at a bench near the front and given the job of measuring small glass rods and arranging them in piles according to lengths. It was monotonous work. The heat from the roof pressed like a weight on my head. I longed to exchange at least names and home towns with my neighbors on either side, but the only sound in the room was the clink of metal parts and the squeak of the officers' boots. They reached the door across from where I sat.

"Production was up again last week," the male officer said in German to a tall slender man with a shaved head and a striped uniform. "You are to be commended for this increase. However we continue to receive complaints of defective wiring. Quality control must improve."

The shaved-headed man made an apologetic gesture. "If there were more food, *Herr Officier*," he murmured. "Since the cutback in rations I see a difference. They grow sleepy, they have trouble concentrating. . . ." His voice reminded me a little of Willem's, deep, cultivated, the German with only a trace of Dutch accent.

"Then you must wake them up! Make them concentrate on the penalties! If the soldiers on the front can fight on half-rations, then these lazy——"

At a terrible look from the woman officer, he stopped and ran his tongue over his lips. "Ah—that is—I speak of course merely as an example. There is naturally no truth in the rumor that rations at the front are reduced. So! I—I hold you responsible!" And together they stalked from the building.

For a moment the prisoner-foreman watched them from the doorway. Slowly he raised his left hand, then dropped it with a slap to his side. The quiet room exploded. From under tables appeared writing paper, books, knitting yarn, tins of biscuits. People left their benches and joined little knots of chattering friends all over the room. Half a dozen crowded around me: Who was I? Where was I from? Did I have any news of the war?

After perhaps half an hour of visiting among the tables, the foreman reminded us that we had a day's quota to meet and people drifted back to their places. The foreman's name, I learned, was Moorman and he had been headmaster of a Roman Catholic boys' school. He himself came over to my workbench the third day I was there; he had heard that I had followed the entire assembly line through the barracks, tracing what became of my dull little piles of rods. "You're the first woman worker," he said, "who has ever shown any interest in what we are making here."

"I am very interested," I said. "I'm a watchmaker."

He stared at me with new interest. "Then I have work you will enjoy more." He took me to the opposite end of the huge shed where the final assembly of relay switches was done. It was intricate and exacting work, though not nearly so hard as watch repair, and Mr. Moorman was right. I enjoyed it and it helped make the eleven-hour workday go faster.

Not only to me but to all the Phillips workers, Mr. Moorman acted more as a kindly older brother than a crew boss. I would watch him, ceaselessly moving among his hundreds of charges, counseling, encouraging, finding a simpler job for the weary, a harder one for the restless. We had been at Vught more than a month before I learned that his twenty-year-old son had been shot here at the camp the week Betsie and I arrived.

No trace of this personal tragedy showed in his care for the rest of us. He stopped frequently at my bench, the first weeks, more to check my frame of mind than my work. But eventually his eyes would travel to the row of relay switches in front of me. . . .

"Dear watch lady! Can you not remember for whom you are working? These radios are for their fighter planes!" And reaching across me he would yank a wire from its housing or twist a tiny tube from an assembly.

"Now solder them back wrong. And not so fast! You're over the day's quota and it's not yet noon."

Lunchtime would have been the best time of day if I could have spent it with Betsie. However, Phillips workers were not allowed to leave the factory compound until the workday ended at 6:00. Prisoners on kitchen detail lugged in great buckets of gruel made of wheat and peas, tasteless but nourishing. Apparently there had been a cutback in rations recently: still the food was better and more plentiful than at Scheveningen where there had been no noonday meal at all.

After eating we were free for a blessed half hour to stroll about within the Phillips compound in the fresh air and the glorious Brabant sun. Most days I found a spot along the fence and stretched out on the warm ground to sleep (the days started with roll call at 5:00 A.M.). Sweet summer smells came in the breezes from the farms around the camp; sometimes I would dream that Karel and I were walking hand in hand along a country lane.

At 6: 00 in the evening there was another roll call, then we marched back to our various sleeping barracks. Betsie always stood in the doorway of ours waiting for me; each evening it was as though a week had passed, there was so much to tell one another.

"That Belgian boy and girl at the bench next to mine? This noon they became engaged!"

"Mrs. Heerma—whose granddaughter was taken to Germany—today she let me pray with her."

One day Betsie's news touched us directly. "A lady from Ermelo was transferred to the sewing detail today. When I introduced myself, she said, 'Another one!' "

"What did she mean?"

"Corrie, do you remember, the day we were arrested, a man came to the shop? You were sick and I had to wake you up."

I remembered very well. Remembered the strange roving eyes, the uneasiness in the pit of my stomach that was more than fever.

"Apparently everyone in Ermelo knew him. He worked with the Gestapo from the first day of occupation. He reported this woman's two brothers for Resistance work, and finally herself and her husband too." When Ermelo had finally caught on to him he had come to Haarlem and teamed up with Willemse and Kapteyn. His name was Jan Vogel.

Flames of fire seemed to leap around that name in my heart. I thought of Father's final hours, alone and confused, in a hospital corridor. Of the underground work so abruptly halted. I thought of Mary Itallie arrested while walking down a street. And I knew that if Jan Vogel stood in front of me now I could kill him.

Betsie drew the little cloth bag from beneath her overalls and held it out to me, but I shook my head. Betsie kept the Bible during the day, since she had more chance to read and teach from it here than I did at the Phillips barracks. In the evenings we held a clandestine prayer meeting for as many as could crowd around our bunk.

"You lead the prayers tonight, Betsie. I have a headache."

More than a headache. All of me ached with the violence of my feelings about the man who had done us so much harm. That night I did not sleep and the next day at my bench scarcely heard the conversation around me. By the end of the week I had worked myself into such a sickness of body and spirit that Mr. Moorman stopped at my bench to ask if something were wrong.

"Wrong? Yes, something's wrong!" And I plunged into an account of that morning. I was only too eager to tell Mr. Moorman and all Holland how Jan Vogel had betrayed his country.

What puzzled me all this time was Betsie. She had suffered everything I had and yet she seemed to carry no burden of rage. "Betsie!" I hissed one dark night when I knew that my restless tossing must be keeping her awake. Three of us now shared this single cot as the crowded camp daily received new arrivals. "Betsie, don't you feel anything about Jan Vogel? Doesn't it bother you?"

"Oh yes, Corrie! Terribly! I've felt for him ever since I knew—and pray for him whenever his name comes into my mind. How dreadfully he must be suffering!"

For a long time I lay silent in the huge shadowy barracks restless with the sighs, snores, and stirrings of hundreds of women. Once again I had the feeling that this sister with whom I had spent all my life belonged somehow to another order of beings. Wasn't she telling me in her gentle way that I was as guilty as Jan Vogel? Didn't he and I stand together before an all-seeing God convicted of the same sin of murder? For I had murdered him with my heart and with my tongue.

"Lord Jesus," I whispered into the lumpy ticking of the bed, "I forgive Jan Vogel as I pray that You will forgive me. I have done him great damage. Bless him now, and his family. . . . " That night for the first time since our betrayer had a name I slept deep and dreamlessly until the whistle summoned us to roll call.

The days in Vught were a baffling mixture of good and bad. Morning roll call was often cruelly long. If the smallest rule had been broken, such as a single prisoner late for evening check-in, the entire barracks would be punished by a 4:00 A.M. or even a 3:30 call and made to stand at parade attention until our backs ached and our legs cramped. But the summer air was warm and alive with birds as the day approached. Gradually, in the east, a pink-and-gold sunrise would light the immense Brabant sky as Betsie and I squeezed each other's hands in awe.

At 5:30 we had black bread and "coffee," bitter and hot, and then fell into marching columns for the various work details. I looked forward to this hike to the Phillips factory. Part of the way we walked beside a small woods, separated only by a roll of barbed wire from a glistening world of dewdrops. We also marched past a section of the men's camp, many of our group straining to identify a husband or a son among the ranks of shaved heads and striped overalls.

This was another of the paradoxes of Vught. I was endlessly, daily grateful to be again with people. But what I had not realized in solitary confinement was that to have companions meant to have their griefs as well. We all suffered with the women whose men were in this camp: the discipline in the male section was much harsher than in the women's; executions were frequent. Almost every day a salvo of shots would send the anguished whispers flying: How many this time? Who were they?

The woman next to me at the relay bench was an intense Communist woman named Floor. She and her husband had managed to get their two small children to friends before their arrest, but she worried aloud all day about them and about Mr. Floor, who had tuberculosis. He worked on the rope-making crew in the compound next to Phillips and each noon they managed to exchange a few words through the barbed wire separating the two enclosures. Although she was expecting a third child in September she would never eat her morning allotment of bread but passed it through the fence to him. She was dangerously thin, I felt, for an expectant mother, and several times I brought her a portion of my own breakfast bread. But this too was always set aside for Mr. Floor.

And yet in spite of sorrow and anxiety—and no one in that place was without both—there was laughter too in the Phillips barracks. An impersonation of the pompous, blustering second lieutenant. A game of blind-man's bluff. A song passed in rounds from bench to bench until——

"Thick clouds! Thick clouds!" The signal might come from any bench which faced a window. The factory barracks was set in the center of the broad Phillips compound; there was no way a camp official could approach it without crossing this open space. In an instant every bench would be filled, the only sound the businesslike rattle of radio parts.

One morning the code words were still being relayed down the long shed when a rather hefty *Aufseherin* stepped through the door. She glanced furiously about, face flushing scarlet as she applied "thick clouds" to her appearance. She shrieked and ranted for a quarter of an hour, then deprived us of our noontime break in the open air that day. After this we adopted the more neutral signal, "fifteen."

"I've assembled fifteen dials!"

During the long hot afternoons pranks and talk died down as each one sat alone with his own thoughts. I scratched on the side of the table the number of days until September 1. There was nothing official about that date, just a chance remark by Mrs. Floor to the effect that six months was the usual prison term for ration-card offenders. Then, if that were the charge and if they included the time served at Scheveningen, September 1 would be our release date!

"Corrie," Betsie warned one evening when I announced triumphantly that August was half over, "we don't know for sure."

I had the feeling, almost, that to Betsie it didn't matter. I looked at her, sitting on our cot in the last moments before lights out, sewing up a split seam in my overalls as she'd so often sat mending under the lamplight in the dining room. Betsie by the very way she sat evoked a high-backed chair behind her and a carpet at her feet instead of this endless row of metal cots on a bare pine floor. The first week we were here she had added extra hooks to the neck of her overalls so that she could fasten the collar high around her throat and, this propriety taken care of, I had the feeling she was as content to be reading the Bible here in Vught to those who had never heard it as she'd been serving soup to hungry people in the hallway of the Beje.

As for me, I set my heart every day more firmly on September 1.

And then, all of a sudden, it looked as though we would not have to wait even this long. The Princess Irene Brigade was rumored to be in France, moving toward Belgium. The Brigade was part of the Dutch forces that had escaped to England during the Five-Day War; now it was marching to reclaim its own.

The guards were noticeably tense. Roll call was an agony. The old and the ill who were slow reaching their places were beaten mercilessly. Even the "red light commando" came in for discipline. These young women were ordinarily a favored group of prisoners. Prostitutes, mostly from Amsterdam, they were in prison not for their profession—which was extolled as a patriotic duty—but for infecting German soldiers. Ordinarily, with the male guards anyway, they had a bold, breezy manner; now even they had to form ruler-straight lines and stand hours at frozen attention.

The sound of the firing squad was heard more and more often. One lunchtime when the bell sounded to return to work, Mrs. Floor did not appear at the bench beside me. It always took a while for my eyes to readjust to the dim factory after the bright sun outside: it was only gradually that I saw the hunk of black bread still resting at her place on the bench. There had been no husband to deliver it to.

And so hanging between hope and horror we waited out the days. Rumor was all we lived on. The Brigade was across the Dutch border. The Brigade was destroyed. The Brigade had never landed. Women who had stayed away from the whispered little prayer service around our cot now crowded close, demanding signs and predictions from the Bible.

On the morning of September 1 Mrs. Floor gave birth to a baby girl. The child lived four hours.

Several days later we awoke to the sound of distant explosions. Long before the roll-call whistle the entire barracks was up and milling about in the dark between the cots. Was it bombs? Artillery fire? Surely the Brigade had reached Brabant. This very day they might be in Vught!

The scowls and threats of the guards when they arrived daunted us not at all. Everyone's mind had turned homeward, everyone talked of what she would do first. "The plants will all be dead," said Betsie, "but we'll get some cuttings from Nollie! We'll wash the windows so the sun can come in."

At the Phillips factory Mr. Moorman tried to calm us. "Those aren't bombs," he said, "and certainly not guns. That's demolition work. Germans. They're probably blowing up bridges. It means they expect an attack but not that it's here. It might not come for weeks."

This dampened us a bit, but as the blasts came closer and closer nothing could keep down hope. Now they were so near they hurt our ears.

"Drop your lower jaw!" Mr. Moorman called down the long room. "Keep your mouth open and it will save your eardrums."

We had our midday meal inside with the doors and windows closed. We'd been working again for an hour—or sitting at our benches, no one could work—when the order came to return to dormitories. With sudden urgency women embraced husbands and sweethearts who worked beside them at Phillips.

Betsie was waiting for me outside our barracks. "Corrie! Has the Brigade come? Are we free?"

"No. Not yet. I don't know. Oh, Betsie, why am I so frightened?"

The loudspeaker in the men's camp was sounding the signal for roll call. No order was given here and we drifted about aimlessly, listening we scarcely knew for what. Names were being read through the men's speaker, though it was too far away to make them out.

And suddenly an insane fear gripped the waiting women. A death-like silence now hung over both sides of the vast camp. The loud-speaker had fallen silent. We exchanged wordless looks, we almost feared to breathe.

Then rifle fire split the air. Around us women began to weep. A second volley. A third. For two hours the executions went on. Someone counted. More than seven hundred male prisoners were killed that day.

There was little sleeping in our barracks that night and no roll call the following morning. About 6:00 a.m. we were ordered to collect our personal things. Betsie and I put our belongings into the pillowcases we had brought from Scheveningen: toothbrushes, needles and thread, a small bottle of Davitamon oil that had come in a Red Cross package, Nollie's blue sweater which was the only thing we had brought with us when we left the quarantine camp ten weeks before. I transferred the Bible in its bag from Betsie's back to my own; she was so thin it made a visible bump between her shoulders.

We were marched to a field where soldiers were passing out blankets from the backs of open trucks. As we filed past, Betsie and I drew two beautiful soft new ones; mine was white with blue stripes, Betsie's white with red stripes—obviously the property of some well-to-do family.

About noon the exodus from camp began. Through the drab streets of barracks we went, past the bunkers, through the maze of barbed-wire compounds and enclosures, and at last onto the rough dirt road through the woods down which we had stumbled that rainy night in June. Betsie hung hard to my arm; she was laboring for breath as she always did when she had to walk any distance.

"March! *Schnell!* Double-time!"

I slipped my arm beneath Betsie's shoulders and half-carried her the final quarter-mile. At last the path ended and we lined up facing the single track, over a thousand women standing toe to heel. Farther along, the men's section was also at the siding; it was impossible to identify individuals among the shaved heads glistening in the autumn sun.

At first I thought our train had not come; then I realized that these freight cars standing on the tracks were for us. Already the men were being prodded aboard, clambering up over the high sides. We could not see the engine, just this row of small, high-wheeled European boxcars stretching out of sight in both directions, machine guns mounted at intervals on the roof. Soldiers were approaching along the track, pausing at each car to haul open the heavy sliding door. In front of us a gaping black interior appeared. Women began to press forward.

Clutching our blankets and pillowcases we were swept along with the others. Betsie's chest was still heaving oddly after the rapid march. I had to boost her over the side of the train.

At first I could make out nothing in the dark car; then in a corner I saw a tall, uneven shape. It was a stack of bread, dozens of flat black loaves piled one on top of another. A long trip then. . . .

The small car was getting crowded. We were shoved against the back wall. Thirty or forty people were all that could fit in. And still the soldiers drove women over the side, cursing, jabbing with their guns. Shrieks rose from the center of the car but still the press increased. It was only when eighty women were packed inside that the door thumped shut and we heard iron bolts driven into place.

Women were sobbing and many fainted, although in the tight-wedged crowd they remained upright. Just when it seemed certain that those in the middle must suffocate or be trampled to death, we worked out a kind of system where, by half-sitting, half-lying with our legs wedged around one another like members of a sledding team, we were able to get down on the floor of the car.

"Do you know what I am thankful for?" Betsie's gentle voice startled me in that squirming madhouse. "I am thankful that Father is in heaven today!"

Father. Yes! Oh Father, how could I have wept for you?

The warm sun beat down on the motionless train, the temperature in the packed car rose, the air grew foul. Beside me someone was tugging at a nail in the ancient wood of the wall. At last it came free; with the point she set to work gouging the hole wider. Others around the sides took up the idea and in a while blessed whiffs of outside air began to circle about us.

It was hours before the train gave a sudden lurch and began to move. Almost at once it stopped again, then again crawled forward. The rest of the day and into the night it was the same, stopping, starting, slamming, jerking. Once when it was my turn at the air-hole I saw in the moonlight trainmen carrying a length of twisted rail. Tracks ahead must be destroyed. I passed the news. Maybe they would not be able to repair them. Maybe we would still be in Holland when liberation came.

Betsie's forehead was hot to my hand. The "red light" girl between whose legs I was wedged squeezed herself into an even tighter crouch so that Betsie could lie almost flat across my lap. I dozed too, from time to time, my head on the shoulder of the friendly girl behind us. Once I dreamed it was storming. I could hear the hailstones on Tante Jans's front windows. I opened my eyes. It really was hailing. I could hear it rattling against the side of the car.

Everyone was awake now and talking. Another storm of hail. And then we heard a burst of machine-gun fire from the roof of the train.

"It's bullets!" someone shouted. "They're attacking the train."

Again we heard that sound like tiny stones striking the wall, and again the machine guns answered. Had the Brigade reached us at last? The firing died away. For an hour the train sat motionless. Then slowly we crawled forward.

At dawn someone called out that we were passing through the border town of Emmerich.

We had arrived in Germany.

13. Ravensbruck

FOR TWO MORE incredible days and two more nights we were carried deeper and deeper into the land of our fears. Occasionally one of the loaves of bread was passed from hand to hand. But not even the most elementary provision had been made for sanitation and the air in the car was such that few could eat.

And gradually, more terrible than the crush of bodies and the filth, the single obsession was: something to drink. Two or three times when the train stopped, the door was slid open a few inches and a pail of water passed in. But we had become animals, incapable of plan or system. Those near the door got it all.

At last, the morning of the fourth day, the train stopped again and the door was opened its full width. Like infants, on hands and knees, we crawled to the opening and lowered ourselves over the side. In front of us was a smiling blue lake. On the far side, among sycamore trees, rose a white church steeple.

The stronger prisoners hauled buckets of water from the lake. We drank through cracked and swollen lips. The train was shorter; the cars carrying the men had disappeared. Only a handful of soldiers—some of them looking no older than fifteen—were there to guard a thousand women. No more were needed. We could scarcely walk, let alone resist.

After a while they got us into straggly columns and marched us off. For a mile the road followed the shore of the lake, then left it to climb a hill. I wondered if Betsie could make it to the top, but the sight of trees and sky seemed to have revived her and she supported me as much as I her. We passed a number of local people on foot and in horse-drawn wagons. The children especially seemed wonderful to me, pink-cheeked and healthy. They returned my stares with wide-eyed interest; I noticed, however, that the adults did not look at us but turned their heads away as we approached.

From the crest of the hill we saw it, like a vast scar on the green German landscape; a city of low gray barracks surrounded by concrete walls on which guard towers rose at intervals. In the very center, a square smokestack emitted a thin gray vapor into the blue sky.

"Ravensbruck!"

Like a whispered curse the word passed back through the lines. This was the notorious women's extermination camp whose name we had heard even in Haarlem. That squat concrete building, that smoke disappearing in the bright sunlight—no! I would not look at it! As Betsie and I stumbled down the hill, I felt the Bible bumping between my shoulder blades. God's good news. Was it to this world that He had spoken it?

Now we were close enough to see the skull-and-crossbones posted at intervals on the walls to warn of electrified wiring along the top. The massive iron gates swung in; we marched between them. Acres of soot-gray barracks stretched ahead of us. Just inside the wall was a row of waist-high water spigots. We charged them, thrusting hands, arms, legs, even heads, under the streams of water, washing away the stench of the boxcars. A squad of women guards in dark blue uniforms rushed at us, hauling and shouting, swinging their short, hard crops.

At last they drove us back from the faucets and herded us down an avenue between barracks. This camp appeared far grimmer than the one we had left. At least, in marches about Vught, we had caught sight of fields and woods. Here, every vista ended in the same concrete barrier; the camp was set down in a vast man-made valley rising on every side to those towering wire-topped walls.

At last we halted. In front of us a vast canvas tent-roof—no sides—covered an acre or more of straw-strewn ground. Betsie and I found a spot on the edge of this area and sank gratefully down. Instantly we were on our feet again. Lice! The straw was literally alive with them. We stood for a while, clutching blankets and pillowcases well away from the infested ground. But at last we spread our blankets over the squirming straw and sat on them.

Some of the prisoners had brought scissors from Vught: everywhere beneath the huge tent women were cutting one another's hair. A pair was passed to us. Of course we must do the same, long hair was folly in such a place. But as I cut Betsie's chestnut waves, I cried.

Toward evening there was a commotion at one end of the tent. A line of S.S. guards was moving across it, driving women out from under the canvas. We scrambled to our feet and snatched up our blankets as they bore down upon us. Perhaps a hundred yards beyond the tent the chase stopped. We stood about, uncertain what to do. Whether a new group of prisoners had arrived or what the reason was for driving us from the tent, no one knew. Women began spreading their blankets on the hard cinder ground. Slowly it dawned on Betsie and me that we were to spend the night here where we stood. We laid my blanket on the ground, stretched out side by side and pulled hers over us.

"The night is dark and I am far from home . . ." Betsie's sweet soprano was picked up by voices all around us. "Lead Thou me on. . . ."

We were waked up some time in the middle of the night by a clap of thunder and a deluge of rain. The blankets soaked through and water gathered in puddles beneath us. In the morning the field was a vast sodden swamp: hands, clothes, and faces were black from the cinder mud.

We were still wringing water from our blankets when the command came to line up for coffee. It was not coffee but a thin liquid of approximately the same color and we were grateful to get it as we shuffled double-file past the makeshift field kitchen. There was a slice of black bread for each prisoner too, then nothing more until we were given a ladle of turnip soup and a small boiled potato late in the afternoon.

In between we were kept standing at rigid attention on the soggy parade ground where we had spent the night. We were near one edge of the huge camp here, close enough to the outer wall to see the triple row of electric wires running along the top. Two entire days we spent this way, stretching out again the second night right where we stood. It did not rain again but ground and blankets were still damp. Betsie began to cough. I took Nollie's blue sweater from my pillowcase, wrapped it around her and gave her a few drops of the vitamin oil. But by morning she had agonizing intestinal cramps. Again and again throughout that second day she had to ask the impatient woman monitor at the head of our row for permission to go to the ditch that served as sanitary facility.

It was the third night as we were getting ready to lie down again under the sky when the order came to report to the processing center for new arrivals. A ten-minute march brought us to the building. We inched along a corridor into a huge reception room. And there under the harsh ceiling lights we saw a dismal sight. As each woman reached a desk where some officers sat she had to lay her blanket, pillowcase, and whatever else she carried onto a growing pile of these things. A few desks further along she had to strip off every scrap of clothes, throw them onto a second pile, and walk naked past the scrutiny of a dozen S.S. men into the shower room. Coming out of the shower she wore only a thin prison dress and a pair of shoes. Nothing more.

But Betsie needed that sweater! She needed the vitamins! Most of all, we needed our Bible. How could we live in this place without it? But how could I ever take it past so many watchful eyes without the overalls covering it?

We were almost at the first desk. I fished desperately in my pillow-case, drew out the bottle of vitamins and closed my fist around them. Reluctantly we dropped the other things on the heap that was fast becoming a mountain. "Dear God," I prayed, "You have given us this precious Book, You have kept it hidden through checkpoints and inspections, You have used it for so many——"

I felt Betsie stagger against me and looked at her in alarm. Her face was white, her lips pressed tight together. A guard was passing by; I begged him in German to show us the toilets. Without so much as a glance, he jerked his head in the direction of the shower room.

Timidly Betsie and I stepped out of line and walked to the door of the big, dank-smelling room with its row on row of overhead spigots. It was empty, waiting for the next batch of fifty naked and shivering women to be admitted.

"Please," I said to the S.S. man guarding the door, "where are the toilets?"

He did not look at me either. "Use the drainholes!" he snapped, and as we stepped inside he slammed the door behind us. We stood alone in the room where a few minutes later we would return stripped even of the clothes on our backs. Here were the prison things we were to put on, piled just inside the door. From the front and back of each otherwise ordinary dress a large "X" had been cut out and replaced with cloth of another color.

And then we saw something else, stacked in the far corner, a pile of old wooden benches. They were slimy with mildew, crawling with cockroaches, but to me they seemed the furniture of heaven itself.

"The sweater! Take the sweater off!" I hissed, fumbling with the string at my neck. Betsie handed it to me and in an instant I had wrapped it around the Bible and the vitamin bottle and stuffed the precious bundle behind the benches.

And so it was that when we were herded into that room ten minutes later we were not poor, but rich. Rich in this new evidence of the care of Him who was God even of Ravensbruck.

We stood beneath the spigots as long as the flow of icy water lasted, feeling it soften our lice-eaten skin. Then we clustered dripping wet around the heap of prison dresses, holding them up, passing them about, looking for approximate fits. I found a loose long-sleeved dress for Betsie that would cover the blue sweater when she would have a chance to put it on. I squirmed into another dress for myself, then reached behind the benches and shoved the little bundle quickly in-side the neck.

It made a bulge you could have seen across the Grote Markt. I flattened it out as best I could, pushing it down, tugging the sweater around my waist, but there was no real concealing it beneath the thin cotton dress. And all the while I had the incredible feeling that it didn't matter, that this was not my business, but God's. That all I had to do was walk straight ahead.

As we trooped back out through the shower room door, the S.S. men ran their hands over every prisoner, front, back, and sides. The woman ahead of me was searched three times. Behind me, Betsie was searched. No hand touched me.

At the exit door to the building was a second ordeal, a line of women guards examining each prisoner again. I slowed down as I reached them but the *Aufseherin* in charge shoved me roughly by the shoulder. "Move along! You're holding up the line!"

And so Betsie and I arrived at Barracks 8 in the small hours of that morning, bringing not only the Bible, but a new knowledge of the power of Him whose story it was. There were three women already asleep in the bed assigned to us. They made room for us as best they could but the mattress sloped and I kept sliding to the floor. At last all five of us lay sideways across the bed and managed to get shoulders and elbows arranged. The blanket was a poor threadbare affair compared with the ones we had given up, but at least the overcrowding produced its own warmth. Betsie had put on the blue sweater beneath her long-sleeved dress and wedged now between me and the others, her shivering gradually subsided and she was asleep. I lay awake a while longer, watching a searchlight sweep the rear wall in long regular arcs, hearing the distant calls of soldiers patrolling the walls. . . .

Morning roll call at Ravensbruck came half an hour earlier than at Vught. By 4:30 A.M. we had to be standing outside in the black predawn chill, standing at parade attention in blocks of one hundred women, ten wide, ten deep. Sometimes after hours of this we would gain the shelter of the barracks only to hear the whistle.

"Everybody out! Fall in for roll call!"

Barracks 8 was in the quarantine compound. Next to us—perhaps as a deliberate warning to newcomers—were located the punishment barracks. From there, all day long and often into the night, came the sounds of hell itself. They were not the sounds of anger, or of any human emotion, but of a cruelty altogether detached: blows landing in regular rhythm, screams keeping pace. We would stand in our ten-deep ranks with our hands trembling at our sides, longing to jam them against our ears, to make the sounds stop.

The instant of dismissal we would mob the door of Barracks 8, stepping on each others' heels in our eagerness to get inside, to shrink the world back to understandable proportions.

It grew harder and harder. Even within these four walls there was too much misery, too much seemingly pointless suffering. Every day something else failed to make sense, something else grew too heavy. "Will You carry this too, Lord Jesus?"

But as the rest of the world grew stranger, one thing became increasingly clear. And that was the reason the two of us were here. Why others should suffer we were not shown. As for us, from morning until lights-out, whenever we were not in ranks for roll call, our Bible was the center of an ever-widening circle of help and hope. Like waifs clustered around a blazing fire, we gathered about it, holding out our hearts to its warmth and light. The blacker the night around us grew, the brighter and truer and more beautiful burned the word of God. "Who shall separate us from the love of Christ? Shall tribulation, or distress, or persecution, or famine, or nakedness, or peril, or sword? . . . Nay, in all these things we are more than conquerors through him that loved us."

I would look about us as Betsie read, watching the light leap from face to face. More than conquerors. . . . It was not a wish. It was a fact. We knew it, we experienced it minute by minute—poor, hated, hungry. We are more than conquerors. Not "we shall be." We are! Life in Ravensbruck took place on two separate levels, mutually impossible. One, the observable, external life, grew every day more horrible. The other, the life we lived with God, grew daily better, truth upon truth, glory upon glory.

Sometimes I would slip the Bible from its little sack with hands that shook, so mysterious had it become to me. It was new; it had just been written. I marveled sometimes that the ink was dry. I had believed the Bible always, but reading it now had nothing to do with belief. It was simply a description of the way things were—of hell and heaven, of how men act and how God acts. I had read a thousand times the story of Jesus' arrest—how soldiers had slapped Him, laughed at Him, flogged Him. Now such happenings had faces and voices.

Fridays—the recurrent humiliation of medical inspection. The hospital corridor in which we waited was unheated, and a fall chill had settled into the walls. Still we were forbidden even to wrap ourselves in our own arms, but had to maintain our erect, hands-at-sides position as we filed slowly past a phalanx of grinning guards. How there could have been any pleasure in the sight of these stick-thin legs and hunger-bloated stomachs I could not imagine. Surely there is no more wretched sight than the human body unloved and uncared for. Nor could I see the necessity for the complete undressing: when we finally reached the examining room a doctor looked down each throat, another—a dentist presumably—at our teeth, a third in between each finger. And that was all. We trooped again down the long, cold corridor and picked up our X-marked dresses at the door.

But it was one of these mornings while we were waiting, shivering, in the corridor, that yet another page in the Bible leapt into life for me.

He hung naked on the cross.

I had not known—I had not thought. . . . The paintings, the carved crucifixes showed at the least a scrap of cloth. But this, I suddenly knew, was the respect and reverence of the artist. But oh—at the time itself, on that other Friday morning—there had been no reverence. No more than I saw in the faces around us now.

I leaned toward Betsie, ahead of me in line. Her shoulder blades stood out sharp and thin beneath her blue-mottled skin.

"Betsie, they took *His* clothes too."

Ahead of me I heard a little gasp. "Oh, Corrie. And I never thanked Him. . . ."

Every day the sun rose a little later, the bite took longer to leave the air. It will be better, everyone assured everyone else, when we move into permanent barracks. We'll have a blanket apiece. A bed of our own. Each of us painted into the picture her own greatest need.

For me it was a dispensary where Betsie could get medication for her cough. "There'll be a nurse assigned to the barracks." I said it so often that I convinced myself. I was doling out a drop of the Davitamon each morning on her piece of black bread, but how much longer could the small bottle last? "Especially," I would tell her, "if you keep sharing it around every time someone sneezes."

The move to permanent quarters came the second week in October. We were marched, ten abreast, along a wide cinder avenue and then into a narrower street of barracks. Several times the column halted while numbers were read out—names were never used at Ravensbruck. At last Betsie's and mine were called: "Prisoner 66729, Prisoner 66730." We stepped out of line with a dozen or so others and stared at the long gray front of Barracks 28. Half its windows seemed to have been broken and replaced with rags. A door in the center let us into a large room where two hundred or more women bent over knitting needles. On tables between them were piles of woolen socks in army gray.

On either side doors opened into two still larger rooms—by far the largest dormitories we had yet seen. Betsie and I followed a prisoner-guide through the door at the right. Because of the broken windows the vast room was in semi-twilight. Our noses told us, first, that the place was filthy: somewhere plumbing had backed up, the bedding was soiled and rancid. Then as our eyes adjusted to the gloom we saw that there were no individual beds at all, but great square piers stacked three high, and wedged side by side and end to end with only an occasional narrow aisle slicing through.

We followed our guide single file—the aisle was not wide enough for two—fighting back the claustrophobia of these platforms rising everywhere above us. The tremendous room was nearly empty of people; they must have been out on various work crews. At last she pointed to a second tier in the center of a large block. To reach it we had to stand on the bottom level, haul ourselves up, and then crawl across three other straw-covered platforms to reach the one that we would share with—how many? The deck above us was too close to let us sit up. We lay back, struggling against the nausea that swept over us from the reeking straw. We could hear the women who had arrived with us finding their places.

Suddenly I sat up, striking my head on the cross-slats above. Something had pinched my leg.

"Fleas!" I cried. "Betsie, the place is swarming with them!"

We scrambled across the intervening platforms, heads low to avoid another bump, dropped down to the aisle, and edged our way to a patch of light.

"Here! And here another one!" I wailed. "Betsie, how can we live in such a place!"

"Show us. Show us how." It was said so matter of factly it took me a second to realize she was praying. More and more the distinction between prayer and the rest of life seemed to be vanishing for Betsie.

"Corrie!" she said excitedly. "He's given us the answer! Before we asked, as He always does! In the Bible this morning. Where was it? Read that part again!"

I glanced down the long dim aisle to make sure no guard was in sight, then drew the Bible from its pouch. "It was in First Thessalonians," I said. We were on our third complete reading of the New Testament since leaving Scheveningen. In the feeble light I turned the pages. "Here it is: 'Comfort the frightened, help the weak, be patient with everyone. See that none of you repays evil for evil, but always seek to do good to one another and to all. . . .'" It seemed written expressly to Ravensbruck.

"Go on," said Betsie. "That wasn't all."

"Oh yes: '. . . to one another and to all. Rejoice always, pray constantly, give thanks in all circumstances; for this is the will of God in Christ Jesus——'"

"That's it, Corrie! That's His answer. 'Give thanks in all circumstances!' That's what we can do. We can start right now to thank God for every single thing about this new barracks!"

I stared at her, then around me at the dark, foul-aired room.

"Such as?" I said.

"Such as being assigned here together."

I bit my lip. "Oh yes, Lord Jesus!"

"Such as what you're holding in your hands."

I looked down at the Bible. "Yes! Thank You, dear Lord, that there was no inspection when we entered here! Thank You for all the women, here in this room, who will meet You in these pages."

"Yes," said Betsie. "Thank You for the very crowding here. Since we're packed so close, that many more will hear!" She looked at me expectantly. "Corrie!" she prodded.

"Oh, all right. Thank You for the jammed, crammed, stuffed, packed, suffocating crowds."

"Thank You," Betsie went on serenely, "for the fleas and for——"

The fleas! This was too much. "Betsie, there's no way even God can make me grateful for a flea."

" 'Give thanks in *all* circumstances,' " she quoted. "It doesn't say, 'in pleasant circumstances.' Fleas are part of this place where God has put us."

And so we stood between piers of bunks and gave thanks for fleas. But this time I was sure Betsie was wrong.

They started arriving soon after 6:00 o'clock, the women of Barracks 28, tired, sweat-stained, and dirty from the long forced-labor details. The building, we learned from one of our platform mates, had been designed to hold four hundred. There were now fourteen hundred quartered here with more arriving weekly as concentration camps in Poland, France, Belgium, Austria, as well as Holland were evacuated toward the center of Germany.

There were nine of us sharing our particular square, designed for four, and some grumbling as the others discovered they would have to make room for Betsie and me. Eight acrid and overflowing toilets served the entire room; to reach them we

had to crawl not only over our own bedmates but over those on the other platforms between us and the closest aisle, always at the risk of adding too much weight
to the already sagging slats and crashing down on the people beneath. It happened
several times, that first night. From somewhere in the room would come a splintering sound, a shriek, smothered cries.

Even when the slats held, the least movement on the upper platforms sent a
shower of dust and straw over the sleepers below—followed by a volley of curses.
In Barracks 8 most of us had been Dutch. Here there was not even a common language and among exhausted, ill-fed people quarrels erupted constantly.

There was one raging now as the women sleeping nearest the windows slammed
them shut against the cold. At once scores of voices demanded that they be raised
again. Brawls were starting all up and down that side of the room; we heard scuffling, slaps, sobs.

In the dark I felt Betsie's hands clasp mine. "Lord Jesus," she said aloud, "send
Your peace into this room. There has been too little praying here. The very walls
know it. But where You come, Lord, the spirit of strife cannot exist. . . ."

The change was gradual, but distinct. One by one the angry sounds let up.

"I'll make you a deal!" The voice spoke German with a strong Scandinavian
accent. "You can sleep in here where it's warmer and I'll take your place by the
window!"

"And add your lice to my own!" But there was a chuckle in the answer. "No
thanks."

"I'll tell you what!" The third voice had a French burr. "We'll open them halfway. That way we'll be only half-frozen and you'll be only half-smothered."

A ripple of laughter widened around the room at this. I lay back on the sour
straw and knew there was one more circumstance for which I could give thanks.
Betsie had come to Barracks 28.

Roll call came at 4:30 A.M. here as it had in quarantine. A whistle roused us at
4:00 when, without even shaking the straw from clothes and hair, the stampede
began for the ration of bread and coffee in the center room. Lastcomers found
none.

The count was made in the *Lagerstrasse,* the wide avenue leading to the hospital. There we joined the occupants of other barracks—some 35,000 at that time—
stretching out of sight in the pale glow of the street lamps, feet growing numb on
the cold cinder ground.

After roll call, work crews were called out. For weeks Betsie and I were assigned
to the Siemens factory. This huge complex of mills and railroad terminals was a
mile and a half from the camp. The "Siemens Brigade," several thousand of us,
marched out the iron gate beneath the charged wires into a world of trees and
grass and horizons. The sun rose as we skirted the little lake; the gold of the late
fall fields lifted our hearts.

The work at Siemens, however, was sheer misery. Betsie and I had to push a heavy handcart to a railroad siding where we unloaded large metal plates from a boxcar and wheeled them to a receiving gate at the factory. The grueling workday lasted eleven hours. At least, at noontime we were given a boiled potato and some thin soup; those who worked inside the camp had no midday meal.

Returning to camp we could barely lift our swollen and aching legs. The soldiers patrolling us bellowed and cursed, but we could only shuffle forward inches at a step. I noticed again how the local people turned their eyes another way.

Back at the barracks we formed yet another line—would there never be an end to columns and waits?—to receive our ladle of turnip soup in the center room. Then, as quickly as we could for the press of people, Betsie and I made our way to the rear of the dormitory room where we held our worship "service." Around our own platform area there was not enough light to read the Bible, but back here a small light bulb cast a wan yellow circle on the wall, and here an ever larger group of women gathered.

They were services like no others, these times in Barracks 28. A single meeting might include a recital of the Magnificat in Latin by a group of Roman Catholics, a whispered hymn by some Lutherans, and a sotto-voce chant by Eastern Orthodox women. With each moment the crowd around us would swell, packing the nearby platforms, hanging over the edges, until the high structures groaned and swayed.

At last either Betsie or I would open the Bible. Because only the Hollanders could understand the Dutch text we would translate aloud in German. And then we would hear the life-giving words passed back along the aisles in French, Polish, Russian, Czech, back into Dutch. They were little previews of heaven, these evenings beneath the light bulb. I would think of Haarlem, each substantial church set behind its wrought-iron fence and its barrier of doctrine. And I would know again that in darkness God's truth shines most clear.

At first Betsie and I called these meetings with great timidity. But as night after night went by and no guard ever came near us, we grew bolder. So many now wanted to join us that we held a second service after evening roll call. There on the *Lagerstrasse* we were under rigid surveillance, guards in their warm wool capes marching constantly up and down. It was the same in the center room of the barracks: half a dozen guards or camp police always present. Yet in the large dormitory room there was almost no supervision at all. We did not understand it.

Another strange thing was happening. The Davitamon bottle was continuing to produce drops. It scarcely seemed possible, so small a bottle, so many doses a day. Now, in addition to Betsie, a dozen others on our pier were taking it.

My instinct was always to hoard it—Betsie was growing so very weak! But others were ill as well. It was hard to say no to eyes that burned with fever, hands that shook with chill. I tried to save it for the very weakest—but even these soon numbered fifteen, twenty, twenty-five. . . .

And still, every time I tilted the little bottle, a drop appeared at the tip of the glass stopper. It just couldn't be! I held it up to the light, trying to see how much was left, but the dark brown glass was too thick to see through.

"There was a woman in the Bible," Betsie said, "whose oil jar was never empty." She turned to it in the Book of Kings, the story of the poor widow of Zarephath who gave Elijah a room in her home: "The jar of meal wasted not, neither did the cruse of oil fail, according to the word of Jehovah which he spoke by Elijah."

Well—but—wonderful things happened all through the Bible. It was one thing to believe that such things were possible thousands of years ago, another to have it happen now, to us, this very day. And yet it happened, this day, and the next, and the next, until an awed little group of spectators stood around watching the drops fall onto the daily rations of bread.

Many nights I lay awake in the shower of straw dust from the mattress above, trying to fathom the marvel of supply lavished upon us. "Maybe," I whispered to Betsie, "only a molecule or two really gets through that little pinhole—and then in the air it expands!"

I heard her soft laughter in the dark. "Don't try too hard to explain it, Corrie. Just accept it as a surprise from a Father who loves you."

And then one day Mien pushed her way to us in the evening food line. "Look what I've got for you!"

Mien was a pretty young Dutch woman we had met in Vught. She was assigned to the hospital and often managed to bring to Barracks 28 some stolen treasure from the staff room—a sheet of newspaper to stuff in a broken window, a slice of bread left untouched on a nurse's plate. Now we peered into the small cloth sack she carried.

"Vitamins!" I cried, and then cast an apprehensive glance at a camp policeman nearby. "Yeast compound!" I whispered.

"Yes!" she hissed back. "There were several huge jars. I emptied each just the same amount."

We gulped the thin turnip water, marveling at our sudden riches. Back at the bunk I took the bottle from the straw. "We'll finish the drops first," I decided.

But that night, no matter how long I held it upside down, or how hard I shook it, not another drop appeared.

On the first of November a coat was issued to each prisoner. Betsie's and mine were both of Russian make, probably once trimmed with fur: threads showed where something had been torn from the collars and cuffs.

Call-ups for the Siemens factory had ceased and we speculated that it had been hit in one of the bombing raids that came within earshot almost nightly now. Betsie and I were put to work leveling some rough ground just inside the camp wall. This too was back-breaking labor. Sometimes as I bent to lift a load my heart cramped strangely; at night spasms of pain gripped my legs.

But the biggest problem was Betsie's strength. One morning after a hard night's rain we arrived to find the ground sodden and heavy. Betsie had never been able to lift much; today her shovels-ful were microscopic and she stumbled frequently as she walked to the low ground where we dumped the loads.

"*Schneller!*" a guard screamed at her. "Can't you go faster?"

Why must they scream, I wondered as I sank my shovel into the black muck. Why couldn't they speak like ordinary human beings? I straightened slowly, the sweat drying on my back. I was remembering where we had first heard this maniac sound. The Beje. In Tante Jans's rooms. A voice coming from the shell-shaped speaker, a scream lingering in the air even after Betsie had leapt to shut it off. . . .

"Loafer! Lazy swine!"

The guard snatched Betsie's shovel from her hands and ran from group to group of the digging crew, exhibiting the handful of dirt that was all Betsie had been able to lift.

"Look what Madame Baroness is carrying! Surely she will over-exert herself!"

The other guards and even some of the prisoners laughed. Encouraged, the guard threw herself into a parody of Betsie's faltering walk. A male guard was with our detail today and in the presence of a man the women guards were always animated.

As the laughter grew, I felt a murderous anger rise. The guard was young and well fed—was it Betsie's fault that she was old and starving? But to my astonishment, Betsie too was laughing.

"That's me all right," she admitted. "But you'd better let me totter along with my little spoonful, or I'll have to stop altogether."

The guard's plump cheeks went crimson. "I'll decide who's to stop!" And snatching the leather crop from her belt she slashed Betsie across the chest and neck.

Without knowing I was doing it I had seized my shovel and rushed at her.

Betsie stepped in front of me before anyone had seen. "Corrie!" she pleaded, dragging my arm to my side. "Corrie, keep working!" She tugged the shovel from my hand and dug it into the mud. Contemptuously the guard tossed Betsie's shovel toward us. I picked it up, still in a daze. A red stain appeared on Betsie's collar; a welt began to swell on her neck.

Betsie saw where I was looking and laid a bird-thin hand over the whip mark. "Don't look at it, Corrie. Look at Jesus only." She drew away her hand: it was sticky with blood.

In mid-November the rains started in earnest, chill, drenching day-long downpours that left beads of moisture even on the inside walls. The *Lagerstrasse* was never dry now; even when the rain let up, deep puddles stood in the road. We were not allowed to step around them as the ranks were formed: often we stood in water up to our ankles, and at night the barracks reeked with rotting shoe leather.

Betsie's cough began to bring up blood. We went to sick call at the hospital, but the thermometer registered only 102°, not enough to admit her to the wards. Alas for my fantasies of a nurse and a dispensary in each barracks. This large bare room in the hospital was where all the sick in the camp had to assemble, often standing outside in the rain for hours just to get through the door.

I hated the dismal place full of sick and suffering women, but we had to go back, again and again, for Betsie's condition was growing worse. She was not repelled by the room as I was. To her it was simply a setting in which to talk about Jesus—as indeed was everyplace else. Wherever she was, at work, in the food line, in the dormitory, Betsie spoke to those around her about His nearness and His yearning to come into their lives. As her body grew weaker, her faith seemed to grow bolder. And sick call was "such an important place, Corrie! Some of these people are at the very threshold of heaven!"

At last one night Betsie's fever registered over the required 104°. There was another long wait until a nurse appeared to lead her and half a dozen others into the hospital proper. I stayed with them as far as the door to the ward, then made my way slowly back to the barracks.

As usual, as I stood in the door of the dormitory, it reminded me most of an anthill. Some women were already asleep after the long workday, but most were stirring about, some waiting for a turn at the toilets, others picking lice off themselves and their neighbors. I twisted and squirmed through the crowded aisles to the rear where the prayer service was just ending. Nights when Betsie and I reported to sick call we left the Bible with Mrs. Wielmaker, a saintly Roman Catholic woman from The Hague who could render the Dutch words in German, French, Latin, or Greek. Women crowded around me, asking after Betsie. How was she? How long would she have to stay?

Lights-out blew and the scramble into the bunks began. I hoisted myself to the middle tier and crawled across those already in place. What a difference since Betsie had come to this room! Where before this had been the moment for scuffles and cursing, tonight the huge dormitory buzzed with "Sorry!" "Excuse me!" And "No harm done!"

I found our section in the dark and squeezed into a spot in the middle. From the doorway a searchlight swept the room, lingering on blocks where anything stirred. Someone's elbow dug into my back, another woman's feet were two inches from my face. How was it possible, packed so close, to be so utterly and miserably alone?

14. The Blue Sweater

IN THE MORNING a cold wet mist hung over the *Lagerstrasse*. I was grateful that Betsie did not have to stand outside.

All day the blanketing fog hung over Ravensbruck, an eerie day when sound was muffled and the sun never rose. I was on potato detail, one of a crew hauling baskets of potatoes to long trenches to be covered with dirt against the freezing weather ahead. I was glad of the hard physical work that drove some of the damp from my bones and for the occasional bite of raw potato when guards were not watching.

Next day when the white pall still lay over the camp, my loneliness for Betsie became too much to bear. As soon as roll call was dismissed, I did a desperate thing. Mien had told me a way to get into the hospital without passing the guardpost inside the door. The latrine at the rear, she said, had a very large window too warped to close tight. Since no visiting was permitted in the hospital, relatives of patients often took this way of getting inside.

In the dense fog it was easy to get to the window unseen. I hoisted myself through it, then clapped my hand to my nose against the stinging odor. A row of lidless, doorless toilets stretched along one wall in the pool of their overflow. I dashed for the door, then stopped, my flesh crawling. Against this opposite wall a dozen naked corpses lay side by side on their backs. Some of the eyes were open and seemed to stare unblinkingly at the ceiling.

I was standing there, lead-footed with horror, when two men pushed through the door carrying a sheet-wrapped bundle between them. They did not even glance at me and I realized they took me for a patient. I ducked round them into the hall

152

and stood a moment, stomach knotting with the sight I had seen. After a while I started aimlessly off to the left.

The hospital was a maze of halls and doors. Already I was not sure of the way back to the latrine. What if the potato crew left before I got back? And then a corridor looked familiar. I hurried, almost running from door to door. At last, the ward where I had left Betsie! No hospital personnel was in sight: I walked eagerly down the aisles of cots looking from face to face.

"Corrie!"

Betsie was sitting up in a cot near the window. She looked stronger, eyes bright, a touch of color in her sunken cheeks. No nurse or doctor had seen her yet, she said, but the chance to lie still and stay indoors had already made a difference.

Three days afterward, Betsie returned to Barracks 28. She still had received no examination or medicine of any kind and her forehead felt feverish to my touch. But the joy of having her back outweighed my anxiety.

Best of all, as a result of her hospitalization, she was given a permanent assignment to the "knitting brigade," the women we had seen the very first day seated about the tables in the center room. This work was reserved for the weakest prisoners, and now overflowed into the dormitories as well.

Those working in the sleeping rooms received far less supervision than those at the tables, and Betsie found herself with most of the day in which to minister to those around her. She was a lightning knitter who completed her quota of socks long before noon. She kept our Bible with her and spent hours each day reading aloud from it, moving from platform to platform.

One evening I got back to the barracks late from a wood-gathering foray outside the walls. A light snow lay on the ground and it was hard to find the sticks and twigs with which a small stove was kept going in each room. Betsie was waiting for me, as always, so that we could wait through the food line together. Her eyes were twinkling.

"You're looking extraordinarily pleased with yourself," I told her.

"You know we've never understood why we had so much freedom in the big room," she said. "Well—I've found out."

That afternoon, she said, there'd been confusion in her knitting group about sock sizes and they'd asked the supervisor to come and settle it.

"But she wouldn't. She wouldn't step through the door and neither would the guards. And you know why?"

Betsie could not keep the triumph from her voice: "Because of the fleas! That's what she said, 'That place is crawling with fleas!'"

My mind rushed back to our first hour in this place. I remembered Betsie's bowed head, remembered her thanks to God for creatures I could see no use for.

Though Betsie was now spared heavy outdoor labor, she still had to stand the twice-daily roll call. As December temperatures fell, they became true endurance tests and many did not survive. One dark morning when ice was forming a halo around each street lamp, a feeble-minded girl two rows ahead of us suddenly soiled herself. A guard rushed at her, swinging her thick leather crop while the girl shrieked in pain and terror. It was always more terrible when one of these innocent ones was beaten. Still the *Aufseherin* continued to whip her. It was the guard we had nicknamed "The Snake" because of the shiny dress she wore. I could see it now beneath her long wool cape, glittering in the light of the lamp as she raised her arm. I was grateful when the screaming girl at last lay still on the cinder street.

"Betsie," I whispered when the The Snake was far enough away, "what can we do for these people? Afterward I mean. Can't we make a home for them and care for them and love them?"

"Corrie, I pray every day that we will be allowed to do this! To show them that love is greater!"

And it wasn't until I was gathering twigs later in the morning that I realized that I had been thinking of the feeble-minded, and Betsie of their persecutors.

Several days later my entire work crew was ordered to the hospital for medical inspection. I dropped my dress onto the pile just inside the door and joined the file of naked women. Ahead of us, to my surprise, a doctor was using a stethoscope with all the deliberateness of a real examination.

"What is this for?" I whispered to the woman ahead of me.

"Transport inspection," she hissed back, not moving her head. "Munitions work."

Transport! But they couldn't! They mustn't send me away! Dear God, don't let them take me away from Betsie!

But to my terror I passed one station after another—heart, lungs, scalp, throat— and still I was in the line. Many were pulled out along the way, but those who remained looked hardly stronger. Swollen stomachs, hollow chests, spindly legs: how desperate for manpower Germany must be!

I halted before a woman in a soiled white coat. She turned me around to face a chart on the wall, her hand cold on my bare shoulder. "Read the lowest line you can."

"I—I can't seem to read any of them. (Lord forgive me!) Just the top letter. That big E." The top letter was an F.

The woman seemed to see me for the first time. "You can see better than that! Do you want to be rejected?"

At Ravensbruck, munitions transport was considered a privilege; food and living conditions in the factories were said to be far better than here in the camp.

"Oh yes, Doctor! My sister's here at Ravensbruck! She's not well! I can't leave her!"

The doctor sat down at her table and scrawled something on a piece of paper. "Come back tomorrow to be fitted for glasses."

Catching up to the line, I unfolded the small blue slip of paper. Prisoner 66730 was instructed to report for an optical fitting at 6:30 the following morning. Six-thirty was the time the transport convoys were loaded.

And so as the huge vans rumbled down the *Lagerstrasse* the next day, I was standing in a corridor of the hospital waiting my turn at the eye clinic. The young man in charge was perhaps a qualified eye doctor, but his entire equipment consisted of a box of framed glasses, from gold-rimmed bifocals to a plastic-framed child's pair. I found none that fitted and at last was ordered back to my work detail.

But, of course, I had no work assignment, having been marked down for transport. I walked back uncertainly toward Barracks 28. I stepped into the center room. The supervisor looked up over the heads of the knitting crew.

"Number?" she said.

I gave it and she wrote it in a black-covered book. "Pick up your yarn and a pattern sheet," she went on. "You'll have to find a place on one of the beds, there's no room here." And she turned back to the pile of finished socks on the table.

I stood blinking in the center of the room. Then grabbing a skein of the dark gray wool I dashed through the dormitory door. And thus began the closest, most joyous weeks of all the time in Ravensbruck. Side by side, in the sanctuary of God's fleas, Betsie and I ministered the word of God to all in the room. We sat by deathbeds that became doorways of heaven. We watched women who had lost everything grow rich in hope. The knitters of Barracks 28 became the praying heart of the vast diseased body that was Ravensbruck, interceding for all in the camp—guards, under Betsie's prodding, as well as prisoners. We prayed beyond the concrete walls for the healing of Germany, of Europe, of the world—as Mama had once done from the prison of a crippled body.

And as we prayed, God spoke to us about the world after the war. It was extraordinary; in this place where whistles and loudspeakers took the place of decisions, God asked us what we were going to do in the years ahead.

Betsie was always very clear about the answer for her and me. We were to have a house, a large one—much larger than the Beje to which people who had been damaged by concentration-camp life would come until they felt ready to live again in the normal world.

"It's such a beautiful house, Corrie! The floors are all inlaid wood, with statues set in the walls and a broad staircase sweeping down. And gardens! Gardens all around it where they can plant flowers. It will do them such good, Corrie, to care for flowers!"

I would stare at Betsie in amazement as she talked about these things. She spoke always as though she were describing things that she saw—as if that wide, winding staircase and those bright gardens were the reality, this cramped and filthy barracks the dream.

But it wasn't a dream. It was really, achingly, endlessly true, and it was always during roll calls that the accumulated misery threatened to overwhelm me.

One morning three women from Barracks 28 lingered inside a few minutes to avoid the cold. All the following week the entire barracks was punished by an extra hour at attention. The lights on the *Lagerstrasse* were not even lit when we were driven from our bunks at 3:30 A.M.

It was during this preinspection lineup one morning that I saw what I had till then refused to believe. Headlights appeared at the far end of the long street, wavering over the snow. Trucks with open flat-beds in the rear were approaching, spattering slush as they passed. They pulled up at the front door of the hospital. The door opened and a nurse appeared, supporting an old woman whose legs buckled as she limped down the steps. The nurse lifted her gently onto the back of a truck. They were pouring out the door now, leaning on the arms of nurses and hospital helpers, the old, the ill. Last of all came orderlies with stretchers between them.

Our eyes took in every detail of the scene; our brains refused. We had known, of course, that when overcrowding reached a certain point, the sickest were taken to the brick building at the foot of the great square smokestack. But, that these women here in front of us—these very ones. It was not possible. Above all I could not put it together with the kindly behavior of the nurses. That one in the truck just ahead, bending solicitously, even tenderly, over her patient. . . . What was passing through her mind just now?

And all the while, it grew colder. One night during evening roll call a platoon somewhere far down the *Lagerstrasse* began a rhythmic stamping. The sound grew as others picked it up. The guards did not stop us and at last the entire street was marching in place, pounding tattered shoes against the frozen ground, driving circulation back into numb feet and legs. From now on this was the sound of roll call, the stamping of thousands of feet on the long dark street.

And as the cold increased, so did the special temptation of concentration-camp life: the temptation to think only of oneself. It took a thousand cunning forms. I quickly discovered that when I maneuvered our way toward the middle of the roll-call formation we had a little protection from the wind.

I knew this was self-centered: when Betsie and I stood in the center, someone else had to stand on the edge. How easy it was to give it other names! I was acting only for Betsie's sake. We were in an important ministry and must keep well. It was colder in Poland than in Holland; these Polish women probably were not feeling the chill the way we were.

Selfishness had a life of its own. As I watched Mien's bag of yeast-compound disappear I began taking it from beneath the straw only after lights-out when others would not see and ask for some. Wasn't Betsie's health more important? (You see, God, she can do so much *for* them! Remember that house, after the war!)

And even if it wasn't right—it wasn't so *very* wrong, was it? Not wrong like sadism and murder and the other monstrous evils we saw in Ravensbruck every day. Oh, this was the great ploy of Satan in that kingdom of his: to display such blatant evil that one could almost believe one's own secret sins didn't matter.

The cancer spread. The second week in December, every occupant of Barracks 28 was issued an extra blanket. The next day a large group of evacuées arrived from Czechoslovakia. One of them assigned to our platform had no blanket at all and Betsie insisted that we give her one of ours. So that evening I "lent" her a blanket. But I didn't "give" it to her. In my heart I held onto the right to that blanket.

Was it coincidence that joy and power imperceptibly drained from my ministry? My prayers took on a mechanical ring. Even Bible reading was dull and lifeless. Betsie tried to take over for me, but her cough made reading aloud impossible.

And so I struggled on with worship and teaching that had ceased to be real. Until one drizzly raw afternoon when just enough light came through the window to read by, I came to Paul's account of his "thorn in the flesh." Three times, he said, he had begged God to take away his weakness, whatever it was. And each time God had said, Rely on Me. At last Paul concluded—the words seemed to leap from the page—that his very weakness was something to give thanks for. Because now Paul knew that none of the wonders and miracles which followed his ministry could be due to his own virtues. It was all Christ's strength, never Paul's.

And there it was.

The truth blazed like sunlight in the shadows of Barracks 28. The real sin I had been committing was not that of inching toward the center of a platoon because I was cold. The real sin lay in thinking that any power to help and transform came from me. Of course it was not my wholeness, but Christ's that made the difference.

The short winter day was fading; I could no longer separate the words on the page. And so I closed the Bible and to that group of women clustering close I told the truth about myself—my self-centeredness, my stinginess, my lack of love. That night real joy returned to my worship.

Each roll call the wind seemed sharper. Whenever she could, Mien smuggled newspapers from the staff room at the hospital, which we placed inside our clothes. Nollie's blue sweater beneath Betsie's dress was black with newsprint.

The cold seemed to be affecting Betsie's legs. Sometimes in the morning she could not move them at all and two of us would have to carry her between us. It was not hard—she weighed no more than a child. But she could no longer stamp her feet as the rest of us did to keep the blood flowing. When we returned to the dormitory I would rub her feet and hands, but my own only picked up the chill from hers.

It was the week before Christmas that Betsie woke up unable to move either legs or arms. I shoved my way through the crowded aisles to the center room. The Snake was on duty.

"Please!" I begged. "Betsie is ill! Oh please, she's got to get to the hospital!"

"Stand at attention. State your number."

"Prisoner 66730 reporting. Please, my sister is sick!"

"All prisoners must report for the count. If she's sick she can register at sick call."

Maryke de Graaf, a Dutch woman on the tier above ours, helped me form a cradle with our arms and carry Betsie outside. The rhythmic stamping had already begun in the *Lagerstrasse*. We carried her to the hospital, then stopped. In the light of the street lamps, the sick call line stretched to the edge of the building and out of sight around the corner. In the sooty snow alongside, three bodies lay where they had fallen.

Without a word Maryke and I turned and carried our load back to the *Lagerstrasse*. After roll call we got her back into bed. Her speech was slow and blurred, but she was trying to say something.

"A camp, Corrie—a concentration camp. But we're . . . in charge . . ." I had to bend very close to hear. The camp was in Germany. It was no longer a prison, but a home where people who had been warped by this philosophy of hate and force could come to learn another way. There were no walls, no barbed wire, and the barracks had windowboxes. "It will be so good for them . . . watching things grow. People can learn to love, from flowers. . . . "

I knew by now which people she meant. The German people. I thought of The Snake standing in the barracks door that morning. "State your number. All prisoners must report for the count."

I looked into Betsie's shrunken face. "We are to have this camp in Germany instead, Betsie? Instead of the big house in Holland?"

"Oh no!" she seemed shocked. "You know we have the house first! It's ready and waiting for us . . . such tall, tall windows! The sun is streaming in——"

A coughing fit seized her; when finally she lay still, a stain of blood blackened the straw. She dozed fitfully during the day and night that followed, waking several times with the excitement of some new detail about our work in Holland or Germany.

"The barracks are gray, Corrie, but we'll paint them green! Bright, light green, like springtime."

"We'll be together, Betsie? We're doing all this together? You're sure about that?"

"Always together, Corrie! You and I . . . always together."

When the siren blew next morning, Maryke and I again carried Betsie from the dormitory. The Snake was standing at the street door. As we started through it with our fragile burden she stepped in front of us. "Take her back to the bunks."

"I thought all pris——"

"Take her back!"

Wonderingly, we replaced Betsie on the bed. Sleet rattled against the windows. Was it possible that the atmosphere of Barracks 28 had affected even this cruel guard? As soon as roll call was dismissed I ran back to the dormitory. There, beside our bed, stood The Snake. Beside her two orderlies from the hospital were setting down a stretcher. The Snake straightened almost guiltily as I approached. "Prisoner is ready for transfer," she snapped.

I looked at the woman more closely: Had she risked fleas and lice to spare Betsie the sick-call line? She did not stop me as I started after the stretcher. Our group of knitters was just entering the big room. As we passed, a Polish friend dropped to her knees and made the sign of the Cross.

Sleet stung us as we reached the outside. I stepped close to the stretcher to form a shield for Betsie. We walked past the waiting line of sick people, through the door and into a large ward. They placed the stretcher on the floor and I leaned down to make out Betsie's words.

". . . must tell people what we have learned here. We must tell them that there is no pit so deep that He is not deeper still. They will listen to us, Corrie, because we have been here."

I stared at her wasted form. "But when will all this happen, Betsie!"

"Now. Right away. Oh, very soon! By the first of the year, Corrie, we will be out of prison!"

A nurse had caught sight of me. I backed to the door of the room and watched as they placed Betsie on a narrow cot close to the window. I ran around to the outside of the building. At last Betsie caught sight of me; we exchanged smiles and soundless words until one of the camp police shouted at me to move along.

About noontime I put down my knitting and went out to the center room. "Prisoner 66730 reporting. Request permission to visit the hospital." I stood ramrod straight.

The Snake glanced up, then scrawled out a pass. Outside it was still sleeting. I reached the door of the ward but the horrible nurse would not let me enter, even with my pass. So I went again to the window next to Betsie's cot. I waited until the nurse left the room, then tapped gently.

Betsie's eyes opened. Slowly she turned her head.

"Are you all right?" I formed with my lips.

She nodded.

"You must get a good rest," I went on.

She moved her lips in reply but I could not follow. She formed the words again. I bent my head to one side, level with hers. The blue lips opened again:

" . . . so much work to do. . . . "

The Snake was off duty during the afternoon and evening and though I asked the other guards repeatedly, I did not again get permission to leave. The minute roll call was dismissed the following morning, I headed for the hospital, permission or no.

I reached the window and cupped my eyes to peer in. A nurse was standing directly between me and Betsie. I ducked out of sight, waited a minute, then looked again. A second nurse had joined the first, both now standing where I wanted to see. They stepped to the head and foot of the bed: I gazed curiously at what lay on it. It was a carving in old yellow ivory. There was no clothing on the figure; I could see each ivory rib, and the outline of the teeth through the parchment cheeks.

It took me a moment to realize it was Betsie.

The nurses had each seized two corners of the sheet. They lifted it between them and carried the bundle from the room before my heart had started to beat again in my chest.

Betsie! But—she had too much to do! She could not——

Where were they taking her? Where had they gone! I turned from the window and began running along the side of the building, chest hurting me as I breathed.

Then I remembered the washroom. That window at the rear—that was where . . .

My feet carried me mechanically around to the back of the building. And there, with my hand on the windowsill, I stopped. Suppose she was there? Suppose they had laid Betsie on that floor?

I started walking again. I walked for a long time, still with that pain in my chest. And each time my feet took me back to the washroom window. I would not go in. I would not look. Betsie could not be there.

I walked some more. Strangely enough, although I passed several camp police, no one stopped or questioned me.

"Corrie!"

I turned around to see Mien running after me. "Corrie, I've looked for you every-where! Oh, Corrie, come!"

She seized my arm and drew me toward the back of the hospital.

When I saw where she was headed I wrenched my arm free. "I know, Mien. I know already."

She didn't seem to hear. She seized me again, led me to the wash-room window, and pushed me in ahead of her. In the reeking room stood a nurse. I drew back in alarm, but Mien was behind me.

"This is the sister," Mien said to the nurse.

I turned my head to the side—I would not look at the bodies that lined the far wall. Mien put an arm around my shoulder and drew me across the room till we were standing above that heart-breaking row.

"Corrie! Do you see her!"

I raised my eyes to Betsie's face. Lord Jesus—what have You done! Oh Lord, what are You saying! What are You giving me!

For there lay Betsie, her eyes closed as if in sleep, her face full and young. The care lines, the grief lines, the deep hollows of hunger and disease were simply gone. In front of me was the Betsie of Haarlem, happy and at peace. Stronger! Freer! This was the Betsie of heaven, bursting with joy and health. Even her hair was graciously in place as if an angel had ministered to her.

At last I turned wonderingly to Mien. The nurse went silently to the door and opened it for us herself. "You can leave through the hall," she said softly.

I looked once more at the radiant face of my sister. Then Mien and I left the room together. A pile of clothes was heaped outside in the hallway; on top lay Nollie's blue sweater.

I stooped to pick it up. The sweater was threadbare and stained with newsprint, but it was a tangible link with Betsie. Mien seized my arm. "Don't touch those things! Black lice! They'll all be burned."

And so I left behind the last physical tie. It was just as well. It was better. Now what tied me to Betsie was the hope of heaven.

15. The Three Visions

THE BEAUTY OF Betsie's face sustained me over the next days, as I went from one to another of the women who had loved her, describing to them her peace and her joy.

Two mornings after her death the count was off at roll call. The other barracks were dismissed, 28 remained in ranks, eyes front. The loudspeaker beeped and a voice came on: a woman was missing; the entire barracks would stand on the *Lagerstrasse* until she was found. Left, right, left, right, endlessly tramping to drive the chill from weary legs. The sun came up, a wan wintry sun that did not warm. I looked down at my feet: my legs and ankles were swelling grotesquely. By noontime there was no feeling in them. Betsie, how happy you are today! No cold, no hunger, nothing between you and the face of Jesus!

The dismissal order came in the afternoon. We learned later that the missing woman had been found dead on one of the upper platforms.

It was the following morning when over the loudspeaker during roll call came the words: "Ten Boom, Cornelia!"

For an instant I stood stupidly where I was. I had been Prisoner 66730 for so long that I almost failed to react to my name. I walked forward.

"Stand to the side!"

What was going to happen? Why had I been singled out? Had someone reported the Bible?

The roll call dragged on. From where I stood I could see almost the entire *Lagerstrasse*, tens of thousands of women stretching out of sight, their breath hanging white in the night air.

The siren blew for dismissal; the guard signaled me to follow her. I splashed through the slush, trying to keep up with the strides of her tall boots. My legs and feet were still painfully swollen from the long count the day before, my shoes were held together with bits of string.

I hobbled behind the guard into the administration barracks at the opposite end of the *Lagerstrasse* from the hospital. Several prisoners were standing in line at a large desk. An officer seated behind it stamped a paper and handed it to the woman in front of him.

"*Entlassen!*" he said.

Entlassen? Released? Was—was the woman free then? Was this—were we all—He called a name and another prisoner stepped to the desk. A signature, a stamp: "*Entlassen!*"

At last "Ten Boom, Cornelia," was called. I stepped to the desk, steadying myself against it. He wrote, brought down the stamp, and then I was holding it in my hand: a piece of paper with my name and birthdate on it, and across the top in large black letters: CERTIFICATE OF DISCHARGE

Dazed, I followed the others through a door at our left. There at another desk I was handed a railway pass entitling me to transportation through Germany to the Dutch border. Outside this office a guard pointed me down a corridor into still another room. There the prisoners who had been ahead of me were tugging their dresses over their heads and lining up against the rear wall.

"Clothing over here!" a smiling prison trusty told me. "*Entlassen* physical," she explained.

I drew the Bible over my head along with the dress, rolled them together and buried the bundle at the bottom of the clothing pile. I joined the others, the wooden wall rough against my bare back. Strange how the very word "Release" had made the procedures of prison a hundred times more hateful. How often Betsie and I had stood like this. But the thought of freedom had stirred in me and the shame of this inspection was greater than all the others.

At last the doctor arrived, a freckled-faced boy in a military uniform. He glanced along the lineup with undisguised contempt. One by one we had to bend, turn around, spread our fingers. When he reached me his eyes traveled down to my feet and his lips puckered in disgust.

"Edema," he said. "Hospital."

He was gone. With one other woman who had not "passed" I scrambled back into my clothes and followed the trusty from the building. Day had broken, a sullen gray sky spitting snow. We started up the *Lagerstrasse,* past the endless streets of barracks.

"Then—we're not—aren't we to be released?"

"I imagine you will be, as soon as the swelling in your legs goes down," the trusty said. "They only release you if you're in good condition." I saw her look at the other prisoner: the woman's skin and eyes were a dull dark yellow.

Sick call stretched around the side of the hospital, but we walked straight through the door and into a ward at the rear. The room was crammed with double-decker cots. I was assigned a place on an upper bunk next to a woman whose body was covered with erupting pustules. But at least it was near a wall where I could keep my swollen legs elevated. That was what mattered now: to get the swelling down, to pass the inspection.

Whether that ray of freedom shed a new, relentless light on Ravensbruck, or whether this was truly the most savage place yet, I could not tell. The suffering was unimaginable. Around me were survivors of a prison train which had been bombed on its way here. The women were horribly mutilated and in terrible pain, but at each moan two of the nurses jeered and mimicked the sounds.

Even in the other patients I saw that stony indifference to others that was the most fatal disease of the concentration camp. I felt it spread to myself: how could one survive if one kept on feeling! The paralyzed and the unconscious kept falling out of the crowded narrow cots; that first night four women fell from upper bunks and died on the floor. It was better to narrow the mind to one's own need, not to see, not to think.

But there was no way to shut out the sounds. All night women cried out a German word I didn't know. *"Schieber!"* Over and over from rasping throats: *"Schieber!"*

Finally I realized that they were calling for bedpans. It was out of the question for most of the women in this room to make it to that filthy latrine next door. At last, reluctant to lower my legs, I climbed down from my cot and set about the chore. The gratitude of the patients was heart-wrenching. "Who are you? Why are you doing this?"—as though cruelty and callousness were the norm, ordinary decency the marvel.

As a wintry dawn crept through the windows, I realized it was Christmas Day.

I went each morning to the clinic at the front of the hospital where I could hear the tramping of feet on the *Lagerstrasse* outside. Each time the verdict was "Edema of the feet and ankles." Many of those who attended the clinic were, like myself, discharged prisoners. Some had been released months ago: their discharge papers and railway passes were ragged from opening and refolding. And—what if Betsie were still alive? Surely our prison term would have been up together. But Betsie would never, never have passed the physical. What if she were here with me? What if I were to pass the inspection and she . . .

There are no "ifs" in God's kingdom. I could hear her soft voice saying it. His timing is perfect. His will is our hiding place. Lord Jesus, keep me in Your will! Don't let me go mad by poking about outside it.

I kept looking for someone to give the Bible to. How easy it would be, back in Holland, to get another—a hundred others. There were not many Hollanders in the ward who would be able to read the Dutch text, but at last I slipped it around the neck of a grateful young woman from Utrecht.

The sixth night I spent in the ward both bedpans were suddenly and mysteriously missing. In an upper bunk on the center aisle were two Hungarian gypsies whose muttering was part of the babble of the room. I never walked past their cot because one of them had a gangrenous foot which she would thrust in the face of anyone who came near. Now someone screamed out that the gypsies had the bedpans, hidden under their blankets to save them the trip to the toilets. I went to their cot and pleaded with them—though I didn't know whether they understood German or not.

Suddenly in the dark something wet and sticky coiled round my face. The woman had taken the bandage from her foot and flung it at me. I ran sobbing down the corridor and washed and washed beneath the wall spigot in the latrine. I would never step into that aisle again! What did I care about the wretched bedpans! I couldn't bear . . .

But of course I did go back. I had learned much, in the past year, about what I could and could not bear. As the gypsies saw me heading down the aisle toward them, both bedpans clattered onto the floor.

The next morning the doctor on duty at the clinic stamped the medical approval on my discharge form. Events that had dragged so slow now moved with bewildering speed. In a dressing shed near the outer gate of the camp I was outfitted with clothes. Underthings; a woolen skirt; a truly beautiful silk blouse; sturdy, almost-new shoes; a hat; an overcoat. I was handed a form to sign stating that I had never been ill at Ravensbruck, never had an accident, and that the treatment had been good. I signed.

In another building I received a day's bread ration and food coupons for three additional days. I was also given back my watch, my Dutch money, and Mama's ring. And then I was standing with a group of ten or twelve just inside the gate.

The heavy iron doors swung open; at the heels of a woman guard we marched through. We climbed the little hill: now I could see the lake, frozen from shore to shore. The pines and the distant church steeple sparkled in the winter sun like an old-fashioned Christmas card.

I could not believe it. Perhaps we were only going to the Siemens factory; tonight we would march back to camp. But at the top of the hill we turned left, toward the center of the small town. I could feel my feet swelling in the tight new shoes, but I bit my lip and made myself stride along. I imagined the guard turning around, pointing a scornful finger: "Edema! Send her back to camp!"

At the small train station the guard turned and left us without a backward glance. Apparently we were all traveling as far as Berlin, then each pursuing her separate route home. There was a long wait on cold iron benches.

The feeling of unreality persisted. Only one thing seemed familiar, the hungry hollow in my stomach. I put off getting into my bread allowance as long as I could, but at last reached into my overcoat pocket. The packet was gone. I sprang up from the bench, looking beneath it, retracing my steps through the station. Whether I had dropped it or it had been stolen, the bread was gone, and with it the ration coupons.

At last a train pulled into the station and we crowded eagerly to it but it was for military personnel only. Late in the afternoon we were allowed aboard a mail train, only to be put off two stops farther on to make room for a food shipment. The trip became a blur. We reached the huge, bomb-gutted terminal in Berlin some-time after midnight.

It was New Year's Day, 1945. Betsie had been right: she and I were out of prison. . . .

Snow drifted down from a shattered skylight as I wandered, confused and fright-ened, through the cavernous station. I knew that I must find the train to Uelzen, but months of being told what to do had left me robbed of initiative. At last some-one directed me to a distant platform. Each step now was agony in the stiff new shoes. When I reached the platform at last, the sign said not Uelzen but Olsztyn, a town in Poland in exactly the opposite direction. I had to cross those acres of concrete floors again.

Ahead of me an elderly man, pink-cheeked from working in the roofless sta-tion, was raking bomb rubble into a pile. When I asked him for directions he took me by the arm and led me himself to the proper platform. "I was to Holland once," he said, voice wistful with recollection. "When the wife was alive, you know. Right on the sea we stayed."

A train was standing on the track and I climbed aboard. It was hours before anyone else arrived, but I did not dare get off for fear I would not find my way back again. By the time the train started up I was dizzy for lack of food. At the first stop outside Berlin I followed the other passengers into the station café. I showed the woman behind the cashbox my Dutch guilders and told her I had lost my coupons.

"That's an old story! Get out of here before I call the police!"

The trip was endless. Many miles of track could be traveled only at a crawl. Some sections were gone altogether and there were interminable, long detours and many changes of train. Often we did not stop in a station at all, for fear of air raids, but exchanged freight and passengers in the countryside.

And all the while, out my window passed once-beautiful Germany. Fire-blackened woods, the gaunt ribs of a church standing over a ruined village. Bremen especially brought tears to my eyes. In all that wasteland I saw one human being, an old woman poking at a heap of bricks.

In Uelzen there was a long wait between trains. It was late at night, the station was deserted. As I dozed in an empty coffee bar my head dropped forward until it rested on the small table in front of me. A blow on my ear sent me sprawling almost to the floor.

"This is not a bedroom!" the furious station agent shrieked. "You can't use our tables to sleep on!"

Trains came. Trains didn't come. I climbed on and off. And then I was standing in a line at a customs shed and the sign on the little station building said *Nieuwerschans*. As I left the building a workman in a blue cap and blue overalls stepped up to me. "Here! You won't get far on those legs! Hang onto my arm."

He spoke Dutch.

I clung to him and hobbled across some tracks to where another train was waiting, engine already puffing smoke. I was in Holland.

We jerked forward. Flat, snow-covered fields glided past the window. Home. It was still occupied Holland, German soldiers still stood at intervals along the tracks—but it was home.

The train was going only as far as Groningen, a Dutch city not far from the border. Beyond that rails were torn up and all except government travel banned. With the last of my strength I limped to a hospital near the station.

A nurse in a sparkling white uniform invited me into a little office. When I had told my story, she left the room. In a few minutes she was back with a tray of tea and rusk. "I left the butter off," she said. "You're suffering from malnutrition. You must be careful what you eat."

Tears tumbled into the hot tea as I drank. Here was someone who felt concern for me. There were no available beds in the hospital, she said, but one of the staff was away and I was to have her room. "Right now I have a hot tub running."

I followed her down gleaming corridors in a kind of happy dream. In a large bathroom clouds of steam were rising from a glistening white tub. Nothing in my life ever felt as good as that bath. I lay submerged to my chin, feeling the warm water soothe my scab-crusted skin. "Just five minutes more!" I would beg each time the nurse rapped at the door.

At last I let her hand me a nightgown and lead me to a room where a bed was turned down and waiting. Sheets. White sheets top and bottom. I could not get enough of running my hands over them. The nurse was tucking a second pillow beneath my swollen feet. I struggled to stay awake: to lie here clean and cared for was such joy I did not want to sleep through a minute of it.

I stayed in the hospital at Groningen ten days, feeling my strength return. For most meals I joined the nurses in their own dining room. The first time I saw the long table set with silverware and glasses, I drew back in alarm.

"You're having a party! Let me take a tray to my room!" I did not feel ready yet for laughter and social chatter.

The young woman beside me laughed as she pulled out a chair for me. "It's not a party! It's just supper—and skimpy enough at that."

I sat down blinking at knives, forks, tablecloth—had I once eaten like this, every day in the year? Like a savage watching his first civilized meal I copied the leisurely gestures of the others as they passed bread and cheese and unhurriedly stirred their coffee.

The ache in my heart was to get to Willem and Nollie—but how could it be done with the travel ban? Telephone service, too, was more limited than ever, but at last the girl at the hospital switchboard reached the telephone operator in Hilversum with the news of Betsie's death and my release.

In the middle of the second week, hospital authorities arranged a ride for me on a food truck headed south. We made the illegal trip at night and without headlights: the food had been diverted from a shipment headed for Germany. In the gray early morning the truck pulled up to Willem's big brick nursing home. A tall, broad-shouldered girl answered my knock, and then went dashing down the hallway with the news that I was here.

In a moment my arms were around Tine and two of my nieces. Willem arrived more slowly, limping down the corridor with the help of a cane. We held each other a long time while I told them the details of Betsie's illness and death.

"Almost," said Willem slowly, "almost I could wish to have this same news of Kik. It would be good for him to be with Betsie and Father." They had had no word of this tall blond son since his deportation to Germany. I remembered his hand on my shoulder, guiding me on our bicycles through the blacked-out streets to Pickwick's. Remembered his patient coaching: "You *have* no cards, Tante Corrie! There *are no Jews.*" Kik! Are the young and brave as vulnerable as the old and slow?

I spent two weeks in Hilversum, trying to adjust to what my eyes had told me that first moment. Willem was dying. Only he seemed unaware of it as he hobbled along the halls of his home bringing comfort and counsel to the sick people in his care. They had over fifty patients at the moment, but what I could not get over was the number of young women in help: nurse's aides, kitchen helpers, secretaries. It was several days before I perceived that most of these "girls" were young men in hiding from the forced-labor conscription which had grown more ruthless than ever.

And still something in me could not rest until I got back to Haarlem. Nollie was there, of course. But it was the Beje, too, something in the house itself that called me, beckoned me, told me to come home.

The problem, again, was getting there. Willem had the use of an official car for nursing-home business, but only within a radius of Hilversum. Finally, after many relayed phone calls, he told me the trip had been arranged.

The roads were deserted as we set out; we passed only two other cars all the way to the rendezvous spot with the car from Haarlem. Ahead, pulled off onto the snow at the side of the road, we saw it, a long black limousine with official government plates and curtained rear windows. I kissed Willem goodbye and then stepped quickly, as instructed, into the rear of the limousine. Even in the curtained gloom the ungainly bulk beside me was unmistakable.

"Oom Herman!" I cried.

"My dear Cornelia." His great hand closed around both of mine. "God permits me to see you again."

I had last seen Pickwick sitting between two soldiers on the prison bus in The Hague, his poor bald head bruised and bleeding. Now here he was, waving aside my sympathy as though that had been an incident too trivial to recall.

He seemed as well informed as ever about everything that went on in Haarlem, and as the uniformed driver sped us along the empty roads, he filled me in on all the details I ached to know. All of our Jews were safe except for Mary Itallie, who had been sent to Poland following her arrest in the street. Our group was still operating, although many of the young men were in hiding.

He warned me to expect changes at the Beje. After the police guard had been removed, a series of homeless families had been housed there, although at the moment he believed the living quarters above the shop were empty. Even before the house was unsealed, loyal Toos had returned from Scheveningen and reopened the watch business. Mr. Beukers, the optician next door, had given her space in his shop from which she had taken orders to give to our repairmen in their homes.

As my eyes adjusted to the dim light I made out my friend's face more clearly. There was perhaps an extra knob or two on the misshapen head, teeth were missing—but to that vast, kindly ugliness the beating had made no real difference at all.

Now the limousine was threading the narrow streets of Haarlem. Over the bridge on the Spaarne. Across the Grote Markt in the shadow of St. Bavo's, into the Barteljorisstraat. I was out of the car almost before it stopped, running down the alley, through the side door, and into Nollie's embrace. She and her girls had been there all morning, sweeping, washing windows, airing sheets for my homecoming. Over Nollie's shoulder I saw Toos standing in the rear door to the shop, laughing and sobbing both at once. Laughing because I was home; crying because Father and Betsie, the only two people she had ever allowed herself to love, would never be.

Together we trooped through the house and shop, looking, stroking—"Remember how Betsie would set out these cups?" "Remember how Meta would scold Eusie for leaving his pipe here?" I stood on the landing outside the dining room and ran my hand over the smooth wood of the Frisian clock. I could see Father stopping here, Kapteyn at his heels.

"We mustn't let the clock run down. . . ."

I opened the glass face, moved the hands to agree with my wristwatch, and slowly drew up the weights. I was home. Life, like the clock, started again: mornings repairing watches in the workshop, noons most often bumping on my tireless bicycle out to Bos en Hoven Straat.

And yet . . . in a strange way, I was not home. I was still waiting, still looking for something. I spent days prowling the alleys and canal banks nearby, calling Maher Shalal Hashbaz by name. The elderly vegetable lady three stores down told me that the cat had mewed at her door the night of our arrest and she had taken him in. For months, she said, the small children of the neighborhood had banded together to bring food to "Opa's kitty." They had brought scraps from garbage pails and even tidbits from their own scanty plates smuggled past watchful mothers, and Mr. Hashbaz had remained sleek and fat.

It was mid-December, she said, when he had not appeared one night to her call, nor had she seen him since. And so I searched, but with a sinking heart: in this winter of Holland's hunger, all my searching brought not one single cat or dog to my call.

I missed more than the cat; the Beje needed people to fill its rooms. I remembered Father's words to the Gestapo chief in The Hague: "I will open my door to anyone in need. . . . " No one in the city was in greater need than its feeble-minded. Since the start of the Nazi occupation they had been sequestered by their families in back rooms, their schools and training centers shut down, hidden from a government which had decided they were not fit to live. Soon a group of them was living at the Beje. They still could not go out on the streets, but here at least they had new surroundings and a program of sorts with the time I could take from the shop.

And still my restlessness continued. I was home, I was working and busy—or was I? Often I would come to with a start at my workbench to realize that I had sat for an hour staring into space. The repairmen Toos had found—trained under Father—were excellent. I spent less and less time in the shop; whatever or whoever I was looking for was not there.

Nor upstairs. I loved the gentle people in my care, but the house itself had ceased to be home. For Betsie's sake I bought plants for every windowsill, but I forgot to water them and they died.

Maybe I missed the challenge of the underground. When the national group approached me with a request, I agreed eagerly. They had false release papers for a prisoner in the Haarlem jail. What could be simpler than to carry this document around the corner and through those familiar wooden doors.

But as the doors closed behind me my heart began to race. What if I couldn't get out? What if I was trapped?

"Yes?" A young police lieutenant with bright orange hair stepped from behind the reception desk. "You had an appointment?"

It was Rolf. Why was he being so stiff with me? Was I under arrest? Were they going to put me in a cell? "Rolf!" I said. "Don't you know me?"

He peered at me as though trying to refresh his memory. "Of course!" he said smoothly. "The lady at the watch shop! I heard you were closed down for a while."

I gaped at him. Why, Rolf knew perfectly—and then I recalled where we were.

In the central foyer of the police station with half a dozen German soldiers looking on. And I had greeted one of our group by name, practically admitted a special relationship between us, when the cardinal rule of the underground was . . . I ran my tongue over my lips. How could I have been so stupid?

Rolf took the forged papers from my shaking hands and glanced through them "These must be passed upon by the police chief and the military overcommand together," he said. "Can you return with them tomorrow afternoon at four? The chief will be in a meeting until——"

I heard no more. At the words "tomorrow afternoon" I had bolted for the door. I stood thankfully on the sidewalk until my knees stopped knocking. If I had ever needed proof that I had no boldness or cleverness of my own, I had it now. Whatever bravery, or skill I had ever shown were gifts of God—sheer loans from Him of the talent needed to do a job. And it was clear, from the absence of such skills now, that this was no longer His work for me.

I crept meekly back to the Beje. And it was at that moment, as I stepped into the alley, that I knew what it was I was looking for.

It was Betsie.

It was Betsie I had missed every moment of every day since I ran to the hospital window and found that she had left Ravensbruck forever. It was Betsie I had thought to find back here in Haarlem, here in the watchshop and in the home she loved.

But she was not here. And now for the first time since her death, I remembered. "We must tell people, Corrie. We must tell them what we learned. . . ."

That very week I began to speak. If this was God's new work for me, then He would provide the courage and the words. Through the streets and suburbs of Haarlem I bumped on my bicycle rims, bringing the message that joy runs deeper than despair.

It was news that people needed to hear that cheerless spring of 1945. No Bride of Haarlem tree filled the air with fragrance; only the stump had been too big to haul off for firewood. No tulips turned fields into carpets of color: the bulbs had all been eaten. No family was without its tragedy. In churches and club rooms and private homes in those desperate days I told the truths Betsie and I had learned in Ravensbruck.

And always at these meetings, I spoke of Betsie's first vision: of a home here in Holland where those who had been hurt could learn to live again unafraid. At the close of one of these talks a slender, aristocratic lady came up to me. I knew her by sight: Mrs. Bierens de Haan whose home in the suburb of Bloemendaal was said to be one of the most beautiful in Holland. I had never seen it, only the trees at the edge of the huge park in which it was set, and so I was astonished when this elegantly dressed lady asked me if I were still living in the ancient little house on the Barteljorisstraat.

"How did you—yes, I do. But——"

"My mother often told me about it. She went there frequently to see an aunt of yours who, I believe, was in charitable work?"

In a rush it all came back. Opening the side door to let in a swish of satin and rustle of feathers. A long gown and a plumed hat brushing both sides of the narrow stairs. Then Tante Jans standing in her doorway with a look that froze in the bones the thought of bouncing a ball.

"I am a widow," Mrs. Bierens de Haan was saying, "but I have five sons in the Resistance. Four are still alive and well. The fifth we have not heard from since he was taken to Germany. As you spoke just now something in me kept saying, 'Jan will come back and in gratitude you will open your home for this vision of Betsie ten Boom.'"

It was two weeks later that a small boy delivered a scented envelope to the side door; inside in slanted purple letters was a single line, "Jan is home."

Mrs. Bierens de Haan herself met me at the entrance to her estate. Together we walked up an avenue of ancient oaks meeting above our heads. Rounding the final bend, we saw it, a fifty-six-room mansion in the center of a vast lawn. Two elderly gardeners were poking about the flowerbeds.

"We've let the gardens go," Mrs. Bierens de Haan said. "But I thought we might put them back in shape. Don't you think released prisoners might find therapy in growing things?"

I didn't answer. I was staring up at the gabled roof and the leaded windows. Such tall, tall windows. . . .

"Are there—" my throat was dry. "Are there inlaid wood floors inside, and a broad gallery around a central hall, and—and bas-relief statues set along the walls?"

Mrs. Bierens de Haan looked at me in surprise. "You've been here then! I don't recall——"

"No," I said. "I heard about it from——"

I stopped. How could I explain what I did not understand?

"From someone who's been here," she finished simply, not understanding my perplexity.

"Yes," I said. "From someone who's been here."

The second week in May the Allies retook Holland. The Dutch flag hung from every window and the "Wilhelmus" was played on the liberated radio day and night. The Canadian army rushed to the cities the food they had stockpiled along the borders.

In June the first of many hundreds of people arrived at the beautiful home in Bloemendaal. Silent or endlessly relating their losses, withdrawn or fiercely aggressive, every one was a damaged human being. Not all had been in concentration camps; some had spent two, three, even four years hidden in attic rooms and back closets here in Holland.

One of the first of these was Mrs. Kan, widow of the watch-shop owner up the street. Mr. Kan had died at the underground address; she came to us alone, a stooped, white-haired woman who startled at every sound. Others came to Bloemendaal, scarred body and soul by bombing raids or loss of family or any of the endless dislocations of war. In 1947 we began to receive Dutch people who had been prisoners of the Japanese in Indonesia.

Though none of this was by design, it proved to be the best possible setting for those who had been imprisoned in Germany. Among themselves they tended to live and relive their special woes; in Bloemendaal they were reminded that they were not the only ones who had suffered. And for all these people alike, the key to healing turned out to be the same. Each had a hurt he had to forgive: the neighbor who had reported him, the brutal guard, the sadistic soldier.

Strangely enough, it was not the Germans or the Japanese that people had most trouble forgiving; it was their fellow Dutchmen who had sided with the enemy. I saw them frequently in the streets, NSBers with their shaved heads and furtive eyes. These former collaborators were now in pitiful condition, turned out of homes and apartments, unable to find jobs, hooted at in the streets.

At first it seemed to me that we should invite them too to Bloemendaal, to live side by side with those they had injured, to seek a new compassion on both sides. But it turned out to be too soon for people working their way back from such hurt: the two times I tried it, it ended in open fights. And so as soon as homes and schools for the feeble-minded opened again around the country I turned the Beje over to these former NSBers.

This was how it went, those years after the war, experimenting, making mistakes, learning. The doctors, psychiatrists, and nutritionists who came free of charge to any place that cared for war victims, sometimes expressed surprise at our loose-run ways. At morning and evening worship people drifted in and out, table manners were atrocious, one man took a walk into Haarlem every morning at 3:00 A.M. I could not bring myself to sound a whistle or to scold, or to consider gates or curfews.

And, sure enough, in their own time and their own way, people worked out the deep pain within them. It most often started, as Betsie had known it would, in the garden. As flowers bloomed or vegetables ripened, talk was less of the bitter past, more of tomorrow's weather. As their horizons broadened, I would tell them about the people living in the Beje, people who never had a visitor, never a piece of mail. When mention of the NSBers no longer brought on a volley of self-righteous wrath, I knew the person's healing was not far away. And the day he said, "Those people you spoke of—I wonder if they'd care for some homegrown carrots," then I knew the miracle had taken place.

I continued to speak, partly because the home in Bloemendaal ran on contributions, partly because the hunger for Betsie's story seemed to increase with time. I traveled all over Holland, to other parts of Europe, to the United States.

But the place where the hunger was greatest was Germany. Germany was a land in ruins, cities of ashes and rubble, but more terrifying still, minds and hearts of ashes. Just to cross the border was to feel the great weight that hung over that land.

It was at a church service in Munich that I saw him, the former S.S. man who had stood guard at the shower room door in the processing center at Ravensbruck. He was the first of our actual jailers that I had seen since that time. And suddenly it was all there—the roomful of mocking men, the heaps of clothing, Betsie's pain-blanched face.

He came up to me as the church was emptying, beaming and bowing. "How grateful I am for your message, *Fraulein,*" he said. "To think that, as you say, He has washed my sins away!"

His hand was thrust out to shake mine. And I, who had preached so often to the people in Bloemendaal the need to forgive, kept my hand at my side.

Even as the angry, vengeful thoughts boiled through me, I saw the sin of them. Jesus Christ had died for this man; was I going to ask for more? Lord Jesus, I prayed, forgive me and help me to forgive him.

I tried to smile, I struggled to raise my hand. I could not. I felt nothing, not the slightest spark of warmth or charity. And so again I breathed a silent prayer. Jesus, I cannot forgive him. Give me Your forgiveness.

As I took his hand the most incredible thing happened. From my shoulder along my arm and through my hand a current seemed to pass from me to him, while into my heart sprang a love for this stranger that almost overwhelmed me.

And so I discovered that it is not on our forgiveness any more than on our goodness that the world's healing hinges, but on His. When He tells us to love our enemies, He gives, along with the command, the love itself.

It took a lot of love. The most pressing need in postwar Germany was homes; nine million people were said to be without them. They were living in rubble heaps, half-standing buildings, and abandoned army trucks. A church group invited me to speak to a hundred families living in an abandoned factory building. Sheets and blankets had been hung between the various living quarters to make a pretense of privacy. But there was no insulating the sounds: the wail of a baby, the din of radios, the angry words of a family quarrel. How could I speak to these people of the reality of God and then go back to my quiet room in the church hostel outside the city? No, before I could bring a message to them, I would have to live among them.

And it was during the months that I spent in the factory that a director of a relief organization came to see me. They had heard of my rehabilitation work in Holland, he said, and they wondered—I was opening my mouth to say that I had no professional training in such things, when his next words silenced me.

"We've located a place for the work," he said. "It was a former concentration camp that's just been released by the government."

We drove to Darmstadt to look over the camp. Rolls of rusting barbed wire still surrounded it. I walked slowly up a cinder path between drab gray barracks. I pushed open a creaking door; I stepped between rows of metal cots.

"Windowboxes" I said. "We'll have them at every window. The barbed wire must come down, of course, and then we'll need paint. Green paint. Bright yellow-green, the color of things coming up new in the spring. . . . "

Since Then

TOGETHER WITH A committee of the German Lutheran Church, Corrie opened the *camp* in Darmstadt in 1946 as a home and place of renewal. It functioned in this way until 1960 when it was torn down to make room for new construction in a thriving new Germany.

The *home* in Bloemendaal served ex-prisoners and other war victims exclusively until 1950, when it also began to receive people in need of rest and care from the population at large. It is still in operation today, in its own new building, with patients from many parts of Europe. Since 1967 it has been governed by the Dutch Reformed Church.

Willem died of tuberculosis of the spine in December 1946. His last book, a study of sacrifice in the Old Testament, was written standing because the pain of his illness would not allow him to sit at a desk.

Just before his death Willem opened his eyes to tell Tine: "It is well—it is very well—with *Kik*." It was not until 1953 that the family learned definitely that his twenty-year-old son had died in 1944 at the concentration camp in Bergen-Belsen. Today a "ten Boom Street" in Hilversum honors Kik.

As a result of his wartime experiences, *Peter* van Woerden dedicated his musical gifts to God's service. He has composed many devotional songs, including a musical setting for the Psalms and Proverbs. Today Peter, his wife, and their five children travel all over Europe and the Near East as a family singing group with a message of God's love.

Well into her eighties, Corrie continued her indefatigable travels in obedience to Betsie's certainty that they must "tell people," working and teaching in sixty-one countries on both sides of the Iron Curtain. To whomever she spoke—African students on the shores of Lake Victoria, farmers in a Cuban sugar field, prisoners in an English penitentiary, factory workers in Uzbekistan—she brought the truth they learned in Ravensbruck: Jesus can turn loss into glory.

When failing health brought an end to her missionary journeys, friends provided Corrie a house in Orange County, California. There, unable to walk and, at the end, even to speak, Corrie continued to minister. Friends who came to cheer the bedridden old lady reported that it was invariably they who went away uplifted.

At 11 o'clock at night on her ninety-first birthday—April 15, 1983—Corrie, in her own phrase, went home at last. The co-author of *The Hiding Place* recalls her reaction to the news:

l tried to be glad for Corrie when the phone call came from California: she'd waited for her "homecoming" so long. But death, from the perspective of earth, means saying goodbye. Missing her already, I roamed our house, touching one by one the physical objects she'd given us over the years. An antique brass kettle. A small square picture frame. An even smaller round one.

Little things that recalled big truths our friend had shared. . . .

The kettle reminded me about priorities. It was Betsie who spied it, dented and soot-encrusted, in a junkyard one morning on her way to the market. She bought it with the meat money.

"Betsie!" cried Corrie, coming upstairs from the watch shop. "What are we going to do with that old thing? Look, it won't even hold water!"

"It's not *meant* to hold water," said Betsie with dignity.

"Well, what's it for, then?"

"It's not 'for' anything. Oh, Corrie, wait till I get the grime off! Can't you just see the morning sun glowing on this spout? I got stew meat instead of a roast," Betsie went on. "You know stew is really easier for Father to chew, and I'm not hungry today. Oh, Corrie, this kettle will go on shining long after we've forgotten what we had for dinner tonight!"

And so it did. It shone for the hunted people who found shelter in the Beje. It shone for Corrie when she returned there alone from the concentration camp, and from her tireless trips to Russia, China, Vietnam. It shines in our home today, saying: What feeds the soul matters as much as what feeds the body.

In the square frame is a piece of yellow cloth cut in the shape of a six-pointed star. Across the star are four black letters: JOOD, the Dutch word for "Jew." When John and I were in Holland doing research for *The Hiding Place*, Corrie took us to the home of Meyer Mossel—"Eusebius" during the Nazi occupation. We sipped tea while Corrie and Eusie reminisced.

"You'd take your pipe with you," Corrie reminded him, recalling the practice drills, "but you'd forget your ashtray, and I'd have to come running after you."

Eusie set down his cup and crossed the room to a massive antique sideboard. From the bottom drawer, buried beneath a pile of table linen, he drew out a scrap of yellow cloth cut in the shape of a star.

"All these years I wondered why I saved this thing," he said. "Now I know it was to give to you, Corrie."

We picked out the frame for Eusie's star that very afternoon: For years it hung on Corrie's wall as it hangs now on ours—a symbol bittersweet as a cross. To me the star says: Whatever in our life is hardest to bear, love can transform into beauty.

And the little round frame? It holds a piece of cloth too—ordinary white cotton, the kind underwear is made of. In fact, it *is* underwear, a fragment of the undershirt Corrie was wearing when the Gestapo raid came.

In prison, in solitary confinement, idleness was eroding Corrie's courage. Nollie smuggled a needle and thread to her, but soon the thread was used up. Then Corrie remembered the undershirt. She unraveled a hem. And now! Animals, houses, faces—she covered the undershirt with embroidery. The design in the round frame is a flower, with elegant curling edges and six leaves on a graceful stem.

You have to look close to see the flower (the thread, of course, is the same color as the cloth). And underwear—even a dear friend's—well, it isn't the most costly of the things Corrie gave us. But it was the one that spoke most clearly, now that she was gone.

The circle of white cotton told me that when we're feeling poorest—when we've lost a friend, when a dream has failed, when we seem to have nothing left in the world to make life beautiful—that's when God says: You're richer than you think.

Elizabeth Sherrill
Chappaqua, New York
April, 1983

Tramp
for the Lord

Contents

Foreword

My wife, Jackie, and I met *Tante* (Aunt) Corrie and her pretty, blond secretary, Ellen de Kroon, at the airport in Melbourne, Florida. Ellen had called the night before saying they were flying in, but that Corrie had been having some severe heart pains. At eighty years of age, that's serious business.

We met the plane and whisked them to our house which is just minutes from the airport. "I'm very tired," *Tante* Corrie said. "I like to rest a while."

Moments later she was stretched out on our daughter's lavender bedspread. I opened the window so the soft, tropical breeze could blow in from the lake behind the house. Gently closing the door, I cautioned the children to speak in whispers, and tiptoed into the kitchen to join Jackie and Ellen.

Ellen had brought us some Gouda cheese and we sliced it, reminiscing over my first meal in Corrie's house in Holland. Ellen couldn't wait to tell Jackie about the expression on my face when Corrie informed me I had a choice of two dishes for lunch: raw mullet dipped in onion, or smoked eel.

Talking softly and munching on cheese and crackers, I glanced up to see *Tante* Corrie coming down the hall, her eyes sparkling.

"Aren't you going to rest?" I asked.

"Oh, I have already a good sleep," she answered in her thick, Dutch accent. "Ten minutes is all you need when God gives the sleep."

It is this remarkable power of recuperation which has allowed *Tante* Corrie, at more than eighty years of age, to tramp the world for the Lord. I saw that same power at work in her life a year later in Pittsburgh. We were both on the program for a Bible conference at the Pittsburgh Theological Seminary. She had spoken three times that day to a congregation made up of everybody from bearded Jesus People to university professors. I was out late that night and, when I returned to the dormitory, I saw Ellen running down the hall. "*Tante* Corrie is having a heart attack," she said.

I raced to Corrie's room. She was stretched out on her bed, her face gray from the pain. "God has told me my time is not yet up," she whispered. "I have sent for a minister to pray that I may be healed."

Moments later, as the young minister arrived and laid his hands on her, I saw her features relax and the color return to her cheeks. "Thank You, Lord," she said softly, "for taking away the pain." Then, signifying she was ready for us to leave, she said, "I go to sleep now."

The next morning at eight o'clock she was behind the pulpit speaking to a thousand persons in the great auditorium—as though nothing extraordinary had happened.

I am convinced that the secret of *Tante* Corrie's great recuperative power, as well as the secret of her popularity as a speaker, lies in her childlikeness. As a little girl believes her Daddy can do anything, so Corrie ten Boom trusts in God—even more. She is living proof of what happens when a woman—when *any* person—is filled with the Holy Spirit.

JAMIE BUCKINGHAM

Introduction:
The World Is My Classroom

THE SCHOOL OF life offers some difficult courses, but it is in the difficult class that one learns the most—especially when your teacher is the Lord Jesus Himself.

The hardest lessons for me were in a cell with four walls. The cell in the prison at Scheveningen, Holland, was six paces in length, two paces in breadth, with a door that could be opened only from the outside. Later there were four barbed-wire fences, charged with electricity, enclosing a concentration camp in Germany. The gates were manned by guards with loaded machine guns. It was there in Ravensbruck that more than ninety-six thousand women died.

After that time in prison, the entire world became my classroom. Since World War II, I have traveled around it twice, speaking in more than sixty countries on all continents. During these three decades I have become familiar with airports, bus stations, and passport offices. Under me have been wheels of every description: wheels of automobiles, trains, jinrikishas, horse-drawn wagons, and the landing gear of airplanes. Wheels, wheels, wheels! Even the wheels of wheelchairs.

I have enjoyed the hospitality in a great number of homes and have slept in many times more than a thousand beds. Sometimes I have slept in comfortable beds with foam rubber mattresses in the United States, and sometimes on straw mats on dirt floors in India. There have been clean rooms and dirty rooms.

One bathroom in Hollywood had a view of exotic plants and flowers from the sunken Roman bathtub; while a bathroom in Borneo was simply a mud hut equipped with nothing but a barrel of cold water. Once, while staying with a group of young Jewish girls in Israel, I had to climb over a mountain of building materi-

185

als, and walk through a junk-filled field to make my way to a tiny outhouse which was nothing more than a hole in the ground. Such a place would have been impossible to find at night.

Always in my travels, even now that I am in my ninth decade of life, I have carried in my hand and in my heart the Bible—the very Word of Life which is almost bursting with Good News. And there has been plenty for everyone. I often feel as the disciples must have felt as they fed more than five thousand with five loaves and two fishes. The secret was that they had received it from the blessed hand of the Master. There was abundance for all and twelve basketfuls of fragments left over.

There has been plenty for the dying ones in the concentration camps—plenty for the thousands gathered in universities, in town halls, and in churches all over the world. Sometimes I have spoken to a few men in prison who stood behind bars and listened hungrily. Once to a group of six missionaries in Japan who offered me hospitality during a twenty-eight-hour rainstorm in which more than a thousand persons perished around us. Groups of hundreds and crowds of thousands have listened under pandals in India and in theaters in South America. I have spoken to tens of thousands at one time in the giant stadiums of America and retreated to the mountains of North Carolina to spend time with a small group of girls in a summer camp.

"God so loved the world . . ." (John 3:16) Jesus said. And that is why I keep going, even into my eightieth years, because we've a story to tell to the nations, a story of love and light.

God has plans—not problems—for our lives. Before she died in the concentration camp in Ravensbruck, my sister Betsie said to me, "Corrie, your whole life has been a training for the work you are doing here in prison—and for the work you will do afterward."

The life of a Christian is an education for higher service. No athlete complains when the training is hard. He thinks of the game, or the race. As the Apostle Paul wrote:

In my opinion, whatever we may have to go through now is less than nothing compared with the magnificent future God has planned for us. The whole creation is on tiptoe to see the wonderful sight of the sons of God coming into their own. The world of creation cannot as yet see reality, not because it chooses to be blind, but because in God's purpose it has been so limited—yet it has been given hope. And the hope is that in the end the whole of created life will be rescued from the tyranny of change and decay and have its share in that magnificent liberty which can only belong to the children of God!

It is plain to anyone with eyes to see that at the present time all created life groans in a sort of universal travail. And it is plain, too, that we who have a foretaste of the Spirit are in a state of painful tension, while we wait for that redemption of our bodies which will mean that at last we have realized our full sonship in him.

Romans 8:18-23 PHILLIPS

Looking back across the years of my life, I can see the working of a divine pattern which is the way of God with His children. When I was in a prison camp in Holland during the war, I often prayed, "Lord, never let the enemy put me in a German concentration camp." God answered *no* to that prayer. Yet in the German camp, with all its horror, I found many prisoners who had never heard of Jesus Christ. If God had not used my sister Betsie and me to bring them to Him, they would never have heard of Him. Many died, or were killed, but many died with the Name of Jesus on their lips. They were well worth all our suffering. Faith is like radar which sees through the fog—the reality of things at a distance that the human eye cannot see.

> My life is but a weaving, between my God and me,
> I do not choose the colors, He worketh steadily,
> Oftimes He weaveth sorrow, and I in foolish pride,
> Forget He sees the upper, and I the underside.
> Not till the loom is silent, and shuttles cease to fly,
> Will God unroll the canvas and explain the reason why.
> The dark threads are as needful in the skillful Weaver's hand,
> As the threads of gold and silver in the pattern He has planned.
>
> ANONYMOUS

Although the threads of my life have often seemed knotted, I know, by faith, that on the other side of the embroidery there is a crown. As I have walked the world— a tramp for the Lord—I have learned a few lessons in God's great classroom. Even as I share these things with those of you who read this book, I pray the Holy Spirit will reveal something of the divine pattern in God's plan for you also.

CORRIE TEN BOOM
Baarn, Holland

My brethren, count it all joy when you fall into [difficult times]. Knowing this, that the trying of your faith worketh patience.

James 1:2, 3

1. A Strange Place to Hope

RANK UPON RANK we stood that hot September morning in 1944, more than a thousand women lining the railroad siding, one unspoken thought among us: *Not Germany!*

Beside me my sister Betsie swayed. I was fifty-two, Betsie fifty-nine. These seven months in a prison and concentration camp since we had been caught concealing Jews in our home had been harder on her. But prisoners though we were, at least till now we had remained in Holland. And now when liberation must come any day, where were they taking us?

Behind us guards were shouting, prodding us with their guns. Instinctively my hand went to the string around my neck. From it, hanging down my back between my shoulder blades, was the small cloth bag that held our Bible, that forbidden Book which had not only sustained Betsie and me throughout these months, but given us strength to share with our fellow prisoners. So far we had kept it hidden. But if we should go to Germany . . . . We had heard tales of the prison inspections there.

A long line of empty boxcars was rolling slowly past. Now they clanged to a halt and a gaping freight door loomed in front of us. I helped Betsie over the steep side. The dark boxcar grew quickly crowded. We were pressed against the wall. It was a small European freight car; thirty or forty people jammed it. And still the guards drove women in, pushing, jabbing with their guns. It was only when eighty women were packed inside that the heavy door slid shut and we heard the iron bolts driven into place outside.

189

Women were sobbing and many fainted, although in the tightly wedged crowd they remained upright. The sun beat down on the motionless train; the temperature in the packed car rose. It was hours before the train gave a sudden lurch and began to move. Almost at once it stopped again, then again crawled forward. The rest of that day and all night long it was the same—stopping, starting, slamming, jerking. Once through a slit in the side of the car I saw trainmen carrying a length of twisted rail. Maybe the tracks ahead were destroyed. Maybe we would still be in Holland when the liberation came.

But at dawn we rolled through the Dutch border town of Emmerich. We were in Germany.

For two more incredible days and two more nights we were carried deeper and deeper into the land of our fears. Worse than the crush of bodies and the filth, was the thirst. Two or three times when the train was stopped the door was slid open a few inches and a pail of water passed in. But we had become animals, incapable of plan. Those near the door got it all.

At last, on the morning of the third day, the door was hauled open its full width. Only a handful of very young soldiers was there to order us out and march us off. No more were needed. We could scarcely walk, let alone resist. From the crest of a small hill we saw it—the end of our journey—a vast gray barracks city surrounded by double concrete walls.

"*Ravensbruck!*"

Like a whispered curse, the word passed back through the line. This was the notorious women's death camp itself, the very symbol to Dutch hearts of all that was evil. As we stumbled down the hill, I felt the little Bible bumping on my back. As long as we had that, I thought, we could face even hell itself. But how could we conceal it through the inspection I knew lay ahead?

It was the middle of the night when Betsie and I reached the processing barracks. And there, under the harsh ceiling lights, we saw a dismaying sight. As each woman reached the head of the line she had to strip off every scrap of clothes, throw them all onto a pile guarded by soldiers, and walk naked past the scrutiny of a dozen guards into the shower room. Coming out of the shower room she wore only a thin regulation prison dress and a pair of shoes.

Our Bible! How could we take it past so many watchful eyes?

"Oh, Betsie!" I began—and then stopped at the sight of her pain-whitened face. As a guard strode by, I begged him in German to show us the toilets. He jerked his head in the direction of the shower room. "Use the drain holes!" he snapped.

Timidly Betsie and I stepped out of line and walked forward to the huge room with its row on row of overhead spigots. It was empty, waiting for the next batch of fifty naked and shivering women.

A few minutes later we would return here stripped of everything we possessed. And then we saw them, stacked in a corner, a pile of old wooden benches crawling with cockroaches, but to us the furniture of heaven itself.

In an instant I had slipped the little bag over my head and, along with my woolen underwear, had stuffed it behind the benches.

And so it was that when we were herded into that room ten minutes later, we were not poor, but rich—rich in the care of Him who was God even of Ravensbruck.

Of course when I put on the flimsy prison dress, the Bible bulged beneath it. But that was His business, not mine. At the exit, guards were feeling every prisoner, front, back, and sides. I prayed, "Oh, Lord, send your angels to surround us." But then I remembered that angels are spirits and you can see through them. What I needed was an angel to shield me so the guards could not see me. "Lord," I prayed again, "make your angels untransparent." How unorthodox you can pray when you are in great need! But God did not mind. He did it.

The woman ahead of me was searched. Behind me, Betsie was searched. They did not touch or even look at me. It was as though I was blocked out of their sight.

Outside the building was a second ordeal, another line of guards examining each prisoner again. I slowed down as I reached them, but the captain shoved me roughly by the shoulder. "Move along! You're holding up the line."

So Betsie and I came to our barracks at Ravensbruck. Before long we were holding clandestine Bible study groups for an ever-growing group of believers, and Barracks 28 became known throughout the camp as "the crazy place, where they hope."

Yes, hoped, in spite of all that human madness could do. We had learned that a stronger power had the final word, even here.

(Reprinted by permission from *Guideposts* magazine, copyright © 1972 by Guideposts Associates, Inc., Carmel, New York 10512.)

2. *Witnesses Unto Me*

IT WAS A week after Betsie had died in Ravensbruck that I took my place in the
ranks of women prisoners standing together in the icy cold of the early morning.

"66730!"

"That is my number," I said weakly as we took our places for roll call.

"ten Boom, Cornelia."

"That is my name," I thought. How strange that they would call me by name
when they always addressed us by number!

"Come forward."

We were falling in line for the roll call. Ten in a line, every one hundredth woman,
one step forward. My friends looked at me sadly.

"What does it mean?" I asked inwardly. "Punishment . . . freedom . . . the gas
chamber . . . sent to another concentration camp?"

There was but one thought that comforted me. "What a joy that Betsie is in
heaven. No matter what terrible things now happen, she will not have to bear it."

The guard, a young German girl, shouted at me. "Nr. 66730!"

I stepped forward, stood at attention and repeated the necessary words.
"Schutzhaftling ten Boom, Cornelia, meldet sich."

"Stand on Number 1 on the roll call."

I went to the place to the far right, where I could overlook the entire square of
the bleak camp. Standing in the crowd I could not feel the draft, but now, standing in the bitter cold, the wind whipped through my ragged prison dress. Another
girl, young and frightened, was sent to stand beside me. Roll call took three hours

and we were almost frozen. She saw how cold I was and rubbed my spine when the guards were not looking.

"Why must I stand here?" I asked through chattering teeth.

Her answer was barely audible as it came from her blue lips. "Death sentence."

I turned back to the Lord. "Perhaps I'll see you soon face-to-face, like Betsie does now, Lord. Let it not be too cruel a killing. Not gas, Lord, nor hanging. I prefer shooting. It is so quick. You see something, you hear something, and it is finished."

I looked back at the young girl beside me. "Lord, this is perhaps the last chance I will have to bring someone to You before I arrive in heaven. Use me, Lord. Give me all the love and wisdom I need."

"What is your name?" I asked her softly, glancing always to see if the guards were looking.

"Tiny."

"I am Corrie," I whispered. "How long have you been here?"

"Two years."

"Did you ever read the Bible?"

"No, I never did."

"Do you believe God exists?"

"I do. I wish I knew more about Him. Do you know Him?"

"I do. Jesus, His Son, came to this world to carry our punishment. He died on the cross, but He rose from the dead and has promised to be with us always. My sister died here. She suffered so much. I, too, have suffered. But Jesus is always with us. He did a miracle in taking away all my hatred and bitterness for my enemies. Jesus is willing to bring into our hearts God's love through His Holy Spirit."

Tiny listened. For almost three hours we talked while the guards completed the roll call. It was a miracle, for I had a chance to explain many things about Jesus. The prisoners behind us listened, too. I felt happy. Perhaps this was my last chance in life, but what joy!

I continued. "Jesus wants to live in your heart. 'Behold, I stand at the door and knock,' He says. 'If anyone opens the door, I'll come in.' Will you open the door of your heart and let Him come in and change you?"

"I will," she said.

"Then talk to Him. Tell Him whatever you think. Now you have a Friend who never leaves you alone."

The siren sounded and the guards shouted at the prisoners. "Get to work!"

Thousands of women prisoners were running to their places where they had to march to their work. Tiny disappeared from sight. Only I was left standing in my place where I had been ordered not to move. I still did not know what fate awaited me.

I did know, however, that the God who never slumbers nor sleeps was now with Tiny. And Tiny knew it, too. Neither of us knew at that time how important that was going to be to her in the next few days. But above the din of the concentration camp, I thought I heard the singing of the angels.

Then I heard my name called. Was it death? Oh, thank God, no. It was life. I was being released. I later learned it was through an administrative blunder, but even then I knew it was not the end of an era—it was just the beginning. Ahead of me was the world.

Then he turned my sorrow into joy! He took
away my clothes of mourning . . . .

Psalms 30:11 LB

3. *Release!*

WHEN YOU ARE dying—when you stand at the gate of eternity—you see things from a different perspective than when you think you may live for a long time. I had been standing at that gate for many months, living in Barracks 28 in the shadow of the crematorium. Every time I saw the smoke pouring from the hideous smokestacks I knew it was the last remains of some poor woman who had been with me in Ravensbruck. Often I asked myself, "When will it be my time to be killed or die?"

But I was not afraid. Following Betsie's death, God's Presence was even more real. Even though I was looking into the valley of the shadow of death, I was not afraid. It is here that Jesus comes the closest, taking our hand, and leading us through.

One week before the order came to kill all the women of my age, I was free. I still do not understand all the details of my release from Ravensbruck. All I know is, it was a miracle of God.

I stood in the prison yard—waiting the final order. Beyond the walls with their strands of barbed wire stood the silent trees of the German forest, looking so much like the gray-green sets on the back of one of our theater stages in Holland.

Mimi, one of the fellow prisoners, came within whispering distance. "Tiny died this morning," she said without looking at me. "And Marie also."

Tiny! "Oh, Lord, thank You for letting me point her to Jesus who has now ushered her safely into Your Presence." And Marie. I knew her well. She lived in my barracks and had attended my Bible talks. Like Tiny, Marie had also accepted Jesus as her Lord. I looked back at the long rows of barracks. "Lord, if it was only for Tiny and Marie—that they might come to know you before they died—then it was all worthwhile."

A guard spoke harshly, telling Mimi to leave the yard. Then he said to me, "Face the gate. Do not turn around."

The gate swung open and I glimpsed the lake in front of the camp. I could smell freedom.

"Follow me," a young girl in an officer's uniform said to me.

I walked slowly through the gate, never looking back. Behind me I heard the hinges squeak as the gate swung shut. I was free, and flooding through my mind were the words of Jesus to the church at Philadelphia:

Behold, I have set before thee an open door, and no man can shut it. . . .

Revelation 3:8

First that door directed me back to Holland. The train ride took three days. Another prisoner, Claire Prins, had been released with me. Her leg was alarmingly swollen and of course both of us were mere skin and bones. But we were *free*!

Arriving in Groningen, we made our way to a Christian hospital called the Deaconess House, where I asked to speak to the superintendent. Perhaps they would help us until I could return to Haarlem, I thought.

"Sister Tavenier cannot come at the moment," the attendant said. "She is helping conduct a Christian service in one of the wards. I'm afraid you will have to wait."

"Would you mind," I said, looking at the attendant, "if I attended the service also?"

She looked at me tenderly, sensing, perhaps, some of my suffering. "Why, of course. You may rest in the waiting room until it starts. I'll come after you."

"Nurse . . . ," I hesitated to ask, "have you anything for me to drink?"

Again the look of compassion crossed her face. "I'll bring you some tea," she said gently.

A few minutes later she placed it before me, saying, "I have not put butter on the toast for I see you are sick. The dry toast and tea will be good for you."

I was deeply touched by this tiny show of consideration. A moment later I was lying in a comfortable chair with my legs outstretched on a bench. A wonderful feeling of rest descended on me. I was in the Netherlands, among good people. My suffering was over.

A nurse came for me, to take me to the ward where the service was to be held. Chairs had been arranged in a semicircle between the beds, facing a table. An elderly minister walked in and a hymnal was handed me. I could see the nurses and patients glancing stealthily at me. My clothes were ragged and filthy, hanging from my gaunt body like rags on a scarecrow. Yet I was so thankful to be free I cared not.

The minister spoke in a well-modulated voice. Then we joined in singing. I could not help but make comparisons: the dirty prison dormitory, infection-ridden and filthy, the beds full of lice, and now this. Clean sheets and pillow cases and a spotless floor. The hoarse voices of the slave drivers and the mature, melodious voice of the minister. Only the singing was the same, for we had sung at Ravensbruck. Singing was one of the ways we kept up our courage.

Following the service the nurse took me to the superintendent's office. "Miss Prins has been taken care of," she said, "and is already in a fresh bed. You both must have had a horrible experience. But now, what must be done with you?"

I sat in a chair across from her desk. For more than a year I had not been allowed to make a decision. All I could do was follow orders. It was difficult even to think. "I don't know, Sister," I said. It was enough just to be surrounded by people who were not angry with me.

"I know what," she said, as she touched a bell. "First we'll give you a warm dinner."

A young nurse appeared and took my arm, guiding me down a hall toward the dining room. "I understand you have just been released from Ravensbruck," she said. "Where are you going? Where is your home?"

"I am going to Haarlem," I replied.

"Oh, Haarlem," she said with excitement. "Do you know Corrie ten Boom who lives there?"

I looked at her. She was one of the YWCA leaders I had worked with before the war. "Truus Benes!" I exclaimed in delight.

"Why, yes, that is my name," she said, bewildered. "But I don't believe I know you."

"I am Corrie ten Boom."

The nurse stopped abruptly in the hall, staring at me. "Oh, no, that is impossible. I know Corrie ten Boom very well. I have been in girls' camps with her several times. She is much younger than you."

"But, really, I am Corrie ten Boom," I argued. Then I thought of how I must have looked. My face was thin and pale, my mouth wide, like skin stretched across a skull. My hair fell queerly about my face. My eyes were hollow. My coat was dirty, for I had at times slept on the floor of the train as we traveled out of Germany. The belt of my dress sagged, for I had not had the energy to fasten it.

The nurse reached out tenderly and touched my chapped hand. "Yes . . . yes . . . it is you. It *is!*" And then we both broke into laughter.

In the dining room we sat opposite each other at a small table and I asked about our mutual acquaintances. Was Mary Barger still living? Jeanne Blooker and . . . ? It was ridiculous to ask such questions, but I wanted to know everything. The world, for me, had stopped while I had been in the concentration camp. Now it was beginning to turn again and I had so much catching up to do.

Then I was eating. Potatoes, brussels sprouts, meat and gravy, and for dessert, pudding with currant juice and an apple!

"I have never seen anyone eat so intensely," one of the nurses from a nearby table commented. I cared not. With every mouthful of food I could feel new life streaming into my body. I had once said to Betsie in camp, "When we get home we shall have to eat carefully, taking only small amounts at a time until our stomachs are ready."

"No," Betsie had said, "God will see to it that we shall be able to retain all sorts of food right from the start."

She was right. How wonderfully good that food did taste. I shall remember that meal as long as I live.

Then came a warm bath. They could hardly get me out of it. My poor sick skin, damaged by lice, seemed to grow softer the moment I slipped into that warm tub.

Afterwards they dressed me. Several of the ex-leaders of the Netherlands Girls' Clubs were among the nurses—girls that I had known before the war. They dressed me up as if I were a doll. One of them had lingerie, another shoes, another a dress and pins for my hair. I felt so happy that I laughed for sheer joy. How sweet they were to me.

These young women had been trained in kindness. How opposite from the concentration camp where men had been trained in cruelty.

I was then taken to a cozy bedroom so I could rest. How lovely was the combination of colors. I was starved for color. In the concentration camp everything was gray. But here in Holland the colors were vivid again. My eyes could not seem to get enough to satisfy them.

And the bed! Delightfully soft and clean with thick woolen blankets. One of the little nurses brought an extra pillow and tucked it under my swollen feet. I wanted to laugh and cry at the same time.

On a shelf was a row of books. Outside I heard the whistle of a boat on a canal and the merry sound of little children calling to one another as they skipped down the street. Far in the distance I heard the sound of a choir singing and then, oh, joy, the chimes of a carillon. I closed my eyes and tears wet my pillow. Only to those who have been in prison does freedom have such great meaning.

Later that afternoon one of the nurses took me up to her room where for the first time in many months I heard the sound of a radio. Gunther Ramin was playing a Bach trio. The organ tones flowed about and enveloped me. I sat on the floor beside a chair and sobbed, unashamedly. It was too much joy. I had rarely cried during all those months of suffering. Now I could not control myself. My life had been given back as a gift. Harmony, beauty, colors, and music. Only those who have suffered as I, and have returned, can fully understand what I mean. I knew my life had been given back for a purpose. I was no longer my own. This time I had been ransomed and released. I knew that God would soon be sending me out as a tramp for the Lord. But right now, He was letting me enjoy the luxury of thanksgiving. I was drinking from a fountain I knew would never run dry—the fountain of praise.

One of the first places I visited, after my release from the concentration camp, was the *Grote Kerk* in Haarlem. Since it was so close to where I had grown up in the Beje, I counted it as much of an old friend as I did the watchmaker's shop.

"May I show you through?" the old usher said as he met me at the door.

"If it is all right," I said. "I would like to be alone."

He nodded, understandingly, and disappeared into the shadows of the sanctuary. I walked over the gravestones that formed the floor of the ancient building. My shoes made a strange, scraping sound that gave forth a hollow echo in the empty cathedral. I remembered the many times I had played here as a child.

My cousin Dot was my closest friend. She was the youngest daughter of my Uncle Arnold who was the previous usher—the caretaker—of the *Grote Kerk*.

Dot and I did everything together, but our favorite pastime was to play hide-and-seek in the big church. There were many wonderful places to hide: pews, old doors giving entrance to spiral staircases, and many closets. There was a world-famous pipe organ in the cathedral and sometimes when there was a concert, Uncle Arnold would allow members of his family to come into the church, sit on a wooden bench without a back and lean against the cold, moist stone wall to hear the magnificent music.

The cathedral was a symphony in gray tones during the day, both inside and outside. In the evening, when the gas lamps were lit on the side transepts, we could see the pillars and ceilings pointing upwards, as the shadows danced about in a mysterious glow.

Only one place was absolutely "off limits" as we played hide-and-seek. That was the old pulpit. We never went there, but for the rest—what a playground that old church was! When we shouted, the echo would ring from transept to transept and our laughter never, never seemed to be sacrilegious. Unlike some of the stern adults who sometimes frowned on our frolic, I had always thought that the laughter of little children in an empty cathedral was the most beautiful of all hymns of praise. And so we grew up, knowing only a God who enjoyed our presence as we skipped, ran, and played through this building which was built for His glory.

One afternoon we played very late and before we knew it, the darkness of the cathedral swallowed us up. I looked around. Through the beautiful stained-glass windows I saw a little light coming in from the streets around. Only the silhouettes of the Gothic pillars stood out in the darkness as they reached upward and upward.

"Let's go home," whispered Dot. "I'm scared."

I was not. Slowly I went to the usher's door that opened out to where Uncle Arnold lived. There was a Presence that comforted me, a deep peace in my heart.

Even in the darkness, smelling the dust and dampness of the church building, I knew that the "Light of the World" was present. Was the Lord preparing me for some time in the future when I would need to know that His light is victorious over all darkness?

It was forty-five years later. Betsie and I walked to the square where roll call was being held in the concentration camp. It was still early, before dawn. The head of our barracks was so cruel that she had sent us out into the very cold outdoors a full hour too early.

Betsie's hand was in mine. We went to the square by a different way from the rest of our barracks-mates. We were three as we walked with the Lord and talked with Him. Betsie spoke. Then I talked. Then the Lord spoke. How? I do not know. But both of us understood. It was the same Presence I had felt years before in the old cathedral in Haarlem.

The brilliant early morning stars were our only light. The cold winter air was so clear. We could faintly see the outlines of the barracks, the crematorium, the gas chamber, and the towers where the guards were standing with loaded machine guns.

"Isn't this a bit of heaven!" Betsie had said. "And, Lord, this is a small fore-taste. One day we will see You face-to-face, but thank You that even now You are giving us the joy of walking and talking with You."

Heaven in the midst of hell. Light in the midst of darkness. What a security!

4. A Song in the Night

THE WAR WAS over. Even before I left the concentration camp, I knew I would be busy helping those who had lost their way. Now I found myself starting just such a work in Bloemendaal. It was more than a home for the homeless; it was a refuge for those who had lost their way spiritually as well as physically.

Yet, because I had lived so close to death, looking it in the face day after day, I often felt like a stranger among my own people—many of whom looked upon money, honor of men, and success as the important issues of life. Standing in front of a crematorium, knowing that any day could be your day, gives one a different perspective on life. The words of an old German motto kept flashing in my mind:

What I spent, I had; what I saved, I lost; what I gave, I have.

How well I understood the feeling of the artist who painted the picture of the corpse of a once wealthy man and entitled it, *Sic transit gloria mundi*—So passes the glory of this world. The material things of this world no longer excited me— nor would they ever again.

It was during this time that I visited Haarlem, the town where I had spent more than fifty years of my life. It was late in the evening as I walked through the streets. Waiting before a traffic light, I had a strange feeling that the people should fall in line five by five, as in the concentration camp. Instead, they chatted about insignificant things and when the light changed, they moved on without anyone shouting at them.

Walking the streets that night, however, I felt growing in me a tremendous desire to tell all men, especially those in bondage to material things, of the One who can set us free from all prisons: Jesus.

It was after midnight when I finally made my way to the Barteljorisstraat. There were few streetlights but the moon and many stars were visible above the ancient rooftops of the familiar houses on the short street. I paused in front of the Beje on the corner of the small alley that came out in the midst of the street. I let my fingertips run across the door of the watchmaker's shop. Even though the Beje was no longer my home, it was still part of my heart. Little did I dream that one day it would be set aside as a museum to commemorate my family and the hiding place of those precious Jews who had been saved from certain death at the hands of the Nazis.

I stood alone in the darkness, allowing myself the sweet luxury of remembering. How often had I put the shutters before the show window. Through this door I had walked on my first day of school, almost fifty years ago. Oh, what an unwilling pupil I had been, crying in fear of leaving the dear old house whose warmth in winter had protected me, whose windows had kept out the rain and mist, whose cheery fire had welcomed me and others in the family each night after the dinner dishes had been put away. Yet my father, knowing my fear, took me by the hand and led me through this door and out into the world of learning, into an unknown world of teachers and classrooms.

Now Father was dead. Only my Heavenly Father remained. I ran my hand over the door, letting my fingers explore the cracks. It was no longer my hiding place. Others lived here now, and the world was my classroom, and my only security came in knowing that underneath were the Everlasting Arms. How thankful I was for my Heavenly Father's strong hand around mine.

I looked into the small alley. It was almost pitch dark. I strained my ears, and in the far off recesses of my heart, could imagine the voices of Father, Betsie, and the others. Had it been only a year ago? It seemed like centuries. "What an honor," Father had said, "to give my life for God's chosen people, the Jews."

I felt the wall with my hands, then gently pressed my face against the cold stones. No, I was not dreaming. It was reality. The old Beje, the old hiding place, was no longer mine. Ravensbruck had taught me much I needed to learn. My hiding place was now in Jesus alone. Even though I was wandering the streets at midnight in a town that used to be my home but was now only a town, I knew the Presence of the Heavenly Father.

Suddenly the cathedral started to play its nostalgic chimes. Day and night through my lifetime I had heard the beautiful music from the *Grote Kerk*. It was not a dream, as I had often experienced in the concentration camp. It was real. I walked out of the shadows of the alley and made my way down the Barteljorisstraat to the *Grote Markt*. I paused to look at the cathedral which was silhouetted against the dark sky, framed into place by a million twinkling stars.

"Thank You, Jesus, that I am alive," I said.

In my heart I heard Him reply, "Lo, I am with you always, even unto the end of the world" (Matthew 28:30).

I stayed there for long minutes as the hands on the face of the great clock moved toward the hour. Then the chimes in the cathedral tower pealed forth once again, this time with the sounds of Luther's famous hymn "A Mighty Fortress Is Our God." I listened and heard myself singing the hymn, not in Dutch, but in German: *"Ein' feste Burg ist unser Gott."*

"How like You, Lord," I half-chuckled, "that You would remind me of Your grace by letting me hear a German hymn."

A policeman passed, looked at me, and spoke a friendly word.

I said, "Good-night, Policeman. A mighty fortress is our God."

I was free.

*By faith Abraham, when he was called to
go out into a place which he should after
receive for an inheritance, obeyed; and he
went out, not knowing whither he went.*

Hebrews 11:8

5. A Great Discovery

WHEN MY PARENTS were married, many years ago, they claimed Psalm
32:8 as their "life verse," the promise which they felt was God's assurance for them.

I will instruct thee and teach thee in the way which thou shalt go: I will guide thee
with mine eye.

Now that Father and Mother were gone, this promise became the special directive for my life as well—God's pledge to guide me in all my journeys. It was especially needed as I set out for my first trip to America.

The war had only been over a short time, and many Europeans wanted to go to
America. However, few, if any, wanted to go for the same reason I did—to carry
the Gospel as a missionary to the Americans. For all of us, however, it was the
same story when we applied for passage to America: "It is impossible to obtain
papers."

I prayed, "Lord, if it is Your will that I go to America, then You must provide
the necessary papers."

I soon discovered that man's importunity is God's opportunity. He uses our
problems as building materials for His miracles. I began to understand that this
was my first lesson in learning to trust Him completely, my first steps on the path
to complete dependence on, and obedience to, His guidance. How much I had to
learn!

At last all my papers were approved, except the final one—the most important
one. I sat alone on a hard wooden bench in the hall of the Immigration Office in

The Hague. Everyone coming out of the office warned those of us waiting in the hall, "That fellow in there is as hard as flint. He passes no one."

"Lord," I prayed silently, "I am willing to go or stay. It is up to You."

"Hello, there! Don't we know each other?" It was the voice of a middle-aged woman standing in front of me. I looked up into her face, trying vainly to recognize her.

"You're Corrie ten Boom," she laughed. "I'm one of your cousins and this is Jan, my husband. I haven't seen you for years, and of course, Jan has never seen you since we were married only six years ago."

"Are you trying to go to America, also?" I asked.

"Oh no," she laughed. "I'm visiting Jan. He has his office in this building."

"Then perhaps you can help me," I said, shaking his hand. I told him my story.

He was polite but said, "I'm sorry. I would like to be of service to my brand-new cousin, but that's not my department. However, if you have trouble, ring me up." He gave me his telephone number and we shook hands again as he left.

I continued to wait. The "man of flint" left the office for coffee and a young clerk took his place. Then it was my turn.

"You had better wait until my boss returns," the clerk said when I told him where I wanted to go and why.

My shoulders sagged. "I cannot wait any longer. Won't you please call this number?" I handed him the card that Jan had handed me earlier.

I prayed while he placed the call. Moments later he hung up. "All is arranged. I am approving your passport. You may make your trip to America."

From there I traveled to Amsterdam to try to arrange passage on a ship of the Holland-America Line. However, another mountain loomed before me. The agent told me they would only put my name on the waiting list. "We will notify you in about a year," he said.

"A year! But I must go now." The agent just shrugged his shoulders and returned to his work.

Disappointed, I returned to the square in the center of the city. God had told me to go to America—of that I was certain. All my papers were in order. God had seen to that also. Now it was up to Him to move this mountain. Glancing across the street I noticed a sign: AMERICAN EXPRESS COMPANY. Stepping into the office I inquired, "Have you passenger accommodations on any of your freighters to America?"

The old clerk looked over his glasses and said, "You may sail tomorrow, Madam, if your papers are in order."

"Oh, tomorrow is too sudden," I said, hardly believing what I heard. "What about next week?"

"That, too, can be arranged," he said. "We don't have very many women your age who ship out on freighters. But if you are willing, so are we."

Several weeks before I had met an American businessman who was visiting relatives in Holland. When I told him of my plans to visit America he tried to discourage me. "It's not easy to make one's way in America," he said.

"I believe you," I told him. "But God has directed me and I must obey."

He then gave me two checks, one small and one larger. "If you need it, use it," he said. "You can repay me later." I tucked them away for safekeeping.

So I arrived in New York as a missionary to America. I was only allowed to bring in fifty dollars, and of course, I knew no one. However, I found my way to the YWCA where I found a room and a place to leave my bags.

I had the address of a group of Hebrew-Christian immigrants who were meeting in New York. I made a phone call and they invited me to come speak. Since they were German, I could not use the English lectures I had prepared on board the ship, but had to speak to them in their native language. It was better, perhaps, for my English was rather hard to understand.

At the end of the week, after wandering around the city in a rather helpless daze, I went downstairs in the YWCA to pay my bill. The clerk looked at me sympathetically. "I am sorry, but our accommodations are so restricted that we cannot allow you to stay here any longer. One week is our limit. Do you have a forwarding address?"

"Yes. I just don't know what it is, yet."

"I don't understand," she said, perplexed.

"God has another room for me," I explained. "He just hasn't told me what the address is. But I am not worried. He led me through Ravensbruck, He will surely see me through America as well."

Suddenly the clerk remembered. "By the way, a letter came for you."

Strange, I thought, as she handed me the envelope. *How could I receive a letter? No one knows where I am staying.* But there it was. I read it hurriedly and then turned to the clerk. "My forwarding address will be this house on 190th Street."

"But why didn't you tell me that before?" she asked.

"I didn't know. It was in this letter. A woman that I do not know writes, 'I heard you speak to the Jewish congregation. I am aware that it is almost impossible to get a room in New York City. My son happens to be in Europe, so you are welcome to use his room as long as you are in New York.'"

The lady at the desk was more amazed than I. However, I reasoned, perhaps she had not experienced miracles before.

I rode the subway to 190th Street. The house at the address was a large, multistoried building occupied by many families. I found the correct apartment at the end of a hall, but no one was home. Certainly my hostess did not expect her invitation to be an eleventh-hour answer to my problem. I arranged myself among my suitcases on the floor, and leaning against the wall, soon began to drift off to sleep.

In those last moments before sleep took over, my mind drifted back to Ravensbruck. I could feel Betsie's bony hand touching my face. It was pitch-black in Barracks 28 where seven hundred other prisoners were asleep. Each day hundreds of women died and their bodies were fed to the ovens. Betsie had grown so weak, and we both knew that death was always moments away.

"Are you awake, Corrie?" Her weak voice sounded so far away.

"Yes, you wakened me."

"I had to. I need to tell you what God has said to me."

"Shhh. We hinder the sleep of the girls around us. Let us lie with our faces toward each other."

The cot was so small. We could only lie like spoons in a box, our knees bumping against the knees of the other. We used our two coats as covers along with the thin black blanket provided by the Nazis.

I pulled the coat over our heads so we could whisper and not be heard. "God showed me," Betsie said, "that after the war we must give to the Germans that which they now try to take away from us: our love for Jesus."

Betsie's breath was coming in short gasps. She was so weak, her body wasted away until there was nothing but her thin skin stretched over brittle bones. "Oh, Betsie," I exclaimed, "you mean if we live we will have to return to Germany?"

Betsie patted my hand under the blanket. "Corrie, there is so much bitterness. We must tell them that the Holy Spirit will fill their hearts with God's love."

I remembered Romans 5:5. Only that morning some of the women in the barracks had huddled with us in the corner while I read from our precious Bible. But I shuddered. Germany. If I were ever released from this horrible place could I ever return to Germany?

Betsie's weak voice whispered on. "This concentration camp here at Ravensbruck has been used to destroy many, many lives. There are many other such camps throughout Germany. After the war they will not have use for them anymore. I have prayed that the Lord will give us one in Germany. We will use it to build up lives."

No, I thought. *I will return to my simple job as a watchmaker in Holland and never again set my boot across the border.*

Betsie's voice was quivering so I could barely understand her. "The Germans are the most wounded of all the people in the world. Think of that young girl guard who swore in such filthy language yesterday. She was only seventeen or eighteen years old, but did you see how she was beating that poor old woman with a whip? What a job there is to do after the war."

I found a place where I could put my hand. It was such a stupid problem, I thought, yet it was a small cot and it was difficult to position my hands and arms. My hand rested on Betsie's left side, just on her heart. I felt her ribs—only skin and bones. How long would she be able to live? Her heart was fluttering inside the rib cage like a dying bird, as though it would stop any moment.

I rested and thought. How close to God's heart was Betsie. Only God could see in such circumstances the possibility for ministry in the future—ministry to those who even now were preparing to kill us. Most of all, to see in such a place as Ravensbruck an opportunity to bless and build up the lives of our enemies. Yes, only the Lord Jesus could have given Betsie such a vision.

"Must we live with them in Germany?" I whispered.

"For a while," Betsie answered. "Then we will travel the whole world bringing the Gospel to all—our friends as well as our enemies."

"To *all* the world? But that will take much money."

"Yes, but God will provide," Betsie said. "We must do nothing else but bring the Gospel and He will take care of us. After all, He owns the cattle on a thousand hills. If we need money we will just ask the Father to sell a few cows."

I was beginning to catch the vision. "What a privilege," I said softly, "to travel the world and be used by the Lord Jesus."

But Betsie did not answer. She had fallen asleep. Three days later she was dead.

Going to bed the night after Betsie died was one of the most difficult tasks of my life. The one electric light bulb was screwed into the ceiling toward the front of the room. Only a feeble ray reached my narrow cot. I lay in the semidarkness—thinking—remembering—trying to reconstruct Betsie's vision.

There was a shuffle of feet near my bed and I looked up. A Russian woman, thin and gaunt, was shuffling down the aisle between the beds looking for a place to sleep. The Russians were not received kindly and everyone turned away. As she neared me I saw the hunted look in her eyes. How awful to be in prison and not have even a place to sleep!

Betsie's place beside me was vacant. I motioned to the woman and threw back the blanket for her. She crept in, gratefully, and stretched out beside me. We were sharing the same pillow and with our faces so close I wanted to speak. But I did not know her language.

"Jesoes Christoes?" I asked softly.

"Oh!" she exclaimed. Quickly making the sign of the cross, she threw her arms about me and kissed me.

She who had been my sister for fifty-two years, with whom I had shared so much of weal and woe, had left me. A Russian woman now claimed my love. And there would be others, too, who would be my sisters and brothers in Christ all across the world.

I was awakened by a gentle hand shaking my shoulder. It was after midnight and I realized I had fallen asleep in the midst of my suitcases, sitting on the floor, and leaning against the wall of the hallway.

"Come," my new friend said softly as she opened the door, "the floor is no place for a child of the King." I rose from my cramped, huddled position and entered her apartment. I was her guest for the next five weeks.

As the weeks passed, however, I realized I was running out of money. Jan ten Have (the publisher of my little book in Holland) was visiting New York. He helped me as much as he could, and I spent most of my time looking up addresses given me in Holland. The Americans were polite and some of them were interested, but none wanted me to come to speak. They were all busy with their own things. Some even said I should have stayed in Holland.

As the weeks slipped by, I found more and more resistance to my ministry. No one was interested in a middle-aged spinster woman from Holland who wanted to preach. "Why did you come to America?" people began to ask.

"God directed me. All I could do was obey."

"That's nonsense," they answered. "There is no such thing as direct guidance from God. Experience proves we must use our common sense. If you are here and out of money, then it is your fault, not God's."

I tried to argue back in God's defense. "But God's guidance is even more important than common sense. I am certain He told me to bring His message to America. I can declare that the deepest darkness is outshone by the light of Jesus."

"We have ministers to tell us such things," was the reply.

"Certainly, but I can tell from my experience in a concentration camp that what such ministers say is true."

"It would have been better for you to have remained in Holland. We don't need any more preachers. Too many Europeans come to America. They should be stopped."

I was growing discouraged. Perhaps the Americans were right. Perhaps I should return to Holland and go back to my job as a watchmaker. My money was gone, and all that remained was the second check given me by the American businessman. Yet I was hesitant to cash it without his approval. I found his address and arrived in an imposing business office in Manhattan. Only this time his face was not as friendly as it had been in Holland.

"Do you mind if I cash your second check?" I asked.

"How do I know if you can return the money?" he asked. "You've been in America five weeks and have found there is no work. I think it would be better if you simply returned the check."

Mustering all my courage I said, "I am sure God has work for me here. I am in His will, and will somehow return all your money."

He snorted, tore up the check and then wrote out another—for a much smaller amount.

I was embarrassed and humbled. I had money in Holland—a balance left from my first book and a small income from the business I had sold. But these funds could not be brought to America. I returned to my room and closed the door. It was time for a long consultation with my Heavenly Father.

Kneeling beside the bed I prayed, "Father, You must help me out. If I must borrow money to return to Holland people will say, 'There, you see, the promises of the Bible are not real. Direct guidance does not exist.' Father, for Your honor's sake, You must help me out."

I fell weeping across the bed. Then, slowly, like a deep realization that dawns in a person's heart, the answer came: "Do not worry about My honor. I will take care of that. In days to come you will give thanks for these days in New York."

A great ocean separated me from my homeland. I had no money. Nobody wanted to hear my lectures. All I had was an inner word from God that He was guiding me. Was it enough? All I could do was press on—and on—and on—for His Name's sake.

Before going to sleep I opened my Bible, my constant companion. My eyes fell on a verse from the Psalms, "The Lord taketh pleasure . . . in those that hope in his mercy" (147:11). It was a thin web—a tiny filament—stretching from heaven to my little room on 190th Street in New York. I fell asleep holding on to it with all my strength.

The next day I attended a Dutch service in a New York church. Dr. Barkay Wolf was the speaker and many Hollanders were present, meeting afterward for coffee in the vestry. The Reverend Burggraaff, who had baptized our Canadian-born princess, was presented to me.

"ten Boom," he mused when he heard my name. "I often tell the story of a nurse by that name. She experienced a miracle in a concentration camp with a bottle of vitamins that never ran out. I tell it to prove that God still performs miracles today, as in Bible times. Do you happen to know that nurse? Is she related to you?"

I felt joy springing in my heart. "She is not a nurse," I replied. "She is a watch-maker. And you are looking at her. It was I who had that experience in 1944."

"Then you must come with me to Staten Island and tell your story to my congregation," he exclaimed.

I spent the next five days in this pleasant parsonage with Rev. and Mrs. Burggraaff. What a joy to eat good Dutch food again. I had been trying to find out how long one could exist on Nedick's ten-cent breakfast which consisted of a cup of coffee, a doughnut, and a small glass of orange juice, eaten while standing at a counter. Now God was resupplying me, not only with food, but with new hope. I could see that the Lord does take pleasure in those that hope in His mercy!

A week later I returned to Manhattan. Walking down the street I saw a church with a notice on the door. Drawing closer I saw it was an invitation to attend the Lord's Supper next Sunday morning, Easter.

Following the service, the minister gave me the address of Irving Harris, the editor of a Christian magazine called *The Evangel.* He encouraged me to go by and see him.

I did. In fact, the very next morning I went up to his office and talked to him. "I know I am walking in the way God has led me," I told him, "but so many declare there is no such thing as direct guidance."

"Pay no attention to them," Mr. Harris advised. "The Bible contains many promises that God will lead those who obey Him. Have you ever heard of a good shepherd who does not lead his sheep?"

Mr. Harris asked if I had any material which he might use in his magazine. I gave him a copy of one of my lectures and told him to use as much as he could.

"There is one drawback," he explained. "We cannot pay. This paper exists only to spread the Gospel, not for financial profit."

"Wonderful!" I exclaimed. "I am in the presence of an American who sees money in its proper perspective."

Mr. Harris gave me a name and address in Washington, D.C. He strongly urged me to make an appointment and go down to see Mr. Abraham Vereide. I knew nothing of Mr. Vereide at the time, although I have since discovered he was one of the great Christian leaders of America. I was suspicious, afraid I was being shrugged off again. But I felt I could trust Mr. Harris and followed through, taking a chance and making a phone call to Washington.

Mr. Vereide received me graciously, inviting me to Washington as his guest. At dinner three other guests were present, all professors who plied me with questions throughout the evening. I felt like a schoolgirl who had been invited out by her headmistress. My English was crude and my mistakes seemed more glaring than ever before. How could I compete with such learned men?

The next afternoon, however, I was asked to address a group of women. They asked specifically that I share my prison experiences with them. This time I felt at home. Certainly I could tell them what the Lord had done in my life.

They received me warmly—enthusiastically—in fact. "Corrie," one of the ladies said afterwards, "this is your message. Share it wherever you go." She then handed me a check that enabled me to return all the money I had borrowed in New York.

Suddenly the tables were turned. Instead of no work, I had to guard against overwork. Abraham Vereide's recommendation brought in calls from everyplace, asking me to come and share my testimony. The calls came from villages and towns, as well as from the big cities. I spoke in churches, prisons, universities, schools, and clubs. For almost ten months I traveled America, everywhere telling the story that Jesus Christ is reality, even in darkest days. I told them that He is the answer to all the problems in the hearts of men and nations. I knew it was so, because of what He had done for me.

As the year drew to a close I began to sense God wanted me to return to Europe. I was homesick for Holland, but this time I felt Him leading me in another direction—Germany. The one land I dreaded.

When I left the German concentration camp I said, "I'll go anywhere God sends me, but I hope never to Germany." Now I understand that was a statement of disobedience. F. B. Meyer said, "God does not fill with His Holy Spirit those who believe in the fullness of the Spirit, or those who desire Him, but those who obey Him." More than anything I desired to be filled with God's Spirit. I knew I had no choice but to go to Germany.

6. *Music From Broken Chords*

THE GERMANS HAD lost face in defeat. Their homes had been destroyed and when they heard the enormity of Hitler's crimes (which many Germans knew nothing about) they were filled with despair. As they returned to their Fatherland they felt they had nothing to live for.

Friends in Darmstadt helped me rent a former concentration camp to use as a home for displaced persons. It was not big, but there was room for about one hundred sixty refugees and soon it was full with a long waiting list. I worked closely with the refugee program of the Lutheran Church (*"das Evangelische Hilfswerk"*) in the Darmstadt camp. Barbed wire disappeared. Flowers, light-colored paint and God's love in the hearts of the people changed a cruel camp into a refuge where people would find the way back to life again.

Marienschwestern, the Lutheran Sisterhood of Mary, whose members had dedicated their lives to serving the Lord and spiritually hungry people, assisted with the children's and women's work. Pastors and members of different churches helped by building homes. I was traveling and helping raise money for the work.

The camp was crowded. Some rooms were jammed with several families. Noise and bedlam were everywhere as families, many without men because they had been killed in the war, tried to carry on the most basic forms of living. Often I would walk through the camp talking with the lonely, defeated people and trying to bring them hope and cheer.

One afternoon I spotted an elderly woman huddled in the corner of a big room. She was obviously new to the camp. She had been put in the big room along with three other families and told she could set up housekeeping in the corner. There she crouched, like a whipped child, her faded, worn dress pulled tightly around her frail, wasted body. I could sense she was distressed by the bedlam of all the crying children, but most of all defeated by life itself.

I went to her, sat beside her on the floor, and asked who she was. I learned she had been a professor of music at the Dresden Conservatory before the war. Now she had nothing.

I asked her to tell me about her life, knowing that sometimes it helps just to have someone willing to listen. She told me that a minister in a nearby town had given her permission to play his piano. She had also learned of several farmers' children nearby who wanted to receive music lessons. But the minister's home was miles away and the only way to get there was on foot. It all seemed so hopeless.

"You were a professor of piano?" I asked excitedly. "I am a great lover of Germany's master musician, Johann Sebastian Bach."

For an instant her eyes lighted up. "Would you care to accompany me to the minister's home?" she asked with great dignity. "I would be most happy to play for you."

It was a great privilege, and even though we had to walk many miles, I sensed God was doing something special.

She seated herself at the battered piano. I looked at the instrument. Even though it had been saved from the bombing it had not been protected from the rain. The strings were exposed through the warped frame and I could see they were rusted. Some were broken and curled around the others. The pedals had long been broken off and the keyboard was almost entirely without ivory. If any of the notes played it would be a miracle.

Looking up the old woman said, "What would you like me to play?"

Silently I prayed, knowing that failure at this moment could crush her forever. Then to my own amazement, I heard myself saying, "Would you please play the 'Chromatic Phantasy' of Bach?"

I was aghast. Why had I picked one of the most difficult of all piano pieces for this old woman to play on such a ruined instrument? Yet the moment I said it, I saw a light flicker behind her eyes and a slight, knowing smile played across her tired face. She nodded, and with great finesse, put her fingers on the broken keyboard.

I could hardly believe my ears. From that damp, battered old piano flowed the beautiful music of Bach as her skilled fingers raced up and down the broken, chipped keys. Tears came to my eyes and ran down my cheeks as I thought of wounded Germany, left with only the remnants of the past, still able to play beautiful music. Such a nation will survive to create again, I thought.

As the notes of Bach faded from the air the words of an old Gospel song, written by the blind composer Fanny J. Crosby, came to mind:

Down in the human heart, crush'd by the tempter,
Feelings lie buried that grace can restore;
Touched by a loving heart, wakened by kindness
Chords that were broken will vibrate once more.

As we walked back to the former concentration camp my companion had a new spring in her step. "It has been many years since I played the 'Chromatic Phantasy,'" she said. "Once I was a concert pianist and many of my pupils are now outstanding musicians. I had a beautiful home in Dresden that was destroyed by the bombs. I had to flee and was not able to take one thing with me."

"Oh, no, you are wrong," I said. "You took with you your most prized possession."

"And what is that?" she asked, shocked.

"Your music. For that which is in your heart can never be taken from you."

Then I told her of what I had learned in Ravensbruck, of Betsie's vision, and that God's love still stands when all else has fallen. "In the concentration camp they took all we had, even made us stand naked for hours at a time without rest, but they could not take Jesus from my heart. Ask Jesus to come into your life. He will give you riches no man can take away from you."

We returned to the camp in silence, but I knew the Holy Spirit was pricking her heart, reminding her of the things that man cannot snatch from us. Soon it was time for me to leave the camp and move on to other fields. The day I left she was sitting in that same corner of the room. A boy was playing his mouth organ, a baby was crying, there were the sounds of shouts and the pounding of a hammer against a wooden crate. The room was full of discord and disharmonic noises, but her eyes were closed and there was a faint smile on her face. I knew God had given her something that no one could ever take from her—ever again.

After the war, Germany was filled with wounds and scars—not all of them on the surface. In one tiny cubicle in the camp at Darmstadt, I found a German lawyer. He was sitting miserably in a wheelchair, the stumps of his legs poking out from under a lap blanket. He was filled with bitterness, hatred, and self-pity. He told me he had once been an active member of his Lutheran church and as a boy had rung the church bell in the village where he lived. Now the horrible injustice of war had taken his legs, and he was bitter against God and man.

I felt attracted to him since some of his experiences were similar to mine. One morning I made a special trip to his room to tell him something of my life.

I found him sitting in his wheelchair, staring at a blank wall. His face was gray, his eyes lifeless. I never was one for introductions so I got right to the point of my visit.

"The only way to get rid of bitterness is to surrender it," I said.

He turned slowly and looked at me. "What do you know about bitterness?" he asked. "You still have your legs."

"Let me tell you a story," I said. "In Holland, during the war, a man came to me begging me to help him liberate his wife. I felt compassion for him and gave him all my money. I also convinced my friends to do the same. But the man was a quisling, a traitor. The only reason he came to me was to trap me so he could have me arrested. Not only did he betray me, but he betrayed my entire family and friends. We were all sent to prison where three members of my family died. You ask me about bitterness and hatred. You only hate circumstances, but I hated a man. Sitting in the prison in my homeland, waiting to be transferred to a concentration camp in Germany, hatred and bitterness filled my heart. I wanted that man to die. I know what it is like to hate. That is why I can understand you."

The lawyer turned his chair to face me. He was listening. "So, you have hated also. What do you suggest I do about my hate?"

"What I have to say is of no importance. Let me tell you what the Son of God had to say. 'For if you forgive men their trespasses, your Heavenly Father will also forgive you. But if you forgive not men their trespasses, neither will your Father forgive your trespasses.' (*See* Matthew 6:14, 15.) If we forgive other people, our hearts are made fit to receive forgiveness."

The lawyer shifted uneasily in his wheelchair. I could see the muscles in his neck stand out as he pushed with his hands to change position. "When we repent," I continued, "God forgives us and cleanses us. That is what I did, believing that if I confessed my sin God would be faithful and just to cleanse my sin and forgive me from all unrighteousness."

The lawyer looked at me and shook his head. "That is easy to say, but my hatred is too deep to have it washed away."

"No deeper than mine," I said. "Yet when I confessed it, not only did Jesus take it away, He filled me with love—even the ability to love my enemy."

"You mean you actually loved the man who betrayed you and who was responsible for the death of your family?"

I nodded. "After the war, when that man was sentenced to death, I corresponded with him and God used me to show him the way of salvation before he was executed."

The lawyer shook his head. "What a miracle! What a miracle! You mean Jesus can do that to a person? I shall have to give this much thought."

Since I have learned not to push a person beyond where God has left him, I bade my friend good-by and returned to my room.

A year later I was in Darmstadt again. My friends had given this man a car with special fixtures so he could drive without legs. He met me at the train station to bring me to the camp. As I got in the car, he laughed at my startled look.

"You taught me that Jesus is victor," he said. "Now surely you are not afraid to drive with a man who has no legs."

"You are right," I answered. "I shall not be afraid. I am so glad to see you again. How are you?"

"Fine. I must tell you at the very beginning that I have surrendered my bitterness to God. I repented and the Lord did just as you said. He forgave me and filled my heart with His love. Now I am working in the refugee camp and am praising God that He can use even a legless man if he is surrendered."

He paused, and then continued. "But there is something I must know. After you forgave your enemies, was it settled once and for all?"

"Oh no," I answered. "Just this month I had a sad experience with friends who behaved like enemies. They promised something but did not keep their promise. In fact, they took great advantage of me. However, I surrendered my bitterness to the Lord, asked forgiveness and He took it away."

We were bouncing over a bumpy road but the lawyer was more intent on me than his driving. "Was the bitterness gone for good, then?"

"No, just the next night, at four o'clock, I awoke and my heart was filled with bitterness again. I thought, *How could my dear friend behave as she did?* Again I brought it to the Lord. He filled my heart with His love. But the next night it came back again. I was so discouraged. God had used me often to help people to love their enemies, and I could always give my testimony about what He had done in my life; but now I felt defeated.

"Then I remembered Ephesians 6:10–20 where Paul describes the 'armour of God.' He said that even after you have come to a standstill, still stand your ground. I was at a standstill, so I decided to stand my ground and the bitterness and resentment fell away before me.

"Corrie ten Boom without the Lord Jesus cannot be victorious. I need the Lord every moment. And I have learned that I am absolutely dependent on Him. Because of this He has made me rich."

We were just arriving at the refugee camp and my lawyer friend parked before the building, turned off the motor, and looked at me with a grin. "I am glad to hear that," he said. "For sometimes my old bitterness returns. Now I shall just stand my ground, claim the victory of Jesus over fear and resentment, and love even when I don't want to."

My friend had learned well the secret of victory. It comes through obedience.

*. . . we feel this warm love everywhere
within us because God has given us the
Holy Spirit to fill our hearts with his love.*

Romans 5:5 LB

7. *Love Your Enemy*

IT WAS IN a church in Munich that I saw him—a balding, heavyset man in a gray overcoat, a brown felt hat clutched between his hands. People were filing out of the basement room where I had just spoken, moving along the rows of wooden chairs to the door at the rear. It was 1947 and I had come from Holland to defeated Germany with the message that God forgives.

It was the truth they needed most to hear in that bitter, bombed-out land, and I gave them my favorite mental picture. Maybe because the sea is never far from a Hollander's mind, I liked to think that that's where forgiven sins were thrown. "When we confess our sins," I said, "God casts them into the deepest ocean, gone forever. And even though I cannot find a Scripture for it, I believe God then places a sign out there that says, NO FISHING ALLOWED."

The solemn faces stared back at me, not quite daring to believe. There were never questions after a talk in Germany in 1947. People stood up in silence, in silence collected their wraps, in silence left the room.

And that's when I saw him, working his way forward against the others. One moment I saw the overcoat and the brown hat; the next, a blue uniform and a visored cap with its skull and crossbones. It came back with a rush: the huge room with its harsh overhead lights; the pathetic pile of dresses and shoes in the center of the floor; the shame of walking naked past this man. I could see my sister's frail form ahead of me, ribs sharp beneath the parchment skin. *Betsie, how thin you were!*

The place was Ravensbruck and the man who was making his way forward had been a guard—one of the most cruel guards.

217

Now he was in front of me, hand thrust out: "A fine message, Fraulein! How good it is to know that, as you say, all our sins are at the bottom of the sea!"

And I, who had spoken so glibly of forgiveness, fumbled in my pocketbook rather than take that hand. He would not remember me, of course—how could he remember one prisoner among those thousands of women?

But I remembered him and the leather crop swinging from his belt. I was face-to-face with one of my captors and my blood seemed to freeze.

"You mentioned Ravensbruck in your talk," he was saying. "I was a guard there." No, he did not remember me.

"But since that time," he went on, "I have become a Christian. I know that God has forgiven me for the cruel things I did there, but I would like to hear it from your lips as well. Fraulein,"—again the hand came out—"will you forgive me?"

And I stood there—I whose sins had again and again to be forgiven—and could not forgive. Betsie had died in that place—could he erase her slow terrible death simply for the asking?

It could not have been many seconds that he stood there—hand held out—but to me it seemed hours as I wrestled with the most difficult thing I had ever had to do.

For I had to do it—I knew that. The message that God forgives has a prior condition: that we forgive those who have injured us. "If you do not forgive men their trespasses," Jesus says, "neither will your Father in heaven forgive your trespasses."

I knew it not only as a commandment of God, but as a daily experience. Since the end of the war I had had a home in Holland for victims of Nazi brutality. Those who were able to forgive their former enemies were able also to return to the outside world and rebuild their lives, no matter what the physical scars. Those who nursed their bitterness remained invalids. It was as simple and as horrible as that.

And still I stood there with the coldness clutching my heart. But forgiveness is not an emotion—I knew that too. Forgiveness is an act of the will, and the will can function regardless of the temperature of the heart. "Jesus, help me!" I prayed silently. "I can lift my hand. I can do that much. You supply the feeling."

And so woodenly, mechanically, I thrust my hand into the one stretched out to me. And as I did, an incredible thing took place. The current started in my shoulder, raced down my arm, sprang into our joined hands. And then this healing warmth seemed to flood my whole being, bringing tears to my eyes.

"I forgive you, brother!" I cried. "With all my heart."

For a long moment we grasped each other's hands, the former guard and the former prisoner. I had never known God's love so intensely as I did then. But even so, I realized it was not my love. I had tried, and did not have the power. It was the power of the Holy Spirit as recorded in Romans 5:5, ". . . because the love of God is shed abroad in our hearts by the Holy Ghost which is given unto us."

And Jesus being full of the Holy Ghost
returned from Jordan, and was led by the
Spirit into the wilderness. . . . And Jesus
returned in the power of the Spirit into
Galilee: and there went out a fame of him
through all the region round about.

Luke 4:1, 14

8. In the Power of the Spirit

AS I STOOD in the railroad station in Basel, Switzerland, waiting for my luggage, I suddenly realized that I did not know where I was supposed to go. For ten years, after my release from prison, I had been traveling all over the world at the direction of God. Many times I did not know why I was to go to a certain place until I arrived. It had become almost second nature not to make my plans and then ask for God's signature. Rather, I had learned to wait for God's plan and then write my name on the schedule.

But this time was different. Suddenly I was in Basel and had no idea why, or whom I was to contact. Besides, I was tired. Sleeping each night in a different bed and always living out of a suitcase had worn me down. I felt a sensation of panic in my heart and sat down, trying to remember to whom I was going. At sixty-three years of age could it be that I was so overworked that I was losing my memory? Or even worse, had God withdrawn His conscious Presence from me and was letting me walk alone for a season?

Inside my suitcase I found an address. It had no meaning to me but it was all I had to go on. I took a taxi to the place but the people at that address were complete strangers and had never heard of me. By now I was desperate—and a little bit frightened.

The people told me of another man I might contact. Perhaps he would know who I was and why I had come to Basel. I took another taxi but this gentleman, too, was unfamiliar with my work.

For ten years the Lord had guided me step-by-step. At no time had I been confused or afraid. Now I was both—unable to recognize the Presence of God. Surely He was still guiding me, but like the pilot who flies into the clouds, I was now having to rely on instruments rather than sight. I decided to turn around and go back home to Holland, there to await further orders.

Because of a severe storm the planes were not flying. I had to travel by train. Arriving in Haarlem, I started toward the phone near the station to call Zonneduin, the house where I was to stay in the outskirts of the city in Bloemendaal.

But on the way to the phone booth I slipped on the wet pavement and before I knew it I was sprawled in the street. A sharp pain shot through my hip and I was unable to stand.

"Oh, Lord," I prayed, "lay Your hand on my hip and take away this horrible pain."

Instantly the pain disappeared, but I was still unable to get up. Kind people assisted me to a taxi where a policeman asked if he could help.

"What is your name?" he asked.

"Corrie ten Boom."

He looked surprised and questioned me further. "Are you a member of the family of that name whom we arrested about ten years ago?"

"That is right."

During the war many of the good Dutch policemen had been in the service of the Gestapo, remaining there for the express purpose of helping political prisoners. This man had been on duty that day my family was arrested.

"I am so sorry about your accident," he said sympathetically, "but I am glad to see you again. I will never forget that night in the police station. You were all sitting or lying on the floor of the station. Your old father was there with all his children and many of your friends. I have often told my colleagues that there was an atmosphere of peace and joy in our station that night, as if you were going to a feast instead of prison and death."

He paused and looked at me kindly as if trying to remember my face. "Your father said before he tried to sleep, 'Let us pray together.' And then he read Psalm 91."

"You remember!" I exclaimed. After ten years that policeman had remembered which psalm my father had read.

For a fleeing moment, sitting in that old taxi on a Haarlem street while the rain pelted the roof, I allowed myself that pain of looking backwards. It was in this same city that we had been arrested. In fact, the prison was only a short distance from where I was now sitting. That was the last time our family had been together. Within ten days Father was dead. Then later Betsie. All gone. Now, ten years later this policeman still remembered.

> He that dwelleth in the secret place of the most High shall abide under the shadow of the Almighty.
>
> verse 1

Now the message was clear. Although there was no light to guide me, I was still in God's will. Actually, when one is abiding under the shadow of the Almighty there will be no light, but that is only because God's Presence is so near.

I leaned back in the seat. "Dear God, when this shadow came over me I thought You had departed. Now I understand it was because You were drawing closer. I eagerly await whatever You have planned for me."

Eager I was, but not so patient. An X ray showed my hip was not broken, only badly bruised. The doctor said I would have to remain in bed for several weeks for it to heal. I was taken from the clinic to Zonneduin where I was put to bed, unable to move or turn over without the help of a nurse.

I was a very impatient patient. I had only five days to get to a student conference in Germany and as the days slipped by and I realized my hip was not healing fast enough to make the conference, I grew irritable.

"Is there not a Christian in all Haarlem who can pray for me to be healed?" I asked.

My friends sent for a particular minister in the city who was known to have laid hands on the sick for healing. That same afternoon he came to my room.

Standing beside my bed he said, "Is there any unconfessed sin in your life?"

What an odd question, I thought. I understood he had agreed to come pray for my healing, but was it his job to get so personal about my sins and attitudes? However, I did not have far to look. My impatience and demanding attitude which I had displayed toward my nurse had been wrong—very wrong. I asked her to come to the room and I repented of my sin, asking both her and God to forgive me.

Satisfied, this gentle man then reached over and laid his hands on my head. Only the year before my sister Nollie had died. Ever since my heart had been broken with mourning. I had the feeling of being left all alone and knew that the insecurity which I had experienced had contributed to my being here in this bed, rather than in Germany with the students. Yet as this tall, handsome man laid his hands on me and prayed, I felt a great stream of power flowing through me. Such great joy. The mourning left and I wanted to sing with David:

Thou hast turned for me my mourning into dancing: thou hast put off my sackcloth, and girded me with gladness.

Psalms 30:11

I felt the Presence of the Lord Jesus all around me and felt His love flowing through me and over me as if I were being immersed in an ocean of grace. My joy became so intense that I finally prayed, "No more, Lord, no more." My heart felt it was about to burst, so great was the joy. I knew it was that wonderful experience promised by Jesus—the Baptism in the Holy Spirit.

I looked at the man who had prayed for me. "Can I walk now?" I asked.

He smiled. "I do not know. All I know is you asked for a cupful and God gave you an ocean."

Ten days later I was on my way to Germany, late, but still filled with joy overflowing. Only after I arrived did I realize why God chose this particular time to fill me with His Holy Spirit. For in Germany, for the first time, I came face-to-face with many people who were demonized. Had I gone in my own power I would have been consumed. Now, going in the power of the Holy Spirit, God was able to work much deliverance through me as we commanded demons to be cast out in the Name of the Lord Jesus Christ.

Jesus specifically warned His followers not to try to minister in His Name without His power. As I found out from my experience in Basel, trying to do the Lord's work in your own strength is the most confusing, exhausting, and tedious of all work. But when you are filled with the Holy Spirit, then the ministry of Jesus just flows out of you.

It was the beginning of a new spiritual blessing that each day brings me into a closer walk with the Lord Jesus. Now, whether I am walking in the bright light of His Presence or abiding under the *shadow* of the Almighty, I know that He is not only with me, He is in me.

. . . greater is he that is in you, than he that is in the world.

1 John 4:4

9. *Conny*

AFTER TWELVE YEARS of traveling alone, someone joined me in my world-wide travels. The Lord saw and supplied my need in the person of Conny van Hoogstraten, a beautiful, young, Dutch woman who became my first constant traveling companion. I met her on one of my visits to England. We worked well as a team (not to say we did not have difficulties—as always happens when people work so close together). However, those hard moments were used to bring us closer to Jesus as we learned to walk in the light with each other. Yes, 1 John 1:7–9 became a reality, and the Lord used Conny in the lives of countless people all over the world to show and teach them the joy of walking in the light.

We laughed much together for the Lord had given Conny an infectious sense of humor and a happy laughter. One of Conny's special gifts was the ability to change a house into a home. People always found an open door and quickly became friends. We were both so different but the Lord molded us into a team fit to do His work. I will never forget the day, now almost eight years ago, that Conny told me of the someone else who had come into her life and that we would have to pray for a new partner. That was one of those very difficult days and the best thing I could do was to go for a long walk. I experienced more than ever before that I was so dependent upon Conny and that I loved her like a sister. I could not understand the Lord's purpose, but during that walk I surrendered Conny to the Lord, and I also surrendered myself in a new way and entrusted my whole being to Him who knew best. Conny was in good hands so why not trust Him for the future? Those last years together were so different from all other years.

In that final year together, the Lord made it clear to me to go to Viet Nam. Conny and I talked it over and Conny shared with me that her fiancé was not in favor of her going there so we had to look around for someone else. It was early spring and I happened to meet a good brother in the Lord who shared that he had been called to go to Viet Nam also. I rejoiced and thanked the Lord as we made plans to go together. The young man was Brother Andrew and he proved to be a very good traveling companion. In Viet Nam, the Lord gave me a very nice nurse who worked with the W.E.C. and she took care of me when I traveled while Brother Andrew was away on other trips to very dangerous places.

I will never forget the tremendous needs I saw in the hospitals and other places I visited, but instead of taking all those needs to Jesus, I kept them in my heavy and overburdened heart. How silly I could be! With that heavy heart and aching body I had to go on to Indonesia. Oh, the Lord worked in spite of me, and the people were very kind to me and helped me in many ways, but the happiest moment came when we landed in Amsterdam. We quickly drove to Soestdijk where a very dear friend, Elisabeth van Heemstra (who was working in Jerusalem at that time) had made her apartment available to me. That was a great gift from the Lord! I had no place I could really call home but now I had one—and what a haven it was! Beautiful surroundings in a quiet section of town. There Conny and I spent our last months together and it was a precious time. Conny was busy with marriage preparations and the new house she and her husband would move into. Many old-time friends came by to say hello. We talked and prayed much and we trusted that the Lord would supply a new partner before Conny's marriage.

How marvelous are His ways! The Lord answered our prayers and gave me another Dutch companion. Her name is Ellen de Kroon, a registered nurse, who loves the Lord very much. I will never forget the first time Ellen visited me. Conny and her fiancé were there also. It was a nice day in June and we decided to sit outside on the balcony. After talking for some time, Ellen noticed that I was getting cold, so she got up, asked me where she could find a shawl and put it around my shoulders. I noticed Conny's face, just beaming, with eyes that seemed to say, "See! You prayed for that 'someone' who would take care of you and love you and here she is." It was a testimony for Conny as well, knowing that Ellen would take her place.

On Conny's wedding day, September 1, 1967, the Lord filled the empty place left behind by Conny with Ellen, the tall, fair-haired nurse. Conny and her husband lived not far from us and she took much time to help Ellen with the work. Almost a year after Conny was married, her husband had to go to India for several weeks. During that time, Conny accompanied me to the United States to start the work on the book *The Hiding Place* while Ellen took care of the work in Holland. Yes, it was Conny who started to type that book which has already blessed so many lives all over the world. I knew that she loved the work we were doing but she also missed her husband. It was so good to bring him daily before the Lord.

Our prayers were answered and Conny's husband returned safely to Holland while I continued my travels with my new companion, Ellen.

Two years had passed when we learned that Conny had been taken ill. We returned to Holland and were on our way to visit Conny in the hospital. I knew that she was very ill, because she had received treatment that would indicate terminal illness unless the Lord would perform a miracle. When we entered Conny's room, it was like stepping into a flower garden and in the midst of it was Conny, almost asleep. Her husband was sitting beside her. That day, her specialist had informed her of her illness and that there was no hope. Conny was prepared to go and be with her Lord and Saviour but to take that trip all by herself was so difficult for her. Would Jesus ask that of her?

Slowly she said, "I have taken many trips in my lifetime but there was always someone with me. Mother was there when I was small, Corrie was with me during many of them, and now my husband is with me. But on this trip, who is going to go with me?"

Her husband gently took her hand and said, "Conny, here is my hand and as soon as Jesus comes for you, I will surrender your hand to Him!"

Conny did not answer but her face looked content. Suddenly she turned to us and asked us to sing Psalm Twenty-Three for her. I swallowed the lump in my throat and asked the Lord to help me in joining the others in the singing, but the phrase we left out was, "though I walk through the valley of the shadow of death . . . . "

When we finished Conny said, "You forgot one phrase—please sing it!"

So we sang, "though I walk through the valley of the shadow of death" while the tears rolled down our cheeks. Then Conny thought of all the friends all over the world whom we had come to know and love, and she asked me to greet them. We began to pray and Conny laid her hands on Ellen's head and said, "Be . . . faithful unto death and I will give thee a crown of life" (Revelation 2:10).

Conny died a victorious death. Her life bore much fruit, and she prepared many people to meet the Master, our Lord Jesus Christ, who came to call her home to be with Him forever.

10. Authority Over Demons

FOR WEEKS I had been traveling through Eastern Europe: Russia, Poland, Czechoslovakia—speaking in many home groups and even, on occasion, in a church. Many churches were still open in Eastern Europe, although the Communists were very strict about who could speak—and what they said. However, as a harmless old Dutch woman I was allowed to sometimes speak in one of the churches.

As if by a miracle, I was invited to speak in a series of meetings in a great cathedral in a large Communist city. I found that the pastors loved the Lord and had a heavy burden for lost souls.

The first several nights I spoke about the abundant life in Jesus Christ—the joy, the unspeakable love, and the peace that passes all understanding. It was as though I was carried by the Holy Spirit through the joyful storehouse of abundance that we possess when we know Jesus. I described in great detail the precious promises made available to us in Christ.

But something was wrong. Although some of the people rejoiced, most of them simply sat rooted to their benches. They were like chained animals, dying of hunger but unable to reach the food. And the more I tried to give them the more I was aware their hearts were shackled so they could not taste the food I was offering them.

Each night I would return to my room with a heavy heart for I knew that although these dear people wanted to receive what I was giving them, they could not. "It is as if the devil keeps a fence around these people that you cannot reach them," my traveling companion said.

"Could it be that demons keep them in bondage?" I wondered.

226

I opened my Bible and read, "In my name shall they cast out devils."

"Lord, what must I do?" I cried out.

"Obey Me!" came the answer.

"But how, Lord? There are *so* many who are bound by demon powers and I cannot meet with each of them individually."

"Where did I say that you can deal only with individuals?" He asked.

I was confused and returned to His Word. It became apparent that the Lord wanted me to send all the evil spirits away in His Name. Yet I knew this type of ministry was forbidden in Communist lands.

That night was the final night of the meetings. The great cathedral was crowded with people, but it was the same as on all the other nights. They were not able to receive what I was giving them. I spoke again on Jesus the Victor. "In the world you will have tribulation, but be of good courage, I have overcome the world." *(See* John 16:33.) They sat like stone images, unable to grasp the joy of the Lord.

I knew God was calling on me to act. I trembled, but I had no choice. "I must interrupt my message for a moment, friends," I said. "Many of you cannot grasp the richness the Lord offers us this evening. The servants of Satan are keeping you in bondage."

Then I obeyed. Taking a deep breath and offering one last quick prayer I said in a loud voice, "In the Name of Jesus I command all dark powers keeping people from the blessings of God to disappear. Go away! Get out of the hearts of these people. Get out of this church. Go to the place where God sends you."

Then, closing my eyes I raised my hands upward and prayed, "Lord, will You now protect us with Your precious blood. *Amen.*"

I was afraid, but I felt secure. I knew God had told me to do it. Then, as I opened my eyes and looked out over the huge congregation, I saw a miracle happen. The people who had been in bondage came alive. They began to rejoice and as I continued my message I could sense their eager hearts drinking in the living water as I poured it out before them.

After the service I was scheduled to meet with a large group of local pastors who had attended the meeting. By the time I was able to break away from the crowd of people who came forward to speak to me, and get to the back room, the pastors were already meeting. Their conversation was very serious.

"How could you do that?" one pastor asked as soon as I entered the room. "Communists do not allow people to speak about demons!"

"I had to obey God," was my only answer.

The pastors resumed their discussion about the meeting. They, too, had seen the bondage. They had also sensed the release when the demons were cast out. But there were some who had studied psychology and others who had studied demonology. They entered into a heated argument about the subject. I had studied none of these. All I knew was God had told me to use my authority in the Name of Jesus. So I sat back while the argument swirled around me.

At last one of the pastors said, "We know God's promises and God's command, but who among us has ever been willing to obey Mark 16:17: 'And these signs shall follow them that believe; In my name shall they cast out devils . . . .'"

There was a long, uncomfortable silence. When the Bible interferes with man's theology, it always causes a strain. The pastor then continued, "God has this evening given Corrie the grace to take the authority of Jesus and in His Name cast out devils. We should be thankful instead of all this arguing."

That was the end of the pastors' meeting, but, oh, what a lesson I learned that night. It is tragic to be around people, especially men of God, who do not recognize the fact that we are surrounded, not only by angels, but also by the powers of darkness.

Someone once asked my opinion of the missionaries in a certain country. My answer was, "They have given all, but they have not taken all. They have given homeland, time, money, luxury, and more; but they have not taken all of the boundless resources of God's promises. Many do not know about two precious weapons: the power of the blood of Jesus—and every Christian's legal right to use the wonderful Name of Jesus to cast out demons."

In *War on the Saints*, Mrs. Jessie Penn-Lewis wrote, ". . . when the existence of evil spirits is recognized by the heathen, it is generally looked upon by the missionary as 'superstition' and ignorance; whereas the ignorance is often on the part of the missionary, who is blinded by the prince of the power of the air to the revelation given in the Scriptures, concerning the satanic powers."

We need to recognize the enemy in order to overcome him. But let us beware of the mistakes that C. S. Lewis described in *Screwtape Letters*. He says, "There are two equal and opposite errors into which our race can fall about the devils. One is to disbelieve in their existence, the other is to believe and to feel an unhealthy interest in them! They themselves are equally pleased by both errors, and they hail a materialist or a magician with the same delight."

We have a good safeguard and guide—the Bible—God's Word. Here we find not only the necessary information about Satan and demons, but also the weapons and the armor that we need for this battle.

God wants and expects us to be conquerors over the powers of darkness—not only for the sake of personal victory and the liberation of other souls—but for His glory, so that His triumph and victory over His enemies may be demonstrated!

First, then, let us see what the Bible says about the powers of darkness. The devil (or Satan) is introduced to us as a person who opposes God and His work. He is the "god of this world" who blinds the minds of the people to the truths of God's Word. Having rebelled against God, he was cast out of heaven; then, he caused man's fall in paradise. Jesus calls him "the father of lies, a liar, a murderer." (*See* John 8:44.) He works often as an "angel of light," seeking the ruin of the elect. But he was cursed of God. Jesus triumphed over him at the Cross of Calvary and in His Resurrection. He has been condemned and will finally be destroyed.

There are many kinds of demons, and they afflict people in various ways. They also bring false doctrine, trying to seduce the elect by oppressing, obsessing, and possessing. They know Jesus, recognize His power, and tremble before Him. For them, hell is the final destination, as it is for Satan.

Second, the Bible gives us direction concerning the stand we have to take against these powers. It is most important to realize that ours is the position *in Christ*. We are called to resist the devil in the "whole armour of God," by virtue of the blood of Jesus, by faith, prayer, and fasting.

I remember in Ravensbruck, for instance, when we had very little to eat, my sister Betsie said, "Let us dedicate this involuntary fast to the Lord that it may become a blessing." Almost immediately we found we had power over the demons that were tormenting us and were able to exercise that power to cast them out of our barracks.

Let us remember that God's Word stands forever, and that His commandments mean for us today exactly the same as for His disciples twenty centuries ago. Those who act on them, in obedience, will in the same way prove God's almighty power. Yes, Jesus said, "In my name shall they cast out devils." And that means us today.

Our fight is not against a physical army, a political party, an atheistic organization—or anything like that. Our fight is against organizations and powers that are spiritual. Demons may come in as a result of occult sin, even from years back. This includes contact with hypnotism, astrology charts, fortune-telling, Ouiji boards and other forms of occultism, sometimes entered into "just for fun." These demons will remain until they are cast out in Jesus' Name.

We are up against the unseen power that controls this dark world and the spiritual agents are from the very headquarters of evil. Therefore, we must wear the "whole armour of God," that we may be able to resist evil in its day of power, and that even when we have fought to a standstill, we may still stand our ground.

Conny and I had traveled throughout Poland. Conny was then my constant companion, and we met many wonderful Christians in that Iron Curtain country. It encouraged us to know that God was using us to bring comfort and strength to the men and women of God. However, the longer we stayed in Poland, the more exhausted we became.

"I do not understand it," Conny said one morning as we were getting up. "I have just wakened from a full night's sleep but already I am weak and tired."

I, too, felt the same way. We thought perhaps it was some kind of sickness we had picked up; yet neither of us seemed to be really sick.

Then in Warsaw one day we happened to meet an old friend from Holland. Kees was in Poland with his wife, traveling with his camping trailer.

"What a joy to meet you," he said. "How are things going?"

I looked at Conny and she looked at me. "You know, Kees, we both feel so tired. It is as if our legs are heavy, like when you have the flu. Yet we are not ill, just tired."

Kees looked at us intently. "Is this your first time to work in Poland?"

"Yes," I answered. "But what does that have to do with it?"

"Let me explain," Kees said. "Your tiredness is nothing less than an attack of the devil. He does not like your work in Poland, for the antichrist is busy here, arranging his army."

Reaching out, he put his hand on my arm. "Corrie and Conny, you must remember you have the protection of the blood of Jesus. Whenever you experience these attacks from the dark powers, you must rebuke them in the Name of Jesus."

I knew what Kees was saying was right. We sat in his car while he read from the Bible. "They overcame him by the blood of the lamb, and by the word of their testimony, and they loved not their lives unto the death" (Revelation 12:11).

Then Kees prayed with us, laying his hands on us in the Name of Jesus and rebuking the dark powers that would attack us. Even as he was praying I felt the darkness leave. By the time the prayer was over, we both felt covered by the blood of the Lamb and all our tiredness had disappeared.

God had taught us a valuable lesson that we would remember in many other areas of the world. We learned that in a country where a godless philosophy reigns, that only by claiming the blood of Jesus can you stand and not fall. The same is true in a city, or school, or even a church building. If Jesus Christ is not recognized as Supreme, then darkness rules.

Since then we have traveled in many countries and felt this same tiredness coming over us. Often I have felt it in American cities. Now I know it simply means that I am in a place where Satan rules. But praise the Lord! I can be an overcomer when I stand in the power of the blood of the Lamb.

But I say unto you, Love your enemies,
bless them that curse you, do good to them
that hate you, and pray for them that
despitefully use you, and persecute you.
Matthew 5:44

11. *Lights From Darkest Africa*

THOMAS WAS A tall black man who lived in a round hut together with his big family in the middle of Africa. He loved the Lord and loved people—an unbeatable combination.

Thomas's neighbor, who lived across the dirt street, hated God—and hated men like Thomas who loved God. The hatred grew stronger and stronger until the man began sneaking over at night and setting fire to the straw roof on Thomas's hut, endangering his small children. Three nights in a row this happened and each time Thomas was able to rush out of his hut and put out the flames before they destroyed the roof and the walls. The fact that he never said an unkind word to his neighbor, only showing him love and forgiveness, made his neighbor hate him even more.

One night the neighbor sneaked across the street and set fire to Thomas's roof. This night, however, a strong wind came up and as Thomas rushed to beat out the fire, the sparks blew across the street and set the neighbor's house on fire. Thomas finished putting out the fire on his roof and then rushed across the street to put out the fire on his neighbor's roof. He was able to extinguish the flames, but in the process he badly burned his hands and arms.

Other neighbors told the chief of the tribe what had happened. The chief was so furious that he sent his police to arrest the neighbor and throw him into prison.

That night Thomas came to the meeting where I was speaking (as he had done each night). I noticed his badly burned hands and asked him what had happened. Reluctantly he told me the story.

231

"It is good that this man is now in prison," I said. "Now your children are no longer in danger and he cannot try again to put your house in flames."

"That is true," he said. "But I am so sorry for that man. He is an unusually gifted man and now he must live together with all those criminals in a horrible prison."

"Then let us pray for him," I said.

Thomas dropped to his knees and holding up his burned and bandaged hands, he began to pray. "Lord, I claim this neighbor of mine for You. Lord, give him his freedom and do the miracle that in the future he and I will become a team to bring the Gospel in our tribe. *Amen.*"

Never had I heard such a prayer.

Two days later I was able to go to the prison. I spoke to the prisoners about God's joy and God's love. Among the group who listened intently was Thomas's neighbor. When I asked who would receive Jesus in his heart, that man was the first one to raise his hand.

After the meeting I told him how Thomas loved him, how he had burned his hands trying to put out the fire to save his house, and how he had prayed that they might become a team to spread the Gospel. The man wept big tears and nodded his head saying, "Yes, yes, that is how it shall be."

The next day I told Thomas. He praised God and said, "You see, God has worked a miracle. We never can expect too much from Him." He left, running off down the path, his face beaming with joy.

I had been in Africa for three weeks when I finally got to visit the prison on the outside of the city. I inquired of the warden if I could talk to the prisoners.

"Impossible," he said, "the prison is on restriction for an entire month due to an uprising that has broken out among the prisoners. Nobody is allowed in to see the men, much less give a sermon."

I felt discouraged but knew that God had brought me to that place for some reason. So, I just stood—looking at the warden.

He grew very uncomfortable (having me stand and look at him). At last he said, "There are some political prisoners who have been sentenced to death. Would you like to speak to them?"

"Certainly," I said.

The warden called three heavily armed soldiers who escorted me down a long hall past many barred doors and into a cell where one man was sitting on a low bench which was also his bed. There was absolutely nothing else in the cell. The only light came from a small window high above the floor that let just a little spot of sunlight fall on the hard-packed dirt floor in that dreary place.

I leaned against the wall. He was a young man with black skin and very white teeth. He looked up, his eyes filled with sadness. What could I say? "Lord, give me some light to pass on to this man who sits in such darkness."

Finally I asked him a question. "Do you know about Jesus?"

"Yes," he said slowly, "I have a Bible at home. I know that Jesus died on a cross for the sins of the world. Many years ago I accepted Him as my Saviour and followed Him for some time until political affairs absorbed all my time. Now I wish I could start again and live a surrendered life, but it is too late. This week I die."

"It is not too late, my friend," I said. "Do you know the ones responsible for your death sentence?"

"I could give you the entire list of those who have put me here," he answered, gritting his teeth. "I know all their names and hate them."

I opened my Bible and read, "But if you do not forgive men their trespasses, neither will your Father forgive your trespasses." Then I closed the Bible and looked at him. "Do you want your Father to forgive you before you die?"

"Of course I want that," he said. "More than anything else in the world. But I cannot meet the conditions. I am not able to forgive. I am young, strong, and healthy. I have a wife and children. These men have wronged me and now this very week they will take away my life. How do I forgive that?"

The man looked at me with eyes full of despair and hopelessness. I felt such a great compassion in my heart, yet I knew I must be stern for much depended on it.

"Let me tell you a story," I said. And then I told him of my experience in the church in Munich when my former guard from the concentration camp asked me to forgive him.

"That moment I felt a great bitterness swelling in my heart," I said. "I remembered the sufferings of my dying sister. But I knew that unforgiveness would do more harm to me than the guard's whip. So I cried out to the Lord, "Lord, thank You for Romans 5:5:

> The love of God is shed abroad in our hearts by the Holy Ghost which is given unto us.

Thank You, Lord, that Your love in me can do that which I cannot do."

"At that moment a great stream of love poured through me and I said, 'Brother, give me your hand. I forgive all.'"

I looked down at the African man sitting on the bench. "I could not do it. I was not able. Jesus in me was able to do it. You see, you never touch so much the ocean of God's love as when you love your enemies."

The man listened as I told him more of Jesus. Then, promising to meet him on the other shore, I prayed with him and left.

The next day a missionary friend came by the place where I was staying. He told me that as soon as I left the prison the prisoner had sent a message to his wife saying, "Don't hate the people who brought me here and who will cause my death. Love them. Forgive them. I cannot, and neither can you, but Jesus in us can do it."

I slept well that night, knowing why God had brought me to Africa.

I had spoken in many prisons in my travels across the world, but the prison in Ruanda, Africa, was the dreariest, darkest prison I had ever seen. The men were all black, their uniforms were black, and they were sitting in the mud on the ground.

I had just entered the prison gate with my interpreter, a missionary lady. Steam (the aftermath of a hard tropical rain) was rising from the mud. The men were sitting on pieces of paper, branches, banana leaves, their legs caked with mud up to their knees.

"Why don't we go into the building?" I asked my interpreter.

"Impossible," she whispered, obviously afraid of the men. "There are so many prisoners that even during the night only half of them can go inside."

I looked at their faces. Like their skin, their eyes were dark. It was the look I had seen so many times in Ravensbruck—the look of those whose hope had died. Unhappiness. Despair. Hopelessness. Anger. How could I speak to them? What could I, an old Dutch woman, say to these miserable men that would help their lives?

"Lord," I prayed, "I am not able to overcome this darkness."

"Take My promise of Galatians 5:22," I heard an inner voice say.

Quickly I took my Bible and opened it to that passage. "But the fruit of the Spirit is love . . . . "

"Thank You, Lord," I whispered. "But I have a great love for these men already or I would not be here."

I read on. "But the fruit of the Spirit is love, joy . . . . "

"Joy?" I asked. "In these surroundings?" Then I remembered what Nehemiah said, "The joy of the Lord is my strength."

"Yes, Lord," I cried out. "That is what I need. That is what I claim. I claim the promise of joy."

Even as I spoke the words I felt a wonderful, lifting sensation in my heart. It was joy—more joy than I had ever felt. It poured like a river out of my inner being; like the rising tide it covered the salt flats of my depression and turned the ugly mud of despair into a shimmering lagoon of blessedness. Moments later I was introduced to the prisoners who all sat, staring at me in hatred. The steam rose around them and the stinging insects swarmed their mud-coated ankles and legs.

I began to talk of the joy that is ours when we know Jesus. What a Friend we have in Him. He is always with us. When we are depressed, He gives us joy. When we do wrong, He gives us the strength to be good. When we hate, He fills us with His forgiveness. When we are afraid, He causes us to love.

Several faces changed and I saw that some of my joy was spilling over on them. But I knew what the rest were thinking. *After your talk you can go home, away from this muddy, stinking prison. It is easy to talk about joy when you are free. But we must stay here.*

Then I told them a story.

"Morning roll call at Ravensbruck was often the hardest time of the day. By 4:30 A.M. we had to be standing outside our barracks in the black predawn chill, in blocks of one hundred women, ten wide, ten deep.

"Names were never used in the concentration camp. It was part of the plan to dehumanize the prisoners—to take away their dignity of life—their worth before God and man. I was known simply as Prisoner 66730.

"Roll call sometimes lasted three hours and every day the sun rose a little later and the icy-cold wind blew a little stronger. Standing in the gray of the dawn I would try to repeat, through shivering lips, that verse of Scripture which had come to mean so much to me: 'Who shall separate us from the love of Christ? shall tribulation, or distress, or persecution, or famine, or nakedness, or peril, or sword? As it is written, for thy sake we are killed all the day long; we are accounted as sheep for the slaughter' (Romans 8:35, 36). In all this there was an overwhelming victory through Jesus who had proved His love for me by dying on the cross.

"But there came a time when repeating the words did not help. I needed more. 'Oh God,' I prayed, 'reveal Yourself somehow.'

"Then one morning the woman directly in front of me sank to the ground. In a moment a young woman guard was standing over her, a whip in her hand.

" 'Get up,' she screamed in a rage. 'How dare you think you can lie down when everyone else is standing!'

"I could hardly bear to see what was happening in front of me. *Surely this is the end of us all,* I thought. Then suddenly a skylark started to sing high in the sky. The sweet, pure notes of the bird rose on the still cold air. Every head turned upward, away from the carnage before us, listening to the song of the skylark soaring over the crematorium. The words of the psalmist ran through my mind: 'For as the heaven is high above the earth, so great is [God's] mercy toward them that fear Him (Psalms 103:11).'"

I looked out at the men who were sitting in front of me. No longer were their faces filled with darkness and anger. They were listening—intently—for they were hearing from someone who had walked where they were now walking. I continued.

"There in that prison I saw things from God's point of view. The reality of God's love was just as sure as the cruelty of men.

> O love of God, how deep and great,
> Far deeper than man's deepest hate.

"Every morning for the next three weeks, just at the time of roll call, the skylark appeared. In his sweet song I heard the call of God to turn my eyes away from the cruelty of men to the ocean of God's love.

"A Jewish doctor, Viktor Frankl, who went through far more suffering in the concentration camps than I, wrote a book. He ends the book with these words: '. . . we have come to know man is that being who has invented the gas chambers of Auschwitz; however, he is also that being who has entered those gas chambers upright with the Lord's Prayer or the *Shema Yisroel* on his lips.'"

Although I was speaking through an interpreter, God's Spirit was working through both of us. I saw joy appearing on the faces of nearly all the men sitting before me.

"Say, men," I said, "do you know Jesus is willing to live in your hearts? He says, 'I stand at the door of your heart and knock. If anyone hears my voice and opens the door, I come in.' Just think: that same Jesus loves you and will live in your heart and give you joy in the midst of all this mud. He who is willing, raise his hand."

I looked around. All the men, including the guards, had raised their hands. It was unbelievable, but their faces showed a joy that only the Holy Spirit could produce. As I left the prison and returned to the car, all the men accompanied me. The guards did not seem worried or anxious that they swarmed around me. In fact, they did not even prevent them from going out the gate to stand around my car. As I opened the door and got in, the men began to shout and chant something, repeating the same words over and over.

"What do they shout?" I asked my interpreter. She smiled and said, "They shout, 'Old woman, come back. Old woman, come back and tell us more of Jesus.'"

The missionary turned to me as we drove off. "I must confess to you that I thought this place was too dark for the light of the Gospel. I had been here once before and was so frightened I said I would never come back. Now, because I had to come interpret for you, I have seen what the Holy Spirit can do. The joy of the Lord is available, even for such a place as this. From now on I shall return every week to tell them about Jesus."

Months later I received a letter from her in which she said, "The fear is gone. The joy remains."

*Carry neither purse, nor scrip, nor shoes:
and salute no man by the way . . . And in
the same house remain, eating and drinking
such things as they give: for the labourer is
worthy of his hire. . . .*

Luke 10:4, 7

12. God Will Provide

THE PEOPLE IN America seem to feel I should not hesitate to ask for money for my ministry, which supports other ministries such as Bible and book translations in many parts of the world. However, from the very beginning of my ministry I have felt it was wrong to ask for money—even to ask for travel expenses. I did not want to be paid for "services rendered." I simply wanted to preach the Gospel and let the Lord provide for me.

I learned this lesson very early in my traveling ministry. I was in England and spoke, among other things, about the former concentration camp where I helped refugees in Germany. My hosts had asked me to do this, saying they know the American people would like to help support it. After the meeting a dignified, well-dressed lady came up and handed me a check for a rather large sum of money. It was designated to my work in Europe.

"It was so very interesting to hear about your work," she said.

"What did you think about the other things I said?" I asked. "Did you find them important also?"

She gave me a quizzical look. I continued. "Of course it is a very good thing to give money for evangelistic work, but today I also spoke about conversion. God does not want a little bit of your money, He wants all of your heart. He wants to possess you completely. God will not let me take your check." I handed it back to her.

As I was speaking I noticed a haughty, proud look come into her eyes. Very deliberately she pulled her fur cape around her neck. Then, without answering at all, she arrogantly walked away.

When I got back to my room I looked sadly at the other checks which had been given me. Was God speaking to me? Was it wrong to speak of my own work while at the same time I urged people to be converted or to forgive their enemies? Was it wrong to listen to these Americans who were urging me to receive collections for my ministry? I dropped to my knees in prayer. God knew my needs.

The answer was very clear from the Lord. "From now on you must never again ask for money."

Great joy entered my heart and I prayed, "Heavenly Father, You know that I need more money than ever before. But from this day on I shall never ask for a penny. No guarantees before I come speak. No travel expenses. Not even a place to stay. I will trust in You believing that you will never forsake me."

That very day I received two letters. One was from a woman in Switzerland. "Corrie, God told me that from now on you must never again ask for money."

The other letter was from my sister in Holland. She wrote, 'When I prayed for your work this morning God made it clear to me that you should not ask anybody for financial support. He will provide everything."

I thought of the night in the concentration camp when my sister, Betsie, had talked with me about our plans for the future. "Corrie, we should never worry about money," she said. "God is willing to supply our every need."

Many years later, when I faced a severe hardship, I was forced to remember this principle. I felt I had received a direct command from the Lord to go to Russia. The price of our tickets and expenses would be five thousand guilders. However, when I looked at my checkbook I found we had only three thousand guilders in the bank.

"Lord," I prayed, "what must I do? You have commanded me to go to Russia but I need two thousand more guilders."

I thought that this time God would let me write a few wealthy friends, telling them of my need, and asking them to send the money for the plane ticket. Instead I heard a very clear directive from God: "Give away two thousand guilders."

"Oh, no, Lord," I said, as I sat at the table in my apartment in Baarn, Holland. "You did not understand. I did not say I wanted to *give* away two thousand guilders. I said I needed someone to give me that amount so I could go to Russia."

However, God seldom listens to my arguments. He waited for me to get through with my objections, and then repeated His original command. This time, though, it was even more specific. I was to give two thousand guilders to a certain mission group that had an immediate need.

I could not understand how anyone's need could be more immediate than my own, but foregoing the "wisdom of the wise," I sat down and wrote a check to this mission group, depleting my bank account down to one thousand guilders.

Later that day I went back down to see if I had received any mail. Among the letters was one from the American publishing company that was to publish *The Hiding Place*. For some months I had been writing back and forth and only two weeks before I had finally signed the contract. I brought the letter back upstairs and opened it. As I pulled it out, a check fluttered to the floor. It was an advance from the publisher, money which I did not think I was going to get until the manuscript was completed. I looked at the figure. It amounted to more than I needed!

God takes His prohibition of asking for money very seriously, just as He means it seriously when He says He will care for and protect us. However, if we seek to raise our own money then God will let us do it—by ourselves. Many times we will be able to raise great amounts of money by human persuasion or downright perseverance in asking. But we will miss the far greater blessing of letting Him supply all our needs according to His own riches. And, as I found out in the case of the guilders needed for the trip to Russia, God always has more for us than we would think of asking.

I would much rather be the trusting child of a rich Father, than a beggar at the door of worldly men.

Yes, the Lord is not only my shepherd; He is my treasurer. He is very wealthy. Sometimes He tries my faith, but when I am obedient then the money always comes in just in time.

My last stop on my first trip to the Orient was Formosa. It was time for me to move on so I went to the travel agency in Taipei and gave the girl a list of all the places I needed to go on the next leg of my journey. Hong Kong, Sydney, Auckland, then back to Sydney, on to Cape Town, Tel Aviv and finally to Amsterdam.

The travel agent wrote it all down and then asked, "What is your final destination?"

"Heaven," I answered simply.

She gave me a puzzled look. "How do you spell that?"

"H-E-A-V-E-N," I spelled out slowly.

After she had written it down she sat looking at the paper. At last she looked up. "Oh, now I understand," she said with a smile. "But I did not mean that."

"But I meant it," I said. "And you do not need to write it down because I already have my ticket."

"You have a ticket to *heaven?*" she asked, astonished. "How did you receive it?"

"About two thousand years ago," I said, noting her genuine interest, "there was One who bought my ticket for me. I only had to accept it from Him. His name is Jesus and He paid my fare when He died on the cross for my sins."

A Chinese clerk, working at the next desk, overheard our conversation and joined in. "What the old woman says is true," he told his companion.

I turned and looked at the Chinese man. "Have you a reservation for heaven?" I asked him.

His face lit up in a smile. "Yes, I have," he said, nodding enthusiastically. "Many years ago, as a child on the mainland, I received Jesus as my Saviour. That makes me a child of God with a place reserved in the house of the Father."

"Then you are also my brother," I said, shaking his hand. Turning back to the other clerk I said, "When you do not have a reservation for a seat on the plane, and try to get aboard, you face difficulty. But when you do not have a place reserved for you in heaven, and the time comes for you to go, you end up in far greater difficulty. I hope my young brother here will not rest until you have made your reservation in heaven."

The Chinese clerk smiled broadly, and nodded. I felt confident he would continue to witness to his fellow worker now that I had opened the door.

I left the travel agency with a good feeling in my heart. Surely God was going to bless this trip since I was already off to such a good start. However, when I arrived in my room and checked my ticket, I found the girl had made a mistake in the route. Instead of sending me from Sydney to Cape Town to Tel Aviv, as I had requested, she had routed me from Sydney to Tel Aviv and then to Cape Town. I went immediately to the phone and called her.

"Why have you changed my schedule?" I asked. "My Chief has told me I must go first to Cape Town and after that to Tel Aviv. However, you have changed the sequence. God is my Master and I must obey Him."

"Then God has made a mistake," she said, half-seriously. "There is no direct flight from Australia to Africa since there is no island in the Indian Ocean for the plane to land and refuel. That is why you must first go overland to Tel Aviv and then down to Cape Town."

"No," I argued. "I cannot follow that route. I must do what my Chief has told me. I'll just have to pray for an island in the Indian Ocean."

We both laughed and hung up. "Lord," I prayed, "if I have made a mistake in hearing Your direction, please show me. But if I heard correctly, then open the way."

An hour later the girl called back. "Did you really pray for an island in the Indian Ocean?" she asked, incredulous. Before I could answer she continued, "I just received a telegram from Qantas, the Australian airline. They have just begun to use the Cocos Islands for a refueling station and beginning tomorrow will have a direct flight from Sydney to Cape Town."

I thanked her and hung up. It was good to know that God does not make a mistake in His plans.

However, I am stubborn and never seem to learn my lessons well. Just a few days later, after I got to Sydney and was to make a short trip to Auckland, New Zealand, and back, I ran into another situation which would have been much easier on me had I remembered the lesson I should have learned back in Formosa.

Since I was only going to be in Auckland for four days before returning to Sydney and then on to Cape Town, I packed all my essential items into one suitcase which I would carry with me. I left the other suitcases with my friends in Sydney, planning to pick them up when I came back through on my way to Africa. Besides my essential clothing, I also took with me my notebooks, Bibles, literature, and colored slides. My slides, taken in many lands, and the manuscripts of my sermons are all very valuable to me. Although I seldom read from my notes when I speak, I feel more comfortable when I have them before me. I have been accused by my friends of ascending the platform with three Bibles and five notebooks. I think it is hardly that bad, but I have met so many people and jotted down so many ideas that I cannot remember them all. So, I try to carry all my notes with me.

As I started to leave the Sydney airport for the plane, one of the pilots spotted me struggling along with my heavy suitcase. He volunteered to help me. "I have to stop by the radio room first," he said, "but then I shall bring your bag directly to your seat."

I hesitated to turn loose my bag, however, since it was filled with everything I needed for the rest of my journey, not to mention a lifetime of treasures.

"You can trust me," he insisted. "I will arrive at the plane before you and shall leave your bag on your seat."

Reluctantly I parted from my suitcase and watched the pilot as he walked out the door. Several minutes later we boarded the plane and I rushed to my seat. The bag was not there. Alarmed, I called the stewardess. She assured me that the bag had been stowed with the rest of the luggage and was perfectly safe. I tried to settle back in my seat as we took off, yet I had an uncomfortable feeling inside.

The plane made a stop in Melbourne before heading out over the Tasman Sea for New Zealand. However, when we landed in Melbourne there was a radio message waiting for me. Like Job, the thing which I greatly feared had come upon me. The message was from Sydney. A bag, belonging to Corrie ten Boom, had been left in the radio room.

I was frustrated—and angry. "Can they send it to me?" I asked the ticket agent.

"I'm sorry," he said, shaking his head. "The only way we can get it to you is to send it on our next plane to London. From there it will go to Rome, then Tel Aviv, and then . . . ."

"Oohhh," I groaned, waving him quiet. "It will never make it. It contains all my earthly treasures and it is not even locked. Tell them just to hold it for me in Sydney. I shall pick it up when I return in four days. In the meantime, I have nothing, not even a toothbrush."

I reboarded the plane and slumped in my seat, dejected, angry, and full of resentment. On the flight from Sydney to Melbourne I had witnessed to the stewardess about my faith in Jesus Christ. I had told her that Jesus was victor in every situation and that He gave us the power to praise Him in all situations. Now, however, I did not feel very much like praising Him at all.

I looked up and the stewardess was bending over me. "How wonderful it must be to be a Christian at a time like this," she said. "Most people would be full of anger and resentment."

I forced a smile and said, "Well, it must be for some reason; nothing happens by chance to a child of God."

Even though I was speaking the truth, I was not walking in the victory. Victory would mean that I had no resentment at all, and at that moment I was overflowing with it.

It was late evening as the plane took off from Melbourne. It would be a night flight to Auckland and I tried to make myself comfortable. Below us was the sea with only the engines of the plane to hold us in the sky. I dozed, fitfully, and then woke to the smell of smoke in the cabin. The other passengers were awake also, and some of them were up in the aisle, expressing alarm. Moments later the stewardess was at my seat.

"I have good news for you," she said softly. "We are returning to Sydney to pick up your bag."

"Yes, indeed, good news for me," I said. "But tell me, are we not in great danger?"

"No," she said, smiling sweetly and patting my pillow, "we are just having some hydraulic difficulties. There is no danger."

I followed her with my eyes as she went from seat to seat, assuring all the passengers that there was no danger. I leaned across the aisle and asked the man in the next seat what was meant by hydraulic difficulties.

"It is bad news," he said. "All the mechanism on the plane depends on the hydraulic system. The wing flaps, the steering mechanism, even the landing gear is controlled by the hydraulic system. Since the fire is in that system it means the pilot could lose control of the plane at any moment."

I sat back in my seat and tried to look out the window. Below was the blackness of the Tasman Sea. The smell of smoke was still very strong in the cabin. I was not afraid of death. Often, as a prisoner I had faced it. I remembered the words of Dwight Moody, "The valley of the shadow of death holds no darkness for the child of God. There must be light, else there could be no shadow. Jesus is the Light. He has overcome death."

Yet I knew I was not right with God because I was not right with man. I still held resentment in my heart and knew it had to be removed before I could even pray. I leaned back in my seat and opened my heart to God, confessing my resentment over my suitcase (which was worthless to me now that we might crash into the sea) and asking Him to forgive me. Then I prayed, "Lord, perhaps I shall see You very soon. I thank You that all my sins have been cleansed by the blood of the Lamb."

I opened my eyes and looked around me. "What of the others?" I wondered. "Are they prepared to die?" No one was sleeping. All were sitting, alert in their seats. I noticed a woman busy applying lipstick and shook my head. How silly to feel you have to enter eternity with painted lips! I had the strongest urge to stand up and say to the people around me, "Friends, perhaps in a few minutes we shall all enter eternity. Do you know where you are going? Are you prepared to appear before God? There is still time to accept the Lord Jesus . . . ."

But I could say nothing. I wanted to stand and urge them to come to Jesus, but I could not. I was ashamed of the Gospel of our Lord Jesus Christ. And not only that, but there was fear in my heart.

We finally made a landing—a safe landing—in Sydney. My bag was returned to me, but there was no joy in my heart. Even though I had been forgiven of my resentment, I had been ashamed of the Lord Jesus. I found a seat in the lounge and sat with my head bowed, my eyes closed.

"Dear Lord, I am not fit to be a missionary. I stood before the very portals of eternity and warned no one."

I opened one of my notebooks and read on the margin of a page a note I had made many years before. "To travel through the desert with others, to suffer thirst, to find a spring, to drink of it, and not tell the others that they may be spared is exactly the same as enjoying Christ and not telling others about Him."

"Oh, Lord," I moaned. "Send me back home. Let me repair watches. I am not worthy to be Your evangelist."

As I sat there, like Jeremiah, trying to resign my commission, I saw a man coming toward me. He introduced himself as a Jewish doctor who had been aboard my flight. "I watched you all through those hours on the plane when our lives were in great danger," he said. "You were neither afraid nor anxious. What is your secret?"

A ray of light. Perhaps God was giving me another chance. "I am a Christian," I said joyfully. "I know the Messiah, Jesus, the Son of God. He died on the cross for my sins, and yours also. If our burning plane had fallen into the sea I had the assurance of going to Heaven."

We sat and talked for a long time before he excused himself. But a few minutes later he was back again. "I must hear more about this Jesus who gives you such peace," he said.

Four times he got up and left, and yet he kept coming back. Each time his request was the same. "Tell me more about Jesus."

I told him how Jesus gives us authority over Satan. How Jesus has promised us mansions in heaven. How He gives to all who believe the power to become the sons of God.

The Jewish doctor drank it all in and finally left saying I had given him much to think about. I sat back in my chair. The Lord, my treasurer, had given me just enough of His wealth that I might share it with one of His hungry children. I had been found worthy to evangelize after all. And in the process I had learned another valuable lesson in the school of life. When I am weak, then am I strong (2 Corinthians 12:10).

13. A Place to Be

EVERYONE NEEDS A place to be. One of the great joys of heaven is that it is a place, a prepared place. I am thankful that there I will have a special house that is reserved just for me.

When I was born, Father and Mother were living on the Korte Prinsegracht, a typical Amsterdam canal. I was born prematurely and my skin was blue. Uncle Hendrik, Tante Jans's husband, looked at me and exclaimed, "I hope the Lord will quickly take this poor little creature to His home in heaven."

But my parents and Tante Anna did not agree with him. They surrounded me with love and care. However, since there were no incubators in those early days, I cried much from the cold. Tante Anna, knowing I missed the warmth of the special place under my mother's heart from which I had come, rolled me in her apron and tied me against her stomach. There I was warm and quiet.

Many years later I was in a primitive house in Africa. The bathtub was made from an old oil drum that had been sawed in half. Missionaries lived there and they invited me in to eat with them. Walking into the kitchen, I saw an African woman with the white missionary child strapped tightly to her back.

"Hey, how nice she has your baby on her back," I said to the missionary mother.

The white mother smiled and said, "The baby was so fearful this morning. All she would do was cry. When the African cook came to the house she took one look at the baby and said, 'Ah, Missee, give me the baby. I will keep her quiet.' So she strapped her on her back and the baby has slept all morning while the cook has been busy around the kitchen."

I could understand that feeling of having a place—of belonging. I was often afraid

244

Here are some pictures taken while
TRAMPING FOR THE LORD

An early photo taken with my own camera and developed by myself.

Below: At the former concentration camp Darmstadt after the war.

I received an Indian garland in Delhi.

Below: At the Christian Literature Crusade bookstore in Ipswich, England.

In North Borneo with a small missionary plane. *Right*: In East Germany.

With missionary children in Africa. *Below*: In South Africa
with Mr. Rowland, a former coworker of Andrew Murray's.

Conny (left) and I bid farewell to Dr. Gwen Shepherd
in Argentina.

Below: In a pedicab in
Formosa.

On the leprosy island at
Ruanda.

With Brother Andrew in Viet
Nam.

In Viet Nam with Tsan, who called me "double old grand-mother."

Below: With two ministers in Tokyo.

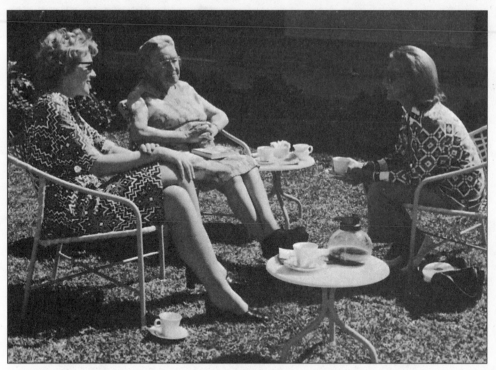

Ellen and I with Mrs. Billy Graham in North Carolina. *Below*: In Bermuda.

as a small child. Sleeping beside my sister, Nollie, who was a year and a half older than me, I begged to be able to hold her hand at night. She refused, and instead gave me the hem of her nightgown. By and by she did not even like me holding on to that, but told me to hold on to the hem of my doll's nightgown.

Then, when I was five years old, the Lord Jesus became a great reality to me. My mother told me how He loved little children and was even willing to live in my heart if I asked Him in. I did, and a feeling of peace and security took the place of the fear I had so often felt. From then on I could go to sleep at night and not be afraid.

As a child I prayed a nursery rhyme:

> Ik ga slapen, ik ben moe;
> 'k Sluit mijn oogjes beiden toe.
> Heere, houd ook deze nacht
> Weder over mij de wacht.

> (I'm going to sleep, I am tired;
> I close both my little eyes.
> Lord, watch over me again
> The whole night long.)

In all these years that I have been a "tramp for the Lord," I have often been afraid. But in those moments I have always reached up and touched the hem of Jesus' garment. He has never failed to wrap me close to Him. Yet, I still long for that time when I shall have a mansion in heaven.

Here on earth, at the age of seventy-seven, for the first time I found a place of my own—a beautiful apartment in Baarn, Holland. Even though I am seldom there (for I intend to keep on traveling until I die in harness), it is still a place to hang up my pictures on the walls and put the few sticks of furniture that I have saved from my days in the Beje. Yet, even with this "home" here on earth, I still long most of all for my heavenly mansion.

When I was a child, Tante Jans composed a children's song. I remember two lines:

> 'k zou zoo graag eens komen, Heiland,
> In dat heerlijk Vaderhuis.

> (I should just like to come, Saviour,
> In that beautiful Father-house.)

As a child, however, I always got the words mixed up when I sang the song. Instead of singing, "to come," I would sing "to peek." The older people laughed at my mistake but I thought they were very stupid. With all my heart I meant what I was singing. As a little child I did not want to go to heaven, I just wanted to peek for a moment. Now, though, that my days have grown long, I no longer sing as I did as a child. Now my greatest desire is to come for all eternity into the beautiful Father-house.

14. *Obedience*

OBEDIENCE IS EASY when you know you are being guided by a God who never makes mistakes.

Conny and I were in Africa and one day during my Quiet Time I began to feel that God was telling me it was time to leave Africa.

"Lord, where do You want us to go?" I asked.

"Argentina," came the answer deep in my heart.

Argentina? I had never been to Argentina. I could not speak a word of Spanish. In those days air travel was sometimes poor in Africa and to fly across the Atlantic Ocean to Buenos Aires would be a trying ordeal. Yet as I sat before the Lord the word *Argentina* became even stronger.

"Yes, but . . . ," I started to answer Him. Then I remembered that obedience never says, "Yes, but . . . . " Rather it always says, "Yes, Lord!" Some months before a missionary by the name of Breson had written me, asking if I would be willing to speak in his church if I ever came to Argentina. I did not know Breson very well, so I had not thought much about the invitation. Now, however, with God speaking to me so strongly, I sat down and wrote Mr. Breson a letter, asking if he could meet us in Buenos Aires and arrange some meetings for me to speak.

We waited almost a month, but there was no answer. "Are you sure it is the Lord's guidance for us to go to Argentina?" Conny asked. "Perhaps this man Breson no longer lives in Buenos Aires. What if we go and there is no one to meet us? Then what will we do?"

I reached out and touched Conny's hand. "Yes, I know it is God's will for us to go to Argentina. Some years ago God spoke to me and told me to go to Japan. I had no money. I knew no one in Japan. I could not speak the language. Yet I knew

God had led me. I finally saved up enough money to fly to Tokyo and stepped off the plane on a dark, rainy night in that strange land and said, 'Lord, here I am. Now what?' I remembered that David Morken was there with Youth for Christ. He found me a room and because of my obedience God opened many doors of ministry. I was alone on that trip, but this time I have you. No, I know we should go to Argentina."

The plane flight was much longer than we expected. Connections were very bad and we had to spend one whole day in a hot, dirty African airport awaiting a connecting flight that would take us on to West Africa for our flight across the ocean. It was almost midnight when we caught our last plane and I could sense Conny's anxiety. However, I was sure of God's guidance.

We finally arrived in the busy Buenos Aires airport. I looked out across the hundreds of hurrying people, hoping I might see Mr. Breson's face. There was no one.

Conny and I struggled with our luggage and at the ticket desk a man asked us, in broken English, if he could send our bags to our address.

"I do not yet know my address," I said. Conny looked worried. I knew her thoughts. *Do you know for sure it is Argentina where God would have you work?* We were both exhausted from all-night plane rides which had been added to the ordeal of waiting in all those African airports. We carried our suitcases to the curb and I sat down. "See if you can find a taxi," I said to Conny. "Perhaps there is a YMCA hotel nearby."

But there were no taxis. The air was heavy and hot. I finally asked a man, "Do you know where there is a YMCA hotel?"

The man gave me a blank stare and moved on. I could speak Dutch, German, and English, but none of those languages helped me here. We sat on our suitcases looking at the streams of traffic passing down the street.

"Aunty, Tante Corrie, are you sure that God's guidance brought us to Argentina?"

I looked at Conny. Her face was dirty and creased with lines of exhaustion. I, too, was hot and tired and unhappy. But I was also sure of God's leadership. "Yes," I said wearily. "I am sure."

"I don't like Argentine mosquitoes," Conny said, slapping her arm. "They are just as cruel as African mosquitoes."

We looked at each other and laughed. Here we were in a strange country with a strange language. Holland was far, far away, yet we were laughing.

Then I heard a man's voice from the other side of the street shouting. *"Bent u Corrie ten Boom?"* ("Are you Corrie ten Boom?")

My name. My language. What joy! I could barely see the man on the far side of the streaming traffic, but he was waving his arms as he shouted.

"Ja, dat ben ik," I shouted back.

The man had to wait for the traffic to thin before he could run across the street. Finally, after dodging cars, he stepped onto the curb. "I am Reverend Mees," he said, extending his hand. "I did not think you would be here but felt I should come and check just the same."

"Do you know Mr. Breson?" I asked. "I had hoped he would meet us."

"Did you not receive Breson's letter?" Reverend Mees asked. There was a look of alarm on his face.

"No, we heard nothing from him."

Reverend Mees put his hand on his forehead and looked toward the sky. "Oh, this is too bad. He wrote you a letter telling you not to come. He could not arrange any meetings and is now on a mission tour in the jungle. He will not be back for two months."

I sat back down on my suitcases, feeling even more tired than before.

"Do you know if there is a YMCA hotel in the city?" I asked, as if this would solve all our problems.

Reverend Mees smiled, "No, I do not know of a YMCA hotel, but a dear friend of mine, a woman doctor, knew about the possibility of your coming. She asked me to bring you to her hospital and from there she will take you to her home. She has a spare bedroom and a little apartment where you can be very comfortable."

Dr. Gwen Shepherd received us graciously at the hospital. I knew at once that she was one of God's precious children and therefore my sister also. She took us to her car and for the first time I experienced what traffic in Buenos Aires is like. Traveling in the jungles of Africa was nothing to the streets of Buenos Aires. There were no traffic lights. At every intersection the cars came racing together, four abreast. Those who arrived first were the first ones through. I never saw an accident (but perhaps that was because I kept my eyes closed most of the time!). However, after bouncing and speeding down the streets, we finally reached her home where she provided wonderful hospitality. That night she invited a number of youth group leaders to her home and I had an opportunity to share with them. The next day another invitation came for me to speak and before long I was even busier than I had been any other place on the earth. Dr. Shepherd had a wonderful gift of administration and arranged much ministry for me. It was indeed God's guidance for me to come to Argentina. What a joy I would have missed had I disobeyed.

Perhaps the greatest joy of the entire trip, however, happened one afternoon in Dr. Shepherd's hospital. I was allowed into a ward where polio patients were being treated. One room was filled with people in iron lungs. I had never seen the wheezing, gasping iron lungs before and they scared me.

"Do you wish to talk to some of the patients?" a kind nurse asked me.

I looked around and said, "No, I think I am unable to talk. I just want to go off somewhere and cry."

Always when I say that I am not able, I get the same answer from the Lord. He says, "I know you can't. I have known it already a long time. I am glad now you know it for yourself for now you can let Me do it."

"All right, Lord, You do it," I said. And surely the Lord did. I went from one iron lung to another telling the men and women about the Lord Jesus Christ who breathes into each one of us His Holy Spirit.

Then I came to a man on a rocking bed. He had a different kind of polio and instead of being in a lung he was on a bed that rocked up and down. When his head was up he could breathe in. When his head went down he breathed out. The nurse told me he was Jewish.

"Ah," I said, "I am happy to meet one of God's chosen people. My old father, my dear sister, and some others in my family died in concentration camps because we loved the Jews. I, too, was in prison for helping Jews. But tell me, do you know the Jew, Jesus, as your personal Messiah?"

The bed rocked up and down and he shook his head for he could not speak. He had a long tube in his nose and could only move one hand slightly to write tiny notes.

"Then is it all right if I tell you about Him?" I asked.

He picked up his stubby pencil and scribbled on a small notebook on the side of his moving bed. "I am ready to listen."

I stayed beside that rocking bed and told my Jewish friend about the great Messiah, the one whom the prophet called, "Wonderful, Counsellor, The mighty God, The everlasting Father, The Prince of Peace" (Isaiah 9:6).

I finished speaking and from my bag took a small embroidery. On one side was stitched a beautiful crown. The other side was quite mixed up. "When I see you on this bed," I said, "not speaking, not moving, I think of this embroidery." I held up the back side of the embroidery. "Your life is like this. See how dark it is. See how the threads are knotted and tangled, mixed up. But when you turn it around then you can see that God is actually weaving a crown for your life. God has a plan for your life and He is working it out in beauty."

He picked up his pencil and wrote again:

thanks God I am already seeing the beautiful side

Thanks God I am already seeing the beautiful side.

What a miracle. He understood God did not want him to become a Gentile. Rather he would become a completed Jew. I prayed and thanked the Lord with him. Then it was time to go and Dr. Shepherd once again took me to her beautiful home.

The next day I returned to the polio ward and asked the nurse if I could speak with my Jewish friend.

"I am sorry," she said, "but your Jewish friend on the rocking bed is no longer with us. Just five minutes after you left he beckoned me to come to his side. There was a wonderful light shining in his eyes and he wrote on a little paper. 'For the first time I prayed in Jesus' name.' Then he closed his eyes and died."

"Then I am not sorry," I answered. "I am glad. I know he has his own crown of life. Praise God."

God has a divine pattern for each of His children. Although the threads may seem knotted—as they did when we were sitting outside the airport in Buenos Aires—on the other side is a crown.

For my thoughts are not your thoughts, neither are your ways my ways, saith the Lord.

Isaiah 55:8

15. *The Real Corrie ten Boom*

WHILE IN HAVANA, Cuba, I was asked to speak at a youth rally in the Salvation Army hall. Of course this was before the Communist take-over so there was still freedom to talk openly about the Lord Jesus Christ.

It was a hot June night and the hall was small and stifling. The meeting was scheduled to begin at seven o'clock, but more and more groups continued to arrive from other parts of the city, so no one seemed to be in a hurry to start. As in most Latin American countries everything was, *"Mañana, mañana,"* even the church services.

Finally, I was seated on the platform between two men with huge drums. One of them, an old Negro with white hair, tried to show his love for the Lord by vigorously beating one of the drums. The sound was almost unbearable. The captain had a very sharp voice and led the singing by shouting, waving his hands, and pounding on the top of the pulpit. The young Cubans sang loudly with much clapping of hands and stomping of feet. By nine o'clock I was already worn out, and all I had done was sit and listen. There was a terrific ringing in my ears and my head was splitting with a headache from the crashing sounds of the drums. Finally, though, I was called on to speak and the hall grew silent. I was grateful for the few moments of peace.

After I spoke the captain introduced a missionary who had brought his slides. The lights were turned out and we all sat in the miserable heat while the missionary began his long slide presentation. Like many missionaries, he had been called upon to do some medical work in the field, so many of his slides dealt with that.

He had photograph after photograph of drugs and medicines which had been given him by various doctors. "This particular bottle of pills was given me by Dr. Smith," he droned on. Then flipping to his next slide he said, "And this box of medicines was sent me by Dr. Jones."

The young people in the hall were not the least bit interested in seeing these boxes, bottles, and jars. The noise grew louder and louder and finally reached such volume that the missionary had to shout to make himself heard. It was ten-thirty when he finally finished his presentation and the lights came back on.

Now the room was filled with flying bugs, moths, insects, and some kind of huge flying beetle which buzzed around the exposed light bulbs and then dropped to the floor or in people's laps. The young people were climbing over the backs of the benches, babies were asleep on the floor, and everybody was sweating profusely. I did not think I could stand much more.

Then the captain came to the front again and began to preach. A flying insect went in my ear and another was caught in my hair. I looked for some way to escape, but I was boxed in by the huge drums on either side. Finally the captain gave an invitation for people to come forward and be saved.

"Surely no one is in a mood to do anything but go home," I said to myself. Then I thought, *I hope nobody comes to the front. I long to get out of here and go to bed.*

Yet, to my great surprise, people began getting up from their seats and coming to the front. They were kneeling around the altar rail. Twenty of them. I saw tears in the eyes of some of the young Cubans and listened as the captain spoke with great persuasion, his voice full of love.

A startling realization swept over me. I was selfish. I had hoped nobody would be saved because of my own weariness. My sleep was more important than the salvation of sinners. Oh, what a terrible egotist I was. Suddenly my bed was no longer important. I was willing to stay up all night if God was working. But what could I do with my guilty feeling for having been so selfish?

Then I began to praise God, for I had learned what to do with my sin. I confessed it to the heavenly Father in Jesus' Name and I claimed His forgiveness. With joy I was able to get up and pray with the twenty young people who had made the important decision to commit their lives to Jesus Christ. It was eleven-thirty when the meeting finally came to a close.

The next morning, Sunday, I spoke in a beautiful church which was filled with the most prominent people in Havana. As I entered the imposing building I was given a copy of the parish magazine which had been handed to all the other people. In it I read an introductory article about my ministry. It said, "Corrie ten Boom is a most popular world evangelist. . . . She is tireless and completely selfless in her absolute dedication to the cause of the Gospel. . . ."

Oh, Lord, I thought, *if only these people knew who the real Corrie ten Boom is, they would not have come out this morning to hear me.*

"Tell them," the Lord answered immediately.

By that time I was seated on the platform looking out over the sea of faces before me. "But Lord, if I tell them, they will reject me."

"Can I bless a lie?" the Lord asked me in my heart. "I can only bless the truth. You do want My blessing, don't you?"

Then it was time for me to speak. The gracious minister gave a flowery introduction and asked me to come to the pulpit. Before I could give my message, however, I knew what I had to do.

Reading first from the parish paper I then said, "Sometimes I get a headache from the heat of the halo that people put around my head. Would you like to know what Corrie ten Boom is really like?" Then I told them what happened the evening before—how my own sleep had been more important in my eyes than the salvation of young people. "That," I said, "was Corrie ten Boom. What egotism! What selfishness! But the joy is that Corrie ten Boom knew what to do with her sins. When I confessed them to the Father, Jesus Christ washed them in His blood. They are now cast into the deepest sea and a sign is put up that says, NO FISHING ALLOWED. Corrie ten Boom is lazy, selfish, and filled with ego. But Jesus in Corrie ten Boom is just the opposite of all these things."

Then I waited. Surely now that the congregation knew what kind of person I was, they would no longer want to hear me. Instead I sensed them all leaning forward, eager to hear what I might say. Instead of rejecting me, they accepted me. Instead of a beautiful church with prominent members and a popular world evangelist, we were all sinners who knew that Jesus died to lift us out of the vicious circle of ego into the light of His love.

God had blessed the truth!

16. *Checkpoint Charlie*

CONNY AND I stood in line, along with other people, outside Checkpoint Charlie, the gate for foreigners into East Berlin. Many of those in line were Dutch and I saw they were being passed without difficulty. Everything seemed routine: Hand your passport to a guard, walk down the line, and receive your passport back with a stamp that allowed you to spend the one day in East Berlin. I hoped it would be as easy for us when it was our turn to be checked.

Finally we were in front of the window. The guard looked at our passports, looked in a book, and then turned and said something to another man behind him.

"Is there a problem?" I asked the man.

He turned and gave me a stern look. "Come with me," he said, motioning for Conny and me to follow him into a small room to one side. We were questioned and then they opened my handbag. There they found two books. One of them was one of my books which had been published in East Germany. The other was a copy of Billy Graham's *Peace With God* which had also been translated into German.

The officer picked up Billy Graham's book and shouted, "What? A book by that machine gun of God!"

I laughed. "I like the name you give to Billy Graham. I will tell him what you called him the next time I see him—God's Machine Gun. However, if I am not allowed to take the books with me into East Berlin, I will just give them to you and you can let us go on."

"Oh, no," he said sternly, "it is not that easy. First we have to write up your deposition."

He searched me to see if I had hidden more books before he began his inquisition. I did not like his rough, crude manner and told him so.

"I really feel as if I am in the hands of the Gestapo again," I said.

"No," he said, abashed, "I am no Gestapo."

"You surely have the same manners," I said bluntly.

He softened his approach but still kept us in the inquisition room for more than three hours. A woman typist copied everything I said and wrote it into a "protocol." I learned that my name was on the blacklist for East Germany, which was the reason I was being so thoroughly questioned. However, I was primarily upset because we had only a few hours to visit the Christians in East Berlin and our time was being wasted here in the guard station.

"Lord," I complained silently, "why are You keeping us here when we need to be about Your business in East Berlin?"

Then slowly it came through my stubborn Dutch mind that God had us in the guard office for a purpose. He not only loved the Christians in East Berlin but He loved these Communist guards also—the officer and the uniformed typist. What a sad mistake we sometimes make when we think that God only cares about Christians. Although God desires that all people become Christians, He does not love one group more than another. In fact, it was for the world that God gave His only begotten Son, and Jesus Himself said He had not come to call the righteous but sinners to repentence *(see* Matthew 9:13). I remembered the words of Jesus when He said, "You will be led before kings and governors for My name's sake. This will be a time, an opportunity, for you to bear testimony. Resolve and settle it in your minds, not to meditate and prepare beforehand how you are to answer." *(See* Matthew 10:18, 19.)

Suddenly my attitude toward the officer changed. Instead of an enemy, I saw him as one of those for whom Christ died. Now I answered every question testifying of my faith in Jesus. It became almost a kind of game.

I asked the officer, "Do you ever read the Bible?"

"No, I am a Marxist," he said stubbornly.

"The Bible was written especially for Marxists," I said. "It says that God so greatly loved the Marxists that He gave His only begotten Son so that any Marxist who believes in Him shall not perish, but have eternal life."

Both the officer and the woman typist were listening with serious faces. I went ahead to talk about the two problems of the human race—sin and death—and stated that the Bible gives us the answer to these problems by telling us about Jesus.

"Why don't you keep my books and read them?" I said. "I will be glad to autograph my book for you and the book by Billy Graham will answer many of your questions."

"Must I read it?" the officer said.

"It will not do you any harm," I laughed.

The officer laughed too, but then, catching himself, became very serious and businesslike again.

"I see, Fraulein, that you are carrying chocolate with you? What is your reason?"

"I am taking it for the minister's children in East Berlin. Don't you bring chocolate with you when you visit a family with children?"

"No, I take flowers with me," he said seriously.

"Flowers are nice for parents, but children prefer chocolate. Besides, I often preach about chocolate."

"What crazy people we have here today," the officer said. "You carry books by a man who talks like a machine gun and then tell me you preach about chocolate. Tell me, what kind of sermon do you get from a chocolate bar, old woman?"

"Several years ago," I answered, "I spoke to a group of Germans who prided themselves as intellectuals. They would not receive me because they felt that they were more profound in their theology than I. So, my last time with them I brought them all some Dutch chocolate. Since chocolate was very rare after the war, they eagerly accepted my gift. Later, when I stood to speak to them, I told them, 'No one has said anything to me about the chocolate.'

"They disagreed, saying that they had all thanked me for it.

"'I did not mean that,' I said. 'I mean no one questioned me about it. No one asked whether it had been manufactured in Holland or Germany, what quantities it contained of cocoa, sugar, milk, or vitamins. Instead of analyzing it, you just ate it.'

"Then I picked up my Bible and said, 'It is the same with this Book. If you try to analyze it as a book of science or even a book of theology, you cannot be nourished by it. Like chocolate, it is to be eaten and enjoyed, not picked apart bit by bit.'"

I stopped talking and noticed, once again, that the officer and the typist were deeply interested in what I was saying. Then the officer straightened up, cleared his throat, and said to the typist, "Please type Fraulein ten Boom's protocol and we will let her pass." With that he stood and left the room, never looking back.

I sat quietly while the typist finished typing her report. Moments later the officer was back. He pulled the paper from the typewriter and read aloud. "When in prison Corrie ten Boom received from God the commission to bring the Gospel of Jesus Christ over the whole world. Her church has taught her to bring chocolate when she visits families with children."

The officer nodded and excused himself, saying he had to read it to his superior officer before I could be approved for entrance into East Berlin. While he was gone I talked with the typist, urging her to accept Jesus as her Lord. She listened intently, reading through some of the pages in my book. However, when the officer returned she straightened up and returned to her typewriter.

I handed Billy Graham's book to the officer. "Sir, be sure and take this book by God's Machine Gun home with you. It will change your life."

He tried to look severe, but behind his eyes I could sense both hunger and thirst. Without saying a word he took the book and slipped it into his briefcase. He handed my book to the typist and motioned her to put it in her purse. Then he opened the door and pointed in the direction of East Berlin. "I am sorry to have detained you so long, Fraulein," he said. "But what we have been doing here is even more important than your visit to your friends."

I shook his hand and Conny and I entered the Communist city, wondering if the officer actually realized the truth of his last statement. What we had to do in East Berlin was important, but even more important was bringing the Good News of Jesus to those who walk in darkness.

17. Facing Death

WATCHMAN NEE ONCE said, "When my feet were whipped my hands suffered pain."

Christians all over the world are bound together as the body of Christ. Many Americans, in particular, do not realize it, but a part of that body is suffering the most terrible persecution and tribulation in the history of mankind. If we are members of that same body—and we are—then we must suffer with them, pray for them, and where it is possible, help them.

I remember hearing of a missionary—a single woman—who turned her back on all her possessions at home and went to China. "Are you not afraid?" a friend asked as she prepared to board the ship. "I am afraid of only one thing," she said, "that I should become a grain of wheat not willing to die."

How much more like Christ that is than the churches who gather at Thanksgiving to sing:

Let thy congregation escape tribulation!

Several years ago I was in Africa in a little country where an enemy had taken over the government. There was great oppression against the Christians by the new government. The first night I was there some of the native Christians were commanded to come to the police station to be registered. When they arrived they were arrested and during the night they were secretly executed. The next day the same thing happened with other Christians. The third day it was the same. By that time the entire district realized that the Christians were being systematically murdered. It was the intent of the new government to eradicate them all—men, women, and children—much as Hitler tried to eradicate all the Jews.

I was to speak in a little church on Sunday morning. The people came, but I could see fear and tension written on every face. All during the service they looked at each other, their eyes asking the same questions: "Will this one I am sitting beside be the next one to be killed? Will I be the next one?"

I looked out on that congregation of black and white faces. The room was hot and stuffy. Moths and other insects came through the screenless windows and swirled around the naked light bulbs hanging over the bare, wooden benches upon which the natives sat. They were all looking at me, expecting, hoping, that I could bring them a word from God for this tragic hour.

I opened my Bible and read 1 Peter 4:12-14 (PHILLIPS).

> And now, dear friends of mine, I beg you not to be unduly alarmed at the fiery ordeals which come to test your faith, as though this were some abnormal experience. You should be glad, because it means you are called to share Christ's sufferings. One day, when he shows himself in full splendor to men, you will be filled with the most tremendous joy. If you are reproached for being Christ's followers, that is a great privilege, for you can be sure that God's Spirit of glory is resting upon you.

I closed the Book and began to talk, simply, as an aunt would talk to her nieces and nephews. "When I was a little girl," I said, "I went to my father and said, 'Daddy, I am afraid that I will never be strong enough to be a martyr for Jesus Christ.'

"'Tell me,' Father said, 'when you take a train trip from Haarlem to Amsterdam, when do I give you the money for the ticket? Three weeks before?'

"'No, Daddy, you give me the money for the ticket just before we get on the train.'

"'That is right,' my father said, 'and so it is with God's strength. Our wise Father in heaven knows when you are going to need things too. Today you do not need the strength to be a martyr; but as soon as you are called upon for the honor of facing death for Jesus, He will supply the strength you need—just in time.'"

I looked out at my African friends. Many of them had already lost loved ones to the firing squad or the headsman's axe. I knew that others would surely die that week. They were listening intently.

"I took great comfort in my father's advice," I said. "Later I had to suffer for Jesus in a concentration camp. He indeed gave me all the courage and power I needed."

My African friends were nodding seriously. They, too, believed God would supply all their needs, even the power to face death bravely.

"Tell us more, Tante Corrie," one grizzled old black man said. It was as though they were storing up all the truth they could so they could draw on it in the day of trial.

I told them of an incident that had taken place in the concentration camp at Ravensbruck. "A group of my fellow prisoners had approached me, asking me to tell them some Bible stories. In the concentration camp the guards called the Bible *das Lügenbuch*—the book of lies. Cruel death punishment had been promised for any prisoner who was found possessing a Bible or talking about the Lord. However, I went to my little cot, found my Bible, and returned to the group of prisoners.

"Suddenly I was aware of a figure behind me. One of the prisoners formed the words with her lips, 'Hide your Bible. It's Lony.' I knew Lony well. She was one of the most cruel of all the *aufseherinen*—the women guards. However, I knew that I had to obey God who had guided me so clearly to bring a Bible message to the prisoners that morning. Lony remained motionless behind me while I finished my teaching and then I said, 'Let's now sing a hymn of praise.'

"I could see the worried, anxious looks on the faces of the prisoners. Before it had been only me speaking. Now they, too, were going to have to use their mouths to sing. But I felt God wanted us to be bold, even in the face of the enemy. So—we sang.

"When the hymn was finished I heard a voice behind me. 'Another song like that one,' she said. It was Lony. She had enjoyed the singing and wanted to hear more. The prisoners took heart and we sang again—and again. Afterwards I went to her and spoke to her about the Lord Jesus Christ. Strangely, her behavior began to change until, in a crude sort of way, she became a friend."

I finished my story and stood silently while the words took their effect on my African friends. "Let me tell you what I learned from that experience," I told them. "I knew that every word I said could mean death. Yet never before had I felt such peace and joy in my heart as while I was giving the Bible message in the presence of mine enemy. God gave me the grace and power I needed—the money for the train ticket arrived just the moment I was to step on the train."

The faces before me broke into broad grins. Gone were the wrinkles of fear and anxiety. Once again their eyes were flashing with joy and their hearts were filled with peace. I closed the service by reading a poem of Amy Carmichael.

> We follow a scarred Captain,
> Should we not have scars?
> Under His faultless orders
> We follow to the wars.
> Lest we forget, Lord, when we meet,
> Show us Thy hands and feet.

The meeting was over and the Africans stood to leave. Then softly, in the back of the room, someone began singing an old gospel song.

There's a land that is fairer than day,
And by faith we can see it afar.
For the Father waits over the way,
To prepare us a dwelling place there.
In the sweet by and by, we shall meet on that beautiful shore,
In the sweet by and by, we shall meet on that beautiful shore.

I don't know how many were killed that week, but someone told me that more than half those who had attended that service met a martyr's death—and thus received a martyr's crown. But I know that God's Spirit of glory had been resting upon them. (*See* 1 Peter 4:14.)

18. *Saved by a Newborn Infant*

ONE OF MY greatest privileges is visiting with missionaries all over the world. Those of us who live in the comfort and security of our homes cannot begin to imagine what the life of a missionary is like. Many of them have no fresh water and only simple food. They constantly face the threat of sickness and infection. Some live in primitive places where their very lives are in danger. Much to my sadness, yet to the glory of God, the list is growing longer each day of men and women who are literally laying down their lives for Jesus' sake on the mission field. These men and women stand on the front lines, often in lonesome places, but knowing that their Master who has placed them there will also stand with them.

Once in a primitive spot in Africa I visited a missionary couple. Their small home was located in a delightful spot that gave a beautiful view of lakes and mountains. They had very little of this world's goods, but were rich in God's grace and had been given a homesite that many wealthy people would pay thousands of dollars to have as their own. Crowded into this tiny shack were six children, the youngest just a few months old. "Come with me," the missionary wife said as she picked up the baby and walked outside. "I want to tell you a story."

We sat on a bench overlooking an awesome scene of grandeur. Spreading before us was a mighty view of the mountains, covered with deep jungle and spotted with lakes and waterfalls.

"To have many little children can be a burden for a missionary," she said. "There comes a time when you have to send them to the homeland because there are no good schools here. But while they are small you try to enjoy them."

She paused and looked down at the sweet baby asleep in her arms. Her voice was tense with emotion as she continued. "But when I learned I was going to have another baby, I rebelled against God. We already had five small children and it did not seem fair that we should have to bear another. My health was not good and I looked upon having another child with great sorrow and unhappiness."

Tears were streaming down her face as she talked. "Was it not enough to have five children? Oh, how my heart cried out at God and there were times when I wished He would take the baby from me.

"The time for the birth was here. I was very weak and there were no doctors nearby. We had no one to leave the other children with, so my husband put us all in the car and drove us into a town where there was a good mission hospital. There we stayed until the baby was born."

The tiny child stirred in her arms, stretched her little arms and yawned. How precious she looked! The mother's voice grew soft. "When we returned to our house with the new baby we learned that in the short days we had been gone the dreaded Mau Mau had come. They had murdered every white person in the entire area. Had we been home we would have all been killed."

She hugged the little baby to her breast, tears flowing down her face. "This little darling was sent by God to save all our lives. Never again shall I rebel against His ways for our lives."

19. *Miracles Every Day*

IT WAS MY first time in India and I was to speak at a conference of missionaries in Vellore. However, when my plane arrived in Bangkok I was told the next plane to Vellore did not leave for three days.

"But this means I will have to miss the first three days of the conference," I said.

"We are sorry, but there is no way," the man at the ticket counter told me. However, the airlines did make arrangements for me to stay at a hotel until the next plane left.

Arriving at the hotel I asked the kindly Indian man who was in charge of my arrangements, "Is there no possibility that I can catch another plane to Vellore?"

"The airlines are making every effort," he assured me.

"Then we must pray that God will help them," I said.

"Do you *profess* to be a Christian?" he asked with a startled look on his face.

"Yes, I do," I answered. "I am a *professor* of Jesus Christ. And what about you?" He hung his head. "I have been, but I am what you call a lost sheep."

"Hallelujah!" I said. "Then you are just the one sheep for whom the Shepherd left the ninety-nine to find."

We talked a long time in the lobby of the hotel. Finally I asked the man if he would be willing to come back to Jesus. "Oh, yes," he said. "For I believe God kept you here just for this reason."

We prayed together in the hotel and then I said to him, "Now that God has used me for this miracle will you pray with me for another miracle—that I might arrive in Vellore in time for the conference?"

The man leaped to his feet. "While you pray I must run an errand. I'll be back shortly." With that he was out the door, leaving me sitting among my suitcases.

Half-an-hour later he was back. "Make quickly ready for the plane," he said. "I think God has performed your miracle. We have discovered another plane going by a different route to Vellore."

"Did you arrange that?" I asked.

"I did," he smiled as he hoisted my bags to his back. "But don't thank me. I must thank you for bringing me back to the Shepherd."

We rushed madly to the airport and I found the plane was supposed to have left long before. However, they were holding it just for me. Panting, I climbed the steps to the plane.

"Ah, Professor," the stewardess said as she closed the door behind me, "we were afraid we would have to leave you."

"Professor?" I asked. "What's this?"

"Oh," she smiled sweetly. "We know all about you. Our hotel agent told us that you are an important *professor* from Holland who has to give significant speeches in Vellore. That is why we have held the plane on the ground until you arrived."

I took my seat near a window. Outside the once-lost sheep was grinning and waving. I waved back. *Surely,* I thought, *God not only had a special reason for keeping me in Bangkok, but He must have an equally important reason for wanting me in Vellore.*

I was right. My first talk to the missionary conference in Vellore was the next morning. I spoke on the reality of God's promises in the Bible. After the service I slipped away from the crowd and strolled in a beautiful garden near the conference center. It was alive with color: green and red crotons mixed their rich colors with the dark orange of the copper plants and the rainbow hues of the flowering shrubs. *How wonderful,* I thought, *to be in the center of God's will.*

"Excuse me," a shy voice said from behind.

I turned and recognized one of the English missionary ladies. Her body seemed weak. She hesitated to speak but at last said, "Do you really believe in God's promises?"

"Yes, I do," I said.

"Do you believe the Lord still heals the sick?"

"Of course," I answered. I motioned for her to sit with me on a stone bench near a flowering hibiscus. First I read to her from the Bible where Jesus said we would lay hands on the sick and they would be healed *(see* Mark 16:18–20). Then I told her of a recent experience in Indonesia.

"I was staying in the house of a dear Chinese pastor and his wife," I said. "Since we were so busy the wife had no time to cook, so a member of their church, another Chinese lady, came every day in a ricksha to fix me a good Chinese meal.

"One morning I was sitting in the house and looked out the window. I saw this dear woman stumbling up the pathway. Her head was bleeding and her dress badly torn. I rushed out to meet her and helped her into the house. Her ricksha had collided with another ricksha and she had been badly injured, hitting her head against a metal part of the primitive vehicle. Since Chinese people were not popular in Indonesia at that time, no doctor would come to see her. Instead they just brought her to the house and let her out.

"I knew her condition was serious and also knew that the doctor would not come to the Chinese pastor's house either. Therefore, I just laid my hands on her and prayed in Jesus' Name that she be healed. She was restored instantly."

The missionary lady was listening intently. "Must you know a person's type of sickness before you pray for them?" she asked.

"No, I'm not a doctor. I do not heal. It is the Lord who heals."

"I am very ill," she said quietly. "Will you lay hands on me and pray?"

"I will," I said. She slipped off the bench and knelt in that beautiful garden while I put my hands on her head and prayed for her to be healed in the Name of Jesus Christ.

She rose slowly to her feet. "Now I will tell you my sickness," she said. "I have leprosy."

I had been in leper colonies and suddenly I was filled with a great fear. *Oh,* I thought, *this is far too difficult for the Lord. I wish now she had told me ahead of time so I would have known not to pray for her.*

Then I felt ashamed and asked forgiveness for my small faith and unbelief. After all, it was not I who said He would heal the sick—but He who had said it.

Some years passed and I lost the name and address of the lady missionary, although many times I remembered that time in the garden and continued to pray for her. Five years later I was back in India, staying with friends of the Pocket Testament League. One afternoon there was a knock at my hotel door. "Do you remember me?" a beautiful lady asked.

I looked at her and said, "I have seen you before but I do not remember who you are."

"Do you remember a time in Vellore when you laid hands on a leper patient and prayed in Jesus' Name that she be healed?"

"Oh, yes," I exclaimed. "I surely remember you. But you are a different person."

She smiled. "The Lord wonderfully healed me. The doctors say I am absolutely healed from leprosy."

"Thank You, Lord," I said aloud. "Your Name be glorified! You are always ready to meet our needs, even when our faith is small."

20. God's Word, the Sword— God's Perfect Weapon

IT HAD BEEN a hectic half year. I had flown from New Zealand to Korea where I had spoken in more than two hundred and fifty meetings in a three-month period. I then returned to Hamilton, New Zealand, for a brief visit before continuing to India.

In New Zealand I had stayed with a family who were memorizing verses of Scripture, using the Navigators' system. I was thrilled to find so many of the new converts in New Zealand studying this course. Since I knew less Scripture in English than I did in Dutch, I, too, determined to start memorizing Scripture. I knew that once the Word of God was hidden in my heart it would be with me always.

Leaving New Zealand full of new zeal, I arrived in the state of Kerala, India, where I was to speak in a series of small conferences far back in the jungle. My Indian companion met me at the airport and took me to a small place on the river where a canoe was waiting. We climbed in and started our slow trip down the peaceful river. Slowly our little craft glided over the shallow waters. Except for the rhythmic sound of the paddle and the occasional murmur of the soft wind in the trees there was nothing to be heard.

My Indian companion was the leader of a home group. Twice a year the home groups in the area come together in a conference to study the Bible, pray, and plead for revival. I was to speak three times a day in several such conferences which would be held in a *pandal*—a wide roof protecting the congregation from the hot sun. There are no walls so the breeze may pass through and the people sit on the grassy floor.

275

As the coolie paddled our canoe down the river, my Indian companion told me of the great longing in his heart to win souls for Jesus Christ.

"Yet I am not successful," he said. "I always give my testimony, but I am not able to persuade people to make a decision."

"Do you use the Sword of the Spirit, the Word of God?" I asked him.

"I fear I am not very adept at handling that Sword," he admitted. "Just at the critical moment I am never able to find a text that fits the situation."

"Yes, I can understand that," I confessed. "I sometimes have the same problem. However, I am now memorizing certain verses of Scripture which I call my First Aid Course. These are emergency Scriptures which I apply to the wound until I can look up the rest of the Scriptures which will bring further healing."

My Indian companion brightened and then I told him of a recent experience in Canada where I had learned that it was not me, but the Word of God coming through me, that won people to Christ anyway.

"I had just finished speaking to a class of university students," I told him as the canoe glided down the quiet river. "I was relaxing on the veranda of one of the dormitories when a very educated woman, who had attended my lectures, sat down with me.

"'What you just told the students was very interesting,' she said. 'But you are too narrow. I am an expert on world religions. I have traveled to many countries and have had long discussions with the leaders of many religious groups. I have discussed the road of life through time and eternity with Muslims, Brahmins, Shintoists, and many others. All of them know God, even though they do not believe in Jesus Christ. I am sorry to have to disagree with your talk this afternoon, but you put too much emphasis on Jesus Christ and do not allow that other religions are just as good as Christianity.'

"I was embarrassed," I told my Indian companion. "Then I remembered something a friend had once told me. 'You are not called to convince anyone,' he had said. 'You are simply called to be an open channel for the Spirit of God to flow through. You can never be anything else, even though you may think so at times. Follow the pathway of obedience, let the Word of God do its own work, and you will be used by God far beyond your own powers.'

"Therefore, I said to the woman, 'Your argument is not with me, but with the Bible. It is not I who say these things, it is the Word of God. Jesus said that no man can come to the Father but by Him. (*See* John 14:6.) If you wish to dispute someone, dispute Him.'"

I looked at my Indian friend. His eyes were fixed on my face as he drank in what I was saying. I continued with the story. "Some time later a reception was held in Ottawa, Canada, for all who wished to meet Prince Bernhard of the Netherlands. It was a pleasure to see so many Hollanders together. The prince looked tired, but he was cheerful and kind to us all. I met many old acquaintances and then, suddenly, I was face-to-face with this same lady who had so adamantly disputed me some time before.

"'I am glad to see you,' she said genuinely. 'I have never been able to forget what you said when you spoke at our university when you quoted Jesus, "No man cometh unto the Father but by me." I have tried to argue with that from every angle, but am unable to get away from the fact that Jesus said it. I can argue with you, but I am having a difficult time arguing with Him.'

"'How wonderful,' I told her. 'Now you are listening to the voice of God. Keep listening. He has much more to say to you.'

" 'Yes,' she said. 'I believe He does.'

"We parted and I have not seen her since, but I know the Sword of the Spirit is still doing its work in her life."

I turned and looked at my Indian friend. He was nodding his head in understanding. "If we diligently read the Bible, the Holy Spirit will give us the right words and Scripture references," I said. "If we depend on Him, we are like the branches of these vines along the river which bear fruit. However, if the branches are broken off, then no fruit will appear."

By this time the forest had thinned out on either side of the river. We could see narrow paths which permitted the people to tread single file through the trees. It was almost dark and I saw, coming down the paths, files of Indian people carrying torches of lighted palm leaves in their hands. The white clothes they wore gave the scene a strange, ethereal appearance as though they were pilgrims walking to heaven. Many had gathered already in the *pandal* away in the distance and were singing a gospel song in a monotone, chanting it over and over as the white-robed pilgrims made their way to the meeting place.

After the meeting that night I lay in my little thatched hut, praising God for the power of the Word of God which had not only drawn these people together, but which had won them to the Lord Jesus Christ. In my mind I listed five reasons why I believe the Bible is inspired:

1. It says so. ". . . holy men of God spake as they were moved by the Holy Ghost" (2 Peter 1:21).
2. The effect it has upon all who believe and follow it.
3. Though some of it was written more than two thousand years before Jesus arrived on earth, yet all the writers agree.
4. The authors do not offer any excuses for their own faults or sins.
5. The writers record some of the most harrowing scenes which affected them greatly, yet they never express one word of emotion. The Holy Spirit wanted the facts recorded, and not their feelings about the facts.

Many persons make the mistake of thinking they can measure the certainty of their salvation by their feelings. It is the Word of God that is their foundation and therefore it is essential for the new convert in Christ to have a practical knowledge of the Bible. More than anyone else it is the new convert who will come under the fire of the enemy. He needs the knowledge of the Sword of the Spirit. As the Lord Jesus used this Sword to overcome the evil one in His temptation experiences, so we must learn to defend ourselves against every sort of attack.

21. *Where Is Heaven?*

HAPPINESS IS NOT dependent on happenings, but on relationship in the happenings.

My father taught me this when I was just a child. He often told me of the early days of his marriage. He had opened a small jewelry store in a narrow house in the heart of the Jewish section of Amsterdam. Poor Mother! She had dreamed of a home with a little garden. She loved beautiful things and spacious views. "I love to see the sky," she often said. Instead, she found herself on a narrow street, in an old house—the kind with only a single room on each story—with worn-out furniture which they had inherited from Grandmother. Yet they were both happy, not because of the circumstances but because of the relationships in the circumstances.

There, in Amsterdam in that narrow street in the ghetto, they met many wonderful Jewish people. They were allowed to participate in their sabbaths and in their feasts. They studied the Old Testament together and, on occasion, even the New Testament.

I have remembered, many times, the lessons I learned from my father about happiness and happenings. But never was it so clear as when I was in Korea, many, many years later.

I had been in the Orient for three months, spending much of the time in Korea. While there I spoke in many meetings in schools, orphanages, children's homes, and churches. One day, after I had spoken in a university, a theological student came to me. I had never seen such gloom on the face of a man who said he wanted to be a minister of the risen Christ.

279

"Why is it that you are so full of unhappiness?" I asked.

"I have lost my way," he said sadly. "When I first became a Christian my pastor taught me the Bible is true. In those days I had great happiness. But now I am studying the famous scholar, Rudolph Bultmann, who says our Bible is full of myths and fables. I have lost my way and no longer know where heaven is."

I was angry. It did not seem right that the simple boys of Korea had to struggle through this horrible theology. They studied many hours at the universities, going to school twice as long as students in America, yet because of what they studied, they often lost their faith. I answered his question about heaven by telling him what I had just seen and heard the day before while driving through the countryside.

There I saw the poorest shack I had ever seen. It was a tiny lean-to, made from materials collected from the garbage heap—pieces of cardboard, tin cans which had been smashed flat, old boards. . . . As we drove past, though, I heard the beautiful voice of a woman singing. Seldom, even in the concert halls of Europe, had I heard such a sweet voice. We stopped the car and listened, for it was like the song of a skylark.

I said to the missionary who was traveling with me, "Do you know that song?"

"Yes," she said, "it says, *Where Jesus is, 'tis heaven there.*"

Oh, how my heart leaped for joy as I heard this beautiful song coming from such a poor place. It is one thing to hear such a song in a dignified church, or pouring through the speakers of an expensive stereo set. But when one hears it coming from the poorest shack in the midst of such poverty, then it means something else.

I looked at the young theological student before me. "Jesus said, 'The Kingdom of heaven is within you' (Luke 17:21). Bultmann is wrong and Jesus is right. Heaven is not a myth or fairy story: heaven is a prepared place for prepared people. Theology in the hands of the Holy Spirit is a beautiful science. But in the hands of unbelievers it is death. If you want to find where heaven is, get out of your stuffy classroom and go back out into the countryside. Listen to the simple faith of those who read only the Bible and trust only in God, not in material things. What do they care if some theologian says that heaven is a fable. They have found Jesus, and where Jesus is, 'tis heaven there."

And how shall they preach, except they be sent?

Romans 10:15

22. *When You Are Tempted to Quit*

THE ENEMY TRIES to make everything work out for the worst. Usually it is not the big problems which depress me, but the multitude of inconveniences which stack up like small rocks to form an immovable mountain. Recently a series of such small incidents almost caused me to resign my commission from the Lord.

In my journeyings I often have to cross borders between countries. Knowing that smuggling is sin, I do not do it. My first irritation came through an encounter with a customs official.

"Do you have anything to declare?" he asked rudely.

"Yes," I replied. "Nylon stockings."

I had put them on top of my luggage to show him, for I knew that at that time it was necessary to pay duty on such items.

"There are four pair here," he said. "You told me one pair."

"No, I did not!" I answered.

But he did not believe me. For the next hour he searched my baggage. He tried all the little boxes to see if they had false bottoms. He squeezed my tooth-paste tube to see if it contained diamonds. He checked my shoes for false heels which might contain drugs. He felt the hem of my dresses to see if I had sewn pearls into them. He almost pulled the lining out of my suitcases. Of course he found nothing at all and finally allowed me to pass—after paying the duty on the four pair of stockings. I was both offended and unhappy.

Later I understood why this incident had made me so upset. I had not surrendered my self-righteousness. I was so sure of my own honesty that I suffered from

281

the consequence of wounded pride. It is easier to surrender one's sins than one's virtues!

Unaware of the reason for my depression, I then discovered that I had missed my plane connections due to the delay in the customs office. I was forced to sleep on a couch in the ladies' room at the airport. However, I am a good sleeper and enjoyed a sound slumber. When I awoke, the amazed cleaning woman (who was sweeping the floor around my couch) said with admiration, "How wonderful to be able to sleep so soundly with so much noise going on around you."

Eventually the plane on which I was traveling flew into a storm making me feel airsick. Then the night following my arrival there was an earthquake. I hate earthquakes for they remind me of the bombs that fell during the war.

Then the kind people who should have arranged my meetings greeted my arrival with, "We thought you needed a holiday and rest so we have not organized anything." Sometimes this is God's plan, but more often it is just a sign of people's laziness to make preparation. So I did not appreciate the fact they had not arranged any meetings for me.

The final inconvenience—the one which caused me almost to give up completely—had to do with my room. My hosts put me in a small room that had no writing table. Ordinarily this would not have disturbed me for I am used to writing on my knee, but on top of everything else that had happened, I crumpled like the camel loaded with straw. I blew up.

The reason was not hard to find. Self-pity had come into my heart. Self-pity is a nasty sin and the devil uses it and always starts his talks with "Poor Corrie."

This time he began by saying, "Why must you always live out of your suitcases? Stay at home and then you won't have trouble with customs officials, passports, luggage, plane connections, and other things. Every night you will be able to sleep in the same comfortable bed; and there are no earthquakes in Holland. After all, you are no longer young. You've lived like a tramp for many, many years. It is time to hang up your harness and retire into a nice green pasture. Let someone else do the work. You've earned your reward."

By this time I was nodding. "Yes, yes, Satan, you are right." So, having listened to his advice I wrote a friend in Holland who managed an international guest house where at the time I had a room kept for me with my own few pieces of furniture.

"I believe the time has now come for me to work in Holland," I wrote. "I am tired of all this traveling and I cannot stand having wheels beneath me any longer. Will you arrange to have a desk—a big one—put in front of the window in my room; and an easy chair—a very easy one—on the right. . . ." In my fantasy I had worked out a lovely dream of heaven here on earth, and me in the middle of it!

That afternoon I posted the letter and then came back to my room to look over my calendar. I jotted down all the names of people I would have to write, canceling my appointments. Everyone would understand. Had not many said, "My, you must be tired at your age!"?

Everything would have gone all right (or perhaps I should be truthful and say "all wrong") had I not picked up my Bible. This old, black Bible has been my guidebook in times of light and in times of darkness. I began to read, asking, "Lord, what would You have me to do?"

I opened to the Book of Romans, chapter 10. "How shall they call on Him in whom they have not believed? And how shall they believe in Him of whom they have not heard? And how shall they hear without a preacher? . . . As it is written, how beautiful are the feet of them that preach the Gospel of peace, and bring glad tidings of good things." *(See* verses 14, 15.)

I remembered the words of a paratrooper instructor. He said that when he had his men in the plane and they were over the battlefield he gave four commands.

FIRST   Attention! *Lift up your eyes* (John 4:35).
SECOND   Stand in the door! *Look upon the fields, for they are white already to harvest* (John 4:35).
THIRD   Hook up! *Be ye filled with the Holy Spirit* (*see* John 20:22).
FORTH   Follow me! *I will make you fishers of men* (Mark 1:17).

I sat for a long time—thinking. It is not our task to give God instructions. We are to simply report for duty.

I laid my Bible on the bed and picked up pen and paper. Balancing the pad clumsily on my knee I wrote my friend in Holland.

Forget about that last letter I wrote. I am not coming home to Holland. I refuse to spend the rest of my life in a pasture when there are so many fields to harvest. I hope to die in harness.

23. *I'll Go Where You Want Me to Go, Dear Lord . . . but Not Up Ten Flights of Stairs*

I HAD SPOKEN that Sunday morning in a church in Copenhagen, Denmark, urging the people to present their bodies as living sacrifices to the Lord. I had said even though I was an old woman that I wanted to give myself completely to Jesus and do whatever He wanted me to do, go wherever He wanted me to go—even if it meant dying.

After the church time, two young nurses approached me. They invited me up to their apartment to have a cup of coffee. I was very tired. At almost eighty years of age I found that standing on my feet for long periods of time was beginning to be exhausting. The cup of coffee sounded good so I accepted their invitation.

But I was not prepared for the walk up to their apartment. Many of the houses in Copenhagen are old, high houses with no elevators. The nurses lived on the tenth floor of such a house and we had to walk up the steps.

"O Lord," I complained as I looked up at the high building, "I do not think I can make it." But the nurses wanted me to come up so badly that I consented to try.

By the time we reached the fifth floor my heart was pounding wildly and my legs were so tired I thought they could not take another step. In the corridor of the fifth floor I saw a chair and pleaded with the Lord, "Lord, let me stay here a time while the nurses go on up the stairs. My heart is so unhappy."

The nurses waited patiently as I collapsed into the chair, resting. "Why, O Lord, must I have this stair-climbing after this busy day of speaking?"

Then I heard God's voice, even louder than my pounding heart. "Because a great blessing is waiting you, a work which will give joy to the angels."

I looked up at the steps, towering above me and almost disappearing into the clouds. Perhaps I am leaving this earth to go to heaven, I thought. Surely that will give joy to the angels. I tried to count the steps. It seemed there were at least one hundred more to climb. However, if God said that the work would give joy to the angels, then I had to go. I rose from my chair and once again started trudging up the long flights of stairs, one nurse in front of me, the other behind me.

We finally reached the apartment on the tenth floor and on entering I found a room with a simple lunch already prepared on the table. Serving the lunch were the mother and father of one of the girls.

I knew there was only a short time and also knew that a blessing of some kind was waiting us. So, without many introductions, I started asking immediate questions.

"Tell me," I asked the nurse's mother, "is it long ago that you found Jesus as your Saviour?"

"I have never met Him," she said, surprised at my question.

"Are you willing to come to Him? He loves you. I have traveled in more than sixty countries and have never found anyone who said they were sorry they had given their hearts to Jesus. You will not be sorry either."

Then I opened my Bible and pointed out the verses about salvation. She listened intently. Then I asked them, "Shall we now talk with the Lord?"

I prayed, then the two nurses prayed and finally the mother folded her hands and said, "Lord Jesus, I know already much about You. I have read much in the Bible, but now I pray You to come into my heart. I need cleansing and salvation. I know that You died at the cross for the sins of the whole world and also for my sins. Please, Lord, come into my heart and make me a child of God. Amen."

I looked up and saw tears of joy on the face of the young nurse. She and her friend had prayed so much for her parents and now the answer was given. I turned and looked at the father, who had sat quietly through all this.

"What about you?' I asked him.

"I have never made such a decision for Jesus Christ either," he said seriously. "But I have listened to all you have told my wife and now I know the way. I, too, would like to pray that Jesus will save me."

He bowed his head and from his lips poured a joyful but very sincere prayer as he gave his life to Jesus Christ. Suddenly the room was filled with great rejoicing and I realized the angels had come down and were standing around, singing praises unto God.

"Thank You, Lord," I prayed as I walked back down the long steps, "for making me walk up all these steps. And next time, Lord, help Corrie ten Boom listen to her own sermon about being willing to go anywhere You tell me to go—even up ten flights of stairs."

For the earth shall be filled with the
knowledge of the glory of the Lord, as the
waters cover the sea.

Habakkuk 2:14

24. To All the World—
Beginning With One

TO GIVE A tract to someone in Russia is always a risk. If the person you are talking to is alone, then there is a little more freedom. However, if a third person is present both are always uneasy—each afraid the other might turn him over to the secret police.

Conny and I had been in a Leningrad hotel for about a week when one morning, on our way down to breakfast, I handed the cleaning woman a tract. It was a simple tract, written in Russian, called "The Way of Salvation." It used only Scripture verses with no commentary.

She glanced at it and then glanced at the other woman cleaning the hall. She pushed the tract back to me, motioning with her hand as if to say, "That is nothing for me."

I felt sorry for her. The answer *no* hurts when you want to help someone. Conny and I continued on down the hall to the elevator, heading to the dining room for breakfast. We were the only ones on the elevator and on the way down I cast this latest burden on the Lord. "Father, I can't reach this woman. Do bring her in contact with someone who can tell her the Gospel in her own language. Lord, I claim her soul for eternity."

I was shocked by the boldness of my prayer. Never in all my life had I prayed that way. Was it proper? Could I actually claim the soul of someone else? In a kind of postscript I asked, "Lord, was this wrong or right? May I say such a prayer?"

Then, even before I could receive His answer, I heard myself praying a prayer that frightened me even more. "Lord Jesus, I claim all of Russia for You."

286

The elevator stopped and Conny and I walked through the huge corridor to the dining room. I was bewildered. My cheeks were red and hot. "Lord, was this right? Was this too much? But no, Lord, Your Word says, 'The earth is the Lord's . . . the world and they that dwell therein' (Psalms 24:1). Surely that means Russia, too."

Still confused, we entered the dining room. It was crowded and the waiter came up and said, "There are only two of you. You cannot eat breakfast here since all the tables are reserved for big groups."

We looked around. A Japanese man had heard the waiter and motioned for us to come to his table where there were two empty places. "Just come," he said. "We will act as if you belong to our group."

But the waiter saw what had happened and refused to wait on us. I felt unhappy and unwelcome. Turning to Conny I said, "At dinner yesterday I took some white buns up to my room in my purse. They are still there and we have some Nescafé. Why should we sit here and wait? Let us go to our room."

It was quiet and peaceful upstairs. Our breakfast tasted good although it was only dry buns and Nescafé without any cream.

Suddenly there was a knock at the door. Conny opened it and there stood the cleaning woman, the one who had refused the tract. Her hair was pulled back in a tight bun and I noticed her heavy leather shoes squeaked when she walked. She closed the door behind herself. From her lips poured a stream of Russian words, not a single one of which we could understand. Then she pointed a finger at my brown bag.

"Conny, she wants to have a tract," I almost shouted.

Conny gave her one but it was not the same one as we had given her the first time. She looked at it, shook her head, and pointed again at the bag.

"Conny, she wants to have 'The Way of Salvation.'"

I got up, rummaged through my bag, and found the original tract. I smiled and handed it to her. She looked at it and her face burst into the great light of joy. Smiling and nodding in appreciation, she backed out of the room.

I was beaming with joy too, for God had answered my prayer. I had not claimed too much after all. The first prayer had already been answered and now I was sure that the second prayer, the one the Holy Spirit had prayed through me without my first thinking up the words, was going to be given a *yes* answer, too.

Conny, who was as excited as I, took her Bible and read "For the earth shall be filled with the knowledge of the glory of the Lord as the waters cover the sea" (Habakkuk 2:14). What a promise—the whole of Russia under the waters of God's glory!

There was another knock at the door. There stood our cleaning woman again. She entered and put a long loaf of fresh white bread on the table. Her face was still wreathed in smiles as she refused payment for it. It was her thank offering to God.

I had never had such a good breakfast in all my life.

25. *Leaving My First Love*

AFTER TWENTY YEARS of wandering the world as a tramp for the Lord I was ill. At seventy-three years of age my body had grown tired. A doctor examined me and said, "Miss ten Boom, if you continue at the same pace you cannot possibly work much longer. However, if you will take a furlough for a year then perhaps you can work for another few years."

I consulted my Lord. He said very clearly that this advice of the doctor was in His plan. It came to mind that I could live during that "Sabbath Year" in Lweza, a beautiful house in Uganda, East Africa. Several years before I had contributed to this place so it could be used as a house of rest for missionaries and other workers in God's Kingdom. Now the bread I had cast upon the waters was coming back to me. I made my plans and soon Conny and I were safely ensconced in Africa.

Lweza was a paradise. Built on a hill in the midst of a garden that must surely resemble Eden, it looked southward out over Lake Victoria. The climate was ideal. Since there were many universities, churches, prisons, and groups in Kampala, the nearby town, I was able to speak in two or three meetings a week. So, while my body rested, my spirit remained active.

The greatest pleasure was to sleep every night in the same bed. During the last twenty years I had slept in more than a thousand different beds, always living out of my suitcases. This year I rested. I put my clothes in a drawer, hung my dresses in a closet, and best of all, each night I laid my head on the same pillow.

In November the Sabbath Year had gone by. Conny and I took a map of the world and stretched it out across my bed, following our usual method of making plans for the next year—the same method I had used for the last twenty years. First we listened to God's plan, then we signed it. This was unlike the method I once used when I made my own plans and then asked God to sign them. Our desire was to be "planned" by the Holy Spirit.

God's plan looked very good to Conny. There would be three months in different countries in Africa, two months in America, and then three months in Eastern Europe behind the Iron Curtain. "Thank You, Jesus," Conny said. But inside I was not so thankful. Conny was young, much younger than I. She loved to travel but I was getting old and was still rather tired.

After Conny left I turned to the Lord. "I prefer to stay here," I said stubbornly. "There is so much to do in Kampala and Entebbe, the two nearest cities. I will work for You. I am willing to have meetings every day, counseling, writing books; but please, let me sleep every night in the same bed. Everyone can understand that at my age I should take it a bit easier."

I got up rejoicing. This new plan of mine made me really happy.

Then Conny called. An African minister from far away Ruanda had come to visit. He started immediately to welcome me: "We are so glad that you are willing to come to Ruanda again. Five years ago you helped us so marvelously when you told what the Lord had been to you in your great need. You said that it was not your faith that helped you through three prisons, for your faith was weak and often wavering. You said it was the Lord Himself who carried you through and that you knew from experience that Jesus' light is stronger than the deepest darkness."

The African brother continued, "Five years ago, however, that was just theory to us. None of us had ever been prisoners. Now there has been a civil war in our country. Many of us have been in prison. I, myself, was in prison for two years. It was then that I remembered everything you had said. I did not have the faith of Corrie ten Boom, I did not even have faith for myself, but I knew to look to the same Jesus who gave you faith. He has also given it to me and that is why we are so happy that you are now coming again to Ruanda."

But I was not happy at all. His words were different from what I wanted to hear. I knew that in such situations I could change the subject by asking a question. Perhaps this would make God stop reminding me of His plans and leave me alone so I could follow mine.

"How is the church in Ruanda?" I asked. "What kind of message do they need now?"

Without hesitating one moment the brother opened his Bible and began to read:

"Write this to the angel of the Church in Ephesus: These words are spoken by the one who holds the seven stars safe in his right hand, and who walks among the seven golden lampstands. I know what you have done; I know how hard you have worked and what you have endured . . . I know your powers of endurance—how you have suffered for the sake of my name and have not grown weary. But I hold this against you, that you [have lost your first love]. Remember then how far you have fallen . . . ."

Revelation 2:1–5 PHILLIPS

This arrow penetrated my heart. Not only Ruanda needed that message, but also Corrie ten Boom. I had lost my first love. Twenty years before I had come out of a concentration camp—starved, weak—but in my heart there was a burning love: a love for the Lord who had carried me through so faithfully—a love for the people around me—a burning desire to tell them that Jesus is a reality, that He lives, that He is victor. I knew it from experience. For this reason I went to Germany and lived in the midst of the ruins. For this reason I had tramped the world for twenty years. I wanted everyone to know that no matter how deep we fall, the Everlasting Arms are always under us to carry us out.

And now? Now I was interested in my bed. I had lost my first love. I asked my African brother to continue to read.

Repent and live as you lived at first. Otherwise, if your heart remains unchanged, I shall come to you and remove your lampstand from its place.

Suddenly joy came in my heart. I could bring my sin, my cold heart, my weary body to Him who is faithful and just. I did it. I confessed my sins and asked for forgiveness. And the same thing happened that always happens when I bring my sin to God in the Name of Jesus: He forgave me. Jesus cleansed my heart with His blood and refilled me with the Holy Spirit.

As God's love—the fruit of the Holy Spirit—was poured out into my heart, I set out again on my journeys—a tramp for the Lord.

What a great joy it was to experience the love of God, who gave me rivers of living water for the thirsty world of Africa, America, and Eastern Europe. Of course, it might be the will of God that some old people retire from their work. In great thankfulness to the Lord they can then enjoy their pensions. But for me, the way of obedience was to travel on, even more so than ever before.

Jesus warned us in Matthew 24:12 that the love of most men waxes cold because iniquity abounds. It is very easy to belong to the "most men." But the gate of repentance is always wide open. *Hallelujah!*

26. *Walking in the Light*

OUR LAST FEW weeks in Lweza proved to be the most fruitful of our entire time spent there, for it was in these weeks that I learned another valuable lesson—the lesson of walking in the light.

One afternoon Conny and I were sitting in the garden looking at the monkeys jumping from one tree to another. The trees and shrubs were a mass of color and sound, causing my heart to be filled with the glory of God's grace.

Yet Conny was discouraged. She had started a girl's club in the YWCA in Kampala and had spent many hours work with it. However, the girls were not interested. I was concerned about her discouragement, feeling it went far deeper than the problems she was having with her class.

I started to ask her about it when we were interrupted by a man walking toward our hill. Conny squinted her eyes into the sun and then shouted, "It is William Nagenda!"

What a joy it was to meet that dear African saint again. I never met an African with whom I could laugh so much and yet learn so much at the same time.

After we exchanged greetings William said, "When I saw you sitting here together a question came to my mind, 'Do they walk in the light together?'"

We answered almost simultaneously. "Oh yes, we do walk in the light together. We are a team."

Just at that moment a boy from the house called that there was a telephone message for me. I excused myself while Conny and William remained behind to talk.

Conny was sitting in a cane and wicker chair while William squatted on his haunches beside the path, his brown knees poking up beside his face.

"I have something to confess to you," Conny said to William.

"And what is that?" he answered gently.

"Your question gripped my heart. I must tell you that I do not really walk in the light with Tante Corrie."

William's face broke into a wide grin and his eyes began to sparkle. "So, that is why God had me ask that strange question."

Conny was serious. "Tante Corrie is so much more mature than I," she continued. "She has walked with Jesus for so many years. She has suffered much for Him in many ways. Thus when I see things in her life that are not right, I hesitate to speak them out to her."

"Oh," William said, startled. "That is not right. The Lord wants you to be very honest with Tante Corrie. That is one reason He has put you with her. Since she is walking in the light then when you also walk in the light, you will help shed light for her path as well as yours."

That night, after we had gone to our room together, Conny sat on the side of the bed and said, "Tante Corrie, this is very difficult for me to say, but I now realize I must walk in the light."

I turned and looked at her. Her face was drawn and solemn. One by one she began listing the things in my life which bothered her—the things I did which she did not believe glorified God. It was not easy for me to hear the things which I had done wrong—things which had caused a shadow to come in Conny's heart. But how wonderful it was that Conny was being completely honest with me. I apologized for the things she had listed and then thanked her for bringing them into the light. "Let us always walk in the light together," I said seriously.

But it was still hard for Conny. She was much younger than I and felt she was still learning. Even though I wanted her to continue to correct me, she found it very difficult. The final breakthrough came after we left Africa and flew to Brazil.

We had been in Rio de Janeiro, one of the most beautiful cities of the world, for a few weeks. As we prepared to leave—to fly south to Buenos Aires—we discovered our suitcases were overweight. The kind people in Rio had given us so many presents we were more than twenty kilograms overweight. It was going to cost us a great deal of extra money to go on to Argentina.

I unpacked my luggage and made three piles: one to send to Holland by sea, one to give away to the poor in Rio, and the smallest one to go back in my suitcase to carry on to our next destination. Finishing my repacking I hurried next door into Conny's room and unpacked her suitcase also. I went through the same procedure, sorting her belongings into three heaps and then repacking only her necessary items. I was in too much of a hurry to notice that Conny said nothing.

A week later, after a beautiful time in Buenos Aires, we were walking along a lonely stretch of beach near our cabin. I was enjoying the beautiful view over a quiet bay when Conny began to talk. Her voice was strained. "I promised God I would walk in the light," she said, "and that means that I must get something settled with you. When you repacked my suitcase and decided what things to send to Holland and what to leave with me, I was not happy about it."

How stupid and tactless I had been to rush in and interfere with Conny's life! I reached out and took her hand. "How thoughtless I have been," I said. "Forgive me for not leaving it up to you."

"I do forgive you," Conny said. Like myself, she had learned not to play lightly with sin, but to hear another's apology and then, instead of passing it off, to forgive it. We walked on for a long time in silence and then Conny spoke again.

"Are you unhappy, Tante Corrie? You are so quiet."

Now it was my time to walk in the light. "There is something hindering me," I said. "Why did you not tell me immediately that you were disturbed? That way it could have been settled on the spot and you would not have had to carry this darkness for all these days. From now on let us both 'speak the truth in love' and never let the sun go down on our misunderstandings."

It was a good lesson. From then until Conny married in 1967 and went to live with her husband, we walked all over the world—always trying to walk in the light.

*I say therefore to the unmarried and
widows, It is good for them if they abide
even as I.*

1 Corinthians 7:8

27. *Secure in Jesus*

IT IS SATAN who tries, in every way, to spoil the peace and joy that God's servants have in their work.

Ellen, my new traveling companion, had gone with me to a lonely mission field in Mexico. Our hostess was a lady missionary, unmarried, in her forties. One evening while we were alone in her little adobe, she confessed her bitterness and resentment over being unmarried.

"Why have I been denied the love of a husband, children, and a home? Why is it that the only men who ever paid any attention to me were married to someone else?" Long into the night she poured out the poison of her frustration. At last she asked me, "Why did you never marry?"

"Because," I said, "the Lord had other plans for me than married life."

"Did you ever fall in love and lose someone, as I have?" she asked bitterly.

"Yes," I said sadly. "I know the pain of a broken heart."

"But you were strong, weren't you," she said in biting tones. "You were willing to let God have His way in your life?"

"Oh, no, not at first," I said. "I had to fight a battle over it. I was twenty-three. I loved a boy and believed he loved me. But I had no money and he married a rich girl. After they were married he brought her to me and putting her hand in mine said, 'I hope you two will be friends.' I wanted to scream. She looked so sweet, so secure and content in his love.

"But I did have Jesus, and eventually I went to Him and prayed, 'Lord Jesus, You know that I belong to You 100 percent. My sex life is yours also. I don't know

294

what plans You have for my life, but Lord, whatever it may be, use me to realize Your victory in every detail. I believe You can take away all my frustrations and feelings of unhappiness. I surrender anew my whole life to You.'"

I looked across the little table at the bitter woman in front of me. Her face was furrowed, her eyes hard with resentment. I sensed she had been trying to run away from her frustrations. Perhaps that was even the reason she was on the mission field. Sadly, there are some of God's children who go to the mission field to escape the pain of not having a husband. I know others, back home, who spend every evening away from their families, attending Christian meetings, because they are unhappy and frustrated in their marriages. Work—even mission work—can become a wrong hiding place.

"Those called by God to live single lives are always happy in that state," I said. "This happiness, this contentment, is the evidence of God's plan."

"But you loved and lost," she exclaimed. "Do you believe that God took away your lover to make you follow Him?"

"Oh, no," I smiled. "God does not take away from us. He might ask us to turn our backs on something, or someone, we should not have. God never takes away, however; God gives. If I reach out and take someone for myself and the Lord steps in between, that does not mean God takes. Rather it means He is protecting us from someone we should not have because He has a far greater purpose for our lives."

We sat for long minutes in the semidark room. Only a small kerosene lamp gave its flickering light, casting faint shadows on the walls and across our faces. I thought back—remembering. I had always been content in the Lord. Back when I was in my thirties God gave me children—the children of missionaries—whom I raised. Betsie, my sister, fed and clothed them while I was responsible for their sports and music. We kept them in our home in Holland, and I found deep satisfaction in seeing them grow to maturity. I also spent a great deal of time speaking and sharing in various clubs for girls. But it was not the work that brought balance to my life, for work cannot balance our feelings. It was because my life was centered in the Lord Jesus that I had balance. Many people try to lose their feelings in work, or sports, or music, or the arts. But the feelings are always there and will eventually, as they had done tonight in this missionary, come boiling to the surface and express their resentment and discontent.

I turned to Ellen, my companion. Ellen is a tall, blond, beautiful Dutch girl then in her early thirties. She is single, yet she has learned the secret of living a balanced life. While I believe God set me apart before I was born to live a single life, Ellen was different. She did not feel that God had called her to a single life; rather she felt that one day, in God's time, she would marry. However, until that time arrived—one year or thirty years from then—I knew she was secure in Jesus and was not looking to a husband or children for her security.

I spoke to the missionary. "There are some, like me, who are called to live a single life," I said softly. "For them it is always easy for they are, by their nature, content. Others, like Ellen, are called to prepare for marriage which may come later in life. They, too, are blessed, for God is using the in-between years to teach them that marriage is not the answer to unhappiness. Happiness is found only in a balanced relationship with the Lord Jesus."

"But it is so hard," she said, tears welling up in her eyes.

"That is so," I said. "The cross is always difficult. 'But you are dead, and your life is hid with Christ in God' (Colossians 3:3). Dear girl, it cannot be safer. That part of you which would cling to a husband is dead. Now you can move into a life where you can be happy with or without a husband—secure in Jesus alone."

I do not know if she really understood me, for often we set our minds on some one thing we think will make us happy—a husband, children, a particular job, or even a "ministry"—and refuse to open our eyes to God's better way. In fact, some believe so strongly that only this thing can bring happiness, that they reject the Lord Jesus Himself. Happiness is not found in marriage; or work; or ministry; or children. Happiness is found by being secure in Jesus.

*After these things the Lord appointed other
seventy also, and sent them two and two
before his face into every city and place....*
Luke 10:1

28. I Have Much People
in This City

MY SECOND TRIP to Cuba was much different from the earlier one because
this time Cuba was in the hands of Communists. Ellen was with me and we had
come from Mexico with our bags loaded with books. Friends had told us that the
Communists in Cuba were burning Bibles and confiscating Christian literature,
so I was not at all sure if we could be allowed to bring all these books in with us.
We had also heard that most of the churches were closed and many of the Christians were in prison—some of them for passing out literature. Thus we were very
cautious.

At customs, in Havana, the officer pointed to my suitcases. "What are these
books?" he asked.

"They are written by me," I said. "I am going to give them to my friends."

I saw him scowl as he picked one of them up. My heart began to beat rapidly.
"Oh, Lord," I prayed inwardly, "what must I do?"

Then I heard myself saying brashly, "Would you like to have one of my books?
Here, I will autograph it especially for you."

The customs officer looked up. I took the book from his hand and wrote my
name in the front and then handed it back. He grinned broadly and thanked me.
Then, glancing once more at my suitcase filled with books, he nodded and motioned
us through the line. I closed the suitcase and stepped out on the streets. Hallelujah! The miracle had happened.

But why were we here? What kind of plans did the Lord have for us on this
island? Had all our former friends been put in prison? Were any of the churches

297

still open? These and many other questions pounded at my mind as we turned our faces toward the city.

An Intourist limousine brought us into the heart of Havana where we found a hotel room. After washing up we went out onto the streets, hoping to find some Christians. But how do you find Christians in a strange city when you cannot even speak their language? We walked up and down the sidewalks, hoping God would show us someone to speak to, but we received no guidance whatsoever.

I finally approached an old man who was leaning against the side of the building. He had a kindly face, I thought. I asked if he knew where there was a church.

He shrugged his shoulders but then, motioning us to wait, went to one of the free telephones along the street. Ellen and I stood praying. Was he going to call the police? Had we broken a law and would we be put in jail? Then we realized he was calling some of his friends, asking if they knew the whereabouts of a church. No one knew anything and he returned, saying he could be of no help.

We were discouraged and to make matters worse, it started to rain. Neither Ellen nor I had a raincoat and soon we were soaked to the skin. We had been walking for hours and I was exhausted.

"Ellen, can we try to get a taxi?" I asked.

"Well, Tante Corrie, we will need a miracle. However, we know that all things are possible with God."

I found a little stool and sat down while Ellen walked on down the street, hoping to find a taxi. I looked out over the sea and felt as if I had just waded out of the surf, so wet was I. I thought of the words of the driver of the Intourist limousine as he had brought us from the airport. "This is the hospital," he had said as we drove by. "Everyone who is ill can go there and it does not cost a penny. Here is a cemetery. When you die, we bury you and even that does not cost your relatives anything."

I had been in many countries, but this was the first place they had offered to bury me!

We knew that the Lord had sent us to Cuba, but we had no idea of our mission. Where were the churches? We had seen some, but they were closed. Some even had trees growing in front of the doors. We had tried to call some Christians, but the ones we knew were no longer living in the area. I sat, waiting, while the water poured down my face. Then I heard a car stopping in front of me. Looking up, I saw Ellen's face in the rear window of the ancient, rusted vehicle.

"Tante Corrie," she called above the sound of the rain, "here I am again." I hobbled to the taxi and got in the back door. "Be careful where you put your feet," Ellen laughed, "or you will touch the street."

The taxi took us to our hotel and soon we were in dry clothes, our wet garments hung across the fixtures in the bathroom where the steady drip, drip of water reminded us of our failure out on the street. I love to walk with Jesus, but after eight decades I realized I was not as young as I used to be. It was in such moments that I started to feel old.

Ellen could not sleep that night. We were supposed to stay in Cuba for two weeks, but if we could not find any Christians then what would we do? She arose in the middle of the night and prayed, "Lord, give me a word so I may know we aren't in vain in this country."

Sitting on the side of her bed, she reached for her Bible which was on the small table. She began to read where she had stopped the night before. She had learned that God does not want His children to be fearful, and the best way to overcome fear is through the Word of God.

She read Acts 18:9, 10.

> Then spake the Lord to Paul . . . Be not afraid, but speak, and hold not thy peace. For I am with thee, and no man shall set on thee to hurt thee: for I have much people in this city.

What an answer!

The next morning Ellen could not wait to find all those people, and neither could I. She had one address which we had not contacted. It was the address of a small house on a side street where some Christians we had once known used to live. Walking from the hotel, she finally found the street and made her way to a dingy door, weatherbeaten and cracked. She knocked boldly.

A small man, deeply tanned and with wrinkles around his eyes, cautiously opened the door. Ellen could speak no Spanish, but she held up her Bible and one of my books (*Amazing Love*) which had been translated into Spanish.

The man glanced at the books and then back to Ellen. Ellen smiled and pointed to my name on the book, then pointed back toward the city. Suddenly his whole face came alive. He threw open the door and shouted, "Corrie! Corrie ten Boom *està aquì. Ella està en Havana!*"

Ellen walked in and found the room was filled with men, all kneeling on the floor. They were pastors who met each week to pray for God's help and guidance in their difficult ministry. Ellen hurried back to the hotel and soon I was meeting with these wonderful men of God. We distributed all our books and made many new friends among God's people. Indeed, God did have "much people" in that city.

29. *The Blessing Box*

MANY TIMES, ON my trips around the world, I am dependent on the hospitality of Christians. From the time of my first trip to America when I was befriended by God's people in New York, and later by Abraham Vereide in Washington, D.C., I have known the love and generosity of others in the Body of Christ.

It was on one of those continual trips, when my only home was my suitcase (that big red one), that I was invited to stay with friends in Colorado. I didn't feel well and needed rest. My hostess escorted me to her lovely house with tall white columns. Taking me up the carpeted stairs she showed me to a beautiful room. From the windows I could see the clear, blue sky which framed the snow-capped Rocky Mountains. She then put her arms around me and said, "Corrie, this is your room. It will always be here for you."

"This room! For me?" I could hardly believe it was true. A place for me to unpack my suitcase! To hang up my clothes! To spread out my writing papers and put my Bible on a desk! Since that gray time in the concentration camp I had longed for bright colors, as a thirsty man yearns for water. This room, and the scenery outside, was filled with color. I wanted to cry, as a child cries when she is happy. But I have learned to control my tears (most of the time, anyway) and was content just to tell the Lord of my deep thankfulness. The Lord is so good for He has given me so many friends, just like this, all over the world.

It was during one of my visits in this Colorado home that I received an early morning telephone call. I was already awake since we intended to leave that afternoon to fly to Washington to speak in a series of meetings arranged by Mr. Vereide.

The phone call was from Alicia Davison, Mr. Vereide's daughter. "Oh, Alicia, I cannot wait to see you today. I am looking forward to it and the meetings in your fellowship house."

There was a pause, then Alicia said, "Tante Corrie, Dad is with the Lord."

"Oh, Alicia . . ." I tried to speak, but nothing else would come out.

"It is all right, Tante Corrie," she said calmly. "I am calling to ask you to please come on to be with all of us. We will not have the meetings, but so many people are coming and we want you to be with us."

"I shall be there this afternoon," I said. After a brief prayer over the phone, I hung up.

I hurried to finish my packing, remembering all the kindnesses that had been poured on me by this wonderful family and their many friends. I have faced death many times, but there is always an empty place in my heart when someone I know and love leaves to be with the Lord. Nor did it ever occur to me that almost two years later I would once again fly to Washington to sit in that same Presbyterian Church not to attend a memorial for Abraham Vereide but to attend the meeting in honor of Alicia, who, although still young and beautiful, would die in Hong Kong while making a mission tour with her husband, Howard Davison.

I was warmly received by my friends in Washington. Although sad, they were rejoicing in the Lord. That night after I had gone to my room, I prayed, "Lord," I asked, "why are people so kind to me? I am just a simple old Dutch woman. Why am I treated so graciously and shown so much hospitality?"

Then the Lord reminded me of my mother's blessing box.

Our house in Haarlem was not really big but it had wide open doors.

I do not suppose that the many guests who were always coming to the Beje ever realized what a struggle it was to make both ends meet. Yet many lonesome people found a place with us and joined in our music, humor, and interesting conversation. There was always a place at the oval dinner table, although perhaps the soup was a bit watery when too many unexpected guests showed up. Our entire home was centered in the ministry of the Gospel. All people who came to us were either workers in the Kingdom of God or people who needed help.

Mother loved all her guests. She often showed her love by dropping a penny in the "blessing box" when they arrived.

The blessing box was a small metal box that sat on the sideboard near the oval dinner table. Here money was collected for the mission that was so close to our hearts. Every time our family was blessed in a particular way, Mother would drop money in the blessing box as a thank offering to God. This was especially true if Father sold an expensive watch or received extra money for repairing an antique clock.

Whenever visitors came Mother would spread her arms wide and welcome them and then to show how she really appreciated their presence would say, "A penny in the blessing box for your coming." If it were a special visitor she might even put in a dime.

Then, at the dinner table, Father would always bless our visitors, thanking God that our house was privileged by their presence. It was always a special occasion for us all.

I well remember the sister-in-law of a minister who spent the night with us. The next morning Tante Anna went to her room and found her sheet twisted into a rope and lying across the bed.

"What is this?" Tante Anna asked.

The woman broke down in tears. "I must confess. Last night I wanted to commit suicide. I made my sheet into a rope and tied it around my neck to jump from the window. But I could not forget the prayer at the dinner table, as Mr. ten Boom thanked God that I could come and share in this hospitality. God spared my life through that prayer."

After a few days in Washington I continued my traveling as a tramp for the Lord. However, fresh on my mind was the hospitality of my dear friends. And I remembered Mother's blessing box, and Father's prayers. Often I am dependent on the hospitality of Christians. God's people have been so generous to open their homes to me and many times when I lay my head on a strange pillow, which has been blessed by the love of my friends, I realize that I am enjoying the reward for the open doors and open hearts of the Beje.

Heaven will be blessed, but here on earth I already am enjoying a "house with many mansions."

If we confess our sins, he is faithful and just to forgive us our sins, and to cleanse us from all unrighteousness.

1 John 1:9

30. *Closing the Circle*

IT WOULD SEEM, after having been a Christian for almost eighty years, that I would no longer do ugly things that need forgiving. Yet I am constantly doing things to others that cause me to have to go back and ask their forgiveness. Sometimes these are things I actually do—other times they are simply attitudes I let creep in which break the circle of God's perfect love.

I first learned the secret of closing the circle from my nephew, Peter van Woerden, who was spending the weekend with me in our little apartment in Baarn, Holland.

"Do you remember that boy, Jan, that we prayed for?" Peter asked.

I well remember Jan. We had prayed for him many times. He had a horrible demon of darkness in his life and although we had fasted and prayed and cast out the demon in the name of the Lord Jesus Christ, the darkness always returned.

Peter continued, "I knew God had brought this boy to me not only so he could be delivered, but to teach me some lessons too."

I looked at Peter. "What could that boy, Jan, so filled with darkness, teach you?"

"I did not learn the lesson from Jan," Peter smiled. "But from God. Once in my intercession time for Jan the Lord told me to open my Bible to 1 John 1:7–9. I read that passage about confessing our sin and asked the Lord what that had to do with the darkness in Jan's life."

Peter got up and walked across the room, holding his open Bible in his hand. "God taught me that if a Christian walks in the light then the blood of Jesus Christ cleanses him from all sin, making his life a closed circle and protecting him from all outside dark powers. But—" he turned and emphatically jabbed his finger into the pages of the Bible—"if there is unconfessed sin in that life, the circle has an opening in it—a gap—and this allows the dark powers to come back in."

Ah, I thought, *Peter has really learned a truth from the Lord.*

"Tante Corrie," Peter continued, "even though I was able to cast out the demon in Jan's life, it always crept back in through the opening in the circle—the opening of Jan's unconfessed sin. But when I led Jan to confess this sin, then the circle was closed and the dark powers could no longer return."

That same week the wife of a good friend came to me for counseling. After I had fixed her a cup of tea she began to tell me about all the people who had prayed for her, yet she was still experiencing horrible dreams at night.

I interrupted her conversation and drew a circle on a piece of paper. "Mary," I said, "do you have unconfessed sin in your life? Is this the reason the circle is still open?"

Mary said nothing, sitting with her head down, her hands tightly clasped in her lap, her feet together. I could see there was a strong battle going on in her life—a battle between spiritual forces.

"Do you really want to be free?" I urged.

"Oh, yes," she said.

Suddenly she began telling me about a strong hatred she had for her mother. Everyone thought she loved her mother, but inside there were things that caused her actually to want to kill her. Yet, even as she spoke, I saw freedom coming into her eyes.

She finished her confession and then quickly asked Jesus to forgive her and cleanse her with His blood. I looked into her eyes and commanded the demon of hatred to leave in the Name of Jesus.

What joy! What freedom!

Mary raised her hands in victory and began to praise the Lord, thanking Him for the liberation and forgiveness He had given her. Then she reached over and embraced me in a hug so tight I thought she would crack my ribs.

"Dear Lord," she prayed, "I thank You for closing the circle with Your blood."

Having thus learned to close the circle by confessing my sins, I wish I could say that ever since then the circle has remained closed in my life. It is not so. For since Satan comes against us so often, then it is necessary to confess often, also. Regardless of how old a person may be, or how long he has ministered in the Name of Jesus Christ, that man still needs to confess his sins again and again—and ask forgiveness.

This truth became painfully clear to me recently when I was invited to Washington, D.C., to speak to a luncheon of businessmen and women. I love to talk to businessmen and was very excited about the meeting. When I arrived, however, I found only women present. This upset me for I felt that men needed to hear the message of forgiveness also.

After the meeting a fine-looking lady came up to me. "I am in charge of arranging the program for the world convention of our ladies' group," she said. "Some of the most influential women in the world will be present. Would you come speak to us in San Francisco?"

I was still miffed that no men had been present for the luncheon. It's not that I disapprove of women's meetings. But I am concerned when men leave the spiritual activity to the women. God is calling *men*. Thus, I gave her a short, discourteous answer. "No, I will not. I must speak to men also. I don't like this business of all women."

She was very gracious. "Don't you feel that you are the right person?" she asked.

"No," I said, "I am not the right person. I do not like this American system where men go about their business leaving the women to act like Christians. I will not come." I turned and walked away.

Later that afternoon I was in my room, packing to catch the plane. The Lord began dealing with me. "You were very rude to that woman," He told me.

I argued with the Lord. "But Lord, I feel that Your message is for all people, not just the women."

"You were very rude to that woman," He said again, gently.

He was right, of course. He always is. I had been speaking on forgiveness, but was unwilling to ask forgiveness for myself. I knew I was going to have to go to that gracious woman and apologize—confess my sin. Until I did, the circle would be open in my life and Satan would be pouring in many other dark thoughts as well.

I looked at my watch and saw I had only enough time to finish my packing and get to the airport. It made no difference. If I left Washington without closing the circle, I would be no good anywhere else. I would just have to miss my plane.

I called the front desk and found which room the woman was in. Then I went to her room. "I must ask your forgiveness," I said as she opened the door. "I spoke to you rudely."

She was embarrassed and tried to pass it off. "Oh, no," she said, "you were not unkind. I understand perfectly. I, too, feel that men should be the spiritual leaders, not women."

She was returning my unkindness with kindness, but that was not what I needed. I needed for her to admit that I was wrong about not speaking to women, and forgive me. I know it is often more difficult to forgive than to ask forgiveness, but it is equally important. To withhold forgiveness often leaves another person in bondage, unable to close the circle, and thus open to further attacks from Satan. It is as important to forgive as it is to ask forgiveness.

This sensitive woman understood. Reaching out and tenderly touching my hand, she said, "I understand, Tante Corrie. I forgive you for your remarks about women's groups and I forgive you for being unkind to me."

That was what I needed to hear. In the future I would indeed speak to women's groups. I would also keep a watch on my lips when tempted to speak unkindly. I missed my plane, but the circle was closed.

> *And there came a certain poor widow, and she threw in two mites . . . And [he] saith unto them, Verily I say unto you, That this poor widow hath cast more in, than all they which have cast into the treasury: For all they did cast in of their abundance; but she of her want did cast in all that she had, even all her living.*
>
> Mark 12:42–44

31. *One Finger for His Glory*

WE ARRIVED AT her apartment by night in order to escape detection. We were in Russia (in the region of Lithuania, on the Baltic Sea). Ellen and I had climbed the steep stairs, coming through a small back door into the one-room apartment. It was jammed with furniture, evidence that the old couple had once lived in a much larger and much finer house.

The old woman was lying on a small sofa, propped up by pillows. Her body was bent and twisted almost beyond recognition by the dread disease of multiple sclerosis. Her aged husband spent all his time caring for her since she was unable to move off the sofa.

I walked across the room and kissed her wrinkled cheek. She tried to look up but the muscles in her neck were atrophied so she could only roll her eyes upward and smile. She raised her right hand, slowly, in jerks. It was the only part of her body she could control and with her gnarled and deformed knuckles she caressed my face. I reached over and kissed the index finger of that hand, for it was with this one finger that she had so long glorified God.

Beside her couch was a vintage typewriter. Each morning her faithful husband would rise, praising the Lord. After caring for his wife's needs and feeding her a simple breakfast, he would prop her into a sitting position on the couch, placing pillows all around her so she wouldn't topple over. Then he would move that ancient black typewriter in front of her on a small table. From an old cupboard he would remove a stack of cheap yellow paper. Then, with that blessed one finger, she would begin to type.

306

All day and far into the night she would type. She translated Christian books into Russian, Latvian, and the language of her people. Always using just that one finger—peck . . . peck . . . peck—she typed out the pages. Portions of the Bible, the books of Billy Graham, Watchman Nee, and Corrie ten Boom—all came from her typewriter. That was why I was there—to thank her.

She was hungry to hear news about these men of God she had never met, yet whose books she had so faithfully translated. We talked about Watchman Nee, who was then in a prison in China, and I told her all I knew of his life and ministry. I also told her of the wonderful ministry of Billy Graham and of the many people who were giving their lives to the Lord.

"Not only does she translate their books," her husband said as he hovered close by during our conversation, "but she prays for these men every day while she types. Sometimes it takes a long time for her finger to hit the key, or for her to get the paper in the machine, but all the time she is praying for those whose books she is working on."

I looked at her wasted form on the sofa, her head pulled down and her feet curled back under her body. "Oh, Lord, why don't You heal her?" I cried inwardly.

Her husband, sensing my anguish of soul, gave the answer. "God has a purpose in her sickness. Every other Christian in the city is watched by the secret police. But because she has been sick so long, no one ever looks in on her. They leave us alone and she is the only person in all the city who can type quietly, undetected by the police."

I looked around at the tiny room, so jammed full of furniture from better days. In one corner was the kitchen. Beside the cupboard was her husband's "office," a battered desk where he sorted the pages that came from her typewriter to pass them on to the Christians. I thought of Jesus sitting over against the treasury, and my heart leaped for joy as I heard Jesus bless this sick old woman who, like the widow, had given all she had.

What a warrior!

> When she enters the beautiful city
> And the saved all around her appear,
> Many people around will tell her:
> It was you that invited me here.
>
> AUTHOR UNKNOWN

Ellen and I returned to Holland where we were able to obtain a new typewriter and have it shipped to her. Now she could make carbon copies of her translations.

Today we got a letter from her husband. In the early morning hours last week she left to be with the Lord. But, he said, she had worked up until midnight that same night, typing with that one finger to the glory of God.

32. *The Ding-Dong Principle*

IN HOLLAND WE have many churches with belfries. The bells in the steeples are rung by hand, with a rope that is pulled from the vestibule of the church.

One day a young Flemish girl, who had repented and received deliverance from lust and impurity, came to me while I was speaking in one of these churches.

"Even though I have been delivered," she said, "at night I still keep dreaming of my old way of life. I am afraid I will slip back into Satan's grasp."

"Up in that church tower," I said, nodding toward the belfry, "is a bell which is rung by pulling on a rope. But you know what? After the sexton lets go of the rope, the bell keeps on swinging. First *ding,* then *dong.* Slower and slower until there's a final *dong* and it stops.

"I believe the same thing is true of deliverance. When the demons are cast out in the name of the Lord Jesus Christ, or when sin is confessed and renounced, then Satan's hand is removed from the rope. But if we worry about our past bondage, Satan will use this opportunity to keep the echoes ringing in our minds."

A sweet light spread across the girl's face. "You mean even though I sometimes have temptations, that I am still free, that Satan is no longer pulling the rope which controls my life?"

"The purity of your life is evidence of your deliverance," I said. "You should not worry about the *dings* and the *dongs,* they are nothing but echoes."

Demons seldom leave without leaving behind their vibrations—*dings* and *dongs.* It is as though they give the clapper one big swing on the way out, scaring us into thinking they are still there. They know that, even though they have to flee at the

Name of Jesus, if we grow fearful over the remaining echoes, other demons can come in and take their place.

The same is true of forgiveness. When we forgive someone, we take our hand off the rope. But if we've been tugging at our grievances for a long time, we mustn't be surprised when the old angry thoughts keep coming up for a while. They're just the *ding-dongs* of the old bell slowing down.

The Bible promises that after we confess and denounce our sins, God cleanses us from them by the blood of Jesus. Indeed, He says, "Your sins and iniquities will I remember no more" *(see* Hebrews 8:12). However, we can do something God cannot do. We can remember our old sins. These are the *dings* and the *dongs* of our past life. When we hear them we need to remember that through Jesus' sacrifice on Calvary, Satan can no longer pull the rope in our life. We may be tempted. We may even fall back occasionally. But we have been delivered from the bondage of sin, and even though the vibrations may still sound in our lives, they will grow less and less and eventually stop completely.

Once Satan has been cast out of the house of your life, he cannot return as long as you walk in obedience. Your body is the temple of the Holy Spirit. However, that does not prevent him (or his demons) from standing outside the house and shouting through the windows, saying, "We're still here!"

But, hallelujah, we know Satan for who he is—the prince of liars. He is *not* still here—he has been cast out. So whenever you hear one of those old echoes in your life—one of the *dings* or *dongs*—you need to stop right then and say, "Thank You, Jesus. You have bought me with Your blood and sin has no right to sound off in my life."

33. The Blacks and Whites of Forgiveness

I WISH I could say that after a long and fruitful life, traveling the world, I had learned to forgive all my enemies. I wish I could say that merciful and charitable thoughts just naturally flowed from me and on to others. But they don't. If there is one thing I've learned since I've passed my eightieth birthday, it's that I can't store up good feelings and behavior—but only draw them fresh from God each day.

Maybe I'm glad it's that way, for every time I go to Him, He teaches me something else. I recall the time—and I was almost seventy—when some Christian friends whom I loved and trusted did something which hurt me. You would have thought that, having been able to forgive the guards in Ravensbruck, forgiving Christian friends would be child's play. It wasn't. For weeks I seethed inside. But at last I asked God again to work His miracle in me. And again it happened: first the cold-blooded decision, then the flood of joy and peace. I had forgiven my friends; I was restored to my Father.

Then, why was I suddenly awake in the middle of the night, rehashing the whole affair again? *My friends!* I thought. *People I loved.* If it had been strangers, I wouldn't have minded so.

I sat up and switched on the light. "Father, I thought it was all forgiven. Please help me do it."

But the next night I woke up again. They'd talked so sweetly too! Never a hint of what they were planning. "Father!" I cried in alarm. "Help me!"

Then it was that another secret of forgiveness became evident. It is not enough to simply say, "I forgive you." I must also begin to live it out. And in my case, that

310

meant acting as though their sins, like mine, were buried in the depths of the deepest sea. If God could remember them no more—and He had said, "[Your] sins and iniquities will I remember no more" (Hebrews 10:17)—then neither should I. And the reason the thoughts kept coming back to me was that I kept turning their sin over in my mind.

And so I discovered another of God's principles: We can trust God not only for our emotions but also for our thoughts. As I asked Him to renew my mind He also took away my thoughts.

He still had more to teach me, however, even from this single episode. Many years later, after I had passed my eightieth birthday, an American friend came to visit me in Holland. As we sat in my little apartment in Baarn he asked me about those people from long ago who had taken advantage of me.

"It is nothing," I said a little smugly. "It is all forgiven."

"By you, yes," he said. "But what about them? Have they accepted your forgiveness?"

"They say there is nothing to forgive! They deny it ever happened. No matter what they say, though, I can prove they were wrong." I went eagerly to my desk. "See, I have it in black and white! I saved all their letters and I can show you where. . . ."

"Corrie!" My friend slipped his arm through mine and gently closed the drawer. "Aren't you the one whose sins are at the bottom of the sea? Yet are the sins of your friends etched in black and white?"

For an astonishing moment I could not find my voice. "Lord Jesus," I whispered at last, "who takes all my sins away, forgive me for preserving all these years the evidence against others! Give me grace to burn all the blacks and whites as a sweet-smelling sacrifice to Your glory."

I did not go to sleep that night until I had gone through my desk and pulled out those letters—curling now with age—and fed them all into my little coal-burning grate. As the flames leaped and glowed, so did my heart. "Forgive us our trespasses," Jesus taught us to pray, "as we forgive those who trespass against us." In the ashes of those letters I was seeing yet another facet of His mercy. What more He would teach me about forgiveness in the days ahead I didn't know, but tonight's was good news enough.

Forgiveness is the key which unlocks the door of resentment and the handcuffs of hatred. It breaks the chains of bitterness and the shackles of selfishness. The forgiveness of Jesus not only takes away our sins, it makes them as if they had never been.

. . . Even so, come, Lord Jesus.
Revelation 22:20

34. *Getting Ready for the End*

SOME TIME AGO, I was with a group of students in the midwest. Some of them were new Christians, but most of them did not know the Lord. They were interested in all kinds of other things, and a Christian professor had organized weekly meetings to answer their questions. So it was that at the last evening meeting of that semester the professor said, "Now you can hear something about Christianity in practice."

First I spoke to those who were Christians. "How long have you known Jesus?" I asked.

One said, "Two weeks." Another said, "Three years." And still another answered and said, "I met Him only yesterday."

Then I said to them, "Well, I have good news. I have known Him seventy-five years, and I can tell you something, men. He will never let you down."

Next I told the other students about Jesus Christ, and what He had done for me, and the great miracles also. When He tells you to love your enemies, He gives you the love that He demands from you. They were listening intently, and I was led by the Holy Spirit not to go into any doctrines or teachings other than the reality of Jesus Christ. I told them of the joy of having Jesus with me, whatever happened, and how I knew from experience that the light of Jesus is stronger than the greatest darkness. I told them of the darkness of my prison experiences, realizing that only those people who were in a German concentration camp could ever fully understand. However, I wanted these students to know that, even though I was there where every day six hundred people either died or were killed, when Jesus is with you the worst can happen and the best remains.

312

Afterwards the students came up and we had coffee. One said to me, "I would love to ask Jesus to come into my heart, but I cannot. I am a Jew."

I said, "You cannot ask Jesus into your heart because you are a Jew? Then you do not understand that with the Jew (Jesus) in your heart—you are a double Jew."

He said, "Oh, then it is possible?"

"On the divine side He was God's Son. On the human side He was a Jew. When you accept Him you do not become a Gentile. You become even more Jewish than before. You will be a completed Jew."

With great joy the boy received the Lord Jesus as his Saviour.

There is a great new surge of interest in spiritual things. Many are interested in Jesus Christ who have never shown any interest before. Churches—which have been dead and cold like mausoleums—are coming to life. All across the world many are being saved and being filled with the Holy Spirit.

At the same time, however, many others are turning away from God. They are openly worshiping Satan. Many others are calling themselves Christians, but are involved in the occult, fortune telling, astrology, mind science, and other things of Satan.

I see over the whole world that there are two huge armies marching—the army of the Antichrist and the army of Jesus Christ. We know from the Bible that Jesus Christ will have the victory, but now the Antichrist is preparing for the time that will come before Jesus returns. The Bible says there will be a time of tribulation, and the Antichrist will take over the whole world. He will be a very "good, religious" man, and he will make one religion for the whole world. After it has been arranged, he will proclaim himself as its god. The Bible prophesies that the time will come when we cannot buy or sell, unless we bear the sign of the Antichrist; that means that world money is coming, and people know this today. If I did not believe in the Bible before, I should believe in it now. Because what was foretold in the Bible you can now read in the newspapers.

At a student meeting in California a theological student approached me saying, "What's all this talk about Jesus' coming again? Don't you know that men have been prophesying for years that He would come, and He never has. Even the early church could not live their religion because they were too busy looking for Christ to return. He is not coming back. It is all foolishness."

I looked at the young man. He was so smug, so full of scoffing, and I felt sorry for him.

"Indeed, Jesus is coming again, and soon," I said. "And you have just proved it to me."

He blinked his eyes. "How did I prove it to you?"

"Because the Bible talks about it in 2 Peter 3:3, that in the last days there shall come scoffers walking after their own lusts and they will say, 'Where is the promise of His Coming? Ever since the early church men have been looking for Him and He has not come.' So you see, my young friend, you are one of the signs of His Coming."

I am not afraid when I think about the Coming of the Lord Jesus. Instead I welcome it. I do not know whether it would be better for me to die and be among that great host of saints who will return with Him, or whether it would be better to remain here and listen for the sound of the trumpet. Either way I like the words of the song that says:

> God is working His purpose out,
> As year succeeds to year:
> God is working His purpose out
> And the time is drawing near—
> Nearer and nearer draws the time
> The time that shall surely be,
> When the earth shall be filled with the glory of God,
> As the waters cover the sea.
>
> A. C. AINGER

I find that when Communists speak of the future of the world, they show a pattern for peace through communism. But when I ask them, "What about when you die?" they say, "Then everything is ended. There is no life after this life." The Bible tells us that the Antichrist can imitate much, even the gifts of the Spirit. But there is one thing he cannot imitate, and that is the peace of God which passes all understanding.

But there are *good* things to tell about the future of the world. For instance, the Bible says the Tree of Life will be used for the healing of the nations. This means that there will be *nations* to heal, and there will be *healing*. I am so thankful that we have the Bible and can know the future of God's plan.

As the end times draw closer and closer, so does the power of God grow greater and greater. One day, on a trip to Russia, I approached the customs officer with a suitcase full of Russian Bibles. I stood in the line and saw how carefully the customs officers checked every suitcase. Suddenly a great fear swept over me. "What will he do when he finds my Bibles? Send me back to Holland? Put me in prison?"

I closed my eyes to shut out the scene around me and said, "Lord, in Jeremiah 1, it is written that 'God watches over his word to perform it' (*see* v. 12). Lord, the Bibles in my suitcase are Your Word. Now, God, please watch over Your Word—my Bibles—so I may take them to Your people in Russia."

Now I know that is not what Jeremiah meant, but I have found that if I pray with my hand on the promises of the open Bible that I do not have to wait until my position is doctrinally sound. God sees my heart.

The moment I prayed I opened my eyes and saw around my suitcase light beings. They were angels. It was the first and only time in my life that I had ever seen them, although I had known many, many times they were present. But this time I saw them, only for a moment, and then they were gone. But so was my fear.

I moved on through the customs line, sliding my suitcase along the stainless steel table toward the officer who was doing such a thorough inspection. At last I was before him.

"Is this your suitcase?" he asked.

"Yes, sir," I answered politely.

"It seems very heavy," he said, grasping it by the handle and picking it up.

"It is very heavy," I said.

He smiled. "Since you are the last one to come through the line I now have time to help you. If you will follow me I shall carry it for you out to your taxi."

My heart almost overflowed with hallelujahs as I followed him through the customs gate and right out to the street where he helped me get a taxi to the hotel.

So, even though we are rapidly approaching the time when the Antichrist will try to take over the world, I am not afraid. For I have an even greater promise of the constant Presence of Jesus who is greater than anything Satan can throw against me.

The Apostle Peter said, "Because, my dear friends, you have a hope like this before you, I urge you to make certain that such a day will find you at peace with God and man, clean and blameless in his sight" (2 Peter 3:14 PHILLIPS).

Surrender to the Lord Jesus Christ must not be partial—but total. Only when we repent and turn away from our sins (using His power, of course) does He fill us with His Holy Spirit. The fruit of the Holy Spirit makes us right with God and God's love in us makes us right with men. Through that we can forgive—even love—our enemies.

Jesus Himself makes us ready for His Coming.

*. . . Suffer little children, and forbid them
not, to come unto me: for of such is the
kingdom of heaven.*

Matthew 19:14

35. *Little Witness for Christ*

TANTE JANS LOST her husband before she was forty years old. He had been a well-known minister in Rotterdam and she had worked faithfully beside him in the church. They had no children and after he died it was clear that her place was to be in our house in Haarlem. She was a poet, author, and organizer—especially was she an organizer! Soon after she moved into the Beje she started a club for girls where she led the meetings and began publishing a small monthly paper for them.

It was long before World War I started, but a detachment of Dutch soldiers was stationed in Haarlem. Seeing many soldiers in the streets, Tante Jans decided to open a club for them too. She approached some wealthy people and within a short time had enough money to build a military home. Twice a week Tante Jans went to the house to lead in a Bible study.

Tante Jans also invited the soldiers to come to our house. Since they were lonely and did not like the street life, many of them accepted. Almost every evening we had soldiers in our home.

One sergeant was a great musician and Tante Jans asked him to teach me and my sister Nollie to play the harmonium—an old pump organ. It wasn't long before I was joining Tante Jans at the military home to accompany the singing.

One night, in my eleventh year, a large group of soldiers had gathered for the Bible study. Before I played, Tante Jans made me sing. The song I sang was about the lost sheep which was found by the shepherd. I sang it slowly and dramatically, climaxing it with the last line:

316

And the sheep that went astray was me.

As I finished singing a big, blond Dutch officer reached out and pulled me to him. Picking me up and sitting me on his knee, he laughed and said, "Tell me, young lady, how did you go astray?"

All the other soldiers laughed, and I was red with embarrassment. It did seem odd that such a little girl would describe herself as a lost sheep.

I had to confess that the line just belonged to the song and that I had never, never been a lost sheep. Then I told him that as a little girl, just five years of age, I had given my heart to Jesus Christ and could never remember not having belonged to Him.

The officer grew very serious and his eyes filled with tears. "Ah, that is the way it should be, little Sweet-Face," he said solemnly. "How much better to come to Jesus as a little child, than to have to stumble, as I have, always seeking the shepherd."

Then he closed his eyes and said softly, "But tonight I think I shall stop seeking, and let Him find me instead."

That night there was deep joy in the Bible meeting. The Lord had used me to lead a man to Christ. It was the first time in my life, and it had taken place not because of what I said, but because of the Holy Spirit who was in me. It was a secret I have remembered all the years of my life as I have traveled the world—a tramp for the Lord.

Jesus is Victor

Contents

Part One   He Cares, He Comforts

Part Two   He Sets the Captive Free

Part Three   Don't Wrestle, Just Nestle

Part One

~

HE CARES,
HE COMFORTS

Preface

Through my traveling over the world, and through my books and films, I have made many friends. When they are ill, I should love to be able to visit and comfort each of them. But I do pray for them, and the Lord gave me this idea—to write them a letter!

That was the beginning of this book. I prayed that the Lord would guide me and give me the thoughts, remembering what I had experienced with sick friends, and He gave me one after the other.

Often friends have the same problem, the same kind of suffering, and that's why I wrote down all I could remember. I'm sure that when a friend is sick he or she will find in one of these stories an answer that the Lord has given me when I needed it.

It is the Lord who has helped me to remember. So I hope that my friends will read this book as a message that the Lord gave—to me, for them.

Dear Friend

You are one of the many people who know me, perhaps even one of the many I have met on my recent journeys, an acquaintance who read one of my books, heard me talk, or saw me on film. And so there grew a real fellowship between you and me. I asked the Lord to give me an opportunity to meet you and He gave me this privilege of writing. He caused me to remember visits, experiences that I had with other sick people, and I'm sure that in these you will find an answer to the question *Why?* or to another problem that you have to face.

My friends had to endure suffering and now you are in the same kind of trouble. I prayed to the Lord to give me a word of comfort and an answer and I wrote them down. I think one of these stories that I tell may be an answer for you, from Corrie, but given to Corrie by the Lord Himself. Oh, it was wonderful that the Lord gave me the thoughts and the answers so quickly! So in some way it is a greeting, a message from the Lord Himself, who loves you and has your life in His hands, who knows of every suffering, every problem, as no human being does.

If you do not know Him, this book will be a challenge, an invitation from the Lord, who said:

Come unto me, all that . . . are heavy laden, and I will give you rest.
                                                                    Matthew 11:28

And if you know Him already, it will be a message from that Friend you and I have in Jesus.

Perhaps you are too ill, too weak to talk much with Him, but then you may lay your weak hand in the strong hand of Him who said:

... him that cometh to me I will in no wise cast out.

John 6:37

How He loves you!

"Jesus Heard You . . . ."

Jesus heard when you prayed last night.
He talked with God about you.
Jesus was there when you fought your fight,
He is going to bring you through.

Jesus knew when you shed those tears,
you did not weep alone.
The burdens you thought too heavy to bear,
He made them His very own.

Jesus Himself was touched by that trial,
you could not understand.
Jesus stood by as you almost fell
and lovingly clasped your hand.

Jesus cared when you bore that pain,
indeed, He bore it too.
He felt each pain, each ache in your heart,
because of His love for you.

Jesus, your Saviour, will always be with you,
no need to be anxious or fret.
Wonderful love, He will be there all the time,
He has never forsaken you yet.

1. *That Wee Little Baby*

YESTERDAY I MET a lady who is expecting a baby. I always like to pray with such a mother and to pray for the baby she has under her heart.

"Lord Jesus, You love that baby already. You know it and You can already fill that tiny little heart with Your love. Lord, will You give the baby and the mother strength and health for the time of pregnancy? And also for the birth? Bless the doctors and the nurses and give them wisdom and love." I was happy that I could pray with that mother, for I know that the Lord hears our prayers.

Some time after that, I was lying in the sunshine and I think I had fallen asleep, for I had a dream. I was talking with that wee baby for whom I had prayed! Often in dreams things happen that cannot take place in reality, for that little baby was talking with me, too!

"I am very happy to be here in this very safe corner of the world. It is so warm and so quiet here under Mama's heart. I have enough food and I do not at all long to be born! I am sure life must be difficult and noisy! No, I want to stay here always."

In my dream, I answered, "No, you must not think about being born as something that is sad or wrong. It is a joy to be born, for then life, the *real* life, begins. You will see your mother's face and her eyes full of love for you. You will rest in her arms; and, you will feel her arms around you. Then you will grow up and become a strong person. After you have lived for a time, there will come a moment when you have to go through another birth: when you go from this world to heaven. It will be like the time when you came from the little place under your mother's heart into life. Then you will see the eyes of Jesus and you will rest in His arms and He will bring you to a beautiful house that He has been preparing for all who believe in Him."

I awoke, and I had to laugh. But I was also happy about that dream. It was good. I took the Living Bible and read:

> You made all the delicate, inner parts of my body, and knit them together in my mother's womb . . . . You saw me before I was born . . . .
>
> Psalms 139:13, 16 LB

Are you afraid to die? Remember that for a child of God, death is only a passing through to a wonderful new world—to the house with many mansions where Jesus has prepared a place for you.

> For we know that when this tent we live in now is taken down—when we die and leave these bodies—we will have wonderful new bodies in heaven, homes that will be ours forevermore, made for us by God himself, and not by human hands.
>
> 2 Corinthians 5:1 LB

If you don't have that assurance, please read on. I will tell you more about how to be ready.

2. The Little Lamb

IT IS ALWAYS a tragic thing when a child dies. People have a tendency to call this an injustice on the part of God. However, God owes us nothing. If He gives our child ten years and then takes him away, we must be grateful for those ten years.

Also, I know how the Lord can use such happenings to accomplish a good purpose. I once heard about a mother who lost her child. She was very embittered and rebellious. One day she walked alone in the fields with a heavy heart. Suddenly she noticed a flock of sheep. The shepherd tried to have the sheep cross over a narrow bridge into another field, but the sheep did not want to set their feet on the shaky little bridge. They went right and left and turned just like stupid sheep do, but they did not obey the shepherd. Finally, the shepherd grabbed a little lamb that had been pressing itself against the soft wool of its mother's body. The man now carried the little lamb across the narrow bridge and put it into the meadow on the other side. Immediately, the mother sheep, bleating loudly, followed across the bridge, and then all the others followed.

The bereaved mother had observed all this with interest. Suddenly she knew that this was a message for her. She realized that for many years she had stubbornly gone her own way instead of following the call of the Good Shepherd: "Come unto me!" Now He had taken away her little son and brought him safely to the other side. His purpose was that she would come to Him, and lead the way for many others to be saved. This is what happened. She went to the Lord and gave Him her heart and life. Then she was able to be a witness to many others and help them to find the way to the Good Shepherd.

3. A Happy Visit

SHE WAS THE mother of one of my club girls and had asked me to visit her in the hospital. When I arrived, she was lying in a bed in a big ward, and she was looking very happy.

"I am really having the time of my life," she said. "Never have I had such good care. I do not have to cook—they bring my meals to my bed—and the nurses even wash me. My, that is different—quite different—from being at home and taking care of my naughty boys."

I understood what she meant. She lived in a narrow alley and had a rather rough husband and many children. "Oh," she said, "it is such a joy that the nurses look after me in every way! I like being ill."

"I understand, but tell me, are you in pain?"

"Yes," she said, "I still have pain, but I must tell you more about why I am so happy. The woman next to me told me more about Jesus. My daughter, who is in your club, also told me about Him, but here I really had time to think. She gave me a tract and a small Bible. I have been reading them and feel so happy! She read Psalm Twenty-three to me and I understood that the Lord *is* my Good Shepherd. Isn't that wonderful? There is only one almost insurmountable obstacle, and that is that next week I must go home again. I feel happy, but I also feel rather weak. I lost so much blood and I do not feel strong. Then to have to go back and start everyday life again . . . ."

I understood and said to her, "Listen. You know now that the Lord is your Shepherd and takes care of His sheep. When you are at home, the same Jesus, who now gives you peace in your heart, will be your Guide and your Friend. What a Friend we have in Jesus! He will help you with all the work you have to do at home. He helped you here! When I was a little girl, five years old, I asked Jesus to come into my heart, and He became my best Friend. Now that was a long time ago, but I know He never lets you down. At home, you will find that He is your teammate. Do you have difficulties and problems?"

"Yes, I have many. Big boys are not easy these days . . . ."

I could tell her that every person in the world is very important in God's eyes and that Jesus, when He died on the cross, bore our sins and sorrows and our punishment. If she would go to Him, He would in no wise cast her out. I prayed with her, and then I heard her whisper, "Jesus, I did not know You, but I would like to be the sheep that You find and take into Your arms. Will You also forgive me my sins? Amen."

I was happy about that and again I saw that there is nobody in the world who can say, "I cannot come to Jesus, He will not accept me."

Come unto me, all . . . .

Matthew 11:28

He loves you and is very happy if you say, "Yes, Jesus, I want to belong to You."

For God so loved the world, that he gave his only begotten Son, that whosoever believeth in him should not perish, but have everlasting life.

John 3:16

4. Pain

I VISITED BOB, a friend who had had a terrible accident. When I entered his room, he opened his eyes and looked at me, saying only one word: "Pain." I saw on his face that his suffering was almost unbearable. I stayed with him that evening.

There came a moment when I saw that he was able to listen and I told him an experience I had in the concentration camp. "Bob, the greatest suffering I had in the concentration camp was to be stripped of all my clothing and to have to stand naked. I told my sister, 'I cannot bear this. This is worse than all other cruelties we have had to endure.' Suddenly it was as if I saw Jesus on the cross, and I remembered that it says in the Bible, 'They took His garments.' Jesus hung there naked. By my own suffering, I understood a fraction of Jesus' suffering. And that gave me strength. Now I could bear my own suffering. Love so amazing—so divine—demands my life, my soul, my all. Bob, do you realize it must have meant almost intolerable pain to Jesus to die on the cross? Just think of His hands, His feet, His body. And He did that for you and for me."

I was silent. Bob had closed his eyes. But a moment later he looked at me and said, "I am looking at Jesus. Yes, I understand only a fraction of the pain He suffered. And it makes me so thankful that He did it all for me."

Bob's face was more relaxed than before and I saw peace in his eyes. A moment later I saw that he had fallen asleep and I quietly left the room.

The next day I was able to visit him again. "Corrie," he said, "every time I had so much pain, and could hardly bear it, I was thinking of Jesus. It made me so thankful! It is as if now I have the strength to bear it. Tell me a little bit of what you thought when you had to suffer in the concentration camp. Have you ever had pain?"

"I surely have, and do you know what helped me then?

> The sufferings of this present time are not worthy to be compared with the glory which shall be revealed in us.
>
> Romans 8:18

"We can look forward to the time when we shall be in the place where there is no pain, no cruelty, no death. Oh, Bob, the best is yet to be! Isn't that a joy?"

I saw him smiling for the first time. "Yes," he said, "what a joy! The best is yet to be!"

> And God shall wipe away all tears from their eyes; and there shall be no more death, neither sorrow, nor crying, neither shall there be any more pain: for the former things are passed away.
>
> Revelation 21:4

5. Can You Forgive?

ONE DAY I visited an old friend in a hospital. When I entered her room, I saw that she was very ill, but also that there was an expression of bitterness on her face. We had many things to talk about, for we had not seen each other for a long time. Then she told me about her husband.

"I know that I will be ill for a long time. The doctor does not give me any hope that I can do my work for a long time to come. My husband did not like having a sick wife. He left me and now lives with a younger woman. He never comes to see me."

"Have you forgiven him?"

"No, I certainly have not!"

"I will tell you something of my own experiences, when I felt bitter about someone. It was in Germany. One day I saw a lady in a meeting who did not look into my eyes. Suddenly I recognized her. She was a nurse who had been very cruel to my dying sister when we were in Ravensbruck Concentration Camp during the war. When I saw her, a feeling of bitterness, almost hatred, came into my heart. How my dying sister had suffered because of her! The moment I felt that hatred in my heart, I knew that I myself had no forgiveness. It was the Lord Jesus who said to us:

If ye forgive not men their trespasses, neither will your Father forgive your trespasses.
Matthew 6:15

340

"I knew I had to forgive her, but I could not. Then I had a good talk with the Lord about it when I was at home later. 'Lord, you know I cannot forgive her. My sister suffered too much because of her cruelties. I know, Lord, that I must forgive, but I cannot.' Then the Lord gave me:

The love of God is shed abroad in our hearts by the Holy Spirit which is given unto us.
Romans 5:5

"The Lord taught me a prayer: 'Thank You, Lord, for Romans 5:5. Thank You, Jesus, that You brought into my heart God's love by the Holy Spirit who is given to me. Thank You, Father, that Your love in me is stronger than my hatred and bitterness.' The same moment I knew I could forgive.

"I told a friend about my experience and she said, 'Oh, I know that nurse. She works in a hospital not far from here.'

"'Can you call her?'

"'Sure I can.' She called the nurse and I had a talk with her over the telephone, telling her that when I had the next meeting that evening, I would have a different message and would very much like her to come.

"Her answer was, 'You would like to see me in your meeting?'

"'Yes, that is why I phoned. I should like it very much.'

"'Then I will come.' She did come, and during the entire evening she looked into my eyes while I spoke. After the meeting, I had a talk with her. I told her that I had been bitter, but that God's Holy Spirit in me had brought His love instead of hatred and that now I loved her. I told her that it was through Jesus Christ who bore our sins on the cross. He forgave us, but He also fills our hearts with God's love through the Holy Spirit, and that is why I could invite her to come to the second meeting.

"I told her more and at the end of our talk that nurse accepted the Lord Jesus Christ as her personal Saviour and Lord. Do you see the miracle? I, who had hated her, was used by God to bring her to the acceptance of Jesus Christ. Not only will the Lord cleanse us by His blood but He will also use us. He used me, who hated her, and God had so absolutely forgiven and cleansed *me* that He could use me to show *her* the way of salvation!

"You are bitter about your husband, but claim Romans 5:5. I know that you love the Lord Jesus. You have known Him for a long time. Trust Him to do the miracle of bringing into your heart so much of God's love that you can forgive your husband!" I prayed with her and left.

A week later I was once more in her room. When I saw her, I knew that God had done something in her heart. "I am absolutely free. The Lord has done in me such a tremendous miracle that I could forgive my husband. You know, now there is a great peace and joy in me."

Yes, we never touch the ocean of God's love so much as when we love our enemies. It is a joy to *accept* forgiveness, but it is almost a greater joy to *give* forgiveness.

The love of God is shed abroad in our hearts by the Holy Spirit which is given unto us.
Romans 5.5

6. *The Foolishness of God*

AFTER WORLD WAR II, my friends and I organized a former concentration camp in Germany as a shelter for the homeless. Once, when I went there, I found a man (a lawyer) who was seriously ill. I asked him if he knew the Lord Jesus. "No," he said, "as long as I do not understand things with my brains, I cannot believe them."

I had a talk with him and I told him that in the Book of 1 Corinthians, chapters one and two tell us about the wisdom of the wise and the foolishness of God. "In the Bible," I said, "you can read very much about the foolishness of God. It is the highest wisdom. It is more important than the wisdom of the wise, because it is only through this that you get the real vision."

It was some weeks later that once more I was in our camp and I went straight to my friend. He was even more ill than the first time I had seen him. I asked, "What do you think of the foolishness of God?"

"I can praise the Lord, for I have seen that it is the greatest wisdom. I have thrown away my pride and I have come to Jesus as a sinner and asked forgiveness. I thank Him for His death on the cross, and I can tell you that He has brought into my heart a peace that passes all understanding. It surpasses everything of the wisdom of the wise, but it is the greatest reality I have ever experienced in my life. I am so thankful for the Bible. During these weeks I have read much in it and I do not fear the future, whatever happens."

Neither death, nor life, nor angels, nor principalities, nor powers, nor things present, nor things to come, Nor height, nor depth, nor any other creature, shall be able to separate us from the love of God, which is in Christ Jesus our Lord.

Romans 8:38, 39

For the first time I saw him look really happy!

. . . hath not God made foolish the wisdom of this world? . . . Because the foolishness of God is wiser than men; and the weakness of God is stronger than men.

1 Corinthians 1:20, 25

7. Alice

IN THE CONCENTRATION camp, a girl once came to me and said, "Please, will you come to Alice a moment? She has such terrible nights. While we sleep, she always turns from one side to the other. She suffers. I don't know what it is. Can you help her?"

"Sure," I said, "I can help her. I can pray for her. But I am busy here with a group. We are studying a portion of the Bible. In a quarter of an hour I will come to Alice."

When I went to her, I saw that she had fallen asleep. She was very restless, tossing from one side to the other. I spoke softly to her, but she did not hear me. Then I prayed and said, "Lord Jesus, You can fill Alice's heart with Your peace. You can fill her subconscious with Your love and then she will sleep well."

As I said amen to that prayer, I saw that Alice was quiet. She slept and I knew that the Lord had answered my prayer.

The next morning, my friend who had called me the day before said, "Oh, Corrie, it was a joy that Alice slept so well. She was so quiet—and I know that God has answered your prayer."

That day Alice died, but I had enjoyed an experience that has given me much courage. When we pray, every word we say is heard by the Lord, and I even read in the Book of Revelation that our prayers are kept in heaven. Our intercession is so important!

Often we cannot reach the others, but the Lord can reach everyone. What a joy to have such a Saviour!

. . . pray one for another . . . .

James 5:16

8. Tommy

HE WAS ONE of a big family. I believe there were fourteen children. Tommy was at a special school for mentally handicapped persons. I gave Bible lessons in that school.

Sometimes I visited Tommy in his home. When I asked where he was his mother always said, "He's in his room upstairs." I knew where to find him—in the little corner of the attic that was his "room." It was nothing more than a bed and a chair. On the chair there was always a small picture of Jesus on the cross.

I remember that once when I visited him, Tommy was on his knees before that chair. His face was full of joy. "Tommy, why are you so happy?" I asked.

"Because Jesus loves me!" he said. "And I love Jesus. He died on the cross for me and my sins, and now I have forgiveness."

His mother told me that Tommy always went straight to his little room when he came home. It was quiet there—a corner of peace in the rather small house. With so many children, the house was often noisy.

One day she found him with his head on the chair. In his hand was the picture of Jesus. Tommy did not move. He was with the Lord.

I'm sure that when he died, he must have felt great joy, because Jesus loved him and had died for him on the cross—and he knew it! Do you know it, too? Jesus, who loved Tommy, loves you just as much.

For God so loved the world, that he gave his only begotten Son, that whosoever believeth in him should not perish, but have everlasting life.

John 3:16

9. Toontje

IN HAARLEM, MY hometown, there was a minister who told me of a little boy who was feebleminded. His name was Toontje. He was always sitting in the front pew of the church. The minister said to his wife, "Toontje doesn't understand one word of my sermons. Nevertheless, he is so faithful—he comes every Sunday."

Once the pastor spoke of the ocean of God's love and told how we knew of it through Jesus Christ. When he was talking, he saw on Toontje's face an expression of great joy. Toontje understood when he talked about God's love. I myself worked among the feebleminded and I know from experience that you can never speak too much about the love of God.

The next day the pastor went to Toontje's home. He thought he would see if the boy still knew something of God's love. But when he arrived at Toontje's house, he heard that the boy had died in his sleep. The pastor told me that on Toontje's dead face was an expression of heavenly joy. "I believe," he said, "that Toontje tried to get too much of God's love into his heart, so that his heart just broke for joy."

If you and I would also accept too much of God's love, our hearts could break for joy. But in heaven we shall have such strong hearts that they will contain much, much more of the love of God. Oh, what a joy that will be! Then we shall praise and thank Him for all He was and is and shall be, for us. Hallelujah! What a Saviour!

We can only see a little of the ocean
when we stand at the rocky shore,
But out there, beyond the eye's horizon,
there's more—there's more!

We can only see a little of God's loving,
a few rich samples of His mighty store,
But out there, beyond the eye's horizon,
there is more—there is more!

AUTHOR UNKNOWN

We can read in the Bible:

When I think of the greatness of this great plan, I fall on my knees before the Father from whom all fatherhood, earthly or heavenly, derives its name, and I pray that out of the glorious richness of his resources he will enable you to know the strength of the Spirit's inner reinforcement—that Christ may actually live in your hearts by your faith. And I pray that you, firmly fixed in love yourselves, may be able to grasp with all Christians how wide and deep and long and high is the love of Christ—and to know for yourselves that love so far beyond our comprehension. May you be filled through all your being with God himself! Now to him who by his power within us is able to do infinitely more than we ever dare to ask or imagine—to him be glory in the Church and in Christ Jesus forever and ever. Amen!

Ephesians 3:14–21
(See PHILLIPS.)

10. Mother

I WOULD LIKE to tell you a little bit about my mother. I loved her so very much. The last years of her life, she was very ill and she could not even talk well— only a few words. But she could love and she could receive love. It was before she fell ill that we had a talk about the Lord.

Mother said, "I am not quite sure if everything is all right between the Lord and me. My faith is so little."

I told her words of Jesus, such as, "Come unto me, all. . . ." I said, "Mother, you, too, belong to the *all.*"

Mother looked sad and answered, "Yes, but. . . ." These words so often interfere when the Lord speaks to us, if we listen more to the spirit of doubt than to the Lord.

And now Mother was ill. She had had a stroke and could only say a few words. One day, I brought her a breakfast tray. She folded her hands and then shook her head. I asked, "Mother, can you not even find words when you pray?"

"No." But then she looked at me and I saw that her face was relaxed and happy.

"But it does not matter that you cannot talk to the Lord," I said. "He talks to you, doesn't He?"

"Yes," she said, and her face was beaming with joy.

"Is it all right with you and the Lord?"

"Absolutely!" was her reply.

I tried to find out the reason she was so changed from doubt to trust. "Did we say something, Mother? Or did someone else who visited you, perhaps the pastor

349

who came to see you yesterday? Or was it a message over the radio that gave you the assurance of salvation?"

Mother smiled and then she pointed upward with her finger.

"Was it the Lord who made it all right?"

"Yes, absolutely, it was the Lord." Six words Mother said, and what a joyful sentence!

My! There I saw that even when we could not reach her, the Lord could always reach her. And He is more concerned about our well-being than we are for each other. When I told Father, he said, "Oh, this is an answer to my prayer!"

"Did you also pray for it? I did, too." We found out that the whole family had been praying that the Lord might give Mother great assurance instead of doubt. How He had answered that prayer! What a joy it was!

Later on, Mother grew worse and was very, very ill; then she could not talk at all. It was as if she had no consciousness, but I felt her pulse and then I talked and asked her some questions. Her heartbeat went quicker when I spoke. "Mother, when you are going to die, you have nothing to fear, for you know that Jesus died on the cross for the sins of the whole world, and also for your sins. And, Mother, He is preparing a beautiful house for you in heaven. Then you may go there and we shall see each other again. For the Lord loves us and we all love Him! Just think of it, Mother, in heaven we shall have no pain. There will be no sickness at all, and, Mother, there you will see Jesus. What a joy it will be to look at His wonderful face!"

I knew that although she could not speak at all, she had understood what I had said. But do you understand what made me happiest? To know that when we cannot reach the other one, the Lord can reach His beloved. And it is He who has said:

Lo, I am with you always, even unto the end of the world.

Matthew 28:20

I know that He was with Mother when she died and went home. He Himself brought her into His wonderful paradise. "Promoted to Glory," the Salvation Army people say.

Thou hast beset me behind and before, and laid thine hand upon me.

Psalms 139:5

11. Pietje

PIETJE WAS A hunchback. She was one of my club girls. We liked each other and had a lot of fun. She could neither walk very far nor very fast and I also had difficulty keeping pace with the other girls of my club. I remember we were on a trip one time through Germany, and we had to cross a rather high mountain. Pietje came to me and said, "Auntie, give me your hand and I will help you." We both had to laugh, for she understood that I needed her help and she needed mine, so we stayed a little behind the rest of my healthy club girls and went arm-in-arm up the mountain.

Yes, Pietje was a dear girl. I remember that in the youth hostel where we stayed that evening, we had a talk about the Judgment Day of God. Pietje said, "I'm afraid to come before the Judgment seat. Have we any advocate who will plead for us?"

"Well, just look in the Bible."

Christ . . . maketh intercession for us.

Romans 8:34

"That is good!" Pietje said. "Who is our judge?"
"Read it yourself."

Who is he that condemneth? It is Christ . . . .

Romans 8:34

"What? Jesus Christ is our Judge *and* our Advocate? Now I am not afraid anymore! He will plead us Not Guilty."

That girl was so happy because she saw what a joy it is that Jesus died for us on the cross and carried our punishment. She knew that one day He will be our Judge and our Advocate. Yes, that was a good talk we had together, there in that youth hostel! I remember there was a lovely view over the mountains and the sun was setting with beautiful colors.

Later, I had to visit Pietje when she was very ill. I found her in the corner of a huge ward in a big hospital. When I saw her, there was nobody with her—no visitors and no nurse—and I talked with her.

"Will you stay with me until I die?" she asked.

"Yes," I said, "I'll do that. Are you sure that you will die soon?"

"Yes," Pietje smiled. "I'm not at all afraid, for, you know, my Judge is the Advocate and my Advocate is the Judge. I am not afraid at all, because it is Jesus Himself who loves me and I love Him."

Say, do *you* sometimes fear when you think of the Judgment Day of God, where we all have to appear whether we believe it or not? Read your Bible! Jesus is *your* Judge and *your* Advocate. Isn't that good? We have nothing to fear—*nothing!*

> Who is he that condemneth? It is Christ that died, yea rather, that is risen again, who is even at the right hand of God, who also maketh intercession for us.
>
> Romans 8:34

12. Debbie

A FRIEND OF mine told me about her sister Debbie. She was very ill and needed some comfort. "I know," my friend said, "that you cannot go all the way to Missouri to visit her, and she cannot come to you. But what about having a talk over the telephone?" That was a good idea. Isn't it wonderful to live in a world where you can talk with each other over the telephone?

It was a good conversation. She told me her difficulties and her worries. "Corrie," she said, "I'm very ill, and some people think I must die. I am afraid of death. Can you help me?"

"Yes, surely, but listen. We haven't much time to talk over the telephone, so let us just ask each other some questions and give answers. Do you know the Lord Jesus? I don't ask if you know *about* Him, but do you know Him?"

"I'm not sure. I have not read much in the Bible. I did not go to church and was really not greatly interested in spiritual things, so I feel that I do not really know Jesus."

"Then first of all you must come to Him, for He is the One who can comfort and help you. He said:

Come unto me, all ye that labour and are heavy laden, and I will give you rest.
Matthew 11:28

. . . him that cometh to me I will in no wise cast out.

John 6:37

"And when you come to Him He is willing to come so close that He will even come into your heart.

Behold, I stand at the door, and knock: if any man hear my voice, and open the door, I will come in . . . .

Revelation 3:20

"Do you understand that *you* must open the door? Then He will come in and you can tell Him everything. He understands far more than I—or any other human being—can. It is true that when you come into contact with the Lord Jesus, you will see your sins, but look at the cross then. You must simply say, 'Lord Jesus, forgive me. I thank You that You died on the cross for my sins.' The Bible says that then He will cast your sins into the depths of the sea, forgiven and forgotten. And I believe that He adds a sign that reads NO FISHING ALLOWED! What about that?"

"I will think about it."

"No, listen! It is all right to think about it, but we have so little time now. Why not do it?"

"Do what?"

"Ask Jesus to come into your heart!"

"Is it so simple?"

"Yes, so simple!"

Then I prayed with her. Oh, it is such a joy that we can always pray with one another over the telephone—the line to the Lord is never busy. He is always ready to listen. "Lord, Debbie would like to ask You to come in, and I thank You, Lord, that You are willing. Will You send away all the doubt, all the 'yes, buts' and the 'if onlies'? I thank You, Lord, that You love Debbie. Hallelujah! Amen!

"Now, Debbie, the way is open. Say, 'Come into my heart, Lord Jesus.'"

And she did. I heard her say, "Lord Jesus, come into my heart. I know that I am not good enough, but, oh, Lord, how I need You! Thank You, Jesus, that You came into my heart. I will tell You all the sins I can remember and I thank You that You have borne them on the cross. Oh, Lord Jesus, You love me, thank You. And I love You. Amen."

Now, wasn't that a wonderful prayer? I was so happy and I know the Lord was happy. I could imagine Him standing there with His arms wide open. I said also, "Debbie, now tell Him all your fears and problems and be sure that when you feel very ill, the Lord Jesus is with you. He will not let you down for one moment."

"Are you sure?"

"Yes, for I know the Lord. I have known Him for a long time and He never gives in. And you two will win, Jesus and you. Bye, Debbie. Until we meet, not in Missouri, but there—in heaven."

"Thank you, Corrie."

I was so happy about that telephone call. But I could do something more for her, and that was to pray! And I did: "Lord, make her very conscious of Your presence. And, Lord, surround her with Your angels and let her room be a room where she is together with You and the angels."

Some time afterward, I met her sister again and she said, "Oh, Corrie, very shortly after you had spoken with Debbie, she became more ill and I went to her to be with her until the end. She repeated all you had said over the telephone. 'I did it,' Debbie told me. 'I didn't understand everything but I know that He came, for since that time there has been such peace and joy and there is no fear at all. I know that I have to die soon, but do you know that I long to go to be with the Lord in heaven?'"

What a blessed telephone talk that was!

> Jesus did it,
> The Bible tells it,
> I believe it.
> That settles it!

Come unto me, all ye that labour and are heavy laden, and I will give you rest.
Matthew 11:28

13. *Passing the Baton*

YOU KNOW THAT I am a *Tramp for the Lord*. I traveled all over the world to tell others about the Lord Jesus. I am already old and I do not like to go alone. That is why I always have a younger woman with me. At one time, the Lord gave me Connie to accompany me. For more than seven years, we went together over a large part of the world. But she married, and then the Lord gave me another companion.

There came a time when Connie became very ill, and she knew that she had to die.

Her husband came home one evening and saw that she was crying. He put his arm around her and asked, "Connie, why do you cry?"

She answered, "I traveled much with Tante Corrie and after that I traveled much with you. But now I must go on a journey all alone and you and Tante Corrie will not be with me . . . ."

"Oh, but listen, Connie," said her husband. "I will keep your hand in mine, and in the moment when you really die, I will give your hand into the hand of Jesus. He will keep you through the valley of the shadow of death and bring you to the beautiful heaven where He has prepared a house for you!"

Connie did not cry anymore. What her husband had said was so true! And it all happened that way when Connie went home.

Oh, that loving hand of God! The men who wrote the Psalms knew much when they wrote what the Holy Spirit told them:

If I take the wings of the morning, and dwell in the uttermost parts of the sea; Even there shall thy hand lead me, and thy right hand shall hold me.

Psalms 139:9, 10

. . . thou art my strength. Into thine hand I commit my spirit.

Psalms 31:4, 5

Connie had a husband who was with her until the last moment of her life. Many, many people have no husband who is able and has the opportunity to stay with them when they are dying, but the great joy is that everyone can know there is a Saviour in Jesus Christ. "What a Friend we have in Jesus!" His hand keeps us, not only when we go through the valley of the shadow of death but also before that. When we pray, "Take my hand, Lord, and hold me tight," the Lord does it. He has every opportunity and every possibility—and how much love He has for us! He is never too busy with others. He takes time to be with us. He himself said:

Lo, I am with you always, even unto the end of the world.

Matthew 28:20

My father used to say to us, when we were children and had to go away from home for a while, "Children, don't forget, when Jesus takes your hand, then He holds you tight. And when Jesus keeps you tight, He guides you through life. And when Jesus guides you through life, one day He brings you safely home."

14. Used by God

ONCE I SLEPT in a hospital in a concentration camp. Many people were ill and many died. In the night, I heard people calling and I went to them. I was ill myself, but not so seriously that I couldn't do this—I went to everyone who called. I saw much, much suffering and loneliness there.

It was in that concentration camp hospital that I experienced God's use of sick people to help others around them. You can feel so weak in illness and unable to do anything, but witnessing for the Lord Jesus is possible because it is really the Lord who witnesses *in us* and it causes us to relax. When we are channels of living water, then it is the Lord who tells us what to say, and He *never* makes a mistake.

Nobody was with these dying people, but I could tell all of them, "Jesus is here. Just put your hand in His hand." And many of them did. And then I saw peace coming into the hearts of these people. There is a little poem in Holland:

> *Als wij de doodsvallei betreen,*
> *laat ons elke aardse vriend alleen,*
> *maar, Hij, de beste Vriend in nood,*
> *geleid ons over graf en dood.*

> When we enter the valley of the shadow of death,
> all our earthly friends leave us alone,
> but He, the best Friend in need,
> accompanies us through the grave and death.

Yes, even for people who are surrounded by friends and relatives, a moment comes when they have to turn to Jesus—the only One who can help them. But what a joy that He is there!

I saw a nurse who looked so worried and tired. Every time she passed my bed, a woman next to me smiled to her, and sometimes she said a kind word.

In the evening the nurse came to her and said, "Do you know that you have helped me? My day was full of disappointments, but your smile has encouraged me."

I learned an important lesson that evening.

15. Nobody Is Too Bad

DURING THE WAR in Vietnam, I was permitted to visit a hospital. I talked to the men who were wounded. In a ward with about twelve patients, I had an opportunity to speak. I told them about the living Jesus, who is with us, who loved us so much that He died for us, and who now lives for us. He is at the same time at the right hand of the Father, praying for us. I also told them that He said:

> Come unto me, all ye that labour and are heavy laden, and I will give you rest.
>
> Matthew 11:28

I showed them what a joy it was that we could come to Him.

Afterwards, I had a talk with the man sitting next to me. He was not much more than a boy, and seriously wounded. He said to me, "What you told about Jesus is so beautiful, so joyful! But I cannot do what you said and go to Him. I have heard about the Lord, but I have always blasphemed. When there were boys in my class who followed the Lord, I teased them. There has been hatred in my heart—hatred against God—and now I know that I am seriously wounded. But I have been too bad, I cannot go to the Lord. I am ashamed of what I have done, of how I have tried to keep others away from Him. Now don't tell me that I can ask Him to help me. I am a very wicked fellow."

"There is only one kind of person who cannot come to Jesus," I told him. "They are the ones who think and say, 'I'm so good, I don't need forgiveness, I don't need the Saviour.' They are the Pharisees, and you can read in the Bible that Jesus

360

could not and would not help the people who were so proud of themselves and who thought they were so good.

"You are quite different. You think you are too bad. You are not. Jesus bore the sins of the whole world and that is a lot. He has also borne your sins on the cross: sins of hatred, of blasphemy, of whatever you did. You *can* go to Him. Jesus hates sins but loves sinners, and all His promises are really for sinners only. *You* are not good enough; *you* are not able. It is *Jesus* who is able and He is your Saviour. Just talk to Him! Tell Him what you have done and what you have been, and then ask forgiveness. The Bible says that when you bring your sins to Him, He will blot them out like a cloud. Did you see that cloud this morning? It is gone. It will never come again. It has absolutely disappeared forever. So when you bring your sins to Jesus, He will make them disappear—He will destroy them forever and ever."

Suddenly I saw that all the men in the ward were listening. I asked, "Who of you will now come to Jesus as a sinner? When you know you are a sinner, you are forgiven." Many men in that ward responded.

If we confess our sins, he is faithful and just to forgive us our sins, and to cleanse us from all unrighteousness.

1 John 1:9

16. Niwanda

I SAW A little paper in my hand. I don't know who put it there, but it was a letter: "Please, come to me. I am in the fifth bed at the right. Niwanda."

I was in Africa and had spoken that morning in a boys' boarding school. I asked the missionary if he could help me find out from whom that letter had come. He smiled and said, "Yes, I know. That boy is very ill. We could not yet take him to the hospital. Fifth bed, that is in room three. I can take you there."

We entered the room where we found Niwanda. Immediately I saw that he was really ill. "I needed some help to find you, boy!"

We both laughed and the missionary said, "I will leave you alone with him."

Niwanda and I had a good talk together. "Tell me something of yourself, boy."

"I am very ill. I have been a Christian for a long time and I have served God, but when I look back on my life, I feel so ashamed. I read in the Bible that Paul said, 'I have fought a good fight.' When I look at the past, I know that I, too, have really done my best to fight the good fight. But no, I didn't make a good job of it as Paul did."

"Listen, Niwanda. It is true that Paul wrote, 'I have fought the fight.' We can quite agree because we have such great respect for him. But he did not write, 'I have fought the fight the right way.' He means, 'I have been fighting in the good fight.' You and I also have to do so—we are both in the good fight. We stand on victory ground, because our fight is under King Jesus, and King Jesus is Victor. He makes us more than conquerors."

I saw that the boy looked happy when I told him this about fighting while standing on victory ground.

I have fought a good fight, I have finished my course, I have kept the faith.

2 Timothy 4:7

17. His Sheep

SOME TIME AGO, I visited a friend of mine. He was a man who had often helped me. When I could not understand something in the Bible, he told me what it meant. He knew a great deal. He knew the Lord. However, there was one strange thing—he was afraid to die.

Now I had heard that he was very ill, so I went to him, thinking that I must try to help him so that he would no longer be afraid to die. It was possible that that moment would soon come. It would be such a pity if he should be afraid, since he had known the Lord for such a long time. I prayed in my heart, "Oh, Lord Jesus, will You touch him, will You take away all fear from his heart?"

When I entered his room, he looked very happy. I asked him, "Are you a little better?"

"No," he said, "I'm very weak and I know that I must die. But what I'm so very happy about is that Jesus said, 'I give My sheep life eternal!' It is good He said it, for I cannot do anything myself. I am so tired that I cannot think properly, but I know that He will take care of me—even . . . even now. I cannot do it, but He is able."

How good it was to see that all the fear had disappeared. The Lord Himself takes care of His own. When there are moments that are difficult, we do not have to fear anything, for He is able to help us. He is faithful. He loves us.

Yes, He gives, and all that we have to do—is accept! Not one of our prayers is lost. All our prayers are kept in heaven.

Another angel came and stood at the altar, having a golden censer; and there was given unto him much incense, that he should offer it with the prayers of all saints upon the golden altar which was before the throne.

Revelation 8:3

18. Little Angel

IN A CHILDREN'S hospital, I stood with my hand in a mother's hand. Her little girl had died. She looked like a little angel. On that little girl's dead face there was such an expression of peace!

"Oh, what joy it must be for that little child to be with Jesus! She will be so happy in heaven."

"I believe that, too," the mother said, "but Corrie, you don't know how wounded I am. I loved my little girl so very much. Why did the Lord take her away from me?"

"I do not know, but God knows. He understands you. He loves you and He loves that little girl."

There are moments when the suffering is so deep that one can hardly talk to a person. What a joy it is then to know that the Lord understands. No pit is so deep that the Lord is not deeper still. Underneath us are the everlasting arms—and the Lord understands.

> He shall cover thee with his feathers, and under his wings shalt thou trust: his truth shall be thy shield and buckler.
>
> Psalms 91:4

19. *The Lost Sheep*

RECENTLY I MET someone who had known the Lord for a long time, but she had turned away from Him. I sang to her, "What a Friend We Have in Jesus."

"I sang that song when I was in Sunday school," she said. "Yes, then I heard about the Lord Jesus every Sunday, but I have gone astray. I did not speak to Him and I did not listen to Him for many years. And now I'm so ill—what can I do?"

I told her of the good shepherd who had a hundred sheep and one of them had also gone astray. "It did not come home with the others. That shepherd left the ninety-nine at home and went to seek that one silly sheep that had lost its way. He found it, took it in his arms, and brought it home. He was very, very happy. So Jesus is on His way looking for you. Won't you let yourself be found by this wonderful Friend who is our Saviour? He is looking for you, and when you call Him, He will take you and carry you home. He will be so happy!"

She closed her eyes and thought about it. Then, opening her eyes again, she said, "Is it as simple as all that?"

"Yes, it is."

She folded her hands. "Lord Jesus, forgive me for having gone my own way. Take me in Your arms and take me back home. Amen."

He was so near that it was as if we heard Him say, ". . . him that cometh to me I will in no wise cast out" (John 6:37).

She looked up and smiled a very happy smile. "What a Friend we have in Jesus!"

20. Worry

"OH, MY CHILDREN! My husband! How can they live without me?"

I was in a hospital in a large town in the United States, and my friend Ann was very ill. She knew it and she did not tell me about her suffering, but about the greatest worry she had. "Just imagine that I should die—who would take care of my family?" I held her hand in mine and just prayed for her. Then suddenly, I remembered a little poem.

> Said the Robin to the Sparrow:
> "I should really like to know
> Why these anxious human beings
> Rush around and worry so."
>
> Said the Sparrow to the Robin:
> "Friend, I think that it must be
> That they have no heavenly Father
> Such as cares for you and me."
>
> ELIZABETH CHENEY

The Bible tells us:

Look at the birds in the sky. They neither sow nor reap nor store away in barns and yet your heavenly Father feeds them.

See Luke 12:24

Aren't you much more valuable to Him than they are? Can any one of you, however much he worries, make himself an inch taller? And why do you worry about clothes? Consider how the flowers grow. They neither work nor weave, but I tell you that even Solomon in all his glory was never arrayed like one of these. Now, if God so clothes the flowers of the field which are alive today and discarded tomorrow, is He not much more likely to clothe you—you of little faith? Don't worry at all, then, about tomorrow. Tomorrow can take care of itself. One day's trouble is enough for one day.

I could easily understand that her children and her husband were reasons to worry about the future. However, our times are in God's hands, and He loves her family even more than she loved them. Worrying is carrying tomorrow's load with today's strength—carrying two days at once. It is moving into tomorrow ahead of time. Worrying does not empty tomorrow of its sorrow—it empties today of its strength.

"Do you know, Ann, I do not believe that worry is from the Lord. It is from the enemy. There has been a man upon the earth of whom Satan is afraid, a man whom he can neither touch nor resist—Jesus Christ. And that is why we can go to Him for help. You are not able to overcome worry, but the Lord Jesus can, and He will—through His Holy Spirit. When we see that worry is a sin—and that is what it really is, for the Bible tells us not to worry—then we know what to do with sin, don't we?"

"Yes, we take it to the Lord, and when we confess our sins, the blood of Jesus cleanses us from all of our sins."

"That is true, so just ask forgiveness for having worried, and then ask Jesus to keep worry away. He gives us peace under all circumstances. I have a little stick here that cannot stand on my hand by itself. But I can even let it stand on the top of my finger, if my hand holds it. In the same way, we cannot keep worry away, but when we surrender to the wounded hands of Jesus, He keeps us from falling. One day He will present us blameless and with unspeakable joy. That will be on the day when He will reveal Himself. Jesus is stronger than all of our problems."

I prayed with Ann and then she said, "I have much to think about and I know one thing—I am not able, but Jesus is. He will do the job."

Cast thy burden upon the Lord, and he shall sustain thee: he shall never suffer the righteous to be moved.

Psalms 55:22

21. Our Times Are in God's Hands

IT IS A feast for me to be in Holland, for I meet friends of former days. I gather them in my home to tell them how much I have experienced during the last year. At one of these gatherings, I missed one of my friends. Somebody told me, "She is ill, so she could not come."

I went to see her. She told me what had happened. "I have been very ill, and everyone—myself, too—thought I had to die. Oh, Corrie, I was not afraid. I was just thinking about the joy of seeing the Lord Jesus as I read in the Bible all the promises that speak of heaven. But then I began to recover. I am not strong, but the doctor said that in a short while I shall be able to do my work again."

"Are you happy?"

"Yes. I can be an eternity in heaven and there is much work for me to do here in this world. I believe I will return to my everyday life richer than I was before I was ill. I see now that our times are in God's hands. I believe I will take the good opportunities, which the Lord will give me in the future, with more thankfulness, because I had thought I had lost them forever. I knew, when I was dying, how serious my condition was, but the Lord gave me grace. I was not afraid. Now I know, as I go back to my everyday life, that I will see the smaller problems in the light of eternity. I am sure I will not be so concerned about the problems of everyday life. I thank God that I had this illness. It made me more ready for life."

All things work together for good to them that love God. . . .

Romans 8:28

The Lord never makes a mistake. One day, when we are in heaven, I'm sure we shall see the answers to the *whys*. My, how often I have asked, "*Why?*" In heaven we shall see God's side of the embroidery. God has no problems—only plans. There is never panic in heaven.

22. When I Saw Death

WHEN I HEARD that my father had died in prison, I was alone in a cell. The prisoner who had been in the cell before me had written on the wall NOT LOST, BUT GONE BEFORE.

After the first shock, I realized what a great joy it was for Father to be with the Lord in the beautiful place that Jesus had prepared for him. Straight from the cell in a prison to that place of peace and love of God. I could thank the Lord that He had taken him home. Yes, he was not lost but gone before.

When I saw Betsie after she had died in the ward of the concentration camp, I saw an expression of intense joy and peace on her face. She even looked young. I could only thank and praise the Lord that He had taken her to Himself. It was as if her face reflected a little bit of the tremendous joy that her soul experienced at that moment, when she went to be with the Lord.

I looked death in the eyes several times myself, and when fear came into my heart I told the Lord Jesus. He did not give me a spirit of fear, but of power and of love and of a sound mind. I knew that I did not have to pass through the valley of the shadow of death alone. Jesus was with me.

The moment I was almost sure that death was coming was when my number was called out when we were standing on roll call. I had to stand as number one in the front row. Many of us thought—also I myself—that we had been called out because they were going to kill us.

I stood there for three hours, and next to me was a Dutch girl I had never seen before. I said to myself: "This is now the last person on earth to whom I can bring the Gospel." And I did. She told me her life story. I told her that Jesus loved her and that He had given His life on the cross to bear her punishment. That girl said *yes* to Jesus.

I was not killed, I was set free.

What do you think about death, about the death of your loved ones, and of yourself? Study the Bible, the answer is there. Talk with the Lord, He understands and loves you. When you come to Him, He will in no wise cast you out or send you away. Are you afraid? Give your fear to Him.

23. Are You Afraid to Die?

IN CHICAGO I met an old friend of mine. I had not seen him for a long time, and I was spending only one day in his town. We had a good talk together, and I remember that I asked him a question. "Are you afraid to die?"

"Yes, I am," he said.

His answer surprised me. He loved the Lord and had known Him a long time. He had a deep faith in God. "Why are you afraid to die? You have been a Christian as long as I have known you. Surely you know that Jesus will not leave you alone for one moment."

"I am afraid, Corrie, because I have never died before. I am afraid because I do not know what it is like to die."

Then we talked about Jesus. Before He went to the cross, He had never died either. Was He also a little afraid?

But today Jesus knows what it is like to die. He has already been through death, and today Jesus says to you and to me, "I will never leave you nor forsake you," and "Lo, I am with you always." That means *even* death.

The old man smiled and said, "Isn't God good to us—that we could talk and think together about this today?"

"Are you afraid to die?"

Fear thou not; for I am with thee: be not dismayed; for I am thy God: I will strengthen thee; . . . yea, I will uphold thee with the right hand of my righteousness.

Isaiah 41:10

No temptation has overtaken you that is not common to man. God is faithful, and he will not let you be tempted beyond your strength, but with the temptation will also provide the way of escape, that you may be able to endure it.

1 Corinthians 10:13 RSV

"Are You Going Home?"

Are you going Home to be with the Lord?
You are not afraid, are you?

Afraid of what?
To feel the Spirit's glad release,
to pass from pain to perfect peace,
the strife and strain of life to cease?
Afraid of that?

Afraid of what?
Afraid to see the Saviour's face?
To hear His welcome and to trace
the glory gleam from wounds of grace?
Afraid of that?

Afraid of what?
To enter into heaven's rest
and yet, to serve the Master blessed,
from service good to service best?
Afraid of that?

Think of stepping on shore and finding it heaven, or taking hold of a hand and finding it God's, or breathing new air and finding it celestial, or feeling invigorated and finding it immortality; of passing through a tempest to a new and unknown ground; of waking up well and happy and finding it home.

You Have His Word

My sheep hear my voice, and I know them, and they follow me: And I give unto them eternal life; and they shall never perish, neither shall any man pluck them out of my hand.

John 10:27, 28

I am the resurrection and the life: He who believes in me will live, even though he dies.

John 11:25 NIV

The gift of God is eternal life through Jesus Christ our Lord.

Romans 6:23

Blessed be the God and Father of our Lord Jesus Christ, which according to his abundant mercy hath begotten us again unto a lively hope by the resurrection of Jesus Christ from the dead, To an inheritance incorruptible, and undefiled, and that fadeth not away, reserved in heaven for you.

1 Peter 1:3, 4

What we suffer now is nothing compared to the glory he will give us later.

Romans 8:18 LB

No mere man has ever seen, heard or even imagined what wonderful things God has ready for those who love the Lord.

1 Corinthians 2:9 LB

If we confess our sins, he is faithful and just to forgive us our sins, and to cleanse us from all unrighteousness.

1 John 1:9

Forasmuch as ye know that ye were not redeemed with corruptible things, as silver and gold, from your vain conversation received by tradition from your fathers; But with the precious blood of Christ, as of a lamb without blemish and without spot.

1 Peter 1:18,19

But God commendeth his love toward us, in that, while we were yet sinners, Christ died for us.

Romans 5:8

Verily, verily, I say unto you, He that heareth my word, and believeth on him that sent me, hath everlasting life, and shall not come into condemnation; but is passed from death unto life.

John 5:24

These things have I written unto you that believe on the name of the Son of God; that ye may know that ye have eternal life, and that ye may believe on the name of the Son of God.

1 John 5:13

For our light affliction, which is but for a moment, worketh for us a far more exceeding and eternal weight of glory.

2 Corinthians 4:17

For we know that if our earthly house of this tabernacle were dissolved, we have a building of God, a house not made with hands, eternal in the heavens.

2 Corinthians 5:1

But thanks be to God, which giveth us the victory through our Lord Jesus Christ.

1 Corinthians 15:57

Part Two

HE SETS THE CAPTIVE FREE

Preface

I KNOW HOW it feels to be behind a door that can be opened only from the outside, for I have been a prisoner in three different prisons. I learned a great deal in prison, as this was a very difficult class in the schoolroom of life. When you are in a difficult class with a good teacher, you learn much—and my teacher was very good. It was Jesus Himself!

I wish I could share with you what I learned during my imprisonment, but I am old and I cannot travel much now. Since we cannot speak personally together, I have decided to visit you through this little book. The conversations, the experiences really happened to me and I want to share them with you—to show you that even when circumstances look utterly bleak, there is a victorious life which is real and available to you.

It is not only behind barbed wire or prison doors that there are prisoners. There are prisoners of sin, of lust, prisoners of wrong philosophies, prisoners of circumstances, prisoners of *self*. There are prisoners everywhere. I pray that this book will help you too to lose your life for Jesus' sake so that you may gain it. Jesus said that those whom He makes free are free indeed. Whether decent or indecent sinners, we all need Jesus. He loves us. Yes, He loves you!

1. *I Was in Prison*

"NAME?" THE INTERROGATOR inquired.

"Cornelia ten Boom, and . . . ."

"Age?"

"Fifty-two."

It was a dark night when we were finally marched out of the building. We could see before us a large canvas-roofed army truck. The truck had no springs and we bounced roughly over the bomb-pitted streets of The Hague. Leaving the downtown section, we seemed to be headed west, toward the suburbs of Scheveningen. Now we knew our destination; the Federal Penitentiary named after this seaside town of Scheveningen.

We turned left into an endless world of steel and concrete.

"Ten Boom, Cornelia!"

Another door rasped open. The cell was deep and narrow, scarcely wider than the door. A woman lay on the single cot, three others on straw ticks on the floor. "Give this one the cot," the matron said. "She's sick."

Soon I was moved to another location. The cell was identical to the one I had just left: six steps long, two wide, a single cot at the back. But this cell was empty. As the guard's footsteps died away down the corridor, I leaned against the cold metal of the door. Alone. Alone behind these walls . . . solitary!

Weeks later, "Get your things together! Get ready to evacuate!" The shouts of the guards echoed up and down the long corridor. I was thankful to see other faces again, . . . but!

Where would we be taken? Where were we headed? One thing I dreaded . . . please . . . not into Germany!

Hours passed as the loaded train sat on the siding. It must have been two or three in the morning when the train at last began to move. The thought uppermost in every mind was: Is it Germany?

Finally we seemed to stop in the middle of a wood. Floodlights mounted in trees lit a broad rough-cleared path lined by soldiers with leveled guns.

Spurred on by the shouts of the guards, I started up the path between the gun barrels. "Close ranks! Keep up! Five abreast!"

The nightmare march lasted a mile or more, when at last we came to a barbed-wire fence surrounding a row of wooden barracks. We went into one of them and fell into an exhausted sleep. So began our stay in this place that we learned was named Vught, after the nearest small village. Vught had been constructed in Holland by the occupation army primarily as a concentration camp for political prisoners.

Several months later we were moved to another camp. After a night punctuated with the hail of bullets and machine-gun fire, we learned at dawn that we were passing through a border town into Germany. For two more incredible days and nights we were carried deeper and deeper into the land of our fears.

From the crest of the hill, we saw a vast scar on the green German landscape; a city of low gray barracks, surrounded by concrete walls on which guard towers rose at intervals. In the very center a square smokestack emitted a thin gray vapor into the blue sky.

"Ravensbruck!"

Like a whispered curse, the word passed back through the lines. This was the notorious extermination camp for women, whose name we had heard even in Holland.

Adapted from *The Hiding Place*

2. Why I Was Sent to Prison

I WANT TO tell you about my experiences in three prisons. During World War II, I was a prisoner of the Gestapo because my family, my friends, and I had saved the lives of Jewish people in Holland. Adolf Hitler was preparing to kill all of them, and our task was to help them to escape to safer countries.

When that was no longer possible, we hid them in our houses. In the end we had a group of eighty people with whom we worked to supply the desperate needs of a hidden people: food, clothing, houses, burials. There were many other factors facing a group of helpless persons hiding in a country already stripped by the occupying army of a powerful enemy.

We were betrayed and all were arrested. My father was eighty-four years old, and lived only a short while in the prison where all his children and a grandson were also incarcerated. We never saw him again, for the prison walls separated us.

Father was a courageous man, but he understood that he was too old for prison life. "If I am imprisoned, I shall die, but it will be an honor for me to give my life for God's chosen people, the Jews," he said before they arrested him. I heard much later that he had died after only ten days' imprisonment.

3. Solitary Confinement

FOR THE FIRST WEEK, they put me in a cell with four or five others, for I was very ill with pleurisy. The prison doctor said it would develop into tuberculosis, so I was sent to solitary confinement. He didn't want me to infect the others.

For the first time ever, I was really alone, and I knew my life was completely in the hands of the enemy. They could kill me or torture me or just forget about me altogether, and there would be no one to know or care.

At night the sounds of distant bombing penetrated the thick walls—and from somewhere within came the muffled cries of people being tortured by the Gestapo—that was a little bit of hell! When I lost courage, I tried singing, but the guards pounded on the door and demanded silence. They threatened to take me to the *dark* cell. In the dark cell you had to stand in water. Time became a very thick thing that I struggled to wade through.

Solitary confinement lasted four months. It wasn't only the isolation that was so hard, but the constant threat that at any moment of the day or night they would come for me. Whenever I heard footsteps outside my cell I would ask myself, "Are they coming to torture or kill me?"

Once I stood with my back against the wall with my hands spread out, as if to try to push away the walls that were closing in on me. I was dead scared. I cried out, "Lord, I'm not strong enough to endure this. I don't have the faith!"

Suddenly I noticed an ant which I had watched roaming the floor of the cell for days. I had just mopped the floor with a wet rag, and the moment the ant felt the water on the stones, he ran straight to his tiny hole in the wall.

Then it was as if the Lord said to me, "What about that ant? He didn't stop to look at the wet rag or his weak feet—he went straight to his hiding place. Corrie, don't look at your faith; it is weak, like the tiny feet of that ant. Don't dwell on the treatment you might receive from these cruel people. I am your hiding place, and you can come running to Me just like that ant disappeared into that hole in the wall."

That brought real peace into my heart. I was then fifty-three years old, and I had always known about Jesus, but there in solitary confinement I began to really understand and experience for myself that His light is stronger than the deepest darkness.

I know there are moments for you when you lose all courage. You feel as a prisoner that you don't exist in the eyes of the people around you, in the eyes of God, or in your own eyes. Then you can read in the Bible a promise from Jesus: "Come to Me, all you who have heavy burdens, and I will give you rest" (Matthew 11:28). When you can believe that, you will *know* Someone is still interested in you. Someone still cares about you—not as a number, but as a person.

4. The Interrogation

AFTER TWO MONTHS in the cell, I was called in for interrogation. The judges, the *Sachbearbeiters,* had a tremendous amount of power, and you had no rights whatever. They could give you a short sentence, a long sentence, or sentence you to death. You were totally in their hands.

I will never forget the moment when I was brought before my judge. I knew that not only my own life was in his hands, but that I could incriminate many friends and co-workers. If I were forced to tell about them, it could mean their death sentence, too.

I prayed for wisdom to answer all the questions of the interrogator, and there were *many* questions! I had to give my whole life history, even what I did in my spare time.

I told him that I taught a Bible class for feebleminded people who could not go to church because they could not understand sermons. "They need the Lord Jesus just as much as you and I do," I said to this National Socialist judge.

He replied, "What a waste of time! Isn't there far more value in converting a normal person than an abnormal one?"

My answer was, "If you knew Jesus, you would know that He has a great love for everyone who is despised or in need. It is possible that a poor, feebleminded child has more value in His eyes than you and I together."

He was angry when I said that, and he called the policemen, saying, "Take her back to her cell."

The next day I was brought again before my judge, who said, "I could not sleep during the night. I was thinking over what you had said about Jesus. I don't know anything about Him. We have plenty of time for the interrogation. First, tell me what you know about Jesus."

Boy, was that an opportunity! I began, "Jesus is a light come into this world. No one who believes in Him remains in darkness. Is there darkness in your life?"

His answer was, "Darkness? There is no light at all in my life. I hate my work. My wife is in Bremen, Germany. I don't even know if she is still alive. The town is being bombed heavily every night now. It is possible that she was killed this very night."

Suddenly the contact between us was on a totally different level. He was no longer the judge, but simply a man in great need, and I, his prisoner, could give him real encouragement as I brought him the Gospel.

I said to him, "Jesus once said, 'Come to me, all who are heavy laden, and I will give you rest.' Come to me—*all*. That means you, too. Come unto Jesus and He will give you rest. Tell Him your sins. He has never sent away any sinner."

I had a good talk with that man, and from then on he was no longer my enemy, but my friend. He helped to save my life and did his utmost, though unsuccessfully, to set me free.

Of course, he still had to do his job, and so he showed me papers found in my house. To my horror I saw names, addresses, and particulars which could mean not only *my* death sentence but the death of my family and my friends as well.

"Can you explain these papers?" he asked.

"No, I cannot." I felt miserable. (You will say, "Why did you have such dangerous papers in your house?" In our underground efforts to save Jewish people, I worked with many young people who did remarkably courageous work. But they were not always careful, so these papers were found in my house.)

The judge knew even better than I how dangerous those papers were. Suddenly he turned around, opened the door of the stove, and threw all the papers into the stove. At that moment it was as if I understood for the first time the text in Colossians 2:13, 14 PHILLIPS:

> . . . God has now made [you] to share in the very life of Christ! He has forgiven you all your sins: Christ has utterly wiped out the damning evidence of broken laws and commandments which always hung over our heads, and has completely annulled it by nailing it over His own Head on the Cross.

In heaven there are dangerous papers for us all, and whether we believe it or not, we will have to come before the judgment seat of God. If we have refused Jesus Christ in this life, then the Judgment Day will be terrible. But if we have received Jesus as our Saviour and Lord, then we have nothing to fear, because Jesus nailed these terrible papers to the cross when He died for the sins of the whole world—your sins and mine. That is what I understood when I saw those papers destroyed by the flames in that stove.

Years later I met that judge in Germany, and I asked him, "Did you bring your sins to Him? It says in the Bible, 'If you confess your sins, He is faithful and just to forgive you, and He will cleanse you from all unrighteousness.'"

His answer was, "No, I did not do that. I am a very good man, and I have never committed sins."

"I am sorry you think that, because that means you cannot have salvation. Jesus will never ever send away anybody who comes to Him. But there is one kind of person in the Bible that I must tell you about.

"That was the Pharisee who said, 'I am good.' And Jesus could not and would not help him. If the time comes when you know you have sins, that you are a sinner, don't forget what I told you. The Bible tells us that Jesus has accepted our punishment at the cross, and the only thing we have to do is to receive Him as our Saviour and come to Him and confess our sins."

He thought a moment and then suddenly said, "I know a sin that I have done."

I said, "All right—bring it to the Lord at once. Ask His forgiveness and thank Him for His forgiveness." He did.

Later in the evening he said, "I see another sin in my life."

"So, you know that you are a sinner. That is good. Just bring it to the Lord and ask forgiveness," I replied. When for the *fourth* time he remembered a sin which needed to be brought to the Lord, I knew he was ready to receive the Lord Jesus Christ as his Saviour.

I said, "Now you can accept Jesus. You know that you need Him."

He did, and I know that his sins were forgiven and that his name was written in the Book of Life.

5. Ravensbruck

THE NAZIS WERE emptying jails everywhere! Male prisoners were sent in one division, and women prisoners in another. My sister Betsie and I, herded together with thousands of other women, were marched into Ravensbruck. It was called a work camp.

When we first came into this concentration camp, they took all our possessions. It was a real miracle that I was able to keep my Bible.

At great risk, I hid it on my back under my dress, and I prayed, "Lord, will You send Your angels to surround me?" Then I thought, *But angels are spirits, and you can see through spirits. I don't want these people to see me!* so I prayed then, in great fear, "Let Your angels *not* be transparent. Let them cover me."

And God did it! As we passed through the inspection, the woman in front of me was searched, then my sister, directly behind me, was searched—out I walked through unsearched!

Our barracks was built for four hundred women, but they packed fourteen hundred of us inside. Bunks were stacked all the way to the ceiling, and we each had a sleeping space only a few inches wide. When they were all working, we had eight toilets for the entire barracks!

In Ravensbruck it was dangerous to use the Word of God. If you were caught teaching the Bible, you were killed in a cruel way, but the guards never knew that I had a Bible meeting twice each day in Barracks 28. The one jammed room was filthy, crawling with fleas and lice, and the guards never came inside the door. You see how the Lord used both angels and lice to keep my Bible in our possession?

6. *Does He Forget Me?*

SOMETIMES I EXPERIENCED moments of great despair. I remember one night when I was outside the barracks on my way to roll call. The stars were beautiful. I remember saying, "Lord, You guide all those stars. You have not forgotten them but You have forgotten Betsie and me."

Then Betsie said: "No, He has not forgotten us. I know that from the Bible. The Lord Jesus said, 'I am with you always, until the end of the world,' and Corrie, He is here with us. We must believe that. It is not what we are *feeling* that counts, but what we believe!"

> Feelings come and feelings go
> And feelings are deceiving.
> My warrant is the Word of God,
> None else is worth believing.

I slowly learned not to trust in myself or my faith or my feelings, but to trust in Him. Feelings come and go—they are deceitful. In all that hell around us, the promises from the Bible kept us sane.

Ravensbruck certainly was a work camp. It was the enemy's plan to work us—to death! Before the war ended, ninety-six thousand women died there. Even my dear Betsie became an old woman before my eyes and slowly starved to death.

The smoke from the crematorium was like a black haze over the camp. Every day seven hundred women died or were killed. There were far too many of us, and death was the only solution to the problem. I looked death in the eye day after day, and I found the Lord to be my refuge still, my only hiding place.

7. The Lifeline

THE GREATEST MOMENT of your life can be when everything seems finished for you. That is the moment when you lay your weak hand in the strong hand of Jesus. For Jesus can make life and death—present and future—victorious! He can give you eternal life; not only life in heaven, but life right now.

It is as when you have fallen in the sea and you think: *Now I will surely drown. I can swim perhaps an hour, but then I will sink!* A lifeline is the only thing that can help you then.

I found that when you are drowning in the terrific misery of the world, Jesus is everything for you—your only lifeline. When you think you have lost everything, then you can be *found* by Jesus Christ.

He died for you. He lives for you, and He loves you more than any human being can love. I have told people about Him for thirty-three years, in sixty-four countries, and in all that time nobody has ever told me he was sorry he asked Jesus to come into his life. You won't be sorry, either.

8. *A Storm Laid Down*

PUNISHMENTS WERE OFTEN general in Ravensbruck. Once we suddenly heard shouting, beating, and swearing in our room. We lived in a crowded room, packed together. Everything was filthy and broken-down. Two people were sharing a very small bunk, and one had thrown the other out of the cot, so they started to fight.

Betsie said, "Corrie, we need to pray. This is dangerous!"

It was dangerous. If the guards had heard the fighting in our barracks, we would all have been cruelly punished. Betsie remained praying. She prayed and prayed. It was as if a storm died down. We heard less beating, less swearing and shouting. Finally, it was quiet, and Betsie said, "Thank You, Father. *Amen.*"

Now, do you see what happened there? There was a room with many prisoners in great danger, and there was one starving old woman—Betsie. God used Betsie to save the situation. That is what God is willing to do and is going to do with you and me when we let Him show us what to do—when He guides us.

The Bible says that we are representatives of heaven on this earth; that we are ambassadors of Jesus Christ. It is terribly important for the world that there are ambassadors—representatives from heaven—in this world, and you and I can be those ambassadors. Often it will save the situation and bless our surroundings. Because we do it so well? No, not at all. Because the Lord is using us to do what *He* wants done.

9. No Wilderness, the Lord's Garden

"YOU MUST TICKLE the hand of God before He is willing to help you," said a prisoner who was sitting on the bed behind me.

"No, girl, that is not true. When you really know the Lord, you know that He is far more ready to bless us than we are ready to ask for His blessing. He loves us. The Bible says, 'You are God's field'" (*see* 1 Corinthians 3:9 RSV). The great preacher and writer C. H. Spurgeon expresses this very clearly:

Oh, to have one's soul as a field under heavenly cultivation,
No wilderness, but a garden of the Lord, walled around by grace,
Planted by instruction, visited by love,
Weeded by heavenly discipline, guarded by divine power.
One's soul thus favored is prepared to yield fruit unto the glory of God.

A garden does not do much. It does bring forth fruit and flowers. But the one who has the responsibility is the gardener, and it is He, our Gardener, who blesses us, surrounds us with grace, and disciplines us. Whether we are willing or not, He does the job. On our part it is necessary to surrender, and then He makes His garden from the wilderness of our lives. It is wonderful what He is willing and able to do.

10. Is Forgiveness Possible?

DO YOU KNOW how it feels when your heart is full of hatred? We were working in an area where wrecked airplanes were piled together. We had to gather the many pieces and load them onto big trucks. It was terribly heavy work for us.

My sister Betsie was a very frail woman, and she could not lift much, but she did her utmost. Suddenly one of the guards noticed that Betsie was picking up only the little pieces, because the big pieces were too heavy for her.

Betsie said kindly to her, "Don't give me more to do than I am trying to do already, because I am not strong enough to lift these heavy parts."

The woman guard said, "You don't decide what you do. *I* decide." Suddenly the guard started to brutally beat Betsie. I have never been so enraged! The other prisoners held me back so I could not grab the guard.

When she had gone, I ran to Betsie, who had blood all over her face. She said, "No, don't hate, Corrie. You must love and forgive."

"I cannot! I am not able."

If there is hate in your heart, you cannot forgive. I knew this, and I also knew that Jesus had said:

> But if you do not forgive, neither will your
> Father who is in heaven forgive your trespasses.
>
> Mark 11:26

After we were back in our barracks, I climbed out of the window and went for a little walk alone, and I talked with the Lord. I said, "Lord, I cannot forgive that

396

brutal woman. It is more difficult to forgive when people you love suffer than when you suffer yourself."

Then the Lord reminded me of a text. I had my little Bible hidden under my dress. I opened it and read:

> ... God's love has been poured into our hearts through the Holy Spirit which has been given to us.
>
> Romans 5:5 RSV

Suddenly I saw that what *I* was not able to do, the Lord, in me, was able to do. I said, "Oh, Lord, I thank You for Romans 5:5. I thank You, Jesus, that You brought into my heart God's love through the Holy Spirit. Thank You, Father, that Your love in me is stronger than my hatred."

At that moment, when I was able to forgive, my hatred disappeared. What a liberation! Forgiveness is the key which unlocks the door of resentment and the handcuffs of hatred. It is a power that breaks the chains of bitterness and the shackles of selfishness. What a liberation it is when you can forgive. Here again we see that we are not a wilderness, but a garden of the Lord, when we give our lives to Jesus. He does the job.

11. Lizzy

WE HAD TO live in beds stacked one on top of another. There were three beds in each stack, and above the cots where my sister Betsie and I slept, there lived a girl, Lizzy, who was a prostitute. Every day Betsie gathered the people around us, and she or I gave a little Bible talk. Lizzy did not join us, but she always listened, and once I heard Betsie talking with her.

"I do not know if I can come to Jesus," Lizzy said to Betsie.

"Why not? The Lord loves you. You are very precious in God's eyes, and when you come to Jesus, He will not send you away. He has never sent anyone away who came to seek forgiveness and to find the answer for his sin or guilt problem.

"God made this world good, and human beings were without sin, but then we people started to do wrong things, and God had to punish us. But He loved us so much that He had a talk with His Son, Jesus, and God said, 'What must I do? I have to punish people, but I love them.'

"Jesus said, 'Father, I will go to the world, and I will carry their punishment.' And the Father agreed. Jesus came to this world and He lived here for thirty-three years. That must have been a difficult time for Him, even from the beginning, for He was used to being in heaven, and then He came to such a dark world, full of problems.

"The most terrible thing He experienced was when He was crucified. Crucifixion is a very cruel, torturous way to kill people. He could have been saved from that. There were many angels around Him, and had Jesus told them to keep Him from the cross, they would have done so. But He did not ask them, because He was willing to suffer and die. It was His purpose, when He came into this world, to die for your sins and mine.

"Now when we believe in Him we do not have to fear any punishment. We are free! There will be a Judgment Day and every one of us will be present there, but we have nothing to fear when we believe in the Lord Jesus Christ. There is no condemnation for those who belong to Him. And Jesus Himself is our Judge and Advocate. You can read that in the Bible."

> Who then will condemn us? Will Christ? No! For he is the one who died for us and came back to life again for us and is sitting at the place of highest honor next to God, pleading for us there in heaven.
>
> Romans 8:34 LB

"But I don't do what I should do!" said Lizzy.

"I don't believe that you must do anything," replied Betsie. "Believe in the Lord Jesus Christ and you will be saved. What had to be done has all been done by Jesus Christ. Your part is to accept that at the cross He died for your sins."

Lizzy folded her hands and said, "Thank You, Jesus, that You did it all at the cross. I surely am not able to do much to change myself, but I thank You that You will do it in me."

12. *The Red Ticket*

"FALL IN FOR the street commando!"

Making streets was heavy work. Betsie and I showed our red tickets, which we had just received from the *Aufseherin*. They were the sign that we were unable to do hard labor. We climbed on our cot and hummed a little song. We picked up the stockings, which we had to knit for the German soldiers.

"You seem to be happy," said the woman behind us.

"We certainly are. We were called to enroll in the street commando, and look what we have." We showed the red tickets.

The woman smiled cynically. "Do you know what your red tickets mean? At the first cleaning up of prisoners, all the red-ticket owners disappear into the gas chamber."

We stopped humming our song. I looked through the window at the smoke which was going up from the crematorium and I thought, "When will my time come to be killed?"

Betsie saw what I was looking at. "Are you afraid, Corrie?"

> Afraid? Of what?
> To feel the Spirit's glad release?
> To pass from pain to perfect peace?
> The strife and strain of life to cease?
> Afraid of that?

I knew that my sins were forgiven, that my name was in the Book of Life, and that I had received Jesus as my Saviour. He had made me a child of God. Jesus gives eternal life. That means the life that belongs to eternity, to heaven. And I had that.

I knew that if they killed me I would go to the Father's house with many mansions. I looked death in the eyes. I saw the valley of the shadow of death. But I was not afraid, for I knew that I would not go alone through that valley. Jesus was going to take my hand and help me through.

How good to know that you belong to Jesus! Do you know it? If not, lay your hand in His strong hand. Those who come to Him, He will in no wise cast out.

13. Ask More—He Will Give

IT WAS CROWDED and filthy and miserable in that room built for two hundred where seven hundred of us lived together. (There were two such rooms.) Although it was a terrible place, yet there were several things for which I was thankful.

One reason for gratitude was that twice a day Betsie or I could gather the prisoners around us for a little Bible message. First I did it only on Sunday, but when I saw that so many people died or were killed from one Sunday to the next, I decided to risk it every day.

Several of my fellow prisoners really came to the Lord and accepted the Lord Jesus as their Saviour. They decided to come every day for the Bible message. Then I gave the talk in the evenings for those prisoners who were assigned to work elsewhere during the day and couldn't attend the daytime meetings in the area where I had to knit stockings.

When I finished teaching, there would be many questions, and I realized that many did not know the simplest truths of the Bible.

I often talked about the fact that when we pray, the Lord hears our prayers. He loves us and loves to have us talk to Him. He always listens when we pray. I told them about the miracles that actually happened to me when God answered my prayers. Sometimes He does not answer our prayers in the way we want or expect Him to answer. We will understand why one day when we are in heaven.

I told them the story of a blind man who came to Jesus during the time that Jesus was in the world with us. Jesus healed him, and then He asked the man, "Can you see?"

The man said, "I see men like trees walking." Jesus touched his eyes again, and the man said "Now I can see clearly." (Read this in Mark 8:23–25.)

You know, sometimes when you first come to Jesus, it is as if you do not see so very much and you do not understand what is happening. You are not able to enjoy your new life. Then the best thing you can do is to tell the Lord that you do not understand it, that you do not see clearly, and that you really see man as the blind man did—like walking trees.

If Jesus had not asked this blind man whether he could see, I am sure that nevertheless the man would have told Him, and said, "Lord, I am glad that I can see a little bit, but I do not see enough." Then Jesus would have healed him.

So it is with you and me. If we do not see as much as we need or want to see, then we must tell it to the Lord. He will heal our eyes so that we see that the love of God is far greater than anything else.

There is an ocean of God's love which we discover when we receive Jesus Christ as our Saviour. He shows it to us through His Holy Spirit. God sees you and me. He knows everything about us, and He loves us so much that He wants to help us and do what we ask.

14. *Is a* No *Answer an Answer?*

WHEN GOD GIVES us the *no* answer, it can be a difficult testing of our faith, but when we study the Bible, we understand more and more that God never makes a mistake. Once we are in heaven, we will understand it all.

> My life is like a weaving between my God and me,
> I do not choose the colors, He worketh steadily.
> Ofttimes He weaveth sorrow and I in foolish pride,
> Forget He sees the upper, and I the underside.

I once prayed for Betsie, my sister. She was so *very* ill. Even in the filthy bunk in our barrack or at our work, it was such a joy and comfort for us just to be together night and day. Now she was in that primitive hospital, and our friends and I, who loved her so, prayed that the Lord would heal her. But when I returned to the hospital after roll call and looked through the window, I saw that she had died. That was one of the darkest moments of my life.

I could not understand why God had not answered my prayer. A few days later, I was called out of lineup and I heard that I was to be set free. I had to go through the office on my way out, and I learned that they did not know my sister had died. I asked them, "What about my sister?" I wanted to find out what would have happened to her if she had still been alive.

They said, "Your sister must remain here for the duration of the war."

"May I remain with my sister?"

"Not for a minute! Now get out!"

I have praised and thanked my Lord for that unanswered prayer. Just imagine how it would have been if she had been healed, and would have had to stay in the hell of Ravensbruck without me. I would have returned to my homeland tormented night and day by the consciousness of her suffering. I saw God's side of the embroidery.

15. Freedom

IT WAS 3:30 A.M. I woke up, and my first thought was, *Roll call*. I looked around me. Clean windows, a chair, a table, a picture on the wall. I was no longer in prison. I was free!

I could sleep for several more hours but I did not. I got up and started to write down what I had experienced in the three prisons. Those writings became my first book, *A Prisoner and Yet* . . . . It became a best seller in Holland, because people were interested in reading about what had happened to the victims of the concentration camps.

For many years of my life I had been the leader of Girl Guide clubs (European Girl Scouts). As soon as I recovered my strength a bit, I got together with all the girls I could locate to tell them what I had experienced, and to find out what had happened to them.

After much talk together, they asked, "What are you going to do?" We were sitting in a clubhouse, cross-legged on the floor. My club girls were interested in all I had learned in prison—that difficult class in life's school.

"Girls, I'm so thankful that all my tomorrows are in God's hands. I want to tell you what happened one night." And this was what I told them:

It was midnight in Ravensbruck, and Betsie tried to wake me up. Sleep was such an important thing. You forgot that you were in prison.

"Why are you waking me up? Leave me, please, in the world of dreams, where there are no guards, no barbed wire, and no lice."

Betsie put her coat over our heads so that we could talk without disturbing our fellow prisoners. "I have to talk with you, Corrie. God has told me several things which we must do after the war, and I am afraid that I may forget some of His instructions.

"We have learned so much here, and now we must go all over the world to tell people what we now know—that Jesus' light is stronger than the deepest darkness. Only prisoners can know how desperate this life is. We can tell from experience that no pit is too deep, because God's everlasting arms always sustain us.

"We must rent a concentration camp after the war, where we can help displaced Germans to get a roof over their heads. I have heard that ninety-five percent of the houses in Germany are bombed out. No one will want these concentration camps after the war, so we must rent one and help the German people find a new life in a destroyed Germany. God has shown me in a vision, a house in Holland in which we will receive the Dutch prisoners who survive the concentration camps. We will help them to find their way through life again."

I asked her, "Must we stay in that camp which we will open for the people here in Germany, or will we be able to stay in the house for the ex-prisoners, at home in Holland?"

"Neither," Betsie said. "You must travel all over the world and tell everybody who will listen what we have learned here—that Jesus is a reality and that He is stronger than all the powers of darkness. Tell them. Tell everyone who will listen! He is our greatest Friend, our hiding place."

A week later Betsie died. A week after that I was set free, and only one week later, the Germans put to death all the women of my age in Ravensbruck.

I looked at my Girl Guides who had listened to my story. "Girls," I said, "I know that you are sincerely interested in what I am going to do. My answer is that I will obey all the instructions that God gave to me through Betsie."

I obeyed. You can read about many of my adventures over the years in my book *Tramp for the Lord*.

Since I have often visited in prisons, now I want to talk with you about some of these experiences.

16. Kimio

WHILE VISITING A prison in Africa, I heard about a young man who was sentenced to die. I asked to see him, but the prison officials would allow me to enter his cell only if three soldiers went in with me.

The cell had a very high ceiling and one small window at the top for light. It was bare, except for a shelf very low to the ground. Sitting on that shelf was a handsome black African who had one more week to live. I was praying very hard! I wanted to be able to talk with him as if we were alone, but the soldiers made me uncomfortable. I always reacted that way when I was around men with guns.

As we talked, I learned that the young man's name was Kimio and that he had a wife and children. Kimio knew about the cross, and that Jesus had died there for the sins of the whole world, including his sins.

I asked him if he knew who was responsible for his arrest and imprisonment. He was a political prisoner, and there came into his eyes the darkness of hatred.

"I can name every person responsible for my being here," he said.

"Can you forgive them?"

"No, I can't."

"I understand that. Once a man betrayed me and my whole family. Because of his betrayal, four of my family died in prison, and I suffered in three of the most horrible prisons in the whole world.

"And, Kimio, I could forgive that man. Not through my own strength—never—but through the Lord. The Holy Spirit can fill your heart with God's love, and He can give you the power to forgive. Kimio, I felt so free after I had forgiven that man. You have to die very soon."

"Yes, and I have a wife and children that I will never see again because of those men."

"I understand, Kimio, but you have to come before God. You have to face a righteous God very soon, and you know about Jesus at the cross.

"Jesus said, 'If you do not forgive those who wrong you, my heavenly Father will not forgive you.' So Kimio, you *have* to forgive.

"You are unable, but the Holy Spirit in you is able. Just pray this prayer with me. 'Thank You, Jesus, that You have brought into my heart God's love through the Holy Spirit. Thank You, Father, that Your love in me is stronger than my hatred.'"

I don't remember what else Kimio and I talked about after that, but I no longer felt the presence of those three armed soldiers. There was the presence of angels in that cell. I learned later that Kimio wrote to his wife: "Love the people who have brought me here. Forgive them. You can't, and I can't, but Jesus in us is able."

Kimio was trapped by the misery of this world, but he learned how to be free.

17. Joy? Is That Possible?

THE WORST PRISON I have ever seen was in another area of Africa. The building was too small for all the prisoners. Only half of them could go inside the building at night; the rest had to stay outside.

During the day they were all kept crammed together in the dirty compound in front of the prison. There had been a tropical rainstorm, and the ground was one large pool of mud. I saw that some men had branches on which they were sitting. Some had small pieces of paper, and others had little shelves. They had all struggled to find something to sit on. Everything was dark and black, but the darkest was the expression of their faces.

I often pray at the same time I am speaking, saying one thing to the Lord and another to the people who are listening to my talk. On this day I said, "Lord, give me a message for these men that will help them in this very difficult place where they live."

The answer from the Lord was, "What is the fruit of the Spirit?" I knew it:

The fruit of the Spirit is love, joy, peace, long-suffering, gentleness, goodness, faith.
See Galatians 5:22 RSV

Then the Lord said, "Speak about joy."

"Lord, how can I speak about joy to these people who live in this terrible place?"

The answer was, "My Holy Spirit is here in this place, and the fruit of the Spirit is available wherever you are."

Then I remembered that when I had been in prison I had found joy even in the midst of the most desperate surroundings. When we are powerless to do a thing, it is a great joy that we can come and step inside the ability of Jesus.

"Lord," I said, "You are able to give joy." Then I heard myself giving a very happy message. The faces of the men lit up when I told them that the joy of the Lord can be our strength, even when we are in very difficult circumstances.

The only thing necessary to begin moving into the joy of the Lord is to tell Jesus Christ that you would like to be His follower. "Receive Jesus Christ as your Saviour and Lord, and He will give you the joy," I said.

Many did. I could see it in their faces. But I also saw faces of people who were not ready or willing. They remained just as dark and unhappy as before.

I said to them, "Fellows, I can understand that you think such joy is not possible for you when you are in this prison, but I can tell you that I was in a prison far worse than yours, where only twenty percent of us came out alive. The rest all starved or were killed in a cruel way. But the Lord Jesus was with us. His Holy Spirit was in our hearts, and there was often a great joy.

"There is joy for you, too, but you must be at peace with God and man—that *is* possible! When you confess your sins to the Lord, He is faithful and just, and He forgives you. He removes your sins, He cleanses your heart, and He fills you with the Holy Spirit. The fruit of the Spirit is joy."

Finally I asked, "Who is willing to receive Jesus Christ? Raise your hand."

All the prisoners did, and even the guards who were there did, too! Now, when *everyone* raises his hand to accept Jesus Christ, then I do not always trust it, but I looked into their faces and saw that this time it was real for all of them.

When I went to the car to leave for the next place, all the men and the guards accompanied me to the street. They were standing around the car, shouting something which I could not understand. I asked the missionary who was with me, "What are these men saying?"

She smiled and said, "They are shouting, 'Come again, old woman. Come again and tell us more about Jesus.'"

I was so glad! You know, I had to leave, but the Lord stayed with these men, and the Holy Spirit filled their hearts. It is true that when you lay your weak hand in the strong hand of Jesus, He keeps you from falling and never leaves you alone.

18. *Three Decent Sinners*

THE APOSTLE PAUL was in prison. It must have been terrible for him. His hands were chained to the hands of two guards night and day. He never knew from one day to the next what the enemy was intending to do with him.

We do know some of the things that Paul did while a prisoner. He wrote letters, which you should read. Some of these "epistles" you should read are called Ephesians, Philippians, Colossians, and the two letters to Timothy.

Another thing we know about Paul is that he used his time in prison to bring the Gospel to the people around him. These men to whom he was chained could not run away when he preached. And what was the result? People were converted! At the very end of his letter to the Philippian Church, Paul writes:

> Greetings to every true Christian, from me and all the brothers here with me. All the Christians here would like to send their best wishes, particularly those who belong to the Emperor's household.
>
> Philippians 4:21, 22 PHILLIPS

I once spoke about this in a prison in New Zealand, because I believe that every prisoner can help his fellow prisoners to know and receive Jesus Christ. Prisoners can be reached by their fellow prisoners better than by people from outside, because they understand one another.

I know some of you are thinking what some of the prisoners there in New Zealand thought: "Perhaps God can use other people, but not me. I am not good enough."

Do you know what happened there? One of the prisoners suddenly stood up and said, "Fellows, this morning I read in the Bible about three murderers. One's name was Paul, one was Moses, and the other was David. We know them as heroes of God, but all three were murderers. What God can do with a totally surrendered murderer! There is hope for you and me, fellows!"

Yes, there is hope for you who read this. I believe I have never heard such a good sermon as that one from a man who was a prisoner. What God can do with you when you surrender all is *tremendous*! There is one condition:

Stay always within the boundaries where God's love can reach and bless you.

Jude 21 LB

I have a glove. This glove cannot do anything, but when my hand is in the glove, the glove can do many things. It can drive a car, it can write.

Yes, I know, it is not the glove that does it, it is the hand inside the glove. You and I are—and Moses, David, and Paul were—just gloves. It was the Holy Spirit in them, and in you and me, who does the work.

What we have to do is to make room for the Holy Spirit, and then miracles can happen in our lives. Perhaps you think, "Oh, that is possible for a *mature* Christian, for somebody who knows the Bible well, and has had training." Perhaps you even think you must first go to a Bible school. All these things are good, but the Lord can also use you when you have none of these opportunities.

19. Hi, Brother!

LET ME TELL you about a prisoner I met some years ago in Bermuda. I had spoken to a big group in the prison, and a black guard asked me, "Will you go with me to some cells where there are people who really need your advice?" I went into that part of the prison where the men were kept who were not even allowed to attend meetings.

I saw two men in a cell. One of them had a round, red tag on his back.

"Has that man tried to run away?" I asked the guard.

"Yes," he replied. "How do you know that?"

"Because of the red tag on the back of his uniform. I have been in three prisons, and we were also forced to wear red tags on our uniforms, if we tried to run away."

"This man is a murderer, and he was sentenced to whippings. He was so afraid of the whippings that he tried to run away. Poor fellow, he has had a double portion."

When I saw him sitting there on the floor, the expression on his face reminded me of a wounded animal, and my heart went out to him. I prayed, "Lord, help me to find a way to his heart." I went to him with my Bible in my hand and asked him, "Say, fellow, have you had a whipping?"

"Yes."

"Was it bad?"

"Yes."

"Did they take you to the hospital afterwards?"

"No, it was not that serious."

414

He stood up and came to the barred door, probably thinking to himself, "That woman is sure asking me strange questions!"

Then I asked, "Did they treat your wounds?"

"Yes, they did. They rubbed them."

"Is there hatred in your heart?"

"Hatred? My whole heart and my whole life are full of hatred."

"I can understand that."

"Ha! You?"

Then I told him how I had felt when they whipped my sister, because she was too frail and weak to shovel sand. How hatred had come into my heart!

But I said, "Fellow, a miracle happened then. Jesus brought into my heart God's love through the Holy Spirit, and I had no hatred. I could forgive.

"And when you receive Jesus Christ as your Saviour, He will fill your heart—not with hatred but with love. How do you do it? You just come to Him and say, 'Lord Jesus, will You be my Saviour?' The Lord is willing to be that. Then you must ask Him to come into your heart. And He *will* come, because it is written in the Bible, and the Bible is true. Jesus said:

Behold, I stand at the door, and knock: if any man hear my voice, and open the door, I will come in to him . . . .

Revelation 3:20

"Fellow, when the Lord Jesus comes into your heart, there is love in your heart. The worst may happen in your life, but the best remains."

I prayed with that man, and then he prayed. I believe I had never heard such a strange prayer. The man had never prayed before, but one of the things he did was thank Jesus that He had died for him on the cross.

Have you ever thanked Jesus for that?

I shook hands with the man. Then he said, "Have you another five minutes?"

"Sure. Why?"

"On the other side of the corridor, in the third cell, is a man in great darkness. Please, tell him also of Jesus."

I went to the man in the third cell. I told him about Jesus, and how I prayed for him! When you speak about Jesus, you can always pray at the same time. You can have the vertical and the horizontal connection at the same moment.

The man in the third cell said his *yes* to Jesus. I mean a real *yes*—a decision.

I had to leave the prison then, but I first passed the cell of the murderer. "Say, fellow, that was good that you sent me to the third cell. He also has accepted Jesus Christ as his Saviour and Lord."

The man looked around me and shouted across the corridor, "Hi, brother!" A babe in Christ, a few minutes old, and he already had a burden for souls. How old are you?

When someone becomes a Christian he becomes a brand new person inside. He is not the same any more. A new life has begun! All these new things are from God who brought us back to himself through what Christ Jesus did. And God has given us the privilege of urging everyone to come into his favor and be reconciled to him. For God was in Christ, restoring the world to himself, no longer counting men's sins against them but blotting them out. This is the wonderful message he has given us to tell others. We are Christ's ambassadors. God is using us to speak to you: we beg you, as though Christ himself were here pleading with you, receive the love he offers you—be reconciled to God.

2 Corinthians 5:17–20 LB

20. Corrie's Message

IN NEW ZEALAND I visited a small prison, where there were probably no more than fourteen men. We had a good time together. The men were sitting with their backs against a wall, and I was sitting in front of them, speaking about the great joy of knowing that you are a child of God.

I told them that when you ask Jesus to come into your heart and you confess your sins, then He does a great miracle in your heart, which He Himself calls "being born into the family of God." At that time you may say to God, "Father, my Father." And He says to you, "My child."

Four of these men made a decision. Each wanted to give his heart to Jesus, to be cleansed and born into the Kingdom of God—to be born a child of God.

Before I left, I shook hands with all the men. One was a very old man. He cried and held my hand and kissed it. I was a little bit amused about that, and finally said, "Now, friend, let me go, and the Lord bless you." Then he let go of my hand.

This man was sentenced to a long imprisonment for the crime of manslaughter. The woman with whom he lived had snored one night when he was drunk. He strangled her because of her noise. When he realized that the woman was dead, he was so scared he ran straight to the police and told them, "I have murdered my wife."

"Why are you crying so?" I asked him.

He replied, "Because I am so happy. I have always had such terrible feelings of guilt because I killed the woman I lived with. Now I have brought it to the Lord Jesus, and I know I am forgiven. I am a child of God! Jesus is in my heart."

A year later I went back to that prison, and I talked with some of the men there. I asked where the old man was, and they told me, "He died some time ago."

One of the men took me aside and said, "I must tell you something. Whenever that man heard me going through the corridor, he called me into his cell. He would say, 'Let us talk about Corrie's message.'"

How happy I was that the Lord had used me to help that man!

21. *Conversations in Prisons*

I KNOW THERE are almost insurmountable problems when you are in prison. I would like to write about some of the problems we discussed when I talked with prisoners in America.

Ann

"What is the most difficult thing that you have to go through?" I asked Ann.

I sat with her in her cell in solitary confinement. She showed me a photograph of her husband and children. "Because of my crime, I have given them such a hard life. They lack a wife and mother and they have to bear the shame—all because of the bad things I have done."

She told me that she had accepted Jesus as her Saviour ten years ago, but had solidly backslid. She knew much about the Bible, so it was easy to talk with her.

"There is an answer to your problem, Ann. It is Jesus. He has told us that we may pray for one another. You can pray for your children and your husband. You can tell the Lord everything. He understands you better than any human being.

"I read in the Book of Revelation that not one of our prayers is lost. They are kept in heaven. That is how important they are in our heavenly Father's eyes.

"You feel guilty that your family has to suffer because of you. You carry that guilt. I have a book here. It must lie somewhere: on my hand, on the table, or on the floor. It is the same with your guilt. It must lie somewhere. It is lying on you. You are carrying it.

419

"Now the Bible teaches us a mystery. When Jesus died on the cross, God laid on Him the guilt of the whole world. Jesus was willing to bear that terrible death, to carry our sins, our guilt. You may bring your sins, your guilt to Jesus, and He will forgive you and make you clean. Then He will fill you with the Holy Spirit. The fruit of the Spirit is peace and joy and love. Then you will be able to think of your husband and children with peace."

Ann said, "I believe all you tell me, but I cannot accept it now. I have been away from the Lord for so long. Ten years ago I could have accepted it, but now it is too late."

"Ann, do you remember the story of the lost sheep? A shepherd had one hundred sheep. One evening when he came home, he saw that one sheep was lost. What did he do?

"He left the ninety-nine at home and went to look for that one lost sheep. He found it, took it on his shoulder, and brought it home.

"You are a lost sheep. Jesus will bring you home. The shepherd rejoiced and organized a feast to celebrate the finding of the lost sheep. Jesus rejoices when He finds you. Only tell Him everything. He loves you. Confess your sins to Him and ask Him to come into your heart. He will rejoice, and you will rejoice."

Ann did it. And I know Jesus rejoiced!

Frank

"Trust and study the Bible, Frank. It is the Word of God. You have asked Jesus to come into your life, and He came. Now all the promises of the Bible are yours."

Frank had seen one of Billy Graham's meetings on television and he had joined the many who came to Jesus that evening.

"Do you know what my problem is when I read the Bible?" Frank said. "It all happened so very long ago. I have seen Christians who were really happy, but after a while they backslid. Their Christianity did not last long."

"Frank, what can help you and give you solid ground to stand on is your faith in Jesus. He is the same yesterday, today, and tomorrow. He never changes. He is the same now as He was in Israel two thousand years ago. He is a solid rock to stand upon.

> On Christ the solid rock, I stand.
> All other ground is sinking sand.

"Talk much with Him. He is here *now*. He loves and understands you."

Roger

He was a young man in a big prison. I had spoken in the chapel, and while he cleaned the table where we had had some refreshments, I had an opportunity to talk with him.

Without looking up, he said, "I am afraid."

"Who are you afraid of? The guards?"

"No, the men around me. They say that they will kill me if I do not do what they ask me to do. They tell me to do dirty things, which I cannot refuse."

"Roger, I was in a prison where the devil was strong, and I was afraid, like you are. I saw then that I was weak, and the devil was stronger, much stronger than I. But then I saw Jesus, who is much stronger than the devil. Jesus and I together could overcome the devil. When I realized that, miracles happened.

"Paul, in the Bible, had a problem in his life. The Bible does not tell us exactly what it was, but he calls it a 'thorn in the flesh, messenger of Satan, to harass me.'

"You can read about it in Second Corinthians 12:7–10. Paul asked God to take it away, but God did not remove that thing. He answered Paul, 'My grace is sufficient for you, for my power is made perfect in weakness.' God does not always remove difficult things from our lives, but His grace in us is sufficient to overcome the difficulties."

> Have you got any rivers you think are uncrossable?
> Got any mountains you can't tunnel through?
> God specializes in things called impossible.
> He can do what no other can do.

22. Mike

"I AM GOING on parole next week."

"Boy, that is good! Are you glad?"

"No, this was my fourth time in prison, and soon it will be my fifth. I know myself."

"No, Mike, Jesus has found you, you have found Jesus, and you and He together will overcome the temptations. Read the story of Gideon in Judges six.

"Gideon was neither strong nor courageous. He hid himself in a barn, in the bottom of a winepress. But how did God see him? The angel who came to him said, 'The Lord is with you, you mighty man of valor.' Because the Lord was with him, Gideon changed from a weakling into a strong overcomer. The Lord said to him, 'Go in this your strength.'

"Mike, the devil is stronger—much stronger than you and me—but Jesus is much stronger than the devil, and with Jesus, we are stronger than the devil.

"It is important that you do what Jude said, 'Stay always within the boundaries where God's love can reach and bless you' (Jude 21 LB).

"If, when you leave prison, you go straight to a bar and get yourself drunk and renew your relationship with the friends who helped you to go to prison through their advice and assistance in your crimes, you can be sure that you will find yourself in this building for the fifth time. You stand on victory ground with Jesus, but you must be willing to go the whole way with Him. You are free to choose."

"That is exactly my problem. I am willing now to be a good guy, but what happens when I am free?"

"Mike, you are not the only one who has this problem, but the Lord knows that. The Bible supplies the answer when it says, 'Be filled with the Spirit' in Ephesians 5:18. A Spirit-filled Christian is a difficult target for the enemy, for he has the fruit of the spirit and the gifts of the Holy Spirit, which are like a good armor and weapons in his hand. A compromise with the enemy is deadly dangerous, just as if a soldier on the front line helps the enemy to attack him and his fellow soldiers.

"If, again and again, you lay your weak hand in the strong hand of Jesus, you will be able to remain within the boundaries where God's love can reach and bless you."

"How do you do that? It all sounds so nice when you say it, but how do I lay my hand in Jesus' hand?"

"Get used to telling Jesus everything. He understands you and loves you. You might say to Him, 'Jesus, I need money badly. I can make a lot of money quickly if I go to that bar and plan a little job with one of my friends. I can also get something to drink there, and I really want a drink. Jesus. Take my hand, fill me with Your Holy Spirit. Keep me from falling!'

"If you say that, Jesus will help you. He is not only willing, but also able to help you. Ask Him to help you find people who love Him and who are willing to show you how to understand the Bible. Fellowship is so important. Read the Bible much. When you find a text that helps you more than others, write it down, and put it in your pocket, and learn it by heart.

"Mike, the most important thing is *trust Jesus*. He will help your faith to grow. In Hebrews twelve He is called the author and finisher of your faith. I like helping you very much, and pray that the Lord will give me wisdom on advising you. Jesus likes to help you even more, and He *really* is able to help."

23. Joe

"I HEARD YOUR talk today about how to become a child of God by Jesus Christ. It made me anxious to do it. But, lady, you do not know what kind of a guy I am. I have murdered people, and don't ask me how! Let's be honest—I am a lousy guy. No, I am not made of the wood from which you can cut and shape a Christian."

"Joe, there are two ways that we know our sins. The devil accuses us night and day. I don't know if you know the devil. I know him. He speaks very clearly, and he says, 'What you have done is what you are, and what you will always be. There is no hope for you.'

"The devil is a liar! The Bible tells us something different. When you bring your sins to Jesus, when you confess your sins, He is faithful and just to forgive you, and He will cleanse you with His blood. You don't understand that? It does not matter. He does it, and it works!

"The Bible also promises that He will put your sins as far away from you as the east is from the west. It is as though He has cast them into the depths of the sea—forgiven and forgotten."

I met Joe again a month later. He looked quite different. The first thing he said was, "I have done it! I was totally miserable! They put me in the hole, which I had feared they would do. I had been in there before for a very long time.

"On my first day in it again, I figured I had nothing to lose and I said, 'God, if You do exist, take this miserable life of mine in Your hand.' At that very moment something happened. It was as if I was no longer alone. I can't tell you exactly how it was, but I felt happier than ever before. Was it the Lord who came to me? I could suddenly talk to Him. I remembered everything you had said and I asked myself, 'Is what she said true?'

"I slept better that night than I had for weeks, and when I woke up, I felt that happy feeling again. I must say that the weeks I spent in that hole were happy. I knew I was not alone, and to my amazement, I was taken out of the hole after only two weeks.

"Now, Miss ten Boom, I believe it all! How good it is to read the Bible. You had told me that Jesus knocks at the door of your heart, and so I said, 'Come in.' I have told Him more than anyone else all that I have done wrong and through that, I believe there was a clearing up of the dirty mess."

"Joe, you can read in John three what took place in your life. In that chapter Jesus tells about what happens when you accept Him. You were born again. Now God is your Father, Joe, and what a Friend you have in Jesus! I'm so glad that the Bible is not fantasy. It is not imagination, not feelings, not philosophy—it is reality! The greatest reality is that Jesus is here on this earth right now, through His Holy Spirit. You are here. I am here. Jesus is here, too."

24. So Long!

WHEN YOU BELIEVE the Lord Jesus Christ and you ask Him to come into your heart and into your life, He gives you *His* freedom and a new dimension of living that circumstances cannot destroy.

We can all get to heaven
Without health—
Without wealth—
Without fame—
Without learning—
Without culture—
Without beauty—
Without friends—
Without ten thousands of things.
But we can never get to heaven without Christ.

God promises us forgiveness for what we have done, but we need His deliverance from what we *are*. He conquered death at the cross and He went to heaven. He pleads for us there.

At the same time He is in heaven, He is also with us! I do not understand it at all, but I know it works. I have experienced His presence in the deepest hell that man can create. I have really tested the promises of the Bible, and believe me, you can count on them.

I know that Jesus Christ can live in us—in you and me—through His Holy Spirit. We can talk with Him. We can tell Him everything. You can talk with Him out loud or in your heart—when you are alone, as I was alone in solitary confinement, or in a place crowded with people. The joy is that He hears each word!

In Ravensbruck, after a terrible winter, it was decided that all prisoners my age and older should be killed. One week before this was to happen, I was set free. Later, I learned that it was done only because of a clerical error. In recording our numbers, my number had mistakenly been transferred from the death column to freedom!

A blunder of man, yes. But I knew it was God's way of telling me that I must share—for the rest of my life—what I had learned about Him.

That is why I wanted to write this book for you. I am eighty-five years old now, and I know that the moment is coming when I will have to die. But I am not afraid of death. I belong to Jesus. All of my tomorrows are in His hands.

You know, eternal life does not start when you go to heaven. It starts the moment you reach out to Jesus. That is where it *all* begins. He never turned His back on anyone, and He is waiting for *you*! God bless you.

Appendix of Helpful Scriptures

THE BIBLE IS a source of strength and wisdom. Read the Word of God often. I have written down some texts which have helped me. I pray that the Lord will bless these texts and this book for *you.*

Feeling Alone

Be strong and of good courage, do not fear or be in dread of them: for it is the Lord your God who goes with you; he will not fail you or forsake you.

Deuteronomy 31:6 RSV

"Come to me, all who labor and are heavy laden, and I will give you rest. Take my yoke upon you, and learn from me; for I am gentle and lowly in heart, and you will find rest for your souls. For my yoke is easy, and my burden is light."

Matthew 11:28–30 RSV

". . . I give them eternal life, and they shall never perish, and no one shall snatch them out of my hand. My Father, who has given them to me, is greater than all, and no one is able to snatch them out of the Father's hand."

John 10:28, 29 RSV

"If a man loves me, he will keep my word, and my Father will love him, and we will come to him and make our home with him."

John 14:23 RSV

[Jesus said,] ". . . I will never fail you nor forsake you." Hence we can confidently say,

> "The Lord is my helper,
> I will not be afraid;
> what can man do to me?"
> Hebrews 13:5, 6 RSV

Temptation

No temptation has overtaken you that is not common to man. God is faithful, and he will not let you be tempted beyond your strength, but with the temptation will also provide the way of escape, that you may be able to endure it.

1 Corinthians 10:13 RSV

Do you want more and more of God's kindness and peace? Then learn to know him better and better. For as you know him better, he will give you, through his great power, everything you need for living a truly good life: he even shares his own glory and his own goodness with us! And by that same mighty power he has given us all the other rich and wonderful blessings he promised; for instance, the promise to save us from the lust and rottenness all around us, and to give us his own character. . . . Then you must learn to know God better and discover what he wants you to do. Next, learn to put aside your own desires so that you will become patient and godly, gladly letting God have his way with you. This will make possible the next step, which is for you to enjoy other people and to like them, and finally you will grow to love them deeply. The more you go on in this way, the more you will grow strong spiritually and become fruitful and useful to our Lord Jesus Christ.

2 Peter 1:2–8 LB

Stay always within the boundaries where God's love can reach and bless you. Wait patiently for the eternal life that our Lord Jesus Christ in his mercy is going to give you. Try to help those who argue against you. Be merciful to those who doubt. Save some by snatching them as from the very flames of hell itself. And as for others, help them to find the Lord by being kind to them, but be careful that you yourselves aren't pulled along into their sins. Hate every trace of their sin while being merciful to them as sinners.

Jude 21–23 LB

How can a young man stay pure? By reading your Word and following its rules. . . . I have thought much about your words, and stored them in my heart so that they would hold me back from sin.

Psalms 119:9, 11 LB

Worry

"Therefore I tell you, do not be anxious about your life, what you shall eat or what you shall drink, nor about your body, what you shall put on. Is not life more than food, and the body more than clothing? Look at the birds of the air; they neither sow nor reap nor gather into barns, and yet your heavenly Father feeds them. Are you not of more value than they? And which of you by being anxious can add one cubit to his span of life? And why are you anxious about clothing? Consider the lilies of the field, how they grow; they neither toil nor spin; yet I tell you, even Solomon in all his glory was not arrayed like one of these. But if God so clothes the grass of the field, which today is alive and tomorrow is thrown into the oven, will he not much more clothe you, O men of little faith? Therefore do not be anxious, saying, 'What shall we eat?' or 'What shall we drink?' or 'What shall we wear?' For the Gentiles seek all these things; and your heavenly Father knows that you need them all. But seek first his kingdom and his righteousness, and all these things shall be yours as well."

Matthew 6:25–33 RSV

Part Three

DON'T WRESTLE,
JUST NESTLE

Foreword

"BABY, JUST CRY. Don't look at the people or mind what they are thinking about you. Just cry." I felt an arm around me, hid my face on her shoulder, and cried. Then I heard her singing softly:

> His eye is on the sparrow,
> And I know He watches me.

Yes, my comforter was Ethel Waters. I had heard her sing those words before, but they had never touched me so. For this time, she was singing that song for me, and I needed her song.

This happened the first time I saw the movie, *The Hiding Place*. In my mind I found myself reliving the suffering of my family. I saw Father and Betsie, both lost in prison. I had to put up with the horrible cruelties again. That was why I cried.

But then my eyes were turned in the right direction by Ethel Waters' song. There *is* One who watches me, and the secret of abundant life is literally "Don't wrestle, just nestle." What a security!

1. *Prescription for Anxiety*

Why should I feel discouraged, Why should the shadows come,
Why should my heart be lonely And long for Heav'n and home,
When Jesus is my portion? My constant Friend is He:
His eye is on the sparrow. And I know He watches me.

"Let not your heart be troubled," His tender word I hear,
And resting on His goodness, I lose my doubts and fear;
Tho' by the path He leadeth But one step I may see:
His eye is on the sparrow, and I know He watches me.

Whenever I am tempted, Whenever clouds arise,
When songs give place to sighing, When hope within me dies,
I draw the closer to Him, From care He sets me free;
His eye is on the sparrow, and I know He cares for me.

MRS. C. D. MARTIN

This century has been called the Age of Anxiety. How fitting that description is! Everywhere I go, I find people tormented by inner tensions, nervous strain, worries, and fears. We are a generation of worriers, always taking pills to cure our anxieties and relax our nerves.

There is a great deal of difference between worry and concern, and we must realize this. Concern makes us do something to ease the situation. It moves us to

take constructive action. But worry burdens our minds and bodies without helping us to find a solution to the problem. Worry is like racing the engine of an
automobile without letting in the clutch. You burn energy, but you don't go
anywhere.

No doctor has a cure for worry. Oh, he can give you an aspirin for your headache or something for your nervous stomach. He may even give you one pill for
your tensions and another pill for your insomnia. But these are not cures. They
just cover up the real problem.

There is a permanent cure for worry. The prescription is not mine—it was given
by Jesus almost two thousand years ago, in His Sermon on the Mount. He devoted
a great deal of this talk to the problem of anxiety. Therefore, here is His prescription for anxiety.

Remember the Power of God

A few weeks before the Sermon on the Mount, Jesus walked along the shore of
the Sea of Galilee and called twelve men to lay down their fishing nets and follow
Him. They would be His disciples. The men saw the presence of God in Jesus. They
wanted to follow Him, but still, they had questions—many questions.

"If we don't fish for a living, how will we support our families?"

"How can we be fishers of men? We're afraid to talk to other people."

"How can we carry the Gospel to the world? Just the thought of doing that fills
us with fear!"

Jesus went up on a mountain to escape the huge crowd that kept following Him.
When He was in a private place, He sat down, gathering His disciples around Him.
He began to teach them about the Kingdom of God. The disciples, who had followed Jesus for a little while now, knew He had no money of His own. Yet He
never worried. He seemed content.

"What is the secret of happiness?" they asked.

Jesus replied:

. . . don't worry about living—wondering what you are going to eat or drink, or what
you are going to wear. Surely life is more important than food, and the body more
important than the clothes you wear. Look at the birds in the sky. They never sow
nor reap nor store away in barns, and yet your Heavenly Father feeds them. Aren't
you much more valuable to him than they are? Can any of you, however much he
worries, make himself even a few inches taller? And why do you worry about clothes?
Consider how the wild flowers grow. They neither work nor weave, but I tell you
that even Solomon in all his glory was not arrayed like one of these! Now if God so
clothes the flowers of the field, which are alive today and burnt in the stove tomorrow, is he not much more likely to clothe you, you "little-faiths?" So don't worry
and don't keep saying, "What shall we eat, what shall we drink or what shall we
wear?" That is what pagans are always looking for; your Heavenly Father knows
that you need them all. Set your heart first on his kingdom and his goodness, and all

these things will come to you as a matter of course. Don't worry at all then about tomorrow. Tomorrow can worry about itself! One day's trouble is enough for one day.

Matthew 6:25–34 PHILLIPS

Actually, Jesus was chiding them a bit, saying "You already have life and a body, and they are far more important than what to eat and wear. Does it not follow that the God who is capable of making a human body is capable of putting clothes on it and providing food to keep it going?"

The next time you find yourself depressed or worried about some big problem, remember the power of God. Remember His great miracle of bringing you into being, and you will know He is more than able to care for you.

I remember reading a story about Bishop Quayle, who must have had a keen sense of humor. He told of a time when he sat up late in his study, worrying over many things. Finally the Lord came to him and said, "Quayle, you go to bed. *I'll* sit up the rest of the night."

A friend of mine told me, "When I worry, I go to the mirror and say to myself, 'This tremendous thing that worries me is beyond solution. It is even too hard for God to handle.' And then I smile."

Remember the Foolishness of Worry

Jesus had a way of asking embarrassing questions. "Which of you by taking thought can add one inch to your height?" Can you worry yourself taller? Or shorter? You might worry yourself dead, but never will you worry yourself happier. That comes by a different method.

Alcoholics Anonymous has sound advice to offer their people—advice all of us could use—in the prayer, "O God, give us serenity to accept what cannot be changed, courage to change what should be changed, and wisdom to distinguish the one from the other."

I like that, for there are two things we should not worry about: the things we can change (we need to get busy and do something about these) and the things we cannot change (no amount of worry will help these). Instead, we should let God give us the courage and strength to master the unavoidable, for with God, nothing is impossible.

"Don't be fools; be wise: make the most of every opportunity you have for doing good. Don't act thoughtlessly, but try to find out and do whatever the Lord wants you to do" (Ephesians 5:16, 17).

Jesus says that God is concerned about us personally. "Look at the birds of the air," Jesus said to His disciples. "God feeds them in spite of the fact they cannot drive a tractor, plough a field, or work a harvesting machine. They can't even build barns to store the grain. Yet God takes care of each one of them." Then He turned to His disciples, and I imagine He had a slight smile on His face. "Are you not of more value than they?"

Next Jesus pointed to the wild flowers that were poking their heads around the rocks in the hard soil of Israel. "Look at them," He said. "They can't run a spindle or loom, they don't even have the ability to sit down at a sewing machine and make their own clothes. But see how beautifully God has dressed them. Why? Because God cares for even the grass of the field." Then He said, "If God so clothes the grass of the field, will he not much more clothe you?" (*See* Matthew 6:25–30.)

Count Your Blessings

I was in Japan, very tired, with a stomach that was upset from the unusual food. How I longed for a good European meal, a table where I would not have to sit cross-legged on the floor, and a soft bed instead of the hard mats the Japanese sleep on. I was filled with self-pity. I wanted to be back in Holland!

That night in church, while I was busy feeling sorry for myself, I saw a man in a wheelchair. After the service my interpreter took me down to meet the man, a bent little fellow with yellow skin and slender hands. His face wore the happiest expression I could imagine.

"What are those little packets on your lap?" I asked the man, pointing to several packages wrapped in brown paper and tied with string.

He broke into a wide grin and tenderly unwrapped one of the packages. It was a sheath of pages covered with Braille, the raised script of the blind. "This is the Gospel of John, written in Braille. I have just finished it," he said.

Then he continued. "This is the fifteenth time I have written the Gospel of John in Braille. I have also written other of the Gospels, as well as many shorter portions of the Bible."

"How did you come to do this?"

"Do you know about the Bible women here in Japan?" he asked. "Bible women go from village to village, bringing copies of the Bible, books, and literature to those who are hungry for God. Our Bible woman is very ill with tuberculosis, but she travels every week to sixteen villages, even though she will soon die. When I heard about it, I asked the Lord what I could do to help her.

"Although my legs are paralyzed, and I cannot get out of the wheelchair, in many ways I am healthier than she. God showed me that though her hands are shaky and my legs paralyzed, I could be the hands, and she the legs. I punch out the pages of Braille, and she takes the Bible around to the villages and gives them to the blind people, who miss so much because they cannot see."

I left the church that night filled not with self-pity, but with shame. Here was I, with two good legs for traveling all over the world, two good lungs, and two good eyes, complaining because I didn't like the food!

These precious people had discovered a sure cure for self-pity—service to others.

Perhaps it is like the slogan I once saw on a church sign in America. "If you are unhappy with your lot in life, build a service station on it." The best antidote I know for self-pity is to help someone else who is worse off than you.

"I complained that I had no shoes, then I saw a man who had no legs, and I stopped complaining."

Walk With God

Does the Lord Jesus say, "Come along now. Take it easy. Don't worry," leaving us to realize that there have never been so many reasons to worry as there are now?

No! The Lord gives an answer.

"Seek first his kingdom and his righteousness" (*see* Matthew 6:33 KJV). It is your relationship with your heavenly Father that is important. That is what determines whether you will be victorious or defeated, however difficult the circumstances are.

The day after He fed the 5,000, Jesus chastised the crowd that followed Him, accusing them of following Him because He had fed them. "But you shouldn't be so concerned about perishable things like food. No, spend your energy seeking the eternal life that I, the Messiah, can give you. For God the Father has sent me for this very purpose" (John 6:27).

Still the crowd was more concerned with food. They asked Him to give them free bread every day, as Moses did in the desert. Jesus told them, "Moses didn't give it to them. My Father did. And now he offers you true Bread from heaven. The true Bread is a Person—the one sent by God from heaven, and he gives life to the world" (John 6:32, 33).

The crowd, still not understanding what Jesus was telling them, asked that they might have every day the bread He was describing.

"I am the Bread of Life. No one coming to me will ever be hungry again. Those believing in me will never thirst," Jesus told them (John 6:35). Although He said this over and over again to the crowd, they still failed to understand or accept. Many of His disciples left Him at this point. Jesus then turned and asked the twelve if they, too, were leaving Him.

Simon Peter answered for all of them: "Master, to whom shall we go? You alone have the words that give eternal life, and we believe them and know you are the holy Son of God" (John 6:68, 69). Peter and the others who stayed with Jesus knew what was important and what was not. They knew the way to victory.

With your hand in the Father's hand, you stand on victory ground. Give room for the Holy Spirit. He gives you the right outlook on troubling events. I know that from the time that I saw my sister Betsie starving in a prison camp. We were surrounded by people who had behind them a training in cruelties, but we had moments when we were conscious that we were walking with the Lord.

Often we had to go too early to roll call, which started at 3:30 A.M. Betsie and I would walk through the camp, and there were three of us present. Betsie said something, I said something, and the Lord said something. I can't tell you how, but both Betsie and I understood clearly what He said. These walks were a bit of heaven in the midst of hell. Everything around us was black and dark, but in us there was a light that belonged to eternity.

Jesus said:

> All who listen to my instructions and follow them are wise, like a man who builds his house on solid rock. Though the rain comes in torrents, and the floods rise and the storm winds beat against his house, it won't collapse, for it is built on rock.
>
> Matthew 7:24, 25

From My Notebook

TODAY IS YESTERDAY'S tomorrow you worried about, and all is well.

If God sends us on stony paths, He provides strong shoes.

Faith is blind—except upward. It is blind to impossibilities, and deaf to doubt. It listens only to God and sees only His power and acts accordingly.

S. D. GORDON

Jesus is always victorious. We only have to get into the right relationship with Him and we shall see His power being demonstrated in our hearts and lives and service. And His victorious life will fill us and overflow through us to others. That is revival in its essence.

ROY HESSION

Worry is the interest you pay on trouble before it comes.

God will not tolerate anything in our life that takes the supreme place which is His by right.
Jesus Christ can transform our . . .

fear into faith
anxiety into adoration
worry into worship.

... Our fears for today, our worries about tomorrow, or where we are—high above the sky, or in the deepest ocean—nothing will ever be able to separate us from the love of God demonstrated by our Lord Jesus Christ when he died for us.

Romans 8:38, 39

2. No Time for Anxiety

WE WERE IN Africa. Prisoners were dancing. The pounding rhythm created an atmosphere of demonical darkness. The expressions of the dancers' faces made me afraid. It was as though they were dancing themselves into a trance, possessed by dark powers. Their shouting influenced the other dancers, causing the gloomy darkness in their eyes to increase every minute.

These people were criminals. They knew what it was to be inspired by hell itself. Next to me were three black Christian brothers, who had accompanied me to this place hidden far away in the jungle—the place where I was to speak. We waited for the prison director to join us.

At last he came. He was a friendly man, but I could see that he knew how to make people obey. "I am so glad you came to speak to my men." He clapped his hands and shouted, "Stop dancing! Sit down and listen to what Miss ten Boom has to tell you."

I saw the anger flash in their eyes. It was hard for these men to part from the spirits who had kept them in their power. About four hundred men settled down in front of me, and about two hundred were standing behind me. I saw not one friendly face among the six hundred: I looked at my three black Christian brothers and felt uneasy that not one white man had accompanied me. I underestimated those men badly, as I later clearly discovered.

I softly prayed, "Lord, I know that those who are with me are more and stronger than those who are against me. Let Your never-failing love fill my heart and mouth, and also the man who will interpret for me."

I spoke rather a long time to those prisoners, and I saw the expressions on their faces change as they heard me say, "Jesus loved you when He died on the cross for the sins of the whole world." I never saw such a dramatic change in people. They came from darkness into light; from the darkness of hell into the light of heaven.

As we waited at the gate while a guard found the key, a prisoner came running toward me. He took my hand and said something. My interpreter translated, "You came to us because God's love is in you. Thank you. Thank Him!"

We squeezed into the tiny car and headed down the primitive path through the jungle, going toward Kampala. The moment we got into the car, my three brothers began to sing and praise the Lord. I was sitting in the front seat, squeezed against the driver. The other two men were crowded into the tiny backseat. But even our cramped positions did not keep them from singing and praising God as we roared through the dense jungle.

What a strange sight we must have been, bouncing down the jungle road, weaving from side to side to miss the holes and puddles, singing and praising the Lord in loud voices!

I saw a man ahead, standing on the side of the narrow road. He had the tire and wheel from a car leaning against his leg. The driver slowed the car to a stop and shouted across me, "What is the matter, my friend?"

"Please bring me to Kampala," he pleaded. "My tire is flat, and my wheel is broken."

What a pity we have no room, I thought.

But my happy black brothers saw no such problem. "Of course," they shouted together. "Join us. We like to help our brothers in the name of Jesus."

The man came around to the other side of the car, to get into the front seat between the driver and me. While he was walking around, one of the men in the backseat leaned forward and whispered. "Pray with us, Tante Corrie, that we bring him to the Lord before we reach Kampala."

How they squeezed him in, I'll never know. But soon we were on our way again, the man jammed between the driver and me holding that big, rusty car wheel and the dirty black tire on his lap. The men in the car began singing and praising the Lord again, keeping time with the bumps in the road.

The driver began to talk to the man in his own language, and the other men enthusiastically entered in. I could not understand what they were saying, but I knew they were talking to him about the Lord Jesus. I prayed, keeping my eyes on the road.

Suddenly the passenger looked at the driver and said something. One of the men in the backseat interpreted for me. The passenger was asking if he knew the driver. Hadn't they met before?

"Sure," the driver answered. "Last year you and I were in the same prison, where we have just been with Miss ten Boom. You know, boy, at that time I served the devil. Now I serve Jesus Christ. He uses me to save lives of other sinners, and He will use you from now on, also."

The man with the big wheel on his lap listened intently. Before long, he accepted Jesus as his Saviour. I wanted to join in the men's happy praises, but I was too concerned about the road and the wild way in which the driver was swerving from side to side. *Surely we'll all be killed,* I worried.

Then, ahead, we saw a woman with two children waiting alongside the road. "Let us give her a lift and also bring her to Jesus," one of the men shouted.

Did he really mean it? There was absolutely no room!

The car stopped, and for a minute I entertained the hope that they were just going to witness to her where she was and drive on. But no, they motioned her to join us in the car!

As she got in the backseat with her two children, I saw a third child come out from under her coat. Somehow they all got in, sitting on top of one another. One of the small children had to crawl over my shoulder and sit on my lap. I could not feel my legs. Never, never had I been in such an overcrowded automobile—and on such a terrible road.

We started up again, the car rolling from right to left, left to right, bouncing off rocks and logs alongside the road, weaving over shaky jungle bridges. But the black men were tremendously happy, believing the Lord had put the woman there so they could pick her up and witness to her. This time, all four of the men—including the one with the big wheel on his lap—eagerly joined in the conversation, telling the woman about the Lord Jesus Christ.

Suddenly the four men began to sing. *"Tuku tenderesa Jesu,"* an African song of praise. The woman had accepted Jesus as her Saviour and Lord.

We arrived in Kampala and swerved through the traffic, the men still singing and banging their hands against the side of the automobile in time with the music. Our fellow travelers left us—the man with the big wheel and the woman with her three children—but not until my friends had obtained their names so they could follow up their work. Then they took me to the place I was staying.

After they had gone, I sat for a long time, rubbing life back into my legs and trying to get some insight into the events of the afternoon. While I, the cautious European, had been so anxious and worried about the fierce prison, the horrible road, the old car, and the discomforts and dangers of the trip, my black brothers had no time for anxiety. They were too busy praising God and sharing the good news with those whom God sent into their path. They did not see the people along the road as problems, but as opportunities.

Perhaps, I thought, as I lay back on the bed to rest my aching body, if I would spend less time worrying whether the car would run, the road was paved, or the bridges would hold—and lose myself in praise and service as these African brothers did—I would not only live longer, but more abundantly. While I was anxious about reaching my destination, they were excited about meeting people along the way. Reaching the destination seemed almost incidental to praising God and serving Him as they went.

Maybe the way in which we travel and the attitude we have while making our way through life is more important than reaching our destination. Or could it be that in God's sight, the way actually is the destination?

Jesus said ". . . I am the Way—yes, and the Truth and the Life . . ." (John 14:6).

From My Notebook

IT IS BETTER to burn out than to smolder out without having warmed one heart for the Lord Jesus.

Happiness is not dependent on happenings, but on the relationship that persists in the happening.

When we act on the Word of God, and not on our feelings, we experience that God means His promises. The fact is that God watches over His Word to perform it.

> Slow me down, Lord,
> I am going too fast,
> I can't see my brother,
> When he is going past.
>
> I miss a lot of good things
> Day by day,
> I can't see a blessing
> When it comes my way

When the heart has learned to trust Him as He should be trusted, utterly without reservations, then the Lord throws wide the doors of the treasure house of grace. He bids us go in with boldness and receive our share of the inheritance of the saints.

Be sure you remain covered with a canopy of praise. It is like a tent over and around you. Satan has no entrance as long as you pin down the sides by praising, and thank God for His wonderful promises.

In the life of the true believer there are no accidents.

My little children, I am telling you this so that you will stay away from sin. But if you sin, there is someone to plead for you before the Father. His name is Jesus Christ . . . .

1 John 2:1

3. *Worry*

BEFORE THE BATTLE, the general always sends his spies into the enemy camp. They take photographs of secret defenses, they learn the enemy's battle positions, their ammunition supply points, even the personal weaknesses of the opposing leaders. But unless the general passes this information on to his own troops, they cannot win the battle.

That is why I want to share with you some of the things I have learned about the enemy and about the Victor, Jesus. I want you to know that God expects us to be conquerors over the powers of darkness—not only for the sake of our personal victory and for the liberation of others who are in bondage to Satan, but for His glory. He wants the world to know that He is triumphant and victorious, and the only way it will ever know is by our demonstration of God's power and authority.

Once a man saved up his money for years and bought the house of his dreams. It was in the countryside, with mountains and streams all around it. He could not wait to begin living in his new house, but because of his business, he could not move in for several months. So he allowed the man who was living there to stay as a caretaker until he was ready to move in himself.

But when the new owner came to move into his dream house, the other man said, "No, I am staying here. You find somewhere else to live."

"But you promised you would move out when I was ready," the owner said.

The man gave a laugh and replied, "This is my home. You cannot come in." Then he slammed the door in the owner's face and locked it.

The owner marched straight to the police station with his papers of ownership.

The next time he knocked on the door of his house, there were two large policemen standing next to him. When the man in the house saw the policemen, he meekly packed his belongings and left the house to its owner.

What the true owner of the house could not do in his own strength, he was able to do when he appeared with authority on his side. It is the same with us. Satan may laugh at us and continue to afflict us with disease, fear, anxiety, and defeat. But when we come to him in the name of Jesus, he knows we have all the authority of the Kingdom of God behind us, and he must flee.

Worry Is Sin

I had to learn that worry is sin before I could get rid of the worry. First I tried to "fear not" as an act of obedience. It was as successful as trying to kill a lion with a toy gun. Then I began to learn the secrets. First you must ask forgiveness for your sin of worry. Then you need to accept the cleansing of the blood of Jesus. Finally, you need to let God fill you with the Holy Spirit. When you are filled with the Holy Spirit, the spirit of fear will flee, forced out by power and love and a sound mind.

In the latter part of 1946, a group of Christian ladies in Ottawa asked me to give my testimony at an evening meeting.

I did not even know where I would sleep that night, but I went in obedience. I felt it was a training in trusting God. How good that the coach was the Lord Himself!

It was the first time that I had been in Canada. I remember that the spirit of worry was very busy with me. Sometimes my traveling went smoothly. God gave me friends who organized my meetings, and I went where He told me to go. But now I was not quite sure of the Lord's guidance. At such moments I felt far from Holland. A big ocean was between my hometown and me.

So often that tramp for the Lord, the prisoner Paul, had helped me. I opened my Bible and read what he wrote from his prison in Rome: "Be careful for nothing; but in every thing by prayer and supplication with thanksgiving let your requests be made known unto God. And the peace of God, which passeth all understanding, shall keep your hearts and minds through Christ Jesus" (Philippians 4:6, 7 KJV).

My, but Paul knew about worry! Still, he found the answer: "I can do all things through Christ which strengtheneth me" (Philippians 4:13 KJV).

I did not even know where I would sleep that night, but God had used Paul to encourage me, and I trusted Him.

That evening, I told my problem to the dear people who heard my talk, and sure enough, a lady came to me and said, "You are very welcome in my home. I have a small guest room you may use." I had been worried about finding a place to sleep, but the Lord had the answer all worked out for me!

What a joy to be surrounded by kind people. Before I fell asleep, I thought of the time shortly before, when enemies were all around me, and how they hated me because of what I had done for the Jews. Soon I was sound asleep.

Suddenly the light in my room came on. I opened my eyes, and a uniformed officer was standing in front of me. My only thought was, *This is the Gestapo. They have found me.* I said to the man, "I am not a Jew." Then I remembered where I was and told him that I was a guest of the lady of the house. Without a word, the man put the light out and left.

What had happened? He was the owner of the house and had come home late. He did not want his wife to see him at that hour, especially since he had been drinking too much that night. He decided to go to the guest room, but his plan misfired because of my presence there. When he told his wife, she was very disturbed. What a shock it must have been for her guest! She put on her robe and ran to my room. There she found me, fast asleep!

Some months later, I met my host again. It was a bitterly cold evening. I had spoken that afternoon in a town some distance from Ottawa, where I was to speak in the evening. Friends had brought me to a house halfway between the two towns, and my former host was waiting there. He told me that he was going to take me to Ottawa, where the meeting was to start at 8 P.M.

The highway was so icy that we skidded from right to left. I looked at my friend and saw that he had given himself courage for the drive by taking some drinks, and it was not a little amount that he had enjoyed. I thought about the coming evening. How could I sit for hours in that car, worrying about the slippery road and his driving, and then still have the power to speak? I couldn't. I was worried— I thought I had reason to be—but I knew that my worry was a sin. I would have to ask forgiveness for my sin and trust the Lord to deliver us safely to Ottawa.

I prayed for strength and then said to the driver, "Jim, I am going to speak tonight, and it is impossible for me to worry for several hours beforehand, while you skid from right to left and left to right. So I hope you don't mind, but I am going to sleep."

Jim smiled and said, "You go ahead. I will drive and not sleep." And he did. The Lord gave me a very good rest.

The young girl who was my secretary at that time was sitting behind me, and she told me later that I snored all the way. That was a comfort to her, because she knew that I was not worried, but she said it was still the most terrible car ride of her life. We arrived safely, on time for the evening meeting, and I was refreshed and ready for my talk.

God's Armor

The battle always has to be fought before the victory is won, though many people think they must have the victory *before* the battle. The conflict with worry and fear is almost always there—each person must overcome or be overcome. But we must fight each battle of our lives in the strength of Jesus' victory. He said, "As the Father has sent me, even so I am sending you" (John 20:21). We are to be like Jesus—One of whom Satan is afraid!

When we worry, we are carrying tomorrow's load with today's strength; carrying two days in one. We are moving into tomorrow ahead of time. There is just one day in the calendar of action—today. The Holy Spirit does not give a clear blueprint of our whole lives, but only of the moments, one by one.

We all have the same enemies—we are all preyed upon by frustration and worry. In India, Australia, Japan, Germany—we need the same Holy Spirit. We need to remember that we are children of God, living within His constant care. God knows and is interested both in the hardest problems we face and the tiniest details that concern us. He knows how to put everything in place, like a jigsaw puzzle, to make a beautiful picture.

But Satan has a very good secret service. The moment you step out from under God's umbrella of grace, you are discovered and attacked by Satan. Recognition of Satan's attack is half the fight. An attacking enemy who is not recognized already has half his battle won. Never knowing where, how, and when Satan will attack us, we should never be unprotected or unprepared. We need to be clothed with the whole armor of God.

> Last of all I want to remind you that your strength must come from the Lord's mighty power within you. Put on all of God's armor so that you will be able to stand safe against all strategies and tricks of Satan. . . . So use every piece of God's armor to resist the enemy whenever he attacks, and when it is all over, you will still be standing up.
>
> Ephesians 6:10, 11, 13 LB

What a relief to know that we do not need to provide the armor! God makes the armor—we just put it on. But the armor has no protection for the back, for God does not expect any deserters. Neither is the armor a museum piece—it is given for us on the battlefield. Jesus is Victor!

Every temptation to worry or fear is an opportunity for victory. It is a signal to fly the flag of our Victor. It is the chance to make the tempter know anew that he is defeated.

> Thine, O Lord, is the greatness, and the power, and the glory, and the victory, and the majesty: for all that is in the heaven and in the earth is thine; thine is the kingdom, O Lord, and thou art exalted as head above all. Both riches and honour come of thee, and thou reignest over all; and in thine hand is power and might; and in thine hand it is to make great, and to give strength unto all.
>
> 1 Chronicles 29:11, 12 KJV

From My Notebook

WORRY IS A cycle of inefficient thoughts, whirling around a center of fear.
Worry is often carrying a load that one should not carry at all.
Worry is distress of mind, not concern. Some people ought to have *more* concern.

It is sinking under the sense of responsibility, yielding to the fear that there may be failure, instead of gripping the lines and whip and determining to ride down the chance of its coming.

S. D. GORDON

God gives us His power to bear all the sorrow of His making. But He does not give us the power to bear the sorrows of our own making, which the anticipation of sorrow most assuredly is.

IAN MACLAREN

The purpose of being guilty is to bring us to Jesus. Once we are there, then its purpose is finished. If we continue to make ourselves guilty—to blame ourselves—then that is sin in itself.

4. May a Christian Worry?

Why, therefore should we do ourselves this wrong,
Or others—that we are not always strong,
That we are ever overborne with care,
That we should ever weak and heartless be,
Anxious or troubled, when with us is prayer,
And joy and strength and courage are with Thee.

AUTHOR UNKNOWN

We imagine that a little anxiety and worry are indications of how wise we are. We think we see the dangers of life clearly. In reality, however, our fears are only an indication of how wicked we really are.

As Charles G. Trumbull says:

Worry is sin; a black, murderous, God-defying, Christ-rejecting sin; worry about anything, at any time whatever. We will never know victory over worry and anxiety until we begin to treat it as sin. For such it is. It is a deep-seated distrust of the Father, who assures us again and again that even the falling sparrow is in His tender care.

The words *fear not* occur many times in the Bible. The Word of God has no suggestions; only commandments. So if we fear and worry, we are being disobedient, and disobedience is always a sin.

The only way blunders and destruction can occur in our lives is when we forget to trust God. When we take things into our own unskilled hands, we get everything knotted and tangled.

Worry is utterly useless. It never serves a good purpose. It brings no good results. One cannot think or see clearly when worrying. Let pagans worry, if they will, but we must not, for we have a living Saviour, our Lord Jesus Christ, and His conquering power. His victory can be our victory. Life at best is brief, and there is so much to be accomplished. If we must burn ourselves out, let us burn out for God.

In this age of increasing pace, it is so easy to follow the crowd and let materialism become our god. But if we do, only too often we find that worry and tension become our masters. The effects of tension are seen in all spheres of life. Tension leads to inefficiency and frayed nerves with our fellow workers and students. In politics, it leads to strain in international relations and fears of war. In the home, tension leads to irritability with our husband or wife, destroying the very thing God meant to be perfect.

For with people who are not content, worry has a fair chance. Paul writes:

"I have learned to be content, whatever the circumstances may be. I know now how to live when things are difficult and I know how to live when things are prosperous. In general and in particular I have learned the secret of facing either plenty or poverty. I am ready for anything through the strength of the One who lives within me" (Philippians 4:11–13 PHILLIPS).

Lonely Contentment

I have never been so poor as the time that I was in solitary confinement. How difficult it was to learn to be content. But Paul wrote once, while in prison, that we are God's workmanship. I experienced the same. The lessons were difficult, but the Teacher was so powerful. The Lord was my all-sufficiency. I wrote home: "The Lord Jesus is everything to me. He never leaves me alone. I concentrate on the Saviour. With Him there is certainty, with the other things, only uncertainty and delayed hope, which hurts the heart. Once I asked to be freed, but the Lord said, 'My grace is sufficient for you.'"

That brought my thoughts to Paul. *He* had to learn a lesson. Three times he asked the Lord to take away the thorn in the flesh (*see* 2 Corinthians 12:8). Then he got this answer: God's grace was sufficient for him. That was true for Paul and it was true for me. In a way I knew that there was a danger that the joy I felt and my security in Him would lose some of their power when I was free; when the securities of the world would once again be a comfortable foundation to rest upon.

When the Lord gives you the ability, through His grace, to accept the situation, that contentment can help you to get rid of your worry, whatever happens. But could I ever accept being a prisoner alone in a cell? I surely could not, but Paul told about all grace, always, in all things (*see* Corinthians 9:8).

Once when I was in the cell, I heard the bolt on the outside of my door being undone. A guard opened the door and commanded, "Follow me!" I was being called out to be questioned. It was the first time I had left the cell during that lonely imprisonment. Yes, lonely—night and day I was alone. First we had to go through long corridors with cell doors on both sides, then through a door which opened onto the outside. I breathed deeply. I was in a courtyard. The walk was almost too short to the small barracks where people were questioned. I looked up to the sky, then around me, and then down and saw blades of grass and some tiny white flowers. The little flower "Shepherd's purse" was growing between the bricks used to pave the courtyard.

When the guard who accompanied me looked the other way, I quickly bent down and picked some of those little flowers and hid them inside my dress. When back in my cell, I took a broken medicine bottle, arranged my bouquet, and put it behind my cup so that the guards could not see it when they looked through the peephole in my door. That tiny bouquet was my garden, and I enjoyed it as the only nice thing in my cell.

I was ready to accept my little bouquet of six blades of grass and three little flowers as my garden because of Him who was in me, and I could say then with Paul, ". . . I look upon everything as loss compared with the overwhelming gain of knowing Christ Jesus my Lord. For his sake I did in fact suffer the loss of everything, but I considered it mere garbage compared with being able to win Christ" (Philippians 3:8 PHILLIPS).

Demon Influence

When we are worrying, we are not trusting. Yet we who have burdens and responsibilities are inclined to worry. Again, it is so important that we recognize the enemy. Worry and depression are sister and brother. I want to tell you about something that I experienced—a time when the influence of depression was practically nationwide.

After I was released from the German concentration camp, I returned to Holland until the war was over. Then God told me to go back to Germany, to carry the good news of Christ's victory over fear and guilt. When I arrived in Germany, however, I found the people in great confusion. Many German people had beloved relatives missing. Were they still in Russian concentration camps? Had they died in battle or in the horrible bombings? This uncertainty drove many people to desperation.

Many of these people were turning to the fortune-tellers to find their answers. While the evil spirits, working through the fortune-tellers, often gave just enough accurate information to keep the people coming back, something else also happened. Many of those who visited the fortune-tellers later developed horrible fears, depression, and anxiety. Their hearts, it seemed, were always in the gloom of darkness. They often had the urge to commit suicide. I immediately recognized this as sure evidence of demon influence.

Jesus said, "I am the Light of the world. So if you follow me, you won't be stumbling through the darkness, for living light will flood your path" (John 8:12). Even if a child of God has visited a fortune-teller and come under demon influence, he does not have to remain in darkness. He can be set free.

Realizing this, I began speaking against the sins of the occult. It was the occult that was putting people in bondage, causing them to break down mentally and spiritually. I often read Deuteronomy 18:10–13 to point out how these sins are an abomination in the sight of God. Instead of depending on God's power, the people were rushing to the enemy for help. And as we know, the enemy is a liar, whose very purpose is to deceive people and lead them away from the truth.

I showed the German Christians how Jesus Christ has provided an answer to this serious problem. Satan is not the Victor, Jesus is. And even if the people had invited the demons in, Christ could overcome that. They did not have to live with their depression or fear any more. They had to be set free. I was able to say to them:

> . . . [God] gave you a share in the very life of Christ, for he forgave all your sins, and blotted out the charges proved against you, the list of his commandments which you had not obeyed. He took this list of sins and destroyed it by nailing it to Christ's cross. In this way God took away Satan's power to accuse you of sin, and God openly displayed to the whole world Christ's triumph at the cross where your sins were all taken away.
>
> Colossians 2:13–15

In the Old Testament there is an interesting story of the lost axhead. A son of the prophets had been chopping wood, and his axhead had fallen into the Jordan River. Since it was a borrowed ax, he was worried and afraid. He ran to Elisha for help. Elisha sent him back to the place where he had made his mistake, so the miracle of restoration could happen. The axhead floated to the surface, the young man grabbed it and replaced it on the handle (see 2 Kings 6:1–6).

Just so, you need to go back to the place where you opened the door of your life to the influence of the spirit of worry. Where did the fear enter? What was it that caused you to start worrying? Remember, the spirit of fear does not come from God. Instead, God gives us power and love and a sound mind (see 2 Timothy 1:7). Therefore, you need to ask the Lord Jesus to close the door that you opened.

How is this done? First you need to recognize that you have sinned. Most fear, anxiety, and worry come through the sin of not trusting God.

Second, confession is necessary. Face yourself. Tell God. And then, if possible, confess to someone close to you. When all of this is done, you may then claim the precious promises for cleansing. You will instantly be freed from the bondage of Satan.

Worry is a demon—fear of demons comes from demons themselves. As children of God, we have nothing to fear. He who is with us is much stronger than he who is against us. "And he asked them, 'Why were you so fearful? Don't you even yet have confidence in me?'" (Mark 4:40.)

"The seed among the thorns represents those who listen and believe God's words but whose faith afterwards is choked out by worry and riches and the responsibilities and pleasures of life . . ." (Luke 8:14).

May we worry? We have a whole Bible as our guide, Jesus Christ as our living Saviour who loves us, and heaven as our future!

From My Notebook

Worry is an old man with bended head,
Carrying a load of feathers which he thinks are lead.

Worry means two enemies—the thing you worry about and the worry!

Why don't we try something lighter than worry? Worrying people are like tight-rope walkers going over a rope from the past to the future. They balance between hope and fear. In one hand they carry a sack with the undigested past, in the other hand a sack with the anticipated future.

The heart lays aside its fears amid the accumulated blessings of our heavenly Father. Worries pass away like cloudlets in the warmth of a summer's morning.

Yesterday He helped me,
Today He did the same.
How long will this continue?
Forever, praise His name.

For God hath not given us the spirit of
fear; but of power, and of love, and of a
sound mind.

2 Timothy 1:7 KJV

5. Fear

FEAR IS THE atmosphere of worry. Nothing weakens us as much as fear. On the other hand, nothing weakens the tempter as much as a quiet, bold, steady fearlessness. Satan cannot operate in the atmosphere of trust.

Oh, but fear and worry can talk so wisely! You may often think they are right, but fear is often a stupid blunder. Once I worked for a month in Los Angeles during a flu epidemic. One morning my secretary woke up with a bad headache, and I feared that she had the flu.

"Girl, please stay in bed. I have to go to a college to speak at nine o'clock, but I will go alone," I told her. Once I was outside, I felt a headache myself. My eyes felt so strange. I knew that headaches and eye problems were sometimes symptoms of the flu, and I worried all the way to the college. I had so much work to do—I didn't have time for the flu!

Once at the college, I opened my Bible to begin my talk and found that I could not read even one letter! Fear whispered, "You have the flu in your eyes." I was not sure that was possible, but I listened to my fear. What would I do if I could not read? I need to prepare for my talks and to study the Bible, if I am to speak about the Lord. Could I go back to my former trade of watchmaking? Impossible! I would need my eyes more for that than for any other trade.

I know that I did not give a happy talk that morning, for when worry and fear are on the throne, you are not an open channel for streams of living water. It is impossible to listen to the Lord's voice while listening to your own fear. Fear is so loud, so insistent, so time-consuming!

459

Near the end of my talk, my secretary came quietly into the room and sat down in the back row of the auditorium. When I finished my talk and the students left, I went to her. "Why didn't you stay in bed, when you had such a headache?"

"Oh, I am not ill. My headache is gone," she answered.

"All right, but it could have been the beginning of the flu. You should have stayed home and started answering the letters that I gave you."

"That's why I came. I couldn't work, because you have *my* glasses!" Both our glasses had exactly the same frame, but far different lenses! We both laughed at our mistake. My flu had gone. So had my headache. Once we traded glasses, I could read perfectly, and I was ashamed to have listened to my silly, blundering fear all morning.

Trust the Vine

Anxiety, fear, and worry are the result of our unwillingness to trust God. To worry is the same as saying to God, "I don't believe You." Do you fear for your finances? Are you afraid you won't be able to feed or shelter your loved ones? Do you lie awake and fear your fears? Listen to what God says!

"Give your burdens to the Lord. He will carry them. He will not permit the godly to slip or fall" (Psalms 55:22).

"And it is he [God] who will supply all your needs from his riches in glory, because of what Christ Jesus has done for us" (Philippians 4:19).

"Stay away from the love of money, be satisfied with what you have. For God has said, 'I will never, never fail you nor forsake you.' That is why we can say without any doubt or fear, 'The Lord is my Helper and I am not afraid of anything that mere man can do to me'" (Hebrews 13:5, 6).

Remember when Jesus told the parable of the vine and the branches in John 15? He said the secret to abundant living is in staying attached to the vine. An unattached branch has something to fear. Not only can it not produce fruit, but it will be burned in the fire. But an attached branch has no fears. All it has to do is nestle close to the vine, and the vine does all the work, sending its sap through the branch and producing luscious grapes. It is not the branch that produces the grapes, it is the vine.

"But if you stay in me and obey my commands, you may ask any request you like, and it will be granted! My true disciples produce bountiful harvests. This brings great glory to my Father" (John 15:7, 8).

Fear does not take away the grief of yesterday, nor does it solve the problems of tomorrow. All it does is rob you of the power of today. Rather than wind up on a psychiatrist's couch or an undertaker's slab, do what God tells you. Seek first His Kingdom and His righteousness. He will add everything else you need.

Fear or Victory?

There are many people who don't realize that fear is the enemy. When the fight is on and blows are being exchanged, fear is a sure element of defeat. Fear sucks the spirit out of one's fighting, takes the nerve out of one's courage, robs vim and zest from one's action. But this is always a false fear, because it tells us the enemy is stronger than we are. That is not true! We know that Jesus is Victor, and a fear that tells us otherwise is false.

When you become a child of God, you are a target for the enemy, and he will do his utmost to tell you that you are crazy. Sometimes you think that you are not a Christian when you have trouble, but I should very much doubt whether you are a Christian at all if you did *not* have trouble.

The whole of the New Testament and the history of the Church shows that when we are children of God, we are in a fight of faith. Not having any troubles in your life is therefore far from being a good sign. It is indeed a serious sign that there is something radically wrong. There is a special reason for my saying that, because we are special objects of the attention of the enemy. Why not have problems when it is God's way to bless you!

". . . count it all joy when ye fall into divers temptations" (James 1:2 KJV). That is the way your faith is proved. The devil cannot rob us of our salvation, thank God! But he can make us miserable. He can fill us with his false fear.

It is the tempter who knows real fear. His fear is founded on fact and experience. He has met One greater and stronger than himself. Satan is afraid of his Victor. He knows what it means to be thwarted and resisted, beaten back steadily and driven clear off the battleground. There has been a man upon the earth whom Satan fears—whom he can neither trust nor resist—Jesus Christ. He learned to fear Him in Nazareth and in the wilderness. Jesus' absolute, steady obedience to the Father beat Satan. Even the storm on Galilee's blue waters, so unusually violent that it frightened the experienced sailors, failed to touch Jesus with fear.

Fear is as common as sin. If we could be wholly free of fear, we would have stronger bodies, minds, spirits, faith, courage, and power. The tempter continually plays on our sense of fear. For instance, people's fear of being in personal want is holding back huge amounts of money—money which could change the condition of the whole heathen world and move forward the date of Jesus' coming.

At our side there is always conflict with the tempter. Each of us must overcome or be overcome. Our victory comes through Jesus' victory, and we must fight in the strength of His victory. Throw out your self-seeking spirit—it allows Satan a free hand to do as he chooses. Yield to the Holy Spirit. He will burn out your self-spirit.

Men as Trees Walking

In his book *Spiritual Depression, Its Causes and Cure,* Dr. D. Martyn Lloyd-Jones wrote about the great importance of living as rich as we are in Jesus Christ.

If all Christians simply began to function as the New Testament would have us do, there would be no problem of evangelism. It is because we are failing as Christian people in our daily lives and witness that the Church counts for so little and so few

are attracted to God. So for that most urgent reason alone, it behooves us to deal
with this question.

We are like the man who was blind and healed, but still saw men as trees walking (*see* Mark 8:22–26). Yes, we have received the healing touch from Jesus—we
were born again the moment we asked Him to come into our hearts—but people
around us are not envious to receive the same. This is simply because we do not
behave like happy, fearless people. We have unlimited riches through the promises of the Bible and the presence of the Lord in our hearts, but we still see men as
trees walking.

Jesus asked the blind man, "Can you see?"

The man answered, "Not quite one hundred percent, Lord." How good it was
that he told the Lord! Jesus gave him another touch of healing, and his eyesight
was perfect. I am sure that even if Jesus had not asked him, the man would have
told the Lord the problem and been satisfied.

So, if your sight is still only partial, tell the Lord, "Thank You, Lord, for what
You did, for what You gave me—but I need more."

For Jesus said, "Blessed are they which do hunger and thirst after righteousness: for they shall be filled" (Matthew 5:6 KJV). He did not tell the blind man,
"Try hard to see." The man had only to ask, and it was given to him.

You and I must ask Jesus to do the job through His Holy Spirit. He is the One
who makes our eyes to see. "But when the Holy Spirit controls our lives he will
produce this kind of fruit in us: love, joy, peace, patience, kindness, goodness,
faithfulness, gentleness and self-control . . ." (Galatians 5:22, 23).

We are often too content with a partial healing. I had an experience of liberation from resentment some time ago. Some friends, fine Christian people, had done
something really mean against me, and I had forgiven them. That is what I thought.

A friend asked me how the situation was, but I told him, "I don't want to talk
about it. I have forgiven it."

"I understand that," he answered, "but I should like to know what they think
about it."

"Oh, they take it easy. They simply say that they have never done it. Perhaps
they forget that I have everything in black and white, in the letters which they wrote
to me at that time."

My friend looked at me and waited a moment. Then be said: "Where are *your*
sins? You told us in your talk this morning that when we confess our sins, God
casts them into the depths of the sea and you even believe that there is a sign saying No Fishing Allowed. But the sins of your friends you have in black and white.
'Lord, I pray that You will give Corrie the grace to burn all the black and white of
the sins of others today as a sweet-smelling sacrifice before she goes to bed.'"

I surely did, and how well I slept that night. Now when I meet these people, I
enjoy a peace that makes our friendship an unusual joy.

No, it was not easy. As a matter of fact, I needed the Lord just as much as when I had to forgive the people who had been cruel to my family. Forgiving is a hard job. But in 2 Corinthians 9:8 Paul tells us that there is always grace, sufficient for everything. The Holy Spirit taught me a prayer that always helps me, "Thank You, Lord Jesus, that You brought into my heart God's love through the Holy Spirit. Thank You, Father, that Your love in me is stronger than my resentment" (*see* Romans 5:5).

No compromise. The Lord is willing and able to give us clear sight. When worry gets static, it becomes depression. When unforgiveness is healed, there is a liberation that makes the enemy run.

Have you the black and white of the sins of others? Burn them today. Together with the Lord, you can.

Children of the Light

One time, artists were invited to paint a picture of peace. The pictures were many and varied, but the winner depicted a little bird sitting calmly on her nest, which was built on a slender branch overhanging Niagara Falls. The peace of the little bird did not depend on her surroundings. And so it is with us. As Christians, our peace of heart and freedom from fear do not depend on our circumstances, but on our trust in God. Fear is want of faith.

Being a Christian does not mean there is no more battle. It means we have a strategic point of attack in the battle. The battle position of the Christian is victory, joy, and abundance. The Lord expects us to do no more than welcome His assistance. The doors of heaven are open. If I hold on to feelings that prevent me from living under an open heaven, then it is no wonder I am fearful and depressed.

A great note of joy and victory is sounded in the book of Philippians—a book, incidentally, written from prison. Here Paul says:

> Don't worry about anything; instead, pray about everything; tell God your needs and don't forget to thank him for his answers. If you do this you will experience God's peace, which is far more wonderful than the human mind can understand. His peace will keep your thoughts and your hearts quiet and at rest as you trust in Christ Jesus.
>
> Philippians 4:6, 7

It is God's intention that we live as children of the light. He wants us to be strong, free, peaceful, and happy. This was the secret Nehemiah learned when he was tempted to come down from the wall he was building around the city of Jerusalem. On every side there were worries and fears, but he grasped God's truth and sang, "The joy of the Lord is my strength" (*see* Nehemiah 8:10).

Now I have a very practical tip for you. Take good notice of all the blessings He gives and all those He has given in your past. As the old hymn says, "Count your many blessings, count them one by one, and it will surprise you, what the Lord has done."

Faith came singing into my room,
And other guests took flight.
Grief, anxiety, fear and gloom,
Sped out into the night.

I wondered that such peace could be,
But Faith said gently, "Don't you see,
That they can never live with me?"

ELIZABETH CHENEY

From My Notebook

THERE IS AN aggressiveness of love that is fearless. Fear is cowardly. Faith is aggressive, like love and goodness are aggressive. Satan is aggressive in evil, but Jesus is more aggressive in love.

Jesus Christ knows no fear, and He expects you to fear nothing while He is with you. When we confess His lordship and our hearts fully agree, then we turn our lives over into His care. That is the end of worry and fear and the beginning of faith.

Worry is double-parking on the avenue of anxiety.

$$- \text{Christ} = + \text{fear}$$
$$+ \text{Christ} = - \text{fear}$$

Courage is fear that has said its prayers.

The folly of being anxious about the near future is just as stupid as worrying about what will happen about a thousand years hence. We have to live in the present moment, because we can do nothing about the past, and God is doing everything about the future.

GEORGE MACDONALD

465

God has made me put my heel on the neck of worry, of weakness, of fear, of inability, and I stand and declare that whosoever believes in Jesus shall not be put to shame.

E. W. KENYON

6. *Frustration*

EVEN IF WE have learned how to deal with anxiety, worry, and fear, the enemy has yet another powerful weapon he uses on us—frustration. Frustration is dangerous because it is so simple to blame it on others, to think there is nothing *we* can do to overcome the problem. And yet even the most frustrating of circumstances can be turned to good, if we use the opportunities we have.

I find it a great frustration to have a message but have no one to give it to. On one trip to Russia I had such a frustrating time! I wanted to tell everybody, especially the communists, about the Lord Jesus Christ. However, whenever I tried to talk to people on the streets of Moscow, I found they would always be looking over their shoulders. Finally they would rush away, afraid someone would see them talking to the old woman with a Bible. I became so frustrated, anxious, and filled with despair. I was in Russia, but I could find no one who would listen!

One afternoon I met a young woman, and we chatted about ordinary things— the weather, the tulips in Holland, the price of gasoline. I sensed she was hungry to hear more about the Lord, but I knew she was afraid to talk in the park. I invited her to come to my hotel room for a good talk.

"Oh, no," she whispered, glancing every which way. "The tourist hotel rooms here are the most dangerous places to talk. There is a hidden microphone in each room. Every word you speak is put on a tape and played before the officials." She excused herself and moved quickly away from me.

The next morning my companion and I were sitting in our hotel room, totally defeated. We had been in Russia one week and had not been able to speak to a single communist about the Lord Jesus.

Suddenly I spotted something on the floor, just under the edge of the bed. It was a pattern of tiny holes, like those in the top of a pepper shaker. Suddenly I had a tremendous inspiration. "Thank You, Lord," I said to myself. "That surely must be the place where the microphone is hidden." Reaching for my Bible, I bent low over the holes in the floor and began to speak in a deliberate voice.

"You who listen have many problems, just like every other human being. Two of these problems are common to all men—sin and death. I have here in my hand a book. It almost bursts with good news. In this book—it is called a Bible—you can read everything you need to know about the answers to these problems. The answer is found in the life of a man, the Son of God, Jesus Christ. He died on the cross for the sins of the whole world, and for your sins also. He carried the punishment you and I deserve. But not only did He die for us, He rose from the dead and is alive today. Yes, He is even willing to live in you through His Holy Spirit. If you will accept Him, He will give you the power to overcome death also and live forever with God in heaven."

For almost five minutes I preached into the hidden microphone, knowing that my sermon was not only being heard, but was being recorded on a tape recorder and passed on to superiors. What a joy! I finished my sermon by saying, "Jesus said once, 'Come unto me, all you who labor and are heavy laden, and I will give you rest.' Since all men in Russia know the meaning of labor, then it means that Jesus must love Russians in a special way. When He says 'all,' He is talking to all who listen to this tape."

From that day on, I gave the microphone a little sermon every morning, bringing a simple Gospel message and hope to my unseen hearers.

After leaving Moscow, we traveled to Leningrad, where once again I discovered the pepper-shaker holes in the floor. That night I gave a five-minute sermon to my hidden listeners. The next morning, two serious men came in and took a seat at the table next to ours at breakfast. From their appearance and the way they dressed, I was sure they were members of the secret police.

For a moment I was disturbed and frustrated. Then I saw what God was doing. My microphone sermon had brought results! Instead of being worried, I should rejoice. This was simply another opportunity to present the Gospel.

I asked my companion, in English, "Do you know that you can become a child of God?"

She immediately grasped what I was doing and began to play her role. "I can never be a child of God," she said, shaking her head. "I am not good enough."

"Ah ha," I answered. "That is exactly what I expected you to say! But you see, only sinners are eligible." As we talked I kept noticing the two men at the next table. They tried to pretend they were not interested. One man had a newspaper in front of his face. But I could see they were leaning in our direction, trying to hear every word.

We continued our conversation, speaking as loudly as we could without making it obvious. We stayed at it until we were satisfied these men could never say they had not heard the Gospel. We even repeated the whole conversation in German, in case they couldn't understand my English!

Do you think I was playing a silly game, talking into hidden microphones and giving my testimony at breakfast? It was no game at all! After one whole week of frustration, I was at last giving my message to the communists. Not in the way I would have preferred, it is true. But who can say that those few men who heard me were not important to the Lord? Even when we are denied a big opportunity, we must make the best of all the little ones that come our way.

I remember a story about the little boy and his sister. They were trying to climb a steep mountain. The little girl began to complain, "Why did God put all these rocks here?"

Her brother reached back and patted her on the shoulder. "These are really stepping stones," he said. "God put them here to help us reach the top."

Many people are worried and frustrated because they never have the opportunity to do what they want to do. I have found the seeming obstacles are really opportunities within themselves. If we do what our hand finds to do, then God will open up broader places of service.

Many years ago I heard of an old Dutchman and his young son. They had to walk home at night across the *polders*, the dried sea bottom where the water had been pumped out and held back by dikes. The little boy was afraid, for he knew there were still deep pockets of water and many patches of quicksand on the polders. All they had to give them light on the walk was a small kerosene lantern.

"Please, Father," the boy begged, "don't make me walk out there. It is so dark, and the lamp only gives light enough for one step at a time."

The father took his son's hand in his own. "That's right, but one step at a time is all the light we need. And if we walk in the light we have, we have enough light for the next step. However, if we stand still, waiting for enough light to see the entire way home, then even the light we have will burn out, and we will be left in the dark."

And so they made their way home safely, one step at a time, walking in the light. Every obstacle, every frustration, can become an opportunity if we trust God and walk in the light we have.

From My Notebook

YOU ARE ON the road to success if you realize that failure is only a detour.

In order to realize the worth of the anchor, we need to feel the stress of the storm.

When a train goes through a tunnel and it gets dark, you don't throw away your ticket and jump off. You sit still and trust the engineer.

Our trust and hope are not in the promises, but in the One who made the promises.

Our faith may falter, but His faithfulness, never!

We are to do heavenly business. The earthly part of it is only a detail.

> Some wish to live within the sound
> Of church and chapel bell
> I want to run a rescue shop
> Within a yard of hell.
>
> C. T. STUDD

We will see more and more that we are chosen not because of our ability but because of His power that will be demonstrated in our not being able.

What can you and I pray for leaders? Pray for the Christian leader that God will guide him. Pray for the non-Christian leader that God will control him.

Faith sees the invisible, believes the unbelievable, and receives the impossible.

Luther said, "Work as though He will not be coming for a thousand years. Be ready as if He should come today."

Men have to go through many experiences in order to get the spiritual vision which is needed to see the divine plan. A film is always developed in a dark room.

7. *Don't Burden Yourself*

MANY YEARS AGO, shortly after World War II had come to a close, I was invited to speak in a Japanese church in Tokyo. The nation was still reeling from the impact of the war. All that the Japanese people had believed in had been snatched away, and two of their greatest cities had been destroyed by the atomic bomb. If ever a people had reason to worry, it was the Japanese.

Because of the language barrier, it seemed practical for me to give them an object lesson. "Do you know the feeling," I began, "when your heart is like a suitcase with a heavy load?"

The sad-faced people in the little church all nodded. They knew the feeling.

I picked up my suitcase and put it on the table. It was very heavy. I told them how weary I was from tramping all over the world, carrying that suitcase filled with heavy objects.

"My heart was like that until just last week, when I read a glorious verse in the Bible. It says, 'Cast all your anxieties on him, for he cares about you.' I did that. I brought all my burdens to the Lord—all my cares—and I cast them upon Him." I opened my suitcase and spread it out on the table to demonstrate. "Lord," I continued, "here are my co-workers. They are so tired." I reached down and took two items out of the suitcase and laid them on the table.

"And here is my trip, Lord—the one I have to make next week to the town where I don't know a single person. You know how worried I am about that, and how afraid I get when I think about it. I cast this care on You, too, Lord." I took a big package out of the suitcase and laid it on the table next to the two smaller packages.

"Here are my friends at home, Lord. They wrote about a car accident. Will You please heal them?" I took out one more object and placed it on the table.

"And here is that boy who refused to give his life to Jesus. Dear Lord, You know how much I have worried about him." I placed a heavy piece on the table.

"This is my unbelief. Almost always when our hearts are heavy, it is because we have an unconfessed sin. Forgive me, Lord, and cleanse me with Your blood. Holy Spirit, give me faith and trust."

I took object after object out of the suitcase, mentioning each one as a particular burden or worry. "This is my pride. This is my self-seeking. . . ." In the end, the suitcase was empty, and I said, "Amen!" I closed the empty suitcase and pretended to walk out of the room, swinging my light bag as though it was made of paper.

The people immediately got my point, and the light of understanding broke on their faces. I could tell by their smiles and polite bows when I was finished that the Holy Spirit had spoken truth to them.

After the meeting I quickly threw all the items back into the suitcase and dashed off with my host, to go to the home of the wonderful Japanese Christians who entertained me until it was time to fly on to Hong Kong.

Many years passed, and then I found myself in Berlin, at an international congress on evangelism. After one of the morning seminars, a distinguished-looking Japanese evangelist approached me. "Corrie ten Boom," he said with a broad smile, "every time I hear your name, I think of your trouble suitcase."

"Oh," I said, flattered, "I am so glad you remembered what I said that night."

"It was not what you said that I remember," he smiled courteously, "it is what you did."

"You remember me taking all those objects out of my suitcase and laying them on the table as an illustration of how to pray?"

"No, that is not what I remember most," he said. "What I remember most is that after you finished your talk, you took all the objects, put them back in your suitcase, and walked out of the hall just as burdened as when you came in."

Oh, what a vivid object lesson! That afternoon, back in my hotel room, I began to take a good look at myself. Was I guilty of doing that in my life? How easy it is to unpack my trouble suitcase each morning and cast all my cares on the Father, because He cares for me. But then, as the day goes on, I keep coming back and picking up first this care and then that one, slipping them back into my suitcase. By the end of the day, I am just as burdened as I was at the beginning, and far more exhausted, for I have had to keep slipping back to pick up the cares originally given to my Father.

What about you? Did you unpack your trouble suitcase this morning? Good! But what did you do afterwards? Is your heart still as burdened and heavy as it was before you prayed? Did you repack your suitcase as soon as you emptied it? If so, perhaps you need to return to the Lord, casting all your cares upon Him—

for He cares for you. Tell it to Him. The Holy Spirit will teach you how to pray and leave your burdens with the Lord.

Live One Day at a Time

When Jesus told His disciples, "Therefore do not be anxious about tomorrow, for tomorrow will be anxious for itself," He was saying, "Don't try to carry today's burden *and* tomorrow's burden at the same time."

One evening a man stepped into the kitchen to help his wife with the dishes. As he was working, he thought, "If that poor woman could just look ahead and see the dishes that remain to be washed in the future, towering like a mountain ahead of her, she would give up right now!" Then he laughed. "But she only has to wash tonight's dishes, and she can handle that."

As you may know, I grew up in a clock shop. My father was a watchmaker, and I was the first woman in Holland to be licensed as a watchmaker. Our home, the Beje, was filled with the sound of ticking clocks. I still remember the old Dutch parable about the clock that had a nervous breakdown.

The little clock had just been finished by the maker, who put it on a shelf in the storeroom. Two older clocks were busy ticking away the noisy seconds next to the young clock.

"Well," said one of the clocks to the newcomer, "so you have started out in life. I am sorry for you. If you'll just think ahead and see how many ticks it takes to tick through one year, you will never make it. It would have been better had the maker never wound you up and set your pendulum swinging."

"Dear me," said the new clock. "I never thought about how many ticks I have to tick in a year."

"Well, you'd better think about it," the old clock said.

So the new clock began to count up the ticks. "Each second requires 2 ticks, which means 120 ticks per minute," he calculated. "That's 7,200 ticks per hour; 172,800 ticks per day; 1,209,600 ticks per week for 52 weeks, which makes a total of 62,899,200 ticks per year. Horrors!" The clock immediately had a nervous breakdown and stopped ticking.

The clock on the other side, who had kept silent during the conversation, now spoke up. "You silly thing! Why do you listen to such words? That old grandfather clock has been unhappy for years. Nobody will buy him, and he just sits around the shop gathering dust. Since he is so unhappy, he tries to make everyone else unhappy, too."

"But," the new clock gasped, "he's right. I've got to tick almost sixty-three million ticks in a year. And they told me I might have to stay on the job for more than one hundred years. Do you know how many ticks that is? That's six billion, two hundred million ticks. I'll never make it!"

"How many ticks do you have to tick at a time?" the wise old clock asked.

"Why, only one, I guess," the new clock answered.

"There, now. That's not so hard, is it? Try it along with me. Tick, tock, tick, tock. See how easy it is? Just one tick at a time."

A light of understanding formed on the face of the clock, and he said, "I believe I can do it. Here I go." He began ticking again.

"One more thing," the wise old clock said. "Don't ever think about the next tick until you have your last tick ticked."

I understand that was seventy-five years ago, and the clock is still ticking perfectly, one tick at a time.

No man sinks under the burden of the day. It is only when yesterday's guilt is added to tomorrow's anxiety that our legs buckle and our backs break. It is delightfully easy to live one day at a time!

From My Notebook

I took a burden to the Lord
To cast and leave it there.
I knelt and told Him of my plight,
And wrestled deep in prayer.

But rising up to go my way
I felt a deep despair,
For as I tried to trudge along,
My burden was still there!

Why didn't You take my burden, Lord?
Oh, won't You take it, please.
Again I asked the Lord for help,
His answering words were these:

My child, I want to help you out
I long to take your load.
I want to bear your burdens too
As you walk along life's road.

But this you must remember,
This one thing you must know . . .
I cannot take your burden
Until you *let it go*.

BETTY CURTI

*Then another angel with a golden censer
came and stood at the altar; and a great
quantity of incense was given to him to mix
with the prayers of God's people, to offer
upon the golden altar before the throne.
And the perfume of the incense mixed with
prayers ascended up to God from the altar
where the angel had poured them out.*
Revelation 8:3, 4

8. Prayer

SOMETIMES WE UNDERESTIMATE the value of our prayers. In the Book of Revelation, we read how precious they are in God's eyes. They are so precious that they are all preserved there.

When I read this text, I understand a little bit of the great value that our prayers have in the eyes of the heavenly Father. Look back on the prayers you have prayed for that person you are worrying about. Not one of those prayers is lost. They are kept in heaven. What a comfort. What an encouragement!

When Do God's Answers Come?

The Bible says that by prayer and supplication with thanksgiving we should let our requests be made known unto God. Have you ever been discouraged about your praying? Does it seem your prayers are never answered? Much of our anxiety comes as we worry about others. This isn't helped, it seems, if we pray for others and then do not see our prayers answered. However, let me tell you a few stories that I think will give you encouragement to go on, despite seeming failure.

Not very long ago, I had a wonderful experience in my home country of Holland. I was invited to appear on national television, to bring the Easter message. More than six million people heard my message, I was told. But the most wonderful result was hearing from some people I had not heard from in years—people I had prayed for many years ago.

One man wrote to me and said, "Twenty-five years ago I came out of a concentration camp, into the house you opened for ex-prisoners. You brought me the Gospel. I thought I was not ready for it, but you told me you were going to keep on praying, anyway. Last night I saw you on TV, and now I can say with all my heart, 'I have accepted the Lord.'" It took twenty-five years, but God answered my prayer for that man's salvation!

Another man telephoned. "Forty-five years ago, you told me exactly the same thing you said tonight on TV—that Jesus was the Son of God and is still alive. I always refused to accept Jesus as my personal Saviour. Now I am ready to say yes to Him. May I come to see you?"

Of course I replied, "Please come."

We talked and prayed together. "Now," I said, "ask Jesus to come into your heart."

He prayed, "Jesus, I cannot open my heart. Please, won't You force the door?" And Jesus did a miracle in the life of that man—an answer to my prayer after forty-five years.

When I was fifteen years of age, I spent some time at a secular domestic-science school. Most of the teachers and students did not want me to talk about the Lord. Therefore I spent time praying for them. Following the TV broadcast, I received a letter saying, "Sixty years ago we were together at the domestic-science school. I suddenly remembered that you often talked about the Lord Jesus when we were together. I saw and heard you on TV. I just want to write and tell you that I am a follower of Jesus Christ." Another answer to prayer—sixty years after.

But the most amazing answer came the week after the TV broadcast. When I was five years old, I accepted the Lord Jesus as my Saviour. After that I developed a burden for the people in my town. We lived in Haarlem, quite near the Smedestraat. In this street there were many pubs. Because of the pubs, I often saw many drunken people, some of whom were dragged into the police station on the same street. I wanted so badly to do something to help, but what can a little girl do in such a sad situation? All I could do was pray—and I did a lot of that.

Mother told me later that for a long time every prayer of mine ended with the words, "Lord Jesus, please save those people in the Smedestraat. And save the policemen, too."

Following my TV appearance, I received a letter. "My husband said that it was so nice to hear that you lived in Haarlem. He lived for seventeen years in the Smedestraat, and he worked in the police station in that street. After I heard you on TV, I knew that you would be interested to know that we now know the Lord personally." It took over seventy years for me to hear that my prayer was answered!

Why do I tell you this? To let you know that no matter how discouraged you may be over your prayers, God never lets you down.

Pray Alone and Together

Prayer is the sturdy answer to worry. I urge you to find a place where you can be alone with the Lord. Let it be your own little private prayer chapel.

I understand that Susanna Wesley, mother of Charles Wesley, had her own little private prayer closet. When things got bad in the Wesley household—the children screaming, money scarce, the roof leaking—she would reach down and grab the hem of her long skirt. Separating it from the many long petticoats women wore in those days, she would pull the outer skirt up over her head and close herself in. There she would meet the Lord and commune with Him, returning to her hectic world refreshed and revived.

Prayer should be informal and to the point: conversations with God, so to speak. Nice words do not count. Be definite. If you have a nervous tummy, do not ask the Lord to take it away. Rather, confess where you got it and ask Him to shut the door on the source of your worry.

Pray specific prayers. God does not give stones for bread. If you ask for specific things, you will receive specific answers. Most of us receive not because we ask not, or if we do ask, we ask amiss.

Go to God the same way you would go to your father or mother. Tell Him about your worries. Tell Him you are a sinner because you are anxious and nervous. Be definite. Prayer opens doors to the power that relieves us from anxiety, for God's power is demonstrated in our weakness.

Remember, prayer is not one-way traffic. If it were, it would be similar to someone coming into your house, asking a question, and then leaving without waiting for an answer. Prayer is both asking and receiving, speaking and listening. Yes, that takes time. But you can learn how to converse with God secretly.

But there is more. Not only do we find help for our anxiety by praying alone, but also when we pray with others and have others pray for us. Jesus says He enjoys joining a small group of even two or three who are praying in His name. ". . . I will be right there among them" (Matthew 18:20). What a marvelous promise! But how many take advantage of it? The best place for group prayer is in the family. Are you a mother? Call the children and ask them to pray with you. Tell them you are anxious and worried, and ask them to join you in prayer.

The devil smiles when we make plans. He laughs when we get too busy. But he trembles when we pray—especially when we pray together. Remember, though, that it is God who answers, and He always answers in a way that He knows is best for everybody.

From My Notebook

PRAYER IS THE signature of the soul on the correspondence with our Creator.

Prayer changes our attention from the problem to the Power, from anxiety to the Almighty.

Is prayer your steering wheel or your spare tire? Keep on top of your circumstances by keeping the morning watch. Don't allow the circumstances to come on top of you.

> We mutter, we sputter—
> We fume and we spurt.
> We mumble and grumble—
> Our feelings get hurt.

> We can't understand things—
> Our vision gets dim,
> When all that we need—
> Is a moment with Him.

To pray only when in peril is to use safety belts only in heavy traffic.

> Fear knocked at the door.
> Faith answered.
> No one was there.

9. God's Answers to Prayer

His love has no limit, His grace has no measure.
His power no boundary known unto men;
For out of His infinite riches in Jesus,
He giveth and giveth and giveth again.

ANNIE JOHNSON FLINT

I KNOW MANY people who trust the Lord for their eternal safety, but they have no faith for the cares of every day. They would find it easy to die, for they know God has promised them a mansion in heaven. In fact, some of them would like to die, just to escape this world. They have no faith for today—just for tomorrow. They do not see that their daily problems are the material from which God builds His miracles.

Once, when I was a little girl, I remember coming to my father with a broken doll. He was busy in the watch shop repairing clocks and watches, but he stopped what he was doing and took special pains to fix my ragged old doll's broken arm. Why did he take this so seriously? Because he saw the doll through the eyes of his little girl. Your heavenly Father loves you. He sees your problems through your eyes. He loves us all and understands our problems. He cares.

When I was in the German concentration camp at Ravensbruck, one bitter winter morning I woke up with a bad cold. My nose was running. Back in Holland I would have been able to adjust to a cold, because I would have a tissue or a hankie to blow my nose. But in the concentration camp, and without a hankie, I felt I could not stand it.

"Well, why don't you pray for a hankie?" Betsie asked.

I started to laugh. There we were, with the world falling apart around us. We were locked in a camp where thousands of people were being executed each week, being beaten to death, or put through unbearable suffering—and Betsie suggests I pray for a hankie! If I were to pray for anything, it would be for something big, not something little, like that.

But before I could object, Betsie began to pray. "Father, in the name of Jesus I now pray for a hankie for Corrie, because she has a bad cold."

I shook my head and walked away. Very shortly after, I was standing by the window when I heard someone call my name. I looked out and spotted a friend of mine, another prisoner, who worked in the hospital.

"Here you are," she said in a matter-of-fact tone. "Take it. I bring you a little present."

I opened the little parcel, and inside was a handkerchief! I could hardly believe my eyes. "How did you know? Did Betsie tell you? Did you know I had a cold?"

She shrugged. "I know nothing. I was busy sewing handkerchiefs out of an old piece of sheet, and there was a voice in my heart saying, 'Take a hankie to Corrie ten Boom.' So, there is your gift. From God."

That pocket handkerchief, made from an old piece of sheet, was a message from heaven for me. It told me that there is a heavenly Father who hears, even if one of His children on this little planet prays for a tiny little thing like a hankie. Not only does He hear, but He speaks to another of His children and says, "Bring a hankie to Corrie ten Boom."

Why should I worry, when I can pray? We are God's children—His own children. Here is an old and well-known story that taught me a deep lesson.

A boy made a little ship. It was a work of art, and he had put many weeks of work into its construction. When it was ready, he took it to the river, and it could really float. He held the rope tightly in his hand, but suddenly a strong wind swept the boat away with such force that the rope broke. The river was deep and wild, and the boy knew that he had lost his ship.

After a few weeks, to his great joy, he saw his ship in the show window of a shop. He went to the shopkeeper and told him that the ship belonged to him, that he had made it. But the man said, "Only the person who gives me the price I am asking for it will have the ship."

The boy went home crying and told his father, who advised him, "I think you must try to make some money and buy the ship."

The boy worked all his spare time until he had enough money and bought his toy from the man. With his ship in his hand, he came home and said, "It's twice mine! I made it, and I bought it."

Can we trust the Lord Jesus, who made us and bought us? We surely can. We are twice His!

A minister in Russia gave me another good illustration. Many people lived in a large apartment house. All the junk was taken to the basement and it was overfull. In a corner stood a harp that was broken, and nobody was able to repair it.

Once a tramp asked if he could spend the night in the house. "There is such a severe snowstorm. May I stay here?"

"We have no room for you, but you could sleep in the basement." They emptied a corner and put some straw on the floor.

After some hours, the owner of the harp suddenly heard music in the basement. She ran downstairs and saw the tramp playing the harp.

"How did you repair my harp? I could not find anybody who was able to do it."

The tramp answered, "When I was young I made this harp, and when you make something, you can repair it."

Who made you? Do you think He can repair you?

The No Answer

When Betsie and I were in Ravensbruck, she became very ill. I took her to the prison hospital and she asked me, "Corrie, please pray with me. Ask the Lord Jesus to heal me. He has said, 'If you shall lay hands upon the sick they shall be healed.' Please do that for me."

I prayed and laid hands on her, and both Betsie and I trusted the Lord for healing. The next morning, I ran from the barracks and looked through the window of the hospital and found Betsie's bed was empty. I ran from window to window, until I finally saw her body. They were getting ready to take it to the crematorium. It was the darkest moment of my life.

Then, just a few days later, I was summoned to the prison office. For some reason, I was being released from prison. Surely it was a clerical error, but whatever the cause, I was free to go. It was a miracle of God.

When I came to the office, I discovered nobody there knew that Betsie was dead. So I asked, "Is my sister also free?"

"No. She stays here until the end of the war."

"Can I stay with her?"

The official became furious and shouted at me. "Disappear! Get out of here!"

Suddenly I saw God's side of what had happened. Suppose Betsie had gotten better and I had to leave her behind? I would have been forced to return to Holland and leave her alone in that horrible camp. I could not have stood it. But she had been released from the concentration camp and was now enjoying all the glory of heaven. I walked out of the camp that day praising and thanking the Lord for that unanswered prayer. Yet it really wasn't unanswered. It was answered in God's way, not mine.

So often we pray and then fret anxiously, waiting for God to hurry up and do

something. All the while God is waiting for us to calm down, so He can do something through us.

There is a vast difference between prayer in faith and faith in prayer. Faith in
prayer is very common. Prayer in faith is so uncommon that our Lord questions if
He will find any of it on earth when He comes back. Prayer in faith is a commanded
duty; it is always reverently making known our requests unto God in full confidence that, if we ask anything according to His will, He hears us; and that according to our faith an answer to our prayers will be granted us.

Praying in faith comes from an abiding faith in the Person prayed to—the confidence is in Him. It is based on a knowledge of who He is, and on a trusted conviction that He is worthy to be trusted. Praying in faith is the act of a simple-hearted
child of God. Can we teach ourselves to pray in faith? We can indeed train ourselves, but the joyful experience is that it is the Spirit of God who does the job. So
give room in your heart for the Holy Spirit.

From My Notebook

Prayer is opening up our sluicegates to the mighty ocean of God.

BISHOP WESTCOTT

> Satan trembles when he sees
> The weakest saint upon his knees.
> The host of hell can that one rout,
> Who meets him with a praiseful shout.

The Holy Spirit does not give a clear blueprint of the rest of your life, but only of a moment, one by one.

We can't solve problems for others. We can introduce them to the Lord.

As a camel kneels before his master to have him remove his burden at the end of the day, so kneel each night and let the Master take your burden.

If a care is too small to be turned into a prayer, it is too small to be made into a burden.

Here then is my charge: First, supplications, prayers, intercessions and thanksgivings should be made on behalf of all men. . . .

1 Timothy 2:1 PHILLIPS

Prayer is the same as the breathing of air for the lungs. Exhaling makes us get rid of our dirty air. Inhaling gives clean air. To exhale is to confess, to inhale is to be filled with the Holy Spirit.

You should therefore be most careful, my brothers, that there should not be in any of you that wickedness of heart which refuses to trust, and deserts the cause of the living God.

Hebrews 3:12 PHILLIPS

10. Trust

WE CONTINUE TO share in all that Christ has for us so long as we steadily maintain, until the end, the trust with which we began. God's love for us never changes—of this we must be confident.

We sin, and our sin comes between our souls and God, as a dark cloud comes between the sun and the earth, and our communion with Him is broken. We are unable to live in the enjoyment of God's love for us when sin stands in our way. Our temptation to sin by worrying comes from the evil one, but we must remember that he can only come through an open door. Calling on Jesus' name sends him back, along with any of his brood, because they hate and fear the name of their Conqueror. They get away from the sound of that name as fast as they can.

Our fearless testimony makes the power of the blood of Jesus effective. There is great need for overcomers in this world, and our Lord earnestly calls for men to follow in His steps and in His strength. He won the decisive victory over our enemies, but everyone must make that victory his own on the battlefield of his own life. In Jesus' great name, we can. By His grace, we will.

Our worry is often due to physical causes. Overwork always makes a sensitive spirit worry and hurry, which in turn overworks our nerves, until we see things in a distorted manner. It is a vicious circle, because worry usually makes us keep working harder, until we finally drop from exhaustion—physical and mental. At that point, we go to God for help, but we have already begun to listen to the devil, so we go to God with a sense of inferiority, which is the devil's message!

Some years ago, I had a very difficult problem and did not see the answer. I talked it over with a good friend. We looked at each other, and on both of our faces there was an expression of defeat. Suddenly my friend stood up. She hit the table with her hand and said, "Do we really think that the enormous power that caused Jesus to come out of the grave is not enough for our problem?" Then I saw the smallness of my faith. Yes, the same Spirit that raised Christ from the dead is willing to work in you.

But if we want to be victorious over our fears through Jesus' victory and strength, we must also be obedient. It was Jesus' obedience that defeated the enemy at every turn, until the climax of Calvary was reached.

Confessed Sins

Once we realize that fear, anxiety, and worry are sins, and then confess these sins to God, what happens? The Bible says, "He has removed our sins as far away from us as the east is from the west" (Psalms 103:12). "I've blotted out your sins; they are gone like morning mist at noon! Oh, return to me, for I have paid the price to set you free" (Isaiah 44:22). "But if we confess our sins to him, he can be depended on to forgive us and to cleanse us from every wrong . . ." (1 John 1:9).

Did you ever see a cloud again, after it had disappeared? No, the cloud that appears afterward is a different one. We do not honor God by asking forgiveness a second time for the same sin. Say, "God has beaten this thing. He had forgiven this sin and forgotten it. I can do the same in His strength." Remember that the victory has been won. Claim that victory as your own, and it will be your own in fact. There is far more victory within your reach than you have realized. Reach out your hand and take as your very own what has been done for you. Reckon yourself dead to the sin of worry.

Say with Paul, ". . . I can do everything God asks me to with the help of Christ who gives me the strength and power" (Philippians 4:13). Commit the past to God, and don't be enchained with it again.

As He cleanses our cups, He fills them to overflowing with His Holy Spirit. We must remember that our cups can be kept clean. Everything that the light of God shows as sin, we can confess and carry to the fountain of water of life, and it is gone, both from God's sight and from our hearts.

A little girl broke a beautiful antique cup. Crying, she brought it to her mother. The mother saw that the little one was sorry, and said, "I forgive you. Throw the pieces in the garbage can."

The next day, the little girl saw the pieces in the garbage can. She took them and brought them to her mother again. "I am sorry, Mother, that I broke your cup yesterday," she cried.

The mother replied, "Leave that in the garbage can, where it belongs. Remember my forgiveness." A confessed sin is dead. Give it a burial.

"Hallelujah!"

Handel's chorus was resounding through the evening air. "Hallelujah! And He shall reign for ever and ever."

I had never heard it sung so perfectly and in such beautiful surroundings.

We were in Japan. The moon and stars were as clear as they can only be in that country. Far away we even saw the white peaks of Mount Fuji.

"Hallelujah! The Lord God omnipotent reigneth."

I had never heard it sung *a capella,* without musical accompaniment. It was as if angels were singing.

I knew the girls. They were the students for whom I had been holding a daily Bible study for the last two weeks, and they were going to the same hall as I, where I was expected to answer questions.

That evening I had to listen most to their worry about sins. I prayed that the Lord would give me a clear answer for them. They were Christian girls, but what a lack of joy they had about the finished work of Jesus at the cross. I asked them a question. "When you rehearsed the 'Hallelujah Chorus,' did you make mistakes?"

The girls giggled. Japanese girls giggle much.

"Many."

"But when you were singing outside in that Japanese moonlit evening, you did not think of those mistakes, otherwise you might have repeated them. Girls, never wait to confess your sins. The devil accuses us night and day. I will tell you something. Sunday morning I spoke in your church."

"Yes, we remember it. You gave us much, but it was so short."

"I thought the same, and your pastor had promised me a long time. I asked him, 'Because I can speak only once in your church, give me as long as possible. Make your preliminaries short.' He promised me, but did not do it. We started the service at 10 o'clock, and at 11 o'clock he was still busy with the *Book of Common Prayer.* That moment the Holy Spirit showed me that I was very impatient. I knew that that was a sin, and at 11 o'clock I brought it to the Lord and asked forgiveness. When we confess our sins, He is faithful and just to forgive us and to cleanse us with His blood. Suddenly I saw that the words of the *Book of Common Prayer* were not just preliminaries, but truths that the Lord uses for His honor.

"Why did I tell you that it was 11 o'clock? Because the devil accuses us before God and our own hearts. It is possible that he said to God at 11:05, 'Do You see Corrie ten Boom in Your church and how impatient she is?' I believe that God answered him, 'I already know it. Five minutes ago Corrie told me. It is forgiven and cleansed.'

"Girls, be sure that you are always five minutes earlier than the accuser. Then you lose your worry about your sins. The reason Jesus came to earth was to save sinners. He died for you, so that you could be forgiven, and He lives for you and in you by His Holy Spirit, to make you overcomers. When you worry about your sins it is because you know them through the accuser who has told you, 'That sin is typically you. That is your nature, and you will remain like that your whole life. There is no hope for you.'

"The devil, the accuser, is a liar. When the Holy Spirit convicts you of sin, it is always in the floodlight of the finished work of Jesus at the cross. He tells you: 'Exactly for these sins Jesus died. Confess and be cleansed.'

"Do you remember what I taught you this week—what the Bible says about repented sins? 'As far as the east is from the west, so far does he remove our transgressions from us' [see Psalms 103]. He throws them into the depths of the sea, forgiven and forgotten, and to warn the accuser, He puts a sign saying No Fishing Allowed. Girls, instead of worrying about your sins, sing again, 'Hallelujah! King of kings and Lord of lords.'"

It sounded even more beautiful than when I had heard it outside, but this time I saw the happy faces, some still wet with tears.

The Word of God

God's promises were never meant to be thrown aside as waste paper. He intended that they should be used. God's gold is not miser's money, but is minted to be traded with. Nothing pleases our Lord better than to see His promises put into circulation; He loves to see His children bring them up to Him, and say, "Lord, do as You have said."

Charles H. Spurgeon

We deny the work of Jesus Christ and stand powerless before the enemy if we doubt the integrity of the Word of God. The bank account of the Bible is not frozen.

Someone told me, "In the Bible there are seventeen thousand promises." I don't know if that is true, but even if there were only seventeen, the quality is so great that the quantity is not too important.

... He has given you the whole world to use, and life and even death are your servants. He has given you all of the present and all of the future. All are yours, and you belong to Christ, and Christ is God's.

1 Corinthians 3:22, 23

When you check your inventory of blessings from God, it shows you have received good measure, pressed down and running over. Do not say, "I am too great a sinner to appropriate God's promises. Perhaps good Christians may do that, but not I." God always hears a prayer of faith. Put all your needs on the table and then say thank You.

Once a factory owner had a very expensive, complicated machine that he needed for his work. It broke down, and there was nobody who could repair it. The owner sent a telegram to the machine factory: "Send an expert." The very next day, an unimpressive man arrived at the airport. The owner sent another telegram to protest that the man they had sent was unsatisfactory. He wore old clothing, he seemed very uneducated—the owner was not at all happy with him. The answer that came back from the machine factory was, "That man is the designer of your machine."

Don't you think our own Creator can find the answers to our problems? Jesus is able to untangle all the snarls in your soul, to banish all complexes, and to transform even your fixed habit patterns. All you must do is trust Him.

From My Notebook

A DYING OLD man said, "I am too sick to remember one promise of God. But I don't worry, because God does not forget them."

If the enemy cannot keep you from working, then he comes up behind you and pushes you and tries to kill you with overwork.

When the devil can't make you bad, he makes you busy.

Elijah was so sure of God that he added difficulties by throwing water over the altar. We, in our unbelief, try to help God.

In the forest fire, there is always one place where the fire cannot reach. It is the place where the fire has already burned itself out. Calvary is the place where the fire of God's judgment against sin burned itself out completely. It is there that we are safe.

The strength we claim from God's Word does not depend on circumstances. Circumstances will be difficult, but our strength will be sufficient.

> Your strength, my weakness—here they always meet,
> When I lay down my burden at Your feet;
> The things that seem to crush will in the end
> Be seen as rungs, on which I did ascend!

Not one sparrow (What do they cost? Two for a penny?) can fall to the ground without your Father knowing it. And the very hairs of your head are all numbered. So don't worry! You are more valuable to him than many sparrows.

Matthew 10:29–31

If you make a compromise with surrender, you can remain interested in the abundant life, all the riches of freedom, love, and peace, but it is the same as looking at a display in a shop window. You look through the window but do not go in and buy. You will not pay the price—Surrender.

E. STANLEY JONES

Jesus told him, "If you want to be perfect, go and sell everything you have and give the money to the poor, and you will have treasure in heaven; and come, follow me." But when the young man heard this, he went away sadly, for he was very rich.

Matthew 19:21, 22

11. Surrender

THAT RICH YOUNG ruler gladly kept all the commandments, and he searched out even more ways to serve his God. But when Jesus told him he would have to give up everything he treasured in his life, the young man simply could not do it.

J. H. Jowett comments on this:

> He hallowed the inch, but not the mile. He would go part of the way, but not to the end. And the peril is upon us all. We give ourselves to the Lord, but we reserve some liberties. We offer Him our home, but we mark some rooms "Private." And that word, "Private," denying the Lord admission, crucifies Him afresh.

My being a tramp for the Lord, going over the whole world, was real training for me in surrender and trust. I learned that the safest place in the world is in the center of the will of God. This is always true, even sometimes when it seems as if following God's will is physically dangerous.

Shortly after the war, I was alone in America. It was Saturday morning in Chicago. I paid the taxi driver and stepped into the YWCA. The lady in the office did not look very happy to see me.

"The office is almost closed, lady," she said.

"Have you a room for me?" I asked.

"No. Come back on Monday."

"Will you telephone the nearest police station, then, and ask them if I can sleep in a cell tonight?"

She looked very surprised. "Why?"

"Well, I come from Holland, and in Holland no woman has to stay in the street during the night. There is always room in a police station, in a cell, and I am sure that in America it will be the same. I would not think of remaining on the street all night in a town like Chicago."

She left the office for a minute, then came back and said, "We have found a room for you."

That was exactly what I had hoped would happen, and I went to my room. It was not the most beautiful room. It was very high up in the building and very small, but much more luxurious than the cell I was living in a year before, in the prison camp.

I did not go out on Sunday. It was raining, and I had discovered that when it rains in America, it pours. I needed some time for rest and for talking with the Lord. As a matter of fact, my first experience in Chicago had scared me. I did not know anyone there, and it was such a big, strange city to face alone.

That Sunday in my room, I had a good talk with the Lord. I confessed my fears to Him and surrendered the whole trip through America to His will. Two weeks after, the Lord blessed my ministry in America in a way that must have made the angels rejoice. The Lord did much good work through the many talks in all the little churches. God opened the doors and the hearts of Chicago for me, and Moody Bible Institute gave me such a welcome that I have never since felt alone in Chicago.

My Lord knows the way through the wilderness—all I have to do is follow and to put my hand into His hand. He holds me.

There is only one force more powerful than fear, and that is faith. Does your need seem big to you? Then make sure that God knows how big it looks to your eyes, and He will treat it as such. He will never belittle it, however trivial. He will not laugh at it, or at us. He never forgets how large our problems look to us.

Does your need seem as big as the throne of grace? Do we not there—and there alone—see it in the right proportion?

We ask, "Do you believe that the Lord is your Shepherd?"

"Yes, but. . . ."

That fatal word *but* shows that we do not believe the Lord is our Shepherd. "Yes, I believe it, *but* I do not have victory over my bad temper, and I am not able to win souls. I worry over things. I do not have peace and joy."

The testimony of victory puts *but* into the right place. "I am passing through a time of great sorrow and trouble, *but* the Lord is my Shepherd. I have been discouraged about my past accomplishment, *but* the Lord is my Shepherd."

Set yourself against being disturbed by disturbing things. Say to yourself, "Being upset is useless. It has bad results, it is sinful. It reproaches my Master. I will not be upset."

Amy Carmichael wrote:

He, Who loved you unto death, is speaking to you. Listen, do not be deaf and blind to Him. And as you keep quiet and listen, you will know, deep down in your heart, that you are loved. As the air is around about you, so is His love around about you now. Trust that love to guide your lives. It will never, never fail. You know how we have watched the great sea washing over the rocks, flooding them till they overflow? That is what the love of God does for us. We have no love in ourselves and our pools would soon be empty if it were not for that glorious inexhaustible sea of love which extends to you and me. Lord, do Thou turn me all into love, and all my love into obedience, and let my obedience be without interruption.

If His will be your will, and His way be your way, then all your insufficiency and inaptitude shall be met by the sufficiency of His grace.

Obey the voice of the Lord Jesus, who says, "Come unto me, all ye that labour and are heavy laden, and I will give you rest" (Matthew 11:28 KJV). Come! Like a mother says to a fearful child, "Come." Nothing else is necessary. When you come to Him, He does the job.

Jesus says, "Behold, I stand at the door, and knock: if any man hear my voice, and open the door, I will come in . . ." (Revelation 3:20 KJV).

"But as many as received him, to them gave he power to become the sons of God . . ." (John 1:12 KJV). That means to become a member of the very family of God, and ". . . Except a man be born again, he cannot see the kingdom of God" (John 3:3 KJV). We cannot expect peace or rest until we personally find it in Jesus Christ. When we do, we can say, ". . . For I know whom I have believed, and am persuaded that he is able to keep that which I have committed unto him against that day" (2 Timothy 1:12 KJV).

Know that Christ is the Lord of all: your mind, your spirit, your body. Let Christ's teachings live in your heart, making you rich in true wisdom. Put everything in His hands.

The first time a cowboy heard the story of Jesus riding on an unbroken colt, he exclaimed, "What wonderful hands He must have had!" Consider the hands of Christ: artist's hands that created all the beauty of this world; love-pierced hands of the kindest Friend that man ever had; hands that are aching to take our own and guide us in ways that are good for us; skillful hands, worthy of our trust and love.

Let us let Him clasp our hands a little tighter, and trust Him a little more than ever before—that our paths may be straighter and gladder than in the past. Let us make more time for prayer, so that we increase the pressure of that hand on ours. Their touch is so light, and the whisper so soft, it is easy to miss them.

A young, discouraged artist fell asleep beside the picture that he was trying to complete. His master quietly entered the room, and, bending over the sleeping pupil, placed on the canvas, with his own skillful hand, the beauty that the painting lacked.

When we, tired and spent, lay down the work done in our own strength, our own great Master will make perfect our picture. He will remove every stain, every blemish, and every failure from our service. He will add the brightest luster to our service, and He will give us the highest honor for our work.

Shall we not surrender to the One who can make us His victorious artists? Paul wrote:

My brothers, I do not consider myself to have grasped it fully even now. But I do concentrate on this: I forget all that lies behind me and with hands outstretched to whatever lies ahead I go straight for the goal—my reward the honour of my high calling by God in Christ Jesus.

Philippians 3:13, 14 PHILLIPS

Now to him who is able to keep you from falling and to present you before his glory without fault and with unspeakable joy, to the only God, our saviour, be glory and majesty, power and authority. . . .

Jude 24 PHILLIPS